Create great-looking Web sites the easy way with
this information-packed, hands-on guide!

W9-ADB-008

WITHDRAWN

Easy
web page creation
149022

Microsoft

Mary Millhollon with Jeff Castrina

PUBLISHED BY
Microsoft Press
A Division of Microsoft Corporation
One Microsoft Way
Redmond, Washington 98052-6399

Library of Congress Cataloging-in-Publication Data
Millhollon, Mary, 1969-
    Easy Web Page Creation / Mary Millhollon, Jeff Castrina.
       p. cm.
    Includes index.
    ISBN 0-7356-1187-4
     1. Web sites--Design. 2. Web Publishing. 3. Microsoft FrontPage. I. Castrina, Jeff. II.
    Title.

  TK5105.888 .M555 2001
  005.7'2--dc21

                                            00-052095

Printed and bound in the United States of America.

1 2 3 4 5 6 7 8 9 QWT 6 5 4 3 2 1

Distributed in Canada by Penguin Books Canada Limited.

A CIP catalogue record for this book is available from the British Library.

Microsoft Press books are available through booksellers and distributors worldwide. For further information about international editions, contact your local Microsoft Corporation office or contact Microsoft Press International directly at fax (425) 936-7329. Visit our Web site at mspress.microsoft.com. Send comments to *mspinput@microsoft.com*.

ActiveX, Encarta, FrontPage, Microsoft, Microsoft Press, MSN, the MSN Logo, PhotoDraw, PowerPoint, Visual InterDev, and Windows are either registered trademarks or trademarks of Microsoft Corporation in the United States and/or other countries. Other product and company names mentioned herein may be the trademarks of their respective owners.

Unless otherwise noted, the example companies, organizations, products, people, and events depicted herein are fictitious. No association with any real company, organization, product, person, or event is intended or should be inferred.

Acquisitions Editor: Casey Doyle
Project Editor: Sally Stickney
Technical Editor: Dail Magee, Jr.

This book is dedicated to the growing number of creative people who keep the Internet dynamic by adding (and updating) their "two cents worth" on the Web.

TABLE OF contents

Acknowledgments   *xi*
Introduction   *xiii*

Part One: The Talk: Web Page Basics

In this first part of the book, you'll learn about Web page creation and design, quell lingering feelings of doubt (you'll see that you *can* create Web pages), and acquire the knowledge you can use to move forward with confidence. By the time you've finished reading the six chapters in this part, you'll be ready to create the four Web sites described in Part Two. So let's get the show on the road (and the pages on the Web)—let's talk!

Chapter 1: Demystifying Your (Future) Home Page   5
  Basic Hoopla   6
    The Internet—Just a Bunch of Hardware   6
    The Web—Some Software for the Hardware   7
    Web Pages—A Few Files on the Net   8
  From Your Head to the Web (and Back Again)   15
    The Client/Server Nature of the Web   15
  Progressing at a Steady Clip   16

Chapter 2: Creating and Shaping Web Text   21
  Text Matters   22
    Readers' Approach to Online Pages   22
  Textual Elements of a Web Page   24
    Title Bar   26
    Content   26
    Hyperlinks   26
    Logos, Graphical Text, and WordArt   26

Forms and Menu Items   27
Plain-Text Navigational Options   27
Date or "Last Modified" Information   27
Writing for the Web   28
Organizing Web Text   29
Writing Effectively for an Online Audience   34
Treating Text as a Design Element   37

**Chapter 3: Illustrating Your Message:
Creating and Using Art on the Web**   41
Welcome to Web Graphics   42
Mechanics of Web Graphics   42
Pixels, Palettes, and Colors   42
Graphics File Formats   46
Size Matters   55
Art of Using Web Graphics   59
Photographs and Illustrations   59
Buttons and Logos   60
Icons, Bullets, and Horizontal Rules   61
Graphical Text   64
Backgrounds   65
Acquiring Art   65
Prepared Art   66
Custom Art   66
Photographs   70

**Chapter 4: Looking Like You Know What You're Doing:
Web Page and Web Site Design**   75
Before You Design   76
Audience Reigns Supreme   76
Storyboarding Your Web Site   78
Web Page Design Rules That Won't Let You Down   80
Web Page Dimensions   80
Page Layout Issues   83
Color   88
Navigation Tools and Hyperlinks   90
Standard Credibility Components   91
Text   92
Graphics   95
Web Site Design Rules to Live By   96
Consistency   97
Structure   97
Case Study Practice   98

Chapter 5: Stockpiling the Goods 105
    Tools of the Trade 106
    Internet Connectivity and Server Space 106
        Free Space Online 107
        Purchasing Server Space 110
    Web Page Creation Tools 113
        Text Editors and HTML Editors 113
        Graphics Applications 119
        FTP Utilities 121
    A Bit About Browsers 123

Chapter 6: Planning Your Attack 127
    Building a Case for Planning 128
    Defining Your Goals 129
    Getting to Know Your Audience 130
    Drawing the Blueprints for Your Site 132
        Keeping Your Files in Line 133
        Site Planning Checklist 136
    Laying Your Home Page's Foundation 138
        Home Page Planning Checklist 140
    Gathering Supplies and Preparing to Build 141
        Supplies Checklist 142

Part Two: The Walk: Creating Web Pages

In this part, you'll find four project chapters designed to help you acquire some well-rounded, hands-on experience as you walk through the Web site creation process. The chapters in this part are arranged progressively, from simplest to hardest, so that you can ease your way into more advanced Web-page-creation tasks.

Chapter 7: Posting a Web Page Within an Hour (or so) 147
    Introducing MSN and Online Communities 148
    Planning an MSN Community Site 152
    Joining an Online Community 153
    Selecting an MSN Communities Template 155
    Setting Up an MSN Communities Web Site 157
    Customizing Your Web Site 160
    Replacing the Default Photograph 162
    Adding Pictures to Your Site's Photos Page 165
    Editing Your Site's Text 167
    Viewing the HTML Behind Your Page 169
    Deleting Your Web Site 171

Expanding Your Web Site   172
Additional Resources   172

Chapter 8: Demystifying Basic HTML   175
Why HTML?   177
HTML Basics   178
    Using HTML Tags   178
    Handling HTML Documents and Web Graphics   186
    Saving and Previewing HTML Documents   187
Planning the HTML Site   188
Getting Your Folders and Graphics in Place   190
Preparing Your Home Page File   192
Specifying the Background and Link Colors   195
Creating a Table   197
Inserting and Linking the Logo   200
Inserting the Home Page Banner Graphic   202
Adding Navigation Links   203
Inserting Footer Information   207
Copying the Home Page Framework to Subpages   211
Inserting Body Text on the Home Page   216
    Creating Headings   216
    Adding Paragraph Text   217
    Formatting Block Quotes and Colored Text   219
    Creating a Linked Unnumbered List   221
Inserting and Linking a Picture   223
Finalizing the Home Page   224
Using the Piano Site's Framework as a Template   226
Additional Resources   228

Chapter 9: Swimming Deeper into Web Waters:
Creating Web Pages with Microsoft Word   231
Introducing the Web Capabilities of Word 2000   232
    Saving a File as an HTML Document   235
    Viewing a Document's HTML Source Code   237
    Creating a Web Page with a Template   238
    Building a Web Page with the Web Page Wizard   241
Planning Your Word 2000 Web Page   242
Formatting a Text Document   244
Following the Wizard's Lead   246
Tweaking the Navigation Bar Settings   251
Adding Text to Subpages   253

Saving and Closing Your Site 254

Creating and Inserting WordArt 255

Adding Clip Art 259

Copying Graphics to Subpages 262

Working with Hyperlinks 264

   Modifying Hyperlink Styles 265

   Adding Hyperlinks 268

   Adding ScreenTips to Existing Hyperlinks 270

   Creating a Mail To Hyperlink 271

   Linking Graphics 273

Previewing Your Word-Generated Web Page 275

Additional Resources 276

Chapter 10: Going All Out: Creating Web Sites with FrontPage 279

Introducing FrontPage: A Full-Featured HTML Editor 281

   Strolling Past the FrontPage Window 282

   The Advantages of Using FrontPage 284

   FrontPage Server Extensions 285

Planning Your FrontPage Web Site 286

Creating a New Web 288

Creating the Subpage Layout 291

   Setting Page Properties 291

   Saving Your Work 294

   Adding the Logo and the Title Bar Graphic 294

   Inserting a Table 297

   Adding Navigation Buttons 301

   Adding Footer Information Below the Table 303

Using the Subpage Layout to Build Web Pages 306

   Preparing to Create Subpages 306

   Adding Text and a Thumbnail Image 307

   Creating an Image Map 311

   Creating Forms 313

Creating a Home Page in FrontPage 322

   Setting Up the Home Page Framework 322

   Assembling the Main Graphic 324

   Creating Links Within the Main Graphic 325

   Adding Dynamic HTML to the Main Graphic 326

   Adding Finishing Touches to the Home Page 327

   A Word About Publishing 328

Additional Resources 329

Part Three: The Rest: Going Live and Moving On

After you post your Web site, you should count on providing at least a small dose of continuing attention to it. Sure you could slap any old Web page onto the Web and leave it there unattended, but your site probably wouldn't be revisited very often. To have a truly successful Web site, you need to tend to your Web pages every so often. The purpose of the chapters in this part is to show you how to *go live* (get your pages online) and keep your site *alive*.

Chapter 11: Sending Your Web Pages Into the Real World   **333**

Now That Your Pages Have Taken Shape   334

Transferring Your Files to the Internet   335

    FTP Applications   335

    Web Folders   339

    Other FTP Options   343

    Browsers as FTP Clients   346

Reviewing Your Work   348

Registering with Search Engines and Directories   349

    META Tags   351

Chapter 12: Updating, Archiving, and Moving On   **355**

After the "Going Live" Dust Settles   356

Updating Your Web Pages   356

    Reasons to Update   356

    Easily Updateable Elements   357

    Updating Tip and Tricks   357

Archiving Web Page Elements   359

Moving Beyond Easy Web Pages   360

    Bonus JavaScript Components   361

Appendix: Web-Safe Colors and HTML Special Characters   **367**

Index   **371**

acknowledgments

First and foremost, we'd like to thank Debbie McKenna, our agent at the Moore Literary Agency, and Casey Doyle, senior acquisitions manager at Microsoft Press, for making this book possible. After the initial plans were in place, we were thrilled to find ourselves working with Sally Stickney, senior editor, and Dail Magee Jr., senior technical editor, at Microsoft Press. We're very grateful for their intelligence, diligence, and wit, which showed throughout the process. (We've never laughed out loud at editorial comments before working with Sally and Dail!) We think everyone should have the chance to work with such enjoyable professionals. We're also very appreciative of all the hard work and attention to detail exerted by the design team at Microsoft Press, including James Kramer and Joel Panchot, and the artists, Michael Kloepfer and Rob Nance. Thanks also go to Dan Latimer, the principal compositor; and Holly Viola, the principal copy editor. It certainly takes a good team to create a good book.

Closer to home, we thank our extremely creative and idiosyncratic (in a good way!) bughouse friends just for "being," and our families, especially Megan Castrina, for loaning us her resume, and Cale, Robert, and Matthew Taylor, for putting up with a writer's schedule. Last but not least, we'd like to thank each other—Jeff thanks Mary, and Mary thanks Jeff—because collaborating on this book was so enjoyable that it hardly felt like we were working at all!

introduction

Recently, while co-teaching a course on graphics and the Web, a nagging suspicion solidified into crystal clarity—everyone wants to build a home page! For several years now, we've been noticing this growing desire wherever we go. Grandparents, Gen-Xers, students, sports teams, committees, small businesses, schools, friends, and established enterprises (especially nontechnical organizations) have expressed that they want (or need) a Web site but they don't have the foggiest idea where to begin.

With that thought in mind, we decided to visit a few bookstores to scope out some Web site creation books so that we could drop a couple book names whenever we heard the increasingly familiar "I want to make a Web site, but…" chant. While rooting around bookstores, we found lots of pretty good Web design and HTML books; surprisingly, though, none wholly met our needs. We were specifically looking for a book or two that kept Web page creation simple yet comprehensive. We wanted an information-packed, easy-to-understand book for everyone—a book for our friends and acquaintances who find computers interesting but don't necessarily want to earn full-fledged geek status anytime soon. When we didn't find what we were looking for, we realized that there is clearly room on the bookshelves for at least one more Web book—*Easy Web Page Creation*.

This Book Could Be for You

We wrote *Easy Web Page Creation* for the great number of individuals, families, organizations, and small businesses who want to create a Web presence but don't have the resources or desire to hire a Webmaster. This book is for you if you have basic computing skills (such as the ability to use a mouse, open folders, run desktop programs, and so forth) and are actively contemplating building a Web site. In *Easy Web Page Creation*, we've consolidated all the facts and tips you need to know to successfully build a Web site. To start, we quickly demystify the "magic" involved in creating Web sites. After reading just a few pages, you'll see how a little knowledge can go a long way toward ensuring that the Web sites you create are successful.

As you'll soon see, the knowledge we impart in this book is designed to build on the knowledge you already have. For example, you might have an inkling that certain applications, such as Microsoft Word and Microsoft FrontPage, can dramatically shorten the Web-page-creation learning curve for most people. Further, you might be aware that your Internet service provider (ISP) grants a certain amount of free server space to you along with your Internet connectivity (many do)—and server space certainly *sounds* like a good resource to have on hand. But even knowing these various bits of information, most would-be Web developers find that the catch lies in the details. Sure, applications and server space are readily available or easily obtainable, but how can you combine these resources to create a Web site? In *Easy Web Page Creation*, we address this very issue, using a friendly, step-by-step (and concept-by-concept) approach to creating, posting, and maintaining Web sites on the Internet. Specifically, the book is divided into three parts, with each part (and each chapter within) building on information presented in prior sections and chapters.

■ **Part One: The Talk: Web Page Basics**   Part One provides the necessary background for Web page and Web site creation. In the chapters in this part, we cover fundamental mechanics as well as design issues associated with Web sites. Chapters 1 through 6 are packed with information and tips about Web page text, graphics, page components, and site-creation techniques and utilities. Further, in this part, we discuss key planning processes and recommend tools that come in handy during Web site creation. By the end of Part One, you'll be ready to tackle creating Web sites, which we explain how to do in detail in Part Two.

■ **Part Two: The Walk: Creating Web Pages**   Part Two provides you with practical, hands-on experience by walking you through the process of creating four Web sites—one per chapter. In this part of the book, you'll find out how to create Web sites in a variety of ways, ranging from stepping through the creation of a simple MSN Communities page to hand-coding HTML in Notepad (which is included with Microsoft Windows) to using the Web Page Wizard in Microsoft Word, and finally, to adding advanced Web page features with Microsoft FrontPage. We dedicate a separate chapter to each Web page creation utility (MSN, Notepad, Word, and FrontPage). Each chapter introduces the utility, presents a planning scenario, provides easy-to-follow procedures for hands-on practice, and lists additional resources.

■ **Part Three: The Rest: Going Live and Moving On**   In Part Three, you'll learn how to upload, archive, and maintain Web pages after you've created them. This part also provides information about future directions you can take in your Web development efforts—both by updating your pages and advancing your skills as a Web developer.

Easy Web Page Creation is written in an easy-going style and is packed with all the information necessary to enable you to create, post, and maintain Web sites. Each chapter begins with introductory text and concludes with a "Key Points" section that summarizes the chapter with a brief bulleted list. Every chapter includes tips, notes, sidebars, "lingo" notes to explain specialized vocabulary, and "Try This" elements that provide you with hands-on experiences directly related to the concepts presented in the text. In addition, we've included an appendix that shows Web-safe color charts (more about that topic beginning in Chapter 3) and a list of common special character codes (called *character entity references*) that you can use in your Web pages (more about character entity references in Chapter 8).

Finally, for maximum assistance and convenience (and because we like to create Web sites), we've created a dynamic online resource, which we call the Creation Guide Web site (located at *www.creationguide.com*), especially for *Easy Web Page Creation*. We opted to put the Internet to work instead of including a CD-ROM with this book because CD-ROMs quickly become outdated (especially when you're talking about the Web). On this book's companion Web site, you'll find numerous samples, resources, and exercise files. Many of the figures in the book are also featured on the Creation Guide site. We strongly encourage you to visit the companion site while you're reading the book (we've liberally sprinkled references to it throughout) as well as anytime after you've finished the book and are searching for additional resources. We'll even post a link to your page on the Creation Guide site if you create a Web site you'd like to share after reading this book.

Understanding System Particulars

At this point, we need to take a couple technical moments to discuss system requirements—nothing too complicated, though, we assure you. Fortunately, you'll find that for the most part we wrote this book for all computer platforms. The theory and Web creation basics described in Parts One and Three are almost completely universal, which means that the text applies to most computer systems and platforms. In Part Two, we do use several specific applications to show you how to create Web sites. In those cases, we opted to use popular applications (and recent versions) for the Microsoft Windows 98, Microsoft Windows Me, and Microsoft Windows 2000 operating systems. Namely, we used Microsoft Word 2000 in Chapter 9 and Microsoft FrontPage 2000 in Chapter 10. Otherwise, the bulk of the book's text is nonspecific to application or operating system. You might notice, though, that we captured all the screens shots on computers running Windows 98 and Windows Me. (In most cases, we've found that computers running Windows 2000 and Macintosh computers have similar results as the Windows 98 and Windows Me screens.) Screen shots of online content are displayed primarily in Microsoft Internet Explorer 5, unless otherwise indicated in the text.

That's about as technical as we need to get at this point. (See—that wasn't so bad.)

Most of All...

Now that we've spent a couple pages summarizing the book's approach and structure, let's put that "practical" information aside. You see, beyond this book, our sincere underlying goal is to get you started—to get you over the hump of thinking that you can't create a Web site and into the realm of realizing that you *can* build a Web site, and pretty easily, too. We designed this book to give you a strong foundation in Web development—a foundation that will serve you well now, while you create an immediate Web presence, as well as in the future, when you work on more advanced Web development endeavors. Most of all, we wrote this book so that you can experience first-hand the enjoyment of building Web pages and the value you can gain from owning your own Web site. We're completely confident that you can build your own Web site. Read on and you'll be a believer—you really can do it!

Support

Every effort has been made to ensure the accuracy of this book. Microsoft Press provides corrections for books at the following address:

http://mspress.microsoft.com/support/

If you have comments, questions, or ideas regarding this book, please send them to Microsoft Press via e-mail to:

mspinput@microsoft.com

or via postal mail to:

Microsoft Press
Attn: *Easy Web Page Creation* Editor
One Microsoft Way
Redmond, WA 98052-6399

You can also contact the authors directly at *mm@creationguide.com* or *jc@creationguide.com* with any comments or suggestions.

Please note that product support is not offered through the above addresses.

PART

one

THE TALK
web page basics

The other day, we went hiking with some friends. But we didn't simply wake up, stretch, walk out the front door, and start climbing. Instead, the event sort of evolved:

"Hey, want to go on a hike on Friday?"

"Sounds good. Where do you want to go?"

And without realizing it, the planning process had begun—we were *talking* about taking a hike. We were calling friends, checking online databases for nearby trails, selecting a time to meet, thinking about supplies—all this, and we hadn't even taken a single step.

Web design follows a similar path. Before you build a Web site, you need to mull it over, talk about it, learn some Web site design principles, plan how to best create your site, and gather your supplies—basically, you need to allow yourself to comfortably slide into the natural progression that takes place whenever you embark on an undertaking. You need to plan. Fortunately, *planning* doesn't have to be synonymous with *boring*.

The goal of Part One is to serve as the "Where do you want to go for a hike, and who's going to drive?" portion of the book. Here's where you satisfy your instinctive planning urges and move beyond gut-level reactions. In this part, you'll learn about Web page creation and design, quell lingering feelings of doubt (you'll see that you *can* create Web pages), and acquire the knowledge you can use to move forward with confidence.

By the time you've finished reading the chapters in this part, you'll be the proud owner of a well-rounded wealth of Web design knowledge, you'll be fully prepared to start planning your own Web sites, and you'll be ready to create the four Web sites described in the project chapters is Part Two. So let's get the show on the road (and the pages on the Web)—let's talk!

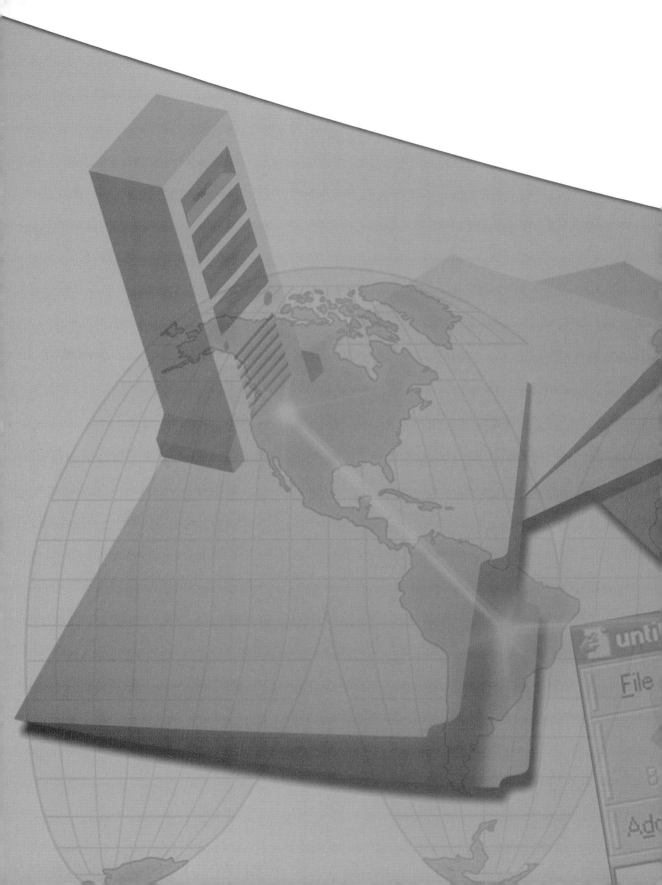

1

demystifying

YOUR (FUTURE) HOME PAGE

Easy—that's the goal. So let's start by pulling back the drapes, opening the shutters extra wide, and cranking open the window. See—same room, different perspective. Opening a few windows and doors and airing out your preconceptions can eliminate a lot of the mystery of creating a Web page.

Basic Hoopla

Most likely, you're fairly familiar with the not-so-newfangled invention called the Internet. Further, we're willing to bet that if you're contemplating the idea of creating a Web presence, then you know how to use a computer on some level. We're also assuming that you've surfed the Web at least a few times, you can use basic applications (such as word processing packages), and you can click a mouse with the best of 'em. Fortunately, your basic computing knowledge is all you need to be able to create Web pages—well, your basic computing knowledge along with this book, of course!

Your first job on the road to becoming a Web page developer entails building on what you already know. For instance, in addition to moderate computing capabilities, you should have an inkling of how the Internet, the Web, and Web pages relate to one another. Therefore, in the spirit of our goal of clarity and simplicity, we'll cut to the chase in this chapter and briefly describe the main elements of the world's largest network—the Internet, the Web, and Web pages. After we get the fundamentals out of the way, we'll spend the remainder of this book talking about planning and building your Web pages.

The Internet—Just a Bunch of Hardware

To put it simply, the Internet, or the Net, is hardware—lots of hardware—connected together to create a massive worldwide network, as illustrated in Figure 1-1. The Internet's hardware encompasses all the components a person can physically touch, including computers, routers, cables, telephone lines, high-speed data circuits, and other physical network pieces.

lingo

The *Internet* is the hardware that's connected together to create a massive worldwide network.

lingo

Routers are relay components between networks.

Figure 1-1
Hardware relationships on the Internet, the world's largest computer network

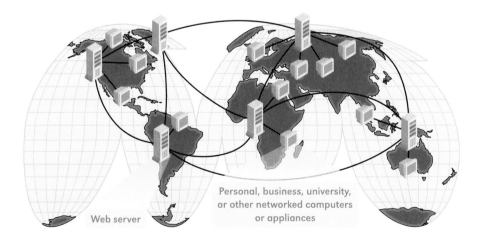

Personal, business, university, or other networked computers or appliances

Web server

For now, that's really all you need to know about the Internet—it's the hardware. No need to regale you with a long diatribe about how the U.S. government's Cold War paranoia spurred the development of a noncentralized computer network. If you're curious about the history of the Internet, you can find information online and at your local bookstore or library. (Also, see the resource section on this book's companion Web page at *www.creationguide.com* for some history-of-the-Internet resources.)

Now that we've clearly identified that the Internet is the hardware, let's take the next logical step. Like all computer hardware (think of your desktop or laptop computer), the Internet needs software—otherwise, the Internet's hardware components would simply sit and gather dust on a worldwide basis. Enter the World Wide Web.

The Web—Some Software for the Hardware

The World Wide Web (also known as WWW or just "the Web") is a little more esoteric than the Internet. That's because the Web consists of software (including programs, documents, and files) that enables information to travel along the Internet's hardware. To help illustrate the Web's role relative to the Internet, here's a short story we first told a few years ago when explaining the role of the Web to Internet newbies:

The *Web* consists of software that enables information sharing on the Internet.

> Long ago (back when insects and arachnids could talk), there lived a spider of unusually bright intellect named Tim. After watching the ants work all day, Tim met up with the lead ant at the time, Bill. The ants, as usual, were incredibly successful at gathering and storing food, but Tim thought the spiders could team up with the ants to make life easier for both groups. Tim approached Bill with this plan, and Bill saw the logic in it. In fact, Bill suggested that they incorporate other creatures into the workgroups as well. Soon, Tim and Bill recruited grasshoppers, flies, and earthworms to become partners in the food-gathering venture. The creatures thought it was a splendid idea, so they got together and created an elaborate labyrinth of anthills, spiderwebs, burrows, and tunnels to assist in the food-gathering venture. The system was in place; it looked perfect; it was time for the work to begin. But, much to the creatures' disappointment, chaos ensued. Even though all the paths and connections were in place, flies had a hard time navigating the tunnels, grasshoppers had difficulty staying in line, earthworms were just too heavy to

walk across the spiderwebs, and, of course, the ants' expectations were much too high for any of the other groups to meet. What the creatures had was a network. What they needed was something or someone who could cross all mediums of the network safely. They needed a universal creature.

This short story provides a good analogy of the Internet-Web relationship. As we said earlier in this chapter, the Internet is the infrastructure for transmitting information—an infrastructure made up of computers, routers, cables, telephone lines, high-speed data circuits, and information bases called *servers* (rather than anthills, spiderwebs, and tunnels). Unfortunately, just as spiderwebs can't support earthworms, not all computers can support all computer file formats. To include every available method (or *protocol*) for understanding the various document formats on all computers would be impractical. So, the Internet community devised its own universal creature, more commonly known as the World Wide Web.

Initially, Tim Berners-Lee conceived and developed the Web at the CERN laboratory in Switzerland for the high-energy physics community. (By the way, although Tim is considered to be of extremely high intellect, he is not a spider!) The Web quickly attracted a great deal of attention and spread beyond the physics arena. As with the history of the Internet, you can find reams of information about the history of the Web online or in numerous computer books.

For our purposes, you only need to know that the Internet is the hardware and the Web is the software. Simple enough. Now, we're ready to move to the next level—the files the Web software supports on the Internet hardware.

Web Pages—A Few Files on the Net

Now we come face-to-face with the heart of the matter—Web pages. Basically, when you strip away all the highfalutin technobabble, Web pages are files. To be specific, Web pages are *Hypertext Markup Language* (HTML) files. No need for your eyes to glaze over at the sight of "HTML"; in Part Two of this book, we'll clear up the mysteries of HTML. At this point, all you need to know is that Web pages are simply files that the Web software can support, just like document (.doc) files that Microsoft Word supports.

lingo

Servers are powerful high-capacity network-linked computers that store files and respond to users' requests to view and access the stored files.

lingo

A *protocol* is a set of rules that describe how data should be transmitted. The Web uses HTTP (Hypertext Transfer Protocol) to transmit HTML documents.

Because Web pages are files, you don't have to stretch your imagination too far to realize that creating a Web page is simply the act of creating a specific type of file on your computer. Word documents, spreadsheets, databases, Web pages—they're all types of files. Clearly, you can see that Web pages aren't mysterious entities. They can't overwhelm you—they're merely computer files, and you've worked with computer files numerous times!

So, don't let Web pages scare you. Of course, this isn't to say that Web pages don't have a few idiosyncrasies that set them apart from other files. Namely, Web pages almost always incorporate multiple files and hyperlinks, and they are frequently rounded up into groups called *Web sites*.

The multifile nature of Web pages

Granted, we just said Web pages are simply files, and we stand by that. But we should clarify a bit regarding the kinds of files we're referring to. While you read the next couple paragraphs, you might think we're providing a little too much information at this point—but we're really not. You should have at least an inkling (not necessarily a firm grasp, just yet) of Web page components and interactions before we get too far along. Enough of the disclaimer; on to the information.

First, at the most basic level, every Web page is a *text document*. A text document is a file that contains words, letters, and numbers without any formatting. For instance, opening Notepad or WordPad in Microsoft Windows (click Start, point to Programs, click Accessories, and then select Notepad or WordPad) and typing your name, a catchy phrase, miscellaneous letters, a few numbers, or anything, really, creates a text document—not

lingo

A *Web site* is a collection of related Web pages, usually including a home page and related subpages.

lingo

A *text document* is a file that contains words, letters, and numbers without any formatting.

Web Pages and Browsers

To view Web pages, you use a *browser* (such as Microsoft Internet Explorer). In most cases, a browser application resides on the local computer (the computer you're working on). You can delete, install, upgrade, and customize your browser just as you delete, install, upgrade, and customize other software applications on your computer (including Microsoft Office programs, such as Word and Microsoft Excel). One slight confusion occasionally crops up regarding where the Internet ends and your computer begins. Clarifying comes easily—when you view a Web page in your browser, the toolbars, menu bars, status bars, and so forth surrounding a Web page are part of the browser application, which resides on your computer; the content within the browser's main window reflects the Internet content.

a Web page, mind you, just a text document. Figure 1-2 shows a simple example of a text document open in Notepad.

Figure 1-2

A text document

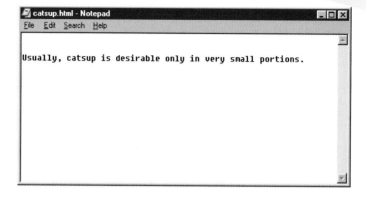

To upgrade your text document to a potential Web page, you simply add specific HTML commands, as shown in Figure 1-3.

Figure 1-3

A text document with fundamental HTML commands

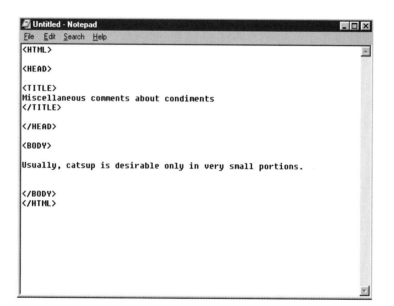

After you add HTML commands, you save the text document with an .html or .htm extension in place of .txt or .doc. (Don't sweat the specifics at this point.) Then, you can open the document in a browser application, such as Internet Explorer.

Figure 1-4 shows how the text document with the HTML commands shown in Figure 1-3 appears in a browser. Notice that only the body text, and not the HTML commands, appears in Figure 1-4. Just the body text shows because HTML commands merely provide instructions to browsers regarding *how* to display information, not *what* to display.

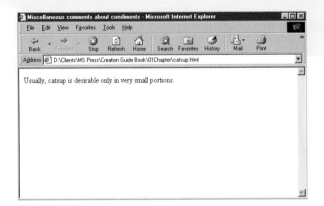

Figure 1-4
A basic text document with HTML commands in a browser

try this! You can see for yourself how HTML works by typing the text shown in Figure 1-3 into a Notepad document. Save the Notepad document as a text (.txt) file, and close Notepad. Next, right-click the text file you just created, select Rename, and replace the .txt extension with an .html extension. Now, open your browser. Finally, open the HTML file in your browser. To do so, type the path to the HTML file in the browser's Address bar, or display both your browser window and the contents of the folder that contains the HTML file and then click and drag the HTML file's icon into the browser window.

Don't worry if this HTML explanation seems a little vague at the moment. We'll walk you through the process of creating a Web page using HTML in Notepad or WordPad later in this book (in Chapter 8). You'll see then that HTML is fairly simple if you take it one step at a time. (And if you want some added inspiration, you'll find that you can create Web pages without knowing HTML at all in other Part Two chapters!) At this point, you mainly need to recognize the following basic premise:

Web pages are text documents.

You might've noticed that a paradox seems to be emerging here because we've adamantly stated that Web pages are text documents. But, if Web pages are text documents, why does the Web overflow with graphics? Fortunately, you can use HTML text documents in conjunction with specific graphics file types on the Web. (Namely, the Web supports graphics files with .gif, .jpeg, and .png extensions—but let's save the graphics file format discussion for Chapter 3.)

Here's the scoop. To show a graphic on a Web page, an HTML (text) document includes commands that tell a browser where to find a particular graphic and how to display it on the page (including position, size, and so forth). Thus, the multifile nature of Web pages is unveiled. Generally, when you look at a Web page online, you're looking at a few files—an HTML (text) file and some graphics files.

To illustrate the multifile concept, take a look at the Arizona Film Society's home page shown in Figure 1-5. As you can see, the Arizona Film Society's home page consists of three files—an HTML document (index.html) and two graphics files (afs_title.gif and 4members.jpg). Figure 1-6 depicts a Windows folder view of the files used to create the home page illustrated in Figure 1-5. (Notice that the Windows folder contains the same HTML file and graphics files.)

A Little More HTML The text and HTML commands used to create a Web page are collectively called the Web page's *source code*. (*Source code* refers to the text and HTML commands used to create a Web page.) Most browsers enable you to display a Web page's source code. For example, to display source code using Internet Explorer, you select Source from the View menu, as shown here:

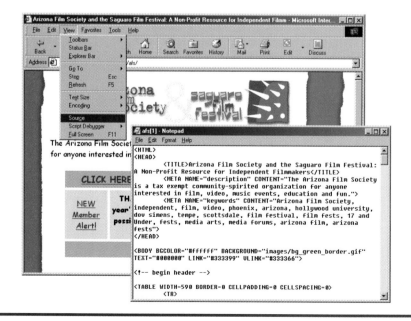

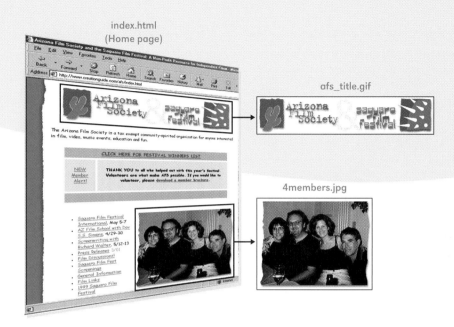

Figure 1-5
An HTML text file and two graphics files combining to create the Arizona Film Society's home page (www.creationguide.com/afs)

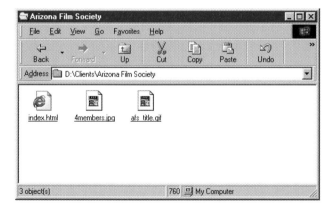

Figure 1-6
Folder view of the Arizona Film Society's home page files

note

As you probably know, one of the Web's major draws is its dynamic nature. Many Web pages are frequently updated and modified. To aid our discussion, we've frozen a copy of the Arizona Film Society's home page on the companion Web site, *www.creationguide.com/afs*. To see Web flux in action, visit the Arizona Film Society's current home page at *www.extracheese.com/afs* and notice that the page has been modified. (Most likely, the page has been modified a number of times since we wrote this chapter.)

After reviewing Figures 1-5 and 1-6, you're ready for another "bottom line" blanket statement. Basically, you need to walk away from this discussion with the following information:

> When you view a Web page in your Internet browser, you're usually viewing a number of files working together to create a single page.

Having safely tucked away the knowledge that a Web page consists of multiple files, you should now consciously consider that a Web page isn't a solo form of communiqué, like a flyer on your windshield. Instead, a Web page almost always uses hyperlinks to link to other Web pages.

lingo

Hyperlinks are clickable text or graphics that enable you to access additional Internet resources.

Hyperlinks and Web sites

As we stated at the beginning of this chapter, we're assuming that if you want to create a Web page, you've surfed the Web. Thus, you've most likely clicked numerous *hyperlinks*. As you probably know, hyperlinks are clickable text or graphics that enable you to access additional Internet resources and Web pages. More technically speaking, hyperlinks are elements included in HTML documents that point to other Web pages or Internet documents (similar to how some HTML commands point to graphics files). Figure 1-7 shows how a couple hyperlinks on the Arizona Film Society's home page point to other Web pages. Clicking a hyperlink displays a linked page—which can be any page on the Internet (not just a Web page you've created), located anywhere in the world.

Figure 1-7
Examples of hyperlinks, which take viewers to other Web pages or Internet resources

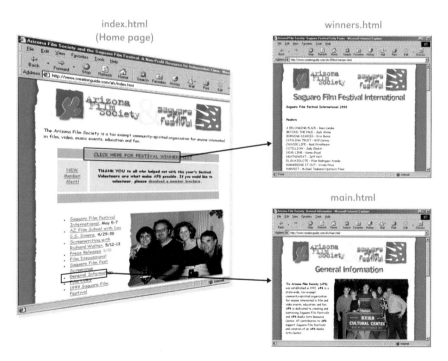

As a Web page designer, using hyperlinks naturally progresses to using multiple Web pages. Generally speaking, you won't want to place all your information on one big, long home page. Instead, you'll probably want to create a series of smaller Web pages that relate and link to one another. This collection of related pages forms your Web site.

From Your Head to the Web (and Back Again)

At this point in the chapter, the components are laid on the table: the Internet, the Web, browsers, Web pages, hyperlinks, and Web sites. This roll call of components is a good start, but we face the small detail of how a text file and a few graphics files that you've created on your computer are turned into a Web page on the Internet. Before we wade too deeply into the muck and mire of Web page transmissions, let's debunk a surprisingly popular myth:

> People who view your Web pages have access to your desktop computer.

The preceding statement is *not* true! Rest assured, Web pages are not stored on personal computers. Instead, Web page files are stored on *servers*. (Refer to Figure 1-1 on page 6 to see an illustration of how servers fit into the Internet's infrastructure.)

The Client/Server Nature of the Web

Servers are simply powerful computers—much more powerful than desktop and laptop computers—that store Internet files and run special software designed to respond to *client requests*. Of course, now we've introduced the term *client*. Let's stop this circuitous approach and briefly indulge in some geekspeak.

Basically, Web files are transmitted using what is known as the *client/server model*. In the client/server model, one system (a server) connected to a network serves the request of another system (the client). For the purposes of Web design, a *client* is a fancy name for a browser (such as Internet Explorer) running on a user's computer, and a *server* is the combination of a powerful computer that stores Web pages and the software that responds to requests to display Web pages stored on the powerful computer. Therefore, when you access a Web page, the following process, which is illustrated in Figure 1-8, takes place:

1   You connect your computer to the Internet and open your browser. Then you enter a Web address (URL) in the Address bar and press Enter, or you click a hyperlink on your browser's start page.

2   The client (your browser) sends the typed URL or the URL associated with a hyperlink across phone lines, cables, and maybe routers to your Internet service provider (ISP). Your ISP is the company you pay to provide you with access to the Internet.

lingo

URL (pronounced "you-are-ell") stands for *Uniform Resource Locator*. A URL refers to an Internet address that tells your Web browser where to look on the Internet to find a specific Web page.

note

Please keep in mind that this chapter presents a simplified (albeit accurate) explanation of the basic Web page retrieval process.

Figure 1-8
The underlying concept of accessing Web pages on remote servers

3 Your ISP then sends your URL request across the Internet via more cables, routers, and other high-speed data circuits to the computer (the server) maintaining the requested Web page.

4 The server sends the Web page information across the Internet to your ISP, and, finally, your ISP forwards the information to your computer.

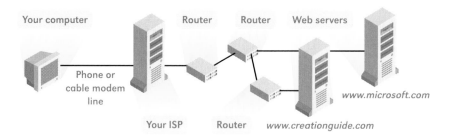

From a Web page designer's perspective, after you create a Web page, you copy your Web page's files to a server that will be hosting your Web page—similar to how you can copy a file from your hard disk onto a floppy disk (except that you copy your Web page's files across Internet lines, as described later in this book in Chapter 11). Using current File Transfer Protocol (FTP) applications or Web publishing wizards, the process of copying your Web page files to a server can be as simple as dragging files from your local folder into a folder on the server you're using to host your Web site. Therefore, when others view your published Web page, they access the server that stores copies of your files, not your computer.

That's a wrap on our fundamentals review. At this point, you're ready to forge ahead with the design and implementation of your Web pages, as described in the upcoming pages. But before closing this chapter, we'd like to brief you on what's coming in the next few chapters.

Progressing at a Steady Clip

As you might suspect, much of the work of creating a Web page entails planning your Web page (and Web site) before you sit down at your computer. You need to spend at least a little time thinking about content—including text and graphics—as well as devising your page's layout. Although designing Web pages is a creative process, it's not a black art devoid of structure. In the course of this book, we'll pass along a few basic tenets that will help make the process of creating your Web page easier.

Our expertise comes not only from our own years of online experience but also from numerous usability studies that many other designers, engineers, and information specialists have performed. From these sources, we have drawn some basic conclusions about text, graphics, and colors on the Web that we have proven in practice. Therefore, the remaining chapters in Part One—Chapters 2 through 6—address the information you should know about Web page design, including issues surrounding text, graphics, colors, helpful programs, and Web page planning. You'll find the next few chapters packed with pertinent Web page creation information that will make your future Web design endeavors more successful. Therefore, we highly recommend that you read (or at least scan) Part One before diving into Part Two.

Of course, we also know that you might be champing at the bit to create a Web presence *now*. We know the feeling. Thus, if you simply can't wait, go ahead and skip to Chapter 7 to get your feet wet by creating your first Web page on MSN's free server space. Similar to some other online services, MSN offers free server space to users who want to create Web pages from scratch or by using templates. You can create a Web page using an MSN Community Web site template within a couple hours and have your first Web page with your very own URL posted today. If you do decide to jump ahead to Chapter 7, be sure to return to Chapters 2 through 6 to brush up on the basics of creating Web pages before you go any further. Then you'll be fully prepared to create the more advanced Web pages presented in Chapters 8 through 10.

Finally, regardless of how you wind your way through this book and onto the Web, when all's said and done, remember to review Chapters 11 and 12. Chapter 11 describes how to go "live" (if you're using any method of Web page publishing other than MSN or another free hosting service), and Chapter 12 addresses updating and archiving your information. Although updating and archiving might sound fairly dull, these processes are critical. After all, if you spend time and effort to create a Web page, you probably won't want it to shrivel and die from neglect within a few weeks.

All in all, by the time you complete this book, you'll have mastered the basics of creating Web pages in a number of ways. You'll no longer cringe when you see expressions like *HTML* and *domain name*, and your skills will serve as a strong foundation that you can build on to create a wide variety of more advanced Web pages.

key points

- The Internet is hardware.

- The Web is software (including programs and documents).

- Browsers are applications that enable you to view Web pages.

- Most basic Web pages consist of multiple files—an HTML (text) file and graphics files.

- A Web site is a group of related Web pages.

- Hyperlinks provide access to other Web pages and Internet resources.

- The Internet uses the client/server model, in which a server responds to client requests for information.

- Internet users access Web pages that are stored on servers.

- If you can use a computer, you can create a Web page!

Home | Bulle

< Previous

Click Here!

creating

Keyword

NEXT

Address http://www.creationguide.com/arts/bullet

2

and shaping

WEB TEXT

Like a great meal, a successful Web page should look good as well as offer rich, satisfying content. A restaurant that serves artistically arranged yet cardboard-flavored dishes or, alternatively, uninspiring-looking piles of palate-pleasing delights rarely earns return visitors. Just as a gourmet restaurant must provide a menu that is prepared to be both tasty and visually attractive if it wants to build a clientele, a well-designed Web page needs to incorporate quality content as well as good design to inspire users to visit time and again.

Text Matters

When people contemplate building Web pages, they usually think of design first—that is, how the page will look rather than what it should say. And that's understandable as well as desirable. In fact, quite a bit of this book is devoted to Web page design. But at the heart of every Web page is *content*. After all, most people build Web pages because they have a message they want to share—even if that message simply asserts, "Look what I've been up to lately!"

To be successful, your Web page must provide information that captures viewers' attention; otherwise, viewers won't stay more than a couple seconds and probably won't return in the future. Therefore, you should start to think about your Web page's content before you get too far into its design.

If you follow along with this text, you'll be well on your way to having your Web page's content fully spelled out and formulated by the end of this chapter. But even if you don't progress that far, you'll be able to identify and create good Web text. Further, you'll know how you can maximize the use of text on your future Web pages. With this know-how in mind, you'll be able to ease into blending content and design when you start to build your Web pages.

Now, back to the matter at hand—online text. Reasonably enough, you might be thinking that you're quite conversant with using words so you don't really need to read about Web page text. But rest assured, even if you're a full-time writer, you can benefit from the tips in this chapter. Although good online text has a lot in common with good printed text, it also varies from printed text in a number of key ways. As you'll see as you progress through the chapter, creating effective online text involves mastering and blending the arts of clarity, marketing, visual appeal, technological limitations, and a little reader psychology.

Room for Improvement
In March 2000, *webreview.com* conducted an informal poll in which readers ranked their general impression of the quality of writing found on the Internet. Of those responding, 55 percent ranked the quality of online writing as fair; 22 percent ranked it as poor; 21 percent ranked it as good; and only 1 percent ranked it as excellent.

Readers' Approach to Online Pages

The first concept you need to address is that readers respond to Web pages differently than they respond to printed pages. Web experts have found that reading a block of text online takes approximately 25 percent longer than reading the same text on a printed page. In other words, in the amount of time you spend reading 75 words online, you could read 100 words on a printed page. Online users have naturally responded to this slowdown by *scanning* Web page text instead of reading every word that flashes across the monitor.

Basically, a user scans a Web page to find an item of interest that encourages the user to click a link or back up and read the content in more depth. If a Web page doesn't grab a user quickly, the user will very likely move on to another page (or another site altogether). Therefore, whenever you create content for a Web page, keep the scanning concept in the forefront of your thought processes. In this chapter, we'll describe a variety of methods you can employ to improve your Web pages' scannability.

To illustrate the scanning concept, compare Figures 2-1 and 2-2. (You can view the Web pages shown in these figures online at *www. creationguide.com/ants/bulletant-bad.html* and *www.creationguide.com/ants/bulletant-good.html*.) Figure 2-1 shows a Web page that doesn't adhere to good online-text practices, whereas Figure 2-2 follows the textual advice presented in this chapter. Notice how much faster you can identify the text's main points in Figure 2-2 than in Figure 2-1. The upcoming text explains why and provides pointers for you to use when creating your own online text.

lingo

You'll notice that we use the words *link* and *hyperlink* interchangeably.

note

On average, most visitors spend less than 30 seconds viewing a Web page.

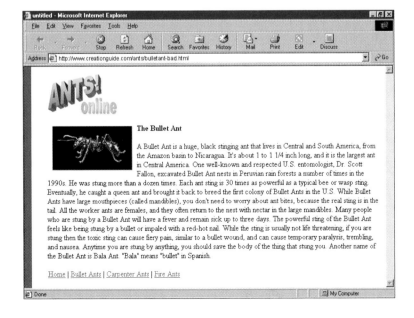

Figure 2-1
An ineffective presentation of Web page text

Figure 2-2
An effective presentation of Web page text

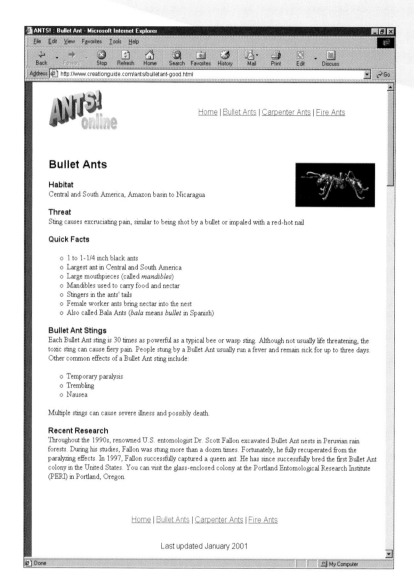

Figure 2-2
An effective presentation of Web page text

Now that we've made a case for thinking about your text and recognizing how readers approach Web pages, let's briefly look at the fundamental roles text plays on a Web page. Then we'll discuss the nitty-gritty details involved in shaping and streamlining online text.

Textual Elements of a Web Page

Most Web pages use a variety of textual components, as illustrated in Figure 2-3. As you can see in the figure (as well as on most Web pages), the textual elements described in the following subsections appear on Web pages.

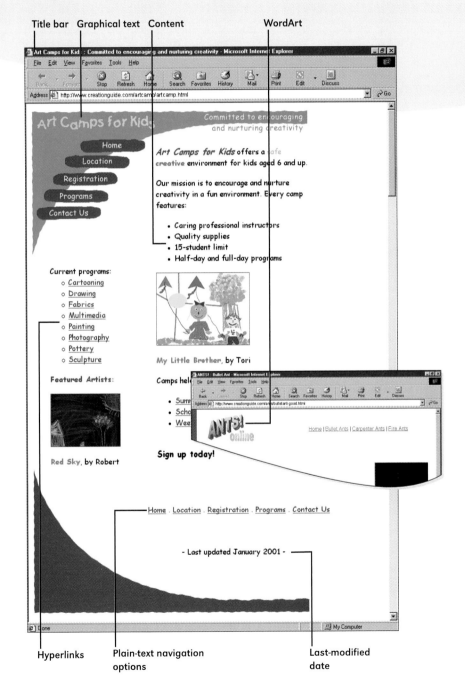

Figure 2-3
The various textual elements of a Web page

Title Bar

When you create a Web page, you create the text that appears in a browser window's title bar. The key to title text is to make it concise, clear, and useful. Notice that when you open a Web page, the Web page's title text also appears in your Microsoft Windows taskbar. Taskbar text simplifies a user's job when switching among a number of open windows. Therefore, although you can insert clever or witty title text if you want to, you should generally lean toward useful and clear instead. Notice the lame vs. helpful title bar text shown earlier in Figures 2-1 and 2-2.

Content

A Web page's content refers to its substance—the reason people are visiting the site. As described in the next few sections, a Web page's content should be clear, brief, easy to scan, informative, timely, and grammatically correct (among other qualities).

Hyperlinks

Hyperlinks provide form and clarity to a group of Web pages (or one long Web page) by linking your home page (as well as ancillary pages) to areas that contain specific related information. Textual hyperlinks should be clear, consistent, and appropriately placed, as we discuss later in this chapter and in Chapter 4.

Logos, Graphical Text, and WordArt

You can use these elements to add a professional look to your Web pages. As we'll explain in Chapter 3, you can use graphical text to add a consistent look and feel to a group of related Web pages. Having all the parts of your Web site appear interrelated clearly indicates to users that they are still within the realm of your Web site even as they click from page to page. Furthermore, logos, graphic text, and WordArt are frequently used to provide a consistent graphical link to a site's home page. You might have discovered while surfing the Web that you can usually click a company's logo to return to the site's home page. (If you haven't discovered this secret, you should test it out during your next Web surfing session.) Whenever possible, take advantage of this practice by linking your logo to your home page throughout your Web site.

try this! If you're viewing the "good" Ants Online page (Figure 2-2) online, you can click the *Ants Online* WordArt logo in the upper-left corner of the page to display the fictitious site's home page.

Forms and Menu Items

Although not illustrated in this chapter's figures, some Web pages use text for forms and menu items. We imagine you've run across online forms (especially if you've purchased a book or CD from Amazon.com or viewed an online map in Microsoft Encarta). The key to forms and menus is clarity—users must clearly know what to select, how to enter text in a form's text boxes, and which action they should perform next. We won't be working with forms and menu items until much later in this book (Chapter 10) because forms and menus are fairly advanced techniques for Web pages. In the meantime, if you're interested in reading up on the role that text plays in creating forms, check out *www.creationguide.com* for a couple references to good graphical user interface (GUI, pronounced "gooey") books that we occasionally refer to.

Plain-Text Navigational Options

Many Web designers opt to format their menu bar and navigation elements (buttons) only as graphics (in Figure 2-3, the blue buttons essentially serve as the home page's navigation elements), but we recommend that you display your navigation hyperlinks as plain text as well. If your Web page's design uses a graphical menu bar or buttons, you can avoid disrupting the layout of your Web pages by showing textual hyperlinks along the bottom of your page. Offering an alternative to graphics-based links is useful because some viewers turn off their browser's graphics capabilities to expedite Web page downloads. If you don't provide text-based navigation components, some users might not discover how to get to your site's ancillary pages.

note

As an added bonus, adding text-based navigation links to the bottom of your Web pages helps users move to other pages in your Web site without having to scroll to the top of the current page to access the main navigation links.

Date or "Last Modified" Information

Generally, you should include a date element on your Web pages. The date can be as nondescript as a small line of text located near the bottom of your page. If regularly updated content is one of your page's main selling points, however, you might want to make the date much more noticeable by placing it higher on your page and nearer the "prime" upper-left area. On the other hand, if you don't plan to update your site regularly, you might opt to omit publishing a last-modified date. (Frankly, we don't recommend that you plan on *not* updating your site, but in some circumstances, you might be able to get away with a static page or two within your site.)

see also | You'll hear more about the importance of Web pages' upper-left corner in Chapter 4.

Now that we've touched on the basic textual elements of Web pages, you're ready to shape and write Web page content.

Writing for the Web

As we mentioned earlier in this chapter, good Web writing shares some basic similarities with well-written printed text. For example, Web text should be clear, grammatical, and well formulated, and it should be written for a specific audience. But Web text requires some unique considerations that don't crop up when you're writing for another medium. One reason Web text requires this unique approach is that Web pages are *nonlinear*. Users don't often methodically read through a Web page or Web site as they would a novel; nor do they "watch" a Web site in the way they would a scripted TV show. Instead, Web surfers scan a page, read a couple snippets of text that interest them, click a link (you hope), possibly read a paragraph or two in depth, check out a picture or other multimedia element, and then click again to access another page or site. Therefore, you need to form and mold your text (and page design) to cater to the desires and habits of Web surfers.

Web Text Attracts Users' Attention Before Graphics Here's yet another reason to take your Web page's text seriously. According to Jakob Nielsen, author of *Designing Web Usability* (New Riders, 2000) and a leading expert on Web page usability, Web text frequently grabs a reader's attention before graphics do. As Nielsen reports, "It is almost twice as common for users to fixate on the text as on the images upon their initial visit to a page. In general, users were first drawn to headlines, article summaries, and captions. They often did not look at the images at all until the second or third visit to a page."

Organizing Web Text

You can effectively shape your Web text by using a combination of methods. Namely, you should adhere to the inverted pyramid methodology (described next), use headings and hyperlinks effectively, and streamline your paragraphs and body text.

Inverted pyramid methodology

Most Web professionals liken Web content to newspaper text. And to an extent, the analogy works. Like news text, Web text should fundamentally take the classic *inverted pyramid* form. An inverted pyramid approach places the most important information at the beginning of a story, including stating the conclusion up front (usually in the heading). In traditional news writing, a good story answers the questions *Who? What? Where? When? Why?* and *How?* as rapidly and succinctly as possible in order of importance. For example, a news report on a freeway car fire would probably first answer the question *What?*—a car fire—and then quickly answer the questions *Where?*—on the freeway—*When?*—during rush hour—and *Why?*—overheated engine. Of course, if the burning car belonged to the president, the story's *Who?* element would jump to the top of the pyramid. After the key points are stated in an inverted pyramid story, the remainder of the article serves to fill in the details and wind down to the least important information at the end.

As we said, you should also generally take an inverted pyramid approach when you're writing Web pages, especially if your page contains substantial textual content. A number of online news sites effectively use a modified approach to the inverted pyramid setup. For example, *iwon.com*, one of our favorite news sites, uses a clear-cut variation of the inverted pyramid. On *iwon.com*, the home page shows links similar to the following hierarchy under a "Today's Headlines" heading:

Top News
> **Headline**
> **Headline**
> ⋮

Sports News
> **Headline**
> **Headline**
> ⋮

Business News

    Headline

    Headline

    ⋮

Entertainment News

    Headline

    Headline

    ⋮

Using the preceding setup, users can click a main heading (such as Top News, Sports News, Business News, or Entertainment News in the preceding example) to view the first few lines of each headline's story. For example, let's say you click the Top News link. You would then see the following layout:

Top story

    A few lines of text providing the main gist of the story

    More Headlines

      Headline

        A few lines of text providing the main gist of the story

      Headline

        A few lines of text providing the main gist of the story

note

To help speed up the trickle-down informational process, you can also click a headline on the *iwon.com* home page to display the full story of any headline that immediately captures your interest.

At this point, you could click a headline to read the full version of the story. Notice the trickle-down effect of the information—main headline, short synopsis, and full story. Imagine if the home page contained every full news story of the day—readers would flee from the text-packed site quicker than the page could download.

Although the news-site setup described here is highly effective, it's probably much more complex than your Web pages need to be. (We're pretty sure you're relieved to hear that!) The setup of *iwon.com* provides a good example of the inverted pyramid methodology. On your pages, you'll be more concerned with ensuring that your most important points (the key points in an inverted pyramid) display quickly and "jump out" at readers. You can achieve this effect by employing a few key techniques, including using headings and hyperlinks wisely and streamlining your text for Web use.

Brainstorms, headings, and hyperlinks

Now that the theory of serving the best information first is firmly in place, you're ready to start thinking about actual content. When it comes to creating text, some people have a hard time getting started. Therefore, we suggest a popular, free-form approach to creating your Web text— brainstorming with a pencil, pen, or keyboard. To effectively brainstorm, follow these steps:

1 Sit down with a pad of paper (or your laptop, if you're lucky), and jot down every concept you want to include in your Web site or Web page. Don't worry about organization or wording. The goal here is to get your ideas out of your head and onto paper (or screen).

2 After you have all the topics that you want to include on your Web page in front of you in hard-copy form (print your electronic notes, if neces- sary), write a keyword next to each topic. You might find that multiple topics can be associated with the same keyword. That's fine—in fact, that will help you group your information later. Again, don't overana- lyze the details; you're working on big umbrella concepts at this point.

3 Review each keyword, and determine which keywords deserve to be headings and which should be hyperlinks. A heading calls attention to a brief amount of information on an existing page; in contrast, a hyperlink indicates that you have enough related text to create a separate Web page from existing information.

Figures 2-1 and 2-2 shown earlier in this chapter provide an ideal example of effective brainstorming. As you can see, Figure 2-1 displays a large block of text—essentially an information brain dump; Figure 2-2 shows where keywords (formatted as headings) come into play to point out the main facts included in the text. If you were brainstorming about bullet ants, you might come up with the paragraph in Figure 2-1. Then when you reviewed your paragraph, you would come up with the head- ing topics shown in Figure 2-2. Remember—clearly calling attention to key points for users is critical. Not only is reading online more arduous than reading printed text, but millions of Web pages are also vying for users' time.

To illustrate how brainstorming can organize a Web *site* as well as a Web *page*, let's view the Ants Online menu bar shown in Figure 2-4. By looking at the menu bar's hyperlinks, you can instantaneously see that

lingo

A *keyword* is a word or phrase that succinctly summarizes the overall essence of a concept or topic. Frequently, a keyword also serves as a main idea that encompasses a group of related concepts.

tip

To determine whether key topics should be hyperlinks on your home page, visualize your home page as a fancy table of contents that summarizes the Web site's main ideas and points users to each area of the site. (See the home page shown in Figure 2-3.)

the Ants Online site includes a home page and three ant species pages. You can almost visualize exactly how the site's brainstorming session might've progressed—the types of ants emerged as the big ideas (thereby necessitating hyperlinks and separate Web pages), and the main facts about each type of ant served to create headings (such as Habitat, Threat, Quick Facts, and so forth, as shown in Figure 2-2). Brainstorming helps you visualize your approach to your Web pages and Web site, which in turn helps you write clear, topic-driven text.

Figure 2-4
The Ants Online menu bar, which clearly defines the site's organization

The shape of body text

At this point, you should have a fair idea of the information you want to include on your home page as well as the logical headings. You should also have a feel for possible ancillary (linked) pages. You're now ready to begin molding the ideas you freely jotted down into user-friendly text. In other words, it's time to write.

Copyrights and Web Text

Because you'll be creating and publishing text on the Web, you should know a little about copyright laws. Copyright laws protect intellectual property. Among other countries, most of Europe, Canada, Japan, and the United States are members of the Bern Union, and they adhere to the rulings of the Bern Convention, which initially laid the groundwork for copyright issues in 1886 and has since passed through a number of revisions.

According to current Bern Convention guidelines, a writer of an original work automatically holds the work's copyright (unless the writer specifically waives that right) for life plus 25 years at a minimum. Some countries guarantee a longer copyright; for example, the United States grants a copyright for life plus 70 years after death. Furthermore, the Bern Convention rulings stipulate that a copyright is granted automatically, without any paperwork or other required formalities.

Keep in mind that the copyright laws protect the actual words used to express an idea—not the idea itself. Therefore, you shouldn't copy text off the Web and paste it into your site. Instead, if you want to include information you found on another site, you should paraphrase relevant text and consider referencing the original source or providing a link to the original source's Web page.

Fortunately, you don't need to stall yourself at this time by fixating on finding the perfect words (which don't exist!) or devising precise sentence structures. Right now, simply formulate your message in rough-draft form. Use the inverted pyramid style to organize your brainstormed ideas. Cut to the chase and display your main topics first. Then convert your brainstormed ideas into readable sentences and clear headings. Most of all, keep in mind that readers will scan your page before they ever read your paragraphs, so begin to implement or at least think about visual cues—such as headings, sidebars, and formatted typography. (In Chapter 4, we'll describe how to use page-layout elements that can add to your page's scannability as well.) That's a lot to keep in mind. To help simplify this stage, here's a checklist of considerations you can refer to as you write Web text:

note

In the next section, we'll describe how to streamline your Web text, so if your paragraphs run a little long at this stage, don't sweat it.

- Introduce one idea per paragraph.

- Keep sentences short without dumbing down.

- Use simple sentence structures. Avoid compound sentences and unnecessary subordinate clauses.

- Think about how you can highlight keywords later during the design phase (such as by inserting hyperlinks or using color or typeface variations, as shown in Figure 2-3).

- Aim to limit paragraphs to approximately 75 words or fewer, if possible. In Figure 2-2, the "*Recent Research*" paragraph shows the approximate maximum length of an online paragraph.

- Use bulleted lists whenever possible.

- Use numbered lists only when you're presenting a series of steps.

- Insert headings and subheadings to break up text and highlight key points.

- Keep headlines simple and direct; choose meaningful over clever wording.

- Ensure that the hierarchy of the headings is clear, both editorially and visually. In other words, make sure your main headings follow a logical system of subordination and are displayed uniquely, such as by formatting main headings larger than subheadings or differentiating them by color or typeface.

- Separate paragraphs within a section by using *white space* (space without any content, either textual or graphical). As you'll see in Chapters 3 and 4 (and beyond), white space is your friend!

- Avoid having too many hyperlinks in body text. Don't embed hyperlinks within paragraphs unless the hyperlinks add extremely pertinent information to your content and you're sure readers will return to your page after clicking the embedded link. Embedding hyperlinks within paragraphs frequently leads readers astray. Generally, hyperlinks should be used to aid navigation.

Writing Effectively for an Online Audience

You've organized your information by topic, written paragraphs, added bulleted lists, inserted headings, and indicated which key points will serve as hyperlinks. Your Web text should be shaping up nicely by now, but the actual wording probably still needs some attention. As with all good writing, you're not finished with the process until you've polished and streamlined your text (as well as read and revised it at least a million times!). One way to fine-tune your text is by looking for and avoiding specific types of writing weaknesses. The number-one way to streamline Web text entails strengthening your sentences.

Strong sentences

Never fear—you won't need steroids or garlic to create strong sentences. Strengthening your sentences merely involves packing as much meaning into each word or clause as possible. As we discussed earlier in this chapter, because you want to limit the number of words you use to convey your Web page's information, you need to make the most out of the words that make the cut.

On Web pages, conciseness is the key (so if you're a Dickensian writer, you'll face a greater challenge than the minimalists out there). To strengthen your text, go through your copy word by word and line by line to ensure that the text implements the following techniques as much as possible:

- **Precise words**   Your text should use clear, easily understood words. If you mean

  Haight & Ashbury

  don't write

  The intersection in which Haight Street crosses across Ashbury Street.

tip

When writing precise Web text, be cautious when using terms that have alternate online significance, such as *home, back, forward, browse,* and so forth.

■ **Strong verbs** Whenever possible, your sentences should use short, solid verbs. For example, instead of writing

This page serves to explain…

simply write

This page explains…

Also, replace *to be* verbs (*is, are, was, were*—you get the idea) with more specific action verbs whenever possible. For example, instead of writing

The TV is on in the background, and it's loud.

replace both instances of *is* with one strong verb:

The TV blares in the background.

When you use strong verbs, you add life to your text and frequently reduce sentence lengths.

■ **Active voice** When you use active voice, your sentences clearly show who or what performs the action. Using active voice works hand in hand with implementing strong verbs. To illustrate, here's a passive-voice sentence:

Many homes were destroyed by the tornado.

Notice that the tornado performed the action (destroyed), yet the word *tornado* appears dead last in the sentence. To make the preceding sentence active, move the word that's performing the action closer to the beginning of the sentence and change the verb, as follows:

The tornado destroyed many homes.

■ **Clear antecedents** Frequently, writers insert pronouns—such as *it, he, she, they,* and so forth—and readers are left wondering just what the pronoun refers to. You can easily eliminate antecedent problems by replacing all unclear pronouns with specific text. (*Hint*: When in doubt, replace the pronoun; better to be overly clear than even slightly vague.) A key antecedent tip is to limit the use of the word *it*, and especially avoid starting sentences with weak "crutch" constructs such as *It is*. For example, the following sentence is grammatically correct but not as strong as it could be:

It is common for cats to sleep all day while you work to put food in their bowls.

tip

To practice reworking sentences, surf the Web for a while. When you see passive text or weak verbs, stop and consider how you could modify the text to be more concise, precise, and active.

You can strengthen this sentence simply by eliminating *It is*, as follows:

Commonly, cats sleep all day while you work to put food in their bowls.

You should also avoid starting your sentences with *There is* and *There are*. Both constructs are weak and almost as commonly overused as *It is*.

Something You Can Do to Keep Things Clear Watch out for all variations of the word *thing*—the term frequently weakens otherwise strong sentences and headings. To quickly eliminate this vagary from your text, use your word processor's Search feature to find each instance of *thing*. (Some writers might be surprised to see how often the term pops up.) Replace the word with more specific terminology whenever you can.

Spelling and grammar

After you streamline your text, the final stage of writing involves checking your spelling and grammar. This step has few gray areas, so we'll put it simply:

Always, always, always run your spelling checker on your Web page's copy. Then print out your text and read it from the hard-copy version— out loud!

Reading your copy out loud slows down your perception of the text so that you can see misspellings as well as hear when your grammar takes a nosedive. If you change your text significantly during your hard-copy read-through, make the changes to your Web text, save the changed text, print it out, and read it aloud again. Finally, when you think you have your text just right, put it down for a couple hours (or longer). Then return to the hard copy with fresh eyes and ears, and read it aloud one last time.

tip

If you need to brush up on your grammar skills, we highly recommend that you snag a copy of *When Words Collide: A Media Writer's Guide to Grammar and Style* (Wadsworth, 1999, now in its fifth edition) by Lauren Kessler and Duncan McDonald. Because the guide targets media writers, you'll also find tips regarding how to streamline your text (including using inverted pyramids, creating active sentence structures, avoiding compound sentences, applying proper punctuation, and more). For further Web writing resources, visit *www.creationguide.com*.

Our recommended polishing process might sound time-consuming and possibly annoying to anyone sitting in your general vicinity, but it's well worth it. (And if you're concerned about wasting paper by repeatedly printing your modified Web text, cross out the old text and print the revised edition on the page's flip side.) Almost no other Web site design error erodes your credibility faster than misspellings and incorrect grammar on your Web pages.

Treating Text as a Design Element

As you know, text on a Web page informs as well as adds to a page's overall design. (Refer to Figure 2-3.) In Chapter 4, we'll delve into how to combine Web text with Web art to create attractive and effective layouts, but you should start to mull over basic text-design issues while you're pulling your text together. Therefore, while you create your content and read Chapters 3 and 4, keep the following text-design issues in mind. (Don't worry if you're not particularly clear about how to implement the following techniques; in Chapter 4, we'll revisit these issues when we discuss Web page layouts in more detail.)

- Create graphical titles and headings for added artistic effect.
- Display pull-quotes and sidebars to lighten text-heavy pages.
- Add WordArt, logos, graphical text, and banners to create a consistent look and feel throughout your site. (In Chapter 9, we'll describe how to use Microsoft Word to create WordArt.)
- Apply color or other typographical formatting (such as boldface or italic) to draw attention to important words and concepts.
- Use drop caps or hung initials (larger first letters in a paragraph) to indicate the beginning of a section.
- Ensure that backgrounds don't interfere with the text's readability.
- Include important data (such as contact information, company name, and so forth) as text, even if the information appears in graphical form elsewhere on the page. Some people turn off their graphics to speed up surfing, which means they'll miss graphical information provided on your page.

- Avoid tiny print—if in doubt, let the users define the text's size via their default browser settings.

- Use easy-to-read, cross-platform compatible fonts. Currently, the fonts most compatible with Windows-based and Apple Macintosh machines include Arial, Arial Narrow, Comic Sans, Courier New, Times New Roman, and Verdana.

Finally, as a parting text tip after all the dos and don'ts outlined in this chapter, we want to suggest that you have fun with your Web page's content. The Web grants you the freedom to quickly and creative impart information in new ways. Think about exactly what you want to say, and then write the parts of your message as clearly and actively as possible. Once you start to write strong concise sentences, you'll be hooked.

key points

- Users scan Web pages instead of reading them linearly.

- Titles, contents, hyperlinks, logos, WordArt creations, graphical text elements, forms, menus, navigation options, and last-modified dates represent typical uses of Web page text.

- The text of a Web page attracts users' attention before the graphics do.

- Web page information should loosely emulate the traditional inverted pyramid news-style writing methodology.

- Brainstorm to clarify your Web page's main points, headings, and hyperlinks.

- Write clear, strong, active sentences and well-formed, concise paragraphs.

- Keep headings and hyperlinks clear and descriptive.

- Use bulleted lists and a heading hierarchy to help readers quickly identify key points.

- Include important information as text to cater to users who opt not to download Web graphics.

- Spell-check, spell-check, and then spell-check again (and don't forget to print and read the text aloud).

- Check your grammar.
- Start to think about text design elements, including typographical formatting, color, and graphical text elements.
- Most of all, after taking into account the strengths and limitations of Web writing, allow the writing experience to be an enjoyable and creative process.

pixel

illustrating

.jpg

your message:

CREATING AND USING ART ON THE WEB

Ever try to give directions without gesturing? It's amazing how a few good hand signals can clarify 10 minutes of rambling. Web graphics offer the same benefit (with the added bonus of pretty colors) as gestures do—a few good graphics and well-placed design elements can transform hard-to-read, text-laden pages into highly communicative and effective works of Web art.

Welcome to Web Graphics

Our goal in this chapter is to simplify the topic of Web graphics. In a perfect world, we'd dedicate pages and pages to the nuances of using graphics on the Web (mostly because we like graphics), but then you'd never get to the rest of the book. We also don't want you to feel intimidated when it comes to using Web graphics. As you might have discovered, you can easily find an overabundance of information about advanced graphics by looking on the Internet and in bookstores everywhere. Fortunately, you can use Web graphics effectively without immersing yourself in gamma theory and rasterizing. Therefore, we've opted to take the practical approach of presenting what we deem to be the most significant and fundamental information about Web page graphics. Think of this chapter as your personal crash course in Web art. By the time you reach the "key points" section at the end of the chapter, you'll have plenty to think about, a few tricks up your sleeve, a cocktail party quip or two, and a number of places to turn to during your search, acquisition, creation, and preparation of Web art.

Mechanics of Web Graphics

Before you start flipping through this chapter to check out the pictures, you really need to read this section to make sure you understand a few key Web graphics issues. As you know, Web graphics look fairly similar to printed graphics, but some Web-specific factors come into play when you're creating and using graphics on the Web. Specifically, online graphics require you to consider color limitations, file formats, and file sizes as well as possible transparency, downloading, and animation issues. Acquiring an awareness of three main factors—colors, file types, and file sizes—enables you to begin using graphics on your Web pages as well as provides a jumping-off point for further graphics study. Therefore, the overall plan of attack here is to tuck some Web graphics fundamentals into a cranial corner or two before opening your mind to the more creative (and fun) prospects of using, gathering, and creating Web graphics. Let's get started by looking at how graphics display color.

Pixels, Palettes, and Colors

First and foremost, every online graphic consists of a bunch of tiny colored squares working together to form an image. In a way, online graphics emulate a painting technique called *pointillism*. Pointillism, introduced by French painter Georges Seurat (1859–1891), is the art of painting pictures one dot (or tiny brush stroke) at a time. Through pointillism, Seurat broke each image on his canvas down into tiny dots of color. When you look closely at a pointillist painting, you can see each dot. As you move away from the painting, the dots blend together to create a picture. Computers display pictures using a technique similar to pointillism, except that instead of painted dots, computers divide pictures into colored squares, called *pixels*. For example, take a look at the cherries in Figure 3-1. (You can display the graphic online by visiting *www.creationguide.com/cherries.*) Figure 3-1 could be any graphic displayed on your screen. As you can see, the graphic looks like most other pictures online (or in printed material, for that matter), and there are no blatant signs of dots, squares, or pixels.

lingo

A *pixel* is one square on a grid of thousands of squares that are individually colored to create an image.

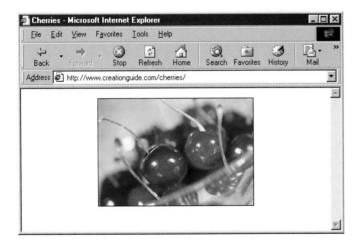

Figure 3-1
A couple cherries standing in as a typical graphic

Now let's look at the graphic a little more closely. If you open the cherries picture in a graphics editing application (such as Jasc Paint Shop Pro, Adobe Photoshop, Microsoft Paint, or Microsoft PhotoDraw) and then dramatically magnify the image, you'll be able to see the actual squares (pixels) that make up the picture, as shown in Figure 3-2. As you can see in Figure 3-2, a picture's colors and shades vary from pixel to pixel.

tip

If you don't have a graphics editing application on your system or if you want to test-drive a popular "full-service" graphics editing application, visit *www.jasc.com* and download a free trial version of Paint Shop Pro.

see also | *We'll have more to say about graphics editing applications later in this chapter as well as in Chapter 5.*

Figure 3-2
The same cherries shown in Figure 3-1 magnified to show the image's pixels

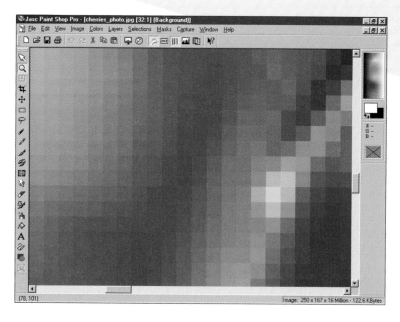

lingo

A *palette* holds the set of colors used in a graphic.

Now that you know about pixels, we can talk a little about *palettes*. A palette is simply the table of colors used in a graphic. Some Web graphics (namely, graphics saved using the GIF format, as described in the next section) use a limited collection of colors. You can assign a palette to an image, or you can let your graphics program generate a palette automatically as you create and edit an image. A GIF palette can hold up to 256 colors, but many images use fewer colors than that. For example, the cherries graphic shown in Figure 3-3 uses 8 colors, and the hot pepper graphic shown in Figure 3-4 (on page 46) uses 128 colors. Notice the pictures' sizes—the cherries graphic is 3 KB (very small), and the hot pepper graphic is 7 KB (almost as small as the cherry GIF graphic).

Figure 3-3
The cherry image's palette (very small)

GIF (8 colors): 3 KB

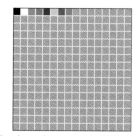

8-color palette used in GIF image

Generally, most graphics applications enable you to view the colors included in a GIF graphic's palette. Further, you can reduce the size of a GIF image by reducing or limiting the number of colors in the picture's palette. And, as you probably know, smaller file sizes equate to quicker download times on the Web.

try this!   To illustrate this section's pixels discussion first hand, display *www.creationguide.com/ cherries* in your browser. Right-click the cherries graphic, and select Save Picture As or Save Image As. (The command varies by browser.) The Save Picture dialog box appears, as shown here:

Save the picture to your computer's hard disk, and be sure to remember *where* you save the figure. (For this exercise, we recommend that you save the picture to your desktop for easy access as well as quick deletion later.) Next, open your graphics program—such as Jasc Paint Shop Pro, Microsoft Paint, or Adobe Photoshop—and then open the file in the application. (You can also import an online picture into your graphics program by right-clicking and choosing Copy, and then opening your graphics program and pasting the image directly into your graphics application.)

To view the image's pixels, enlarge the picture by using your graphics program's Zoom Tool or Magnifying Glass. To further illustrate how pixels work, incrementally decrease the image's view (or "zoom out") to a slightly more viewable size, as shown here:

If you zoom out slowly, you can see how the pixels start to blend to create a clear image.

Figure 3-4
The hot pepper image's palette (small enough for quick down-loading)

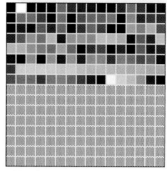

GIF (128 colors): 7 KB

128-color palette used in GIF image

try this! To view a color palette, display *www.creationguide.com/palettes/samples.html* and then right-click and save either the cherries or hot pepper GIF image to your computer's hard disk. Next, open the GIF image in your graphics editor. To display the image's palette in Paint Shop Pro, select Edit Palette from the Colors menu. In Photoshop, select Mode from the Image menu, and then select Color Table. (We realize that every graphics package has its own menu options; we provide the preceding two commands to give you an idea of the type of command you should look for in your graphics application.)

note

In some Web graphics applications and documentation, a palette is also referred to as a *color look-up table* (CLUT) or simply a *color table*.

As we just mentioned, palettes come into play when you use GIF images. We realize we haven't defined GIFs yet—or any Web-friendly image formats for that matter. Now that you have a feel for the nature of pixels and palettes, however, let's move on and discuss graphics file formats that you can use on the Web. We'll talk more about palettes when we discuss GIFs later in this chapter. (We'll also cover palettes in Chapter 4, when we talk about choosing colors for your Web site.)

Graphics File Formats

As you might recall, in Chapter 1 we said that every graphic on a Web page is stored as a separate file. As a refresher, look at Figure 3-5, which shows the sample Web page introduced in Chapter 1 (Figure 1-5). Notice the names of the two image files used in Figure 3-5.

The title bar figure's file name ends with a .gif file extension (afs_title.gif), and the other figure's file name ends with a .jpg file extension (4members.jpg). Graphics file extensions work on the same principles as other file formats. For example, if you see a file on your desktop named holiday_gift_list.doc, you know by the .doc extension that the file is probably a Microsoft Word document, and you'll want to open

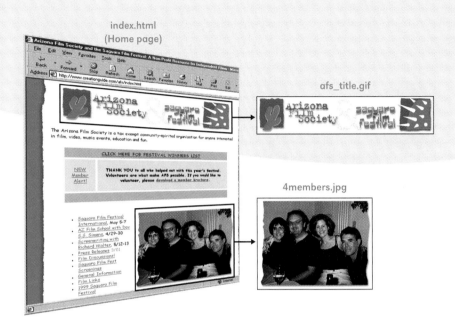

Figure 3-5
GIF and JPEG files used on a Web page

the document in Word (especially if you're one of the people listed on the holiday gift list!). Similarly, if you see a file on your desktop named bills.xls, you know the .xls indicates a Microsoft Excel document, so you could open the file in Excel (although you might want to avoid files named *bills*). In relation to Web graphics, your Web pages can include graphics images that use the .gif and .jpeg (or .jpg) file extensions because most popular Web browsers can display GIF and JPEG (pronounced "jay-peg") files.

GIFs

GIFs are the most widely supported graphics type on the Web (which means that almost all browsers—old, new, and in-between—can display GIF images). *GIF* stands for *Graphics Interchange Format*. CompuServe created this format in the 1980s as an efficient means to transmit images across data networks. The GIF format's main strength is that GIF images are usually small, which means that they download and display quickly.

As we mentioned earlier in this chapter, GIF images use palettes and support up to 256 colors (which makes them 8-bit graphics). Because GIFs support a limited number of colors, you should use GIFs for flat color areas (such as the blue and green areas in the Art Camps for Kids Web page in Figure 3-7), logos, line art, icons, cartoonlike illustrations, buttons,

lingo

GIF (Graphics Interchange Format) is a graphics file format used to create images for use on the Internet. GIF images can contain up to 256 colors.

horizontal rules, bullets, backgrounds, and other graphic elements that require few colors. Figures 3-6 and 3-7 show examples of GIF images.

Figure 3-6
Line art, horizontal rules, but-tons, bullets, and graphical text examples of GIF files

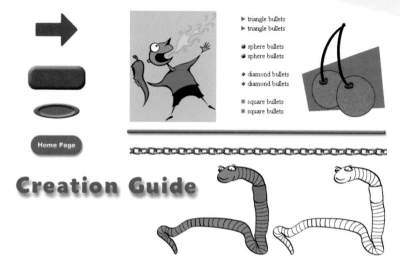

In addition to being palette-reliant, small, and efficient, GIFs perform three special tricks: interlacing, transparency, and animation.

Interlaced GIFs   Normally, a GIF image appears on-screen row by row, from top to bottom of the image, like pulling down a window shade. If you want to, you (as a Web page designer) can change how a GIF down-loads onto viewers' monitors by saving your GIF file as an *interlaced GIF file*. An interlaced GIF graphic displays on users' screens as blurred or jagged at first and then gradually becomes clearer. Figure 3-8 shows an interlaced GIF in the midst of downloading. The figure on the left shows the image before it's fully downloaded, and the figure on the right shows the fully downloaded image. (To view the interlaced GIF online, visit *www.creationguide.com/interlaced*.)

Interlaced GIFs are good to use when you want to transmit an image's main idea to readers while they wait for the complete download. The drawback of interlaced GIFs is that they have slightly larger file sizes than conventional (noninterlaced) GIF images. Therefore, for buttons, icons, and small graphics, you're better off sticking to the conventional GIF file format.

note

If you're using a fast Internet connection, such as a cable modem, you probably won't see the effects of interlacing.

Figure 3-7
GIF images used for large, flat color areas

Figure 3-8
Downloading an interlaced GIF

Transparent GIFs   Transparent GIFs (GIFs that use the GIF89a format) enable you to design icons, logos, and other elements that appear to be cut out, thereby allowing the Web page's background to show through areas of the image. For example, as you can see in the right side of Figure 3-9 (and online at *www.creationguide.com/transparent*), the yellow background shows through in the transparent GIF to create the illusion of a nonrectangular image.

Figure 3-9
Comparing a standard GIF with a transparent GIF

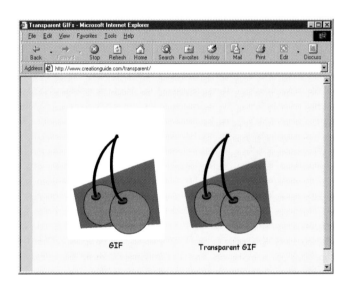

When you create a transparent GIF, you essentially specify a unique color in your image to serve as your transparent color. For example, you could color the background of your picture hot pink and then assign hot pink to be the picture's transparent color—just make sure hot pink doesn't show up elsewhere in your image or you'll create unwanted transparent spots. When a browser encounters the transparent color, the browser doesn't show any graphics information in the color's area, which enables the Web page's background to show through.

note

If a GIF's background color matches your Web page's background color—such as an image with a white background on a Web page with a white background— you automatically achieve the illusion of transparency.

Animated GIFs   The last GIF "trick" involves animation. Using GIF animation tools and graphics editing programs, you can layer GIFs and save the layers in a "stack" to create simple animations. When a browser displays the stacked GIF images, it displays each image one after the other. This technique is similar to the old flip-card "movies" that were popular long before most of us came into existence. Moving icons are a prime example of animated GIFs. Figure 3-10 illustrates the theory behind animated GIFs. To see the smiley animation in action, visit *www.creationguide.com/*

animated_gifs. As you'll see later in this chapter, you can download free animated GIFs and GIF animation tools from the Web.

An animated GIF uses layers of GIF images to achieve animation.

frame 01 frame 02 frame 03 frame 04 frame 05 frame 06 frame 07 frame 08 frame 09 frame 10

Figure 3-10
The GIF images used to create a spinning-smiley-face animated GIF

"Safe" Colors for the Web

As you know, all computer systems are not created equal. Many people have a heck of a time keeping up with the computer industry's rapid pace of hardware development. Therefore, when you design Web pages, you should keep in mind that not all people will be able to access your pages if your pages require the latest and greatest display hardware. In fact, approximately 10 percent of all Web surfers are restricted to viewing Web pages in 256 colors (although most new systems display millions of colors, so the 256-color design issue will probably soon be a design consideration of the past). Therefore, for the next couple years, when you design your Web pages and create GIF images, you might consider relying on colors that 256-color monitors can display without a hitch. The universal colors are referred to as the *Web-safe* or *browser-safe* colors. If your Web page uses colors other than Web-safe colors, systems that support only 256 colors will resort to *dithering* the nonstandard colors.

Dither refers to the random dot pattern that results when colors are approximated by mixing similar and available colors from a limited palette. To avoid dither, stick to the 216 Web-safe colors. (The other 40 colors out of the 256 colors are reserved for the computer system's use.) The figure below shows the Web-safe color palette. Graphics editing programs usually provide a Web-safe palette that you can load when working with GIF images, or you can copy the palette shown below off the Web (at *www.creationguide.com/palettes*) and create your own Web-safe color palette based on the Web image. For example, open the color palette image in Paint Shop Pro, and choose Save Palette from the Colors menu. The Web-safe color palette is also shown in the appendix of this book (along with a few other color resources).

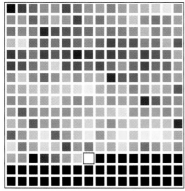

216 Web-safe colors

JPEGs

In addition to GIF graphics, your Web pages will probably include JPEG images. The JPEG image file format was created by and named after the *Joint Photographic Experts Group*. This image format supports millions of colors, and JPEGs are almost universally supported by browsers. (Technically speaking, JPEGs support 24-bit color, which is also referred to as *full color* or *true color*.) Because JPEGs can contain millions of colors, JPEG graphics frequently display photographic images online.

When you're working with JPEGs for your Web pages, you can specify whether you want to save your JPEGs as standard or progressive:

- ■ **Standard** When you save an image as a standard JPEG file, the image loads line by line from the top of the screen down, similar to how GIFs download by default. Figure 3-11 shows a standard JPEG image that is about four-fifths downloaded.

Figure 3-11
Standard JPEG images load line by line from the top down

Standard JPEG - 58 KB
No compression

- ■ **Progressive** When you save an image as a progressive JPEG file, the image first appears blurry and then becomes more focused as the image data is downloaded (similar to interlaced GIFs). With fast Internet connection speeds, the progressive rendering might not be readily apparent to viewers; instead, after a delay, the image will seem to "pop up" onto the page. In our experience, progressive JPEGs seem to create smaller file sizes and download slightly quicker than standard JPEG files.

Another JPEG configuration parameter that you can use to your advantage is *compression*. Compression is a process that reduces an image's file size by throwing out some color information. JPEG compression is called a "lossy" compression scheme because once you compress an image the deleted information is lost. Fortunately, if you're careful, people viewing the image online can't easily discern the information loss.

Keep in mind that the more you compress an image, the smaller the image's file size becomes, but the resulting image won't be as sharp as a less compressed image. Therefore, you should experiment with various compression settings when configuring JPEG images for your Web pages.

tip

When compressing JPEG images, always save an original uncompressed version of your graphic. Once an image is compressed using JPEG's compression scheme, the data is lost.

try this! To view online images using standard and progressive rendering as well as to compare compressed images, visit *www.creationguide.com/jpegs* (also shown below). Watch the page closely as the pictures download, and notice which image displays first. Also notice the quality and size of each JPEG image. (If you're using a fast Internet connection, you might not see a speed difference.)

At this point, you should be comfortable with the idea of progressive and compressed JPEG files, but we haven't yet explained how to configure these types of settings for a JPEG image. Fortunately, most image editing programs make specifying JPEG file parameters fairly easy. To access JPEG file settings in Paint Shop Pro, follow the steps on the next page.

1 Open your JPEG image in Paint Shop Pro. (Feel free to practice with any of the fruit.jpg images shown on *www.creationguide.com/jpegs.*)

2 Choose Save As from the File menu to display the Save As dialog box.

3 Enter a new filename, and then click Options to access the Save Options dialog box, shown in Figure 3-12.

Figure 3-12
Configuring JPEG compression and rendering settings in Paint Shop Pro

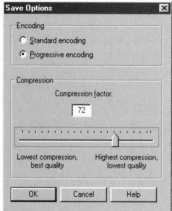

4 Specify an encoding option (Standard or Progressive), select a compression setting, click OK, and then click Save.

To configure JPEG settings in Photoshop, follow these steps:

1 Open your JPEG image in Photoshop. (Feel free to practice with any of the fruit.jpg images shown on *www.creationguide.com/jpegs.*)

2 Choose Save from the File menu.

3 Enter a file name, and click Save. The JPEG Options dialog box opens, as shown in Figure 3-13. Specify compression settings by moving the Quality slider in the JPEG Options dialog box, and then click OK.

Figure 3-13
Configuring JPEG compression and rendering settings in Photoshop

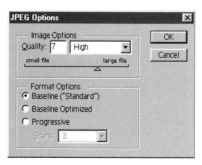

PNG

The third (and final) graphic type we'll discuss in this chapter is the PNG file format. PNG (pronounced "ping") stands for *Portable Network Graphics*. Similar to GIFs, PNG files are small, they load quickly, and they're limited to 256 colors. PNG files transmit faster than GIFs, but only the newer browsers support them.

Initially, the PNG file format was devised because Unisys, the makers of the GIF compression algorithm, decided to enforce the patents for that algorithm—meaning that software vendors had to pay to use it. But you really don't need to know the details about the PNG vs. GIF debate. Just know that newer major browsers (including Microsoft Internet Explorer 5 and later) can display PNG images, but most Web designers don't use PNGs in deference to users who surf the Web with older or less technologically advanced browsers. At this point, your Web pages probably shouldn't use PNGs either.

Size Matters

The last major "technical" Web graphics consideration that we cover in this chapter is file size, which is directly related to download speeds. As a Web surfer, you've probably caught yourself drumming your mouse impatiently while waiting for pages that take longer than 10 seconds to display (or, even more likely, clicking away before the slow page ever fully displays). As a Web designer, you need to hold on to that impatient feeling. When you design Web pages and use Web art, you should always keep one eye on your design and another eye on the user's perspective. (That almost sounds painful!)

When you use Web art, you can take advantage of a few techniques that will help keep your file sizes manageable. We already covered a few key topics earlier in this chapter that can help to reduce file sizes and speed download times, including these:

- ■ Avoid dither in GIF images by using Web-safe colors whenever possible, especially in large, flat color areas. (Just think—before reading this chapter, the preceding sentence wouldn't have made a bit of sense to you!)

- ■ Configure JPEG images to render progressively.

- ■ Compress JPEG images to reduce file sizes.

lingo

PNG (Portable Network Graphics) is a graphics file format designed to replace GIF images on the Internet.

note

Internet Explorer for Microsoft Windows began to incorporate some PNG support in 1997 and just barely began providing PNG support in Macintosh versions of Internet Explorer in 2000. Therefore, the PNG file format is taking a while to catch on because developers know that all users don't have access to the most up-to-date or most technologically advanced browsers. From a developer's perspective, there's currently no reason to risk losing viewers by using a PNG file format when the GIF file format is readily available, just as easy to use, and widely recognized in almost all browsers (regardless of version).

In addition to using the three preceding graphics file techniques, you can control download speeds by resizing your images, cropping images, and using thumbnails. We briefly describe each technique in the following sections. Please keep in mind that the actual mechanics of accomplishing certain tasks vary among graphics editing tools.

Resizing graphics

One of the best ways to conserve download time is to physically resize your images in a graphics editor. Note that we're talking about resizing the image, not simply changing your view. Zooming in and out changes your view of an image, but it doesn't affect the file's actual size or dimensions. Try to size your images to the approximate size you want to display them on your Web page. Figure 3-14 shows the Resize dialog box you use in Paint Shop Pro to resize an image. To access the Resize dialog box, open the image and then select Resize from the Image menu.

Figure 3-14
Resizing an image in Paint Shop Pro

Keep in mind that smaller images result in smaller file sizes, which result in quicker download times.

Cropping images

In addition to resizing an image, you can *crop* the image to reduce its size. When you crop an image, you cut out the portion of the image that you don't want to use. Cropping is frequently used to remove any unwanted or unneeded portions of your photograph. For example, you might want to crop the apples.jpg image shown in Figure 3-14 to show a close up of the green apple amidst the red apples in the colander. Figure 3-15 shows crop lines (the dashed lines that surround the portion of the image you want to retain) in the apples.jpg image, which is 50 KB, and Figure 3-16 shows the result of cropping apples.jpg. The cropped version in Figure 3-16 is only 6 KB.

lingo

Cropping refers to cutting off a part of an image, such as unnecessary portions of a graphic.

Figure 3-15
Crop marks indicating the portion of an image that you want to use as a Web graphic

Figure 3-16
The cropped image

try this! To crop an image, follow these steps:

1 Open an image in your graphics editor.

2 Click the selection tool (which usually looks like a dashed rectangle or square in the application's toolbar).

3 Click and drag in your image to outline the area of the image you want to retain. (If you outline the wrong area, press Esc and try again.)

4 After you have an area selected, choose Crop To Selection (in Paint Shop Pro) or Crop (in Photoshop) from the Image menu, or select a similar command in your graphics editing program.

lingo

A *thumbnail* is a miniature version or small portion of a graphic. Frequently, on Web pages, thumbnail graphics are hyperlinked to larger versions of the graphic.

Using thumbnails

After you master the art of resizing and cropping images, you're ready to use *thumbnails*. A thumbnail is a small picture that links to a larger image. (The larger image is usually the same as the thumbnail, but we've seen some creative uses of thumbnails in our day.) When you use thumbnails, viewers can choose to view the small image and be done with it or they can click the thumbnail to view the larger image. In other words, when you use thumbnails, you grant viewers the option to download large images if they're willing to endure the longer download times.

The trick to using thumbnails is to create two graphics with different names. Usually, you use the same image for both graphics, and you make one image small with a quick download time and the other image (while optimized to the best of your ability, of course) larger with a longer download time. Then you display the small image on your Web page, and you link the small image to the larger image. (We'll show you how to link images in Part Two of this book.) Figure 3-17 shows two thumbnails. The left thumbnail displays the entire linked image, and the right thumbnail shows a cropped portion of the linked graphic. Figure 3-17 also shows the larger graphic that's linked to the thumbnails. By clicking either thumbnail shown in Figure 3-17, you can open a window displaying a large view of the apples.jpg image.

try this! You can view thumbnails in action by clicking the thumbnails at *www.creationguide.com/ sizing*.

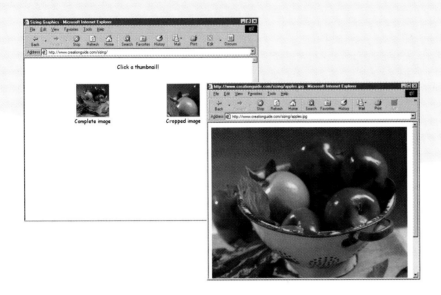

Figure 3-17
*Thumbnails that link to a sizable
rendition of the apples.jpg image*

Art of Using Web Graphics

Now that we've gotten the technical aspects of graphics out of the way, let's talk briefly about graphic design. The overriding premise of Web graphics is that your Web page's graphics should serve two masters— esthetics and utility. Ideally, every piece of art on your Web page should contribute to both causes by looking good and serving a purpose. There- fore, this chapter helps you to brush up on the various types of estheti- cally appealing and useful graphics that you should start to consider for your Web pages, including these:

- Photographs and illustrations

- Buttons and logos

- Icons, bullets, and horizontal rules

- Graphical text

- Backgrounds

In the next few sections, we'll take a quick look at each of the pre- ceding graphical elements.

Photographs and Illustrations

We won't dwell too long on photographs and illustrations given our ex- tended discussion of image formats earlier in this chapter. As we've mentioned numerous times, the key to using photographs and illustrations is to keep the file sizes as small as possible so that they download quickly. Further, you should ensure that your photographs and illustrations add to your page's content instead of detract from your message. Imagine waiting patiently for a movie review Web page to download only to find that the page contains a couple links to reviews and a large picture of the Web designer's dog wearing sunglasses. Without a second thought, you'd probably dash off to find a faster, more useful movie review site for future reference.

One use of photographs and illustrations that we haven't mentioned yet is *image maps*. Images maps are graphics that have clickable areas that enable you to visit various Web pages. Quite possibly, you've clicked your state or country on an online map to get local information. If done properly, image maps represent a good mix of esthetics and utility, but they should be used judiciously. Image maps involve mildly complex HTML coding, plus you need to ensure that you don't create an image map with a graphic that takes forever to download. In Chapter 10, we'll show you how you can create an image map using Microsoft FrontPage.

Buttons and Logos

Buttons and logos are a Web page's bread-and-butter graphics. No doubt, you've clicked a countless number of buttons and caught sight of more than a few logos. Thus, you're well aware that buttons help you to navigate around a site and logos brand a Web page as well as provide a quick link to a site's home page. The MSN logo in Figure 3-18 (and online at *www.msn.com*) is easy to spot, appears consistently on every page, and serves as a reliable hyperlink to the MSN home page.

On your Web pages, the key to successfully using graphic buttons and logos is consistency. If you're using a logo, ensure that the logo is instantly identifiable and easily visible on every page. For example, your logo should use the same colors throughout your site and appear in the same area on every page. (We'll talk more about page setup in later chapters.) It should also link to your site's home page in every instance. If you're using custom buttons, use the same buttons on every page in your site and position them in the same location on each page, if possible.

Consistently displaying buttons and logos adds an overall feeling of unity to your site as well as speeds up the downloading process. Once a viewer downloads your home page, your button and logo graphics will be stored in the temporary cache (or temporary memory) of the user's

lingo

An *image map* is a graphic that's formatted so that various areas of the graphic serve as hyperlinks to related Web pages. For example, in Chapter 10, we show you how to create an image map out of a solar system graphic, in which viewers can click a planet to access a related Web page that contains details about the selected planet.

tip

Later in this chapter, we'll show you a quick and dirty way to create simple custom buttons by using Word.

MSN logo

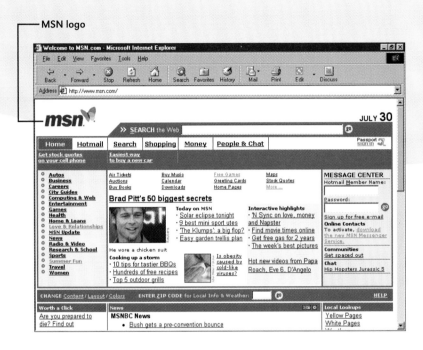

Figure 3-18
The MSN logo, which appears on every page in the site

machine. If the same button and logo images appear on your Web site's ancillary pages, the user's browser won't have to redownload the button graphics because the graphics will already be stored on the user's computer. In turn, less downloading means quicker page displays. Kind of a sneaky design tactic, but it's great for reducing download times.

Icons, Bullets, and Horizontal Rules

Icons, bullets, and horizontal rules help draw attention to elements on your Web pages as well as quickly communicate information in place of text. But tread lightly when you're using these elements. A fine line exists between clarifying and cluttering. When used sparingly and with discretion, icons, bullets, and rules can add a professional look to a page. When overused, these elements can make your page look amateurish and bury your message in visual mayhem.

Icons are small graphics used to call attention to a particular feature or to communicate a brief message. For example, you might use a graphic icon entitled "New" on your Web page to quickly identify recently updated content. To get a feel for the effective use of icons, surf around a few online auction sites (such as Amazon and eBay), and you'll see all sorts of icons. Notice how each icon is a simple graphic that clearly denotes a particular message.

tip

You can combine icons and button features to create picture buttons. For example, you might use a small picture of a house to serve as your Home button.

Bullets are small graphics added at the beginning of entries in a list or series. When you add graphical bullets to your Web pages, make sure that the graphics you use draw attention to your list and not to the bullets themselves. For example, any of the small bullets shown in Figure 3-19 are effective bullet graphics; in contrast, spinning rainbow-colored bouncing bullets will drive most users away from your page before they even attempt to read your content.

Figure 3-19
A sampler of bullets and rules

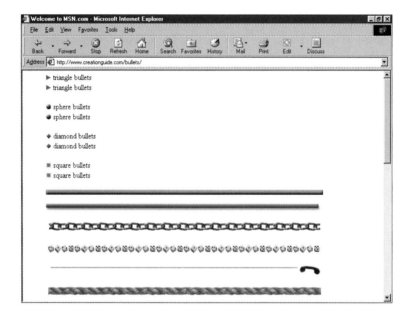

Horizontal rules denote sections in your Web pages. You can insert a graphical rule (as shown in Figure 3-19), or you can create a standard horizontal rule by using HTML code, as described in the following Try This! feature. In our opinion, you should limit your use of horizontal rules. Horizontal rules tend to chop up pages (thereby making them harder to read), and, 9 times out of 10, a little white space or a heading might serve your needs better than adding a horizontal rule. Used appropriately, horizontal rules can be useful, especially in long, text-heavy pages.

try this! You can add bullets and rules to your Web pages without creating a graphic. To create a bulleted list in HTML (without adding custom graphical bullets), you use the following tags:

```
<UL>        (identifies the beginning of the list)
<LI>        (marks the beginning of each list item)
</UL>       (identifies the end of the list)
```

To create a horizontal rule, you use the <HR> tag, in which you can specify the following properties for a horizontal rule:

SIZE	(the height of the rule line in pixels)
WIDTH	(either in percentage of page width or in absolute pixels)
ALIGN	(center, left, or right justified)
NOSHADE	(By default, HTML horizontal rules display with a shadow.)

To see HTML bullets and rules in action, open a blank Notepad document, and type the following:

```
<HTML>
<HEAD>
<TITLE>
Bulleted Lists and Horizontal Rules
</TITLE>
</HEAD>
<BODY>
<H1> Fruit </H1>
<UL>
     <LI> Grapes
     <LI> Kiwis
     <LI> Watermelon
</UL>
<HR SIZE="8" WIDTH="80%" ALIGN="CENTER" NOSHADE>
</BODY>
</HTML>
```

Save the file as test.html, and then open the document in your browser. Your bulleted list and horizontal rule should look similar to those shown here in Microsoft Internet Explorer:

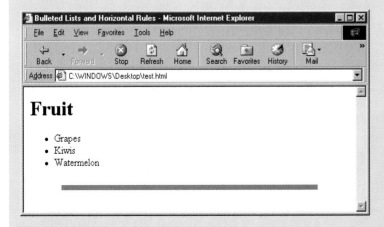

By the way, as you might've noticed, we snuck in the <H1> heading tag just for fun.

Graphical Text

As you may or may not know, browsers display text differently based on the browser's make, model, and year. But sticking with standard text when designing a Web page is rarely exciting or desirable. Fortunately, graphics provide a livable workaround. Basically, *graphical text* refers to text elements that have been created and then saved as a GIF or JPEG image that you can insert into your Web page as a picture. Graphical text includes titles, headings, and page banners. (A *banner* is generally a rectangular graphic that blends art and text, and usually runs across the top of a Web page.) Using graphical text, you can customize text without relying on fonts that might or might not be installed on users' computers. Figure 3-20 shows some text that can be imported into a graphics editing program, cropped, and used as graphical text on a Web page. Notice the bottom entry in Figure 3-20.

see also | *In Chapter 9, we'll show you how to create WordArt in Microsoft Word.*

Figure 3-20
Samples of graphical text

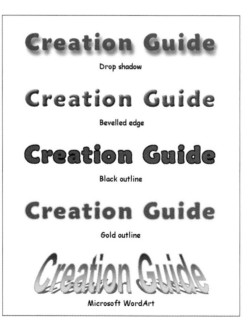

Backgrounds

You can modify your Web page's background in two ways: by coloring the background or by displaying a graphic beneath your Web page's contents. The key to using backgrounds is to ensure that together your content and the background create a striking contrast. Above all else, your content must be easy to read. If your background makes your page hard to read, lose the background (no matter how cool the color or pattern).

Adding background color to a Web page simply entails adding to your Web page an instruction that tells browsers which color to display. When you add a background image to your Web page, the image displays repeatedly across and down a user's screen (in a pattern called *tiling*) to create the illusion of a large graphical background. We'll cover background commands, colors, and images throughout Part Two of this book. In the meantime, Figure 3-21 shows some sample background images. You can visit the background samples online at *www.creationguide.com/backgrounds*. Click any sample to see a Web page filled with the background image.

tip

You can find lots of free background patterns on the Web. (We'll point you to these sources later in this chapter.) Some Web page editor programs, such as Microsoft FrontPage, also provide a selection of background patterns.

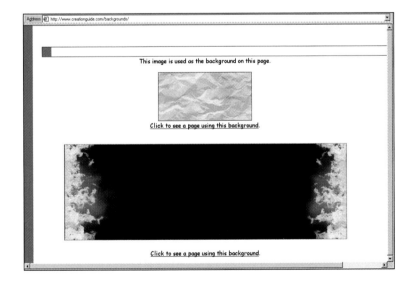

Figure 3-21
Sample background images

Acquiring Art

Now that you're on top of some of the *what* and *how* of graphics, you're ready for the *where*—as in, *where* are you going to find graphics for your Web page? Years ago, when we first started designing Web pages, we

tip

As you acquire and create images for your Web site, keep the files stored together in a folder on your desktop and give each graphic a unique, clearly identifiable name. You'll thank yourself later if you keep your images somewhat organized now.

note

When you save Web graphics from the Internet for your own use, make sure the artwork is truly freeware; otherwise, you might violate copyright laws. If you're unsure about whether a graphic is free for use, send an e-mail message to the site's Webmaster and ask permission to use the artwork.

tip

For up-to-date links to free online graphics, online art vendor Web pages, and graphic designers, visit *www.creationguide.com/ resources/graphics*.

asked ourselves the same question. Today, we're more interested in where we can store all the graphics we've collected! Fortunately for you, acquiring graphics is very easy, and becoming easier all the time. In this section, we'll briefly describe where you can find graphics as well as introduce you to the art of creating your own graphics. Specifically, we'll talk about acquiring prepared art, custom art (that you create), and photographs.

Prepared Art

Prepared art is plentiful—you just need to know where to look. You can obtain Web graphics from a number of resources, including these:

- **Clip art**   You can buy clip art CD-ROMs wherever software is sold, or you can use the clip art that comes with applications such as Word.

- **Free online art**   Many Web sites provide art free (making the art *freeware*) from their Web sites. You simply use the "right-click and save" method to copy the images to your disk.

- **Online art vendors**   A number of major vendors sell artwork online.

- **Graphic designers**   If you have a specific need and want a professional product, you can hire computer artists and graphic designers to create custom art for you.

Custom Art

Sometimes, Web pages beg for custom art. You can pay a designer to create the custom art (as mentioned in the preceding section), or you can try your hand at creating your own art (which we recommend in most cases). Creating custom art isn't as difficult as some people believe. Like any endeavor, the more you work at it, the better your results. But we're not here to give you a pep talk, so instead let's focus on how you can create your own custom art.

At this point, the most useful types of custom art that you can create are graphical text elements (such as title text and banners) and buttons. Fortunately, you can create custom art in almost any graphics editor as well as desktop applications, such as Word. Therefore, to ease any drawing anxiety issues you might be facing, we'll start right off with a brief exercise in creating a button in Word. We provide this exercise simply to prove to you that you can create custom art, but if you like the buttons you create, you should save them for later. (In Part Two, we show you how to insert and link buttons on your Web pages.) Here's how to create a button in Word:

1 Open a new document in Word.

2 Display your Drawing toolbar (if necessary) by pointing to Toolbars on the View menu and choosing Drawing from the submenu. Figure 3-22 shows the Drawing toolbar in Word.

Figure 3-22
The Word Drawing toolbar, which contains all the tools you need to design a Web page button

3 In the Drawing toolbar, click AutoShapes, point to Basic Shapes, and click Rounded Rectangle, as shown in Figure 3-23.

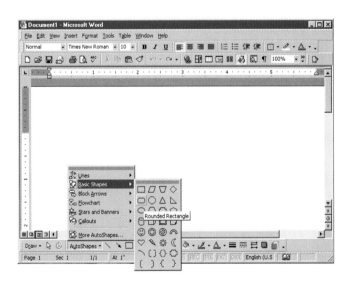

Figure 3-23
Selecting a shape for your button

tip

You can hold your mouse arrow over a button or graphical menu option to see the name of the button or option.

4 Click on the blank Word document, and then drag to create the button's outline, as shown in Figure 3-24. The button shown in Figure 3-24 is approximately 1 inch tall and 1¾ inches wide.

Figure 3-24
Drawing your button in a Word document

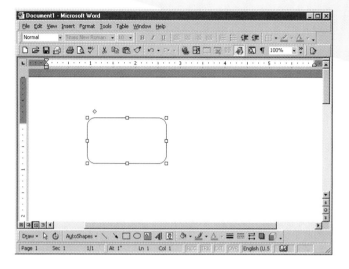

5 In the Drawing toolbar, click the Text Box icon, click inside the button's outline, and type *Click Here*.

6 Select the *Click Here* text, click the Font drop-down arrow in the Formatting toolbar, select Arial Rounded MT Bold (or any other font if you prefer), click the Font Size drop-down arrow in the Formatting toolbar, select 24, and, finally, click the Center button in the Formatting toolbar. Click in an area inside the button, but off your text. Your button should now look similar to the one shown in Figure 3-25.

Figure 3-25
Adding text to your button image

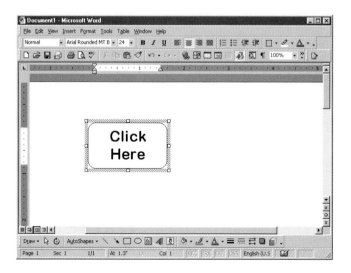

7 On the Drawing toolbar, click the Fill Color (the paint can icon) arrow and then click a color. The button's background color displays. You can change the button's fill color by selecting another color with the Fill Color tool.

8 In the Drawing toolbar, click the Shadow button and then click Shadow Style 6. Click anywhere in the Word document to deselect the button. Your button should look similar to the one shown in Figure 3-26.

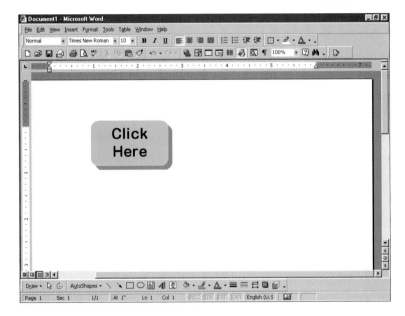

Figure 3-26
Viewing the finished button

The next step involves saving your button as a GIF image for your Web page. You can convert your image to a GIF file in a number of ways in Word, but for now, we'll show you a quick and easy way to use Paint Shop Pro to make the conversion.

9 With your newly designed button displaying, press the Print Scrn button on your keyboard.

10 Open Paint Shop Pro, and choose Paste As New Image from the Edit menu. Your Word document view should be pasted into Paint Shop Pro, as shown in Figure 3-27.

Figure 3-27
*Pasting your button into Paint
Shop Pro*

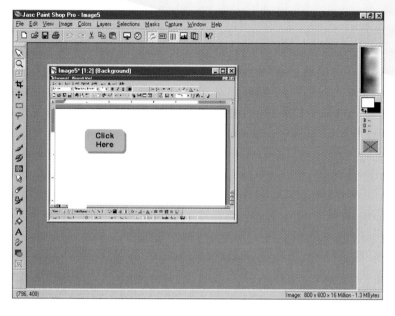

Figure 3-27
*Pasting your button into Paint
Shop Pro*

11 In Paint Shop Pro, click the Selection tool, outline the button, and then choose Crop To Selection from the Image menu to cut out the button.

12 Choose Save As from the File menu to open the Save As dialog box. Save the button as a GIF file.

In this section, we've barely skimmed the surface of creating custom art, but as you can see, custom art provides a lot of leeway for creativity. In addition to using Word and Paint Shop Pro, you can use other graphics programs, as described in Chapter 5, as well as scan hand-drawn art pieces for use in your Web pages. (We'll describe scanning in the next section.)

Photographs

You probably have at least one boxful of prime Web art resources lying around your home—photographs. You can use new and old photographs to add art to your Web pages. The trick is getting the hard-copy picture turned into information your computer can understand. To do that, you can use any of the following options:

■ **Scanners**   Basically, a scanner takes a picture of your photograph and saves the picture information as a file on your computer. After you have a scanned picture, you can manipulate the file just as you manipulate other graphics files. You can use any flatbed scanner on the market to create Web graphics. You don't need to get a top-of-the-line machine, either. We use moderately priced ($200 to $300 range) scanners to scan most of our pictures. If you don't have a scanner and you aren't planning to purchase one, you can pay others to scan your pictures for you. For example, many copy centers also scan pictures for a small fee.

■ **Film developers**   The next time you drop off a roll of film for development, check out the services that the film developer offers. Many film developers can develop your film on CD and offer other digitizing services as well. For example, visit Kodak's PhotoNet site at *www.photonet.kodak.com*. Other developers will send your pictures to you as e-mail attachments, scanned and ready to include on your Web pages. (PhotoWorks' site at *www.photoworks.com* provides such a service.)

■ **Digital cameras**   A third option for obtaining photographic images is to use a digital camera. Digital cameras enable you to snap a photo and then instantly send the picture into your computer. If you're thinking about buying a digital camera, keep in mind that instead of using film you'll be going through a lot of batteries. (So check out how much the camera's batteries cost before you plunk down any cash.) Also look for a camera with an infrared port. (Infrared ports look like small, dark-red circles.) Eventually, when all systems have infrared ports (most laptops and new systems now come equipped with them), you'll be able to transfer information from one piece of hardware to another via the infrared ports without attaching any wires between the components. This capability is pretty slick, and it's very handy when you're using a digital camera.

Finally, as the last bit of advice in this chapter, regardless of how and where you obtain your Web page graphics, remember to optimize your images and save them as GIF and JPEG files. Make sure your images' file sizes are as small as possible without compromising quality. Further, store your images in a central location on your hard disk, and don't forget to uniquely name every graphic.

key points

- Online graphics are made up of pixels.
- Most browsers support GIF and JPEG images.
- GIF images are small, limited to 256-color palettes, and quick to download.
- GIFs can be interlaced, transparent, or animated.
- JPEG images can contain millions of colors and are frequently used to display photographs.
- By default, GIFs and JPEGs display line by line from the top down, but you can change the default by creating interlaced GIFs or progressive JPEGs.
- JPEG's compression scheme enables you to reduce the size of JPEG images, but the compression is "lossy," so compress with care.
- Size graphics in your graphics editing program to help make your Web page's graphics files as small as possible.
- Cropping images reduces file sizes as well.
- Consider using thumbnails to link to large online graphics.
- Graphic Web page elements include photographs, illustrations, buttons, logos, icons, bullets, horizontal rules, graphical text, and backgrounds.
- You can acquire Web graphics from clip art collections on CD-ROMs, online freeware, online art vendors, and graphic designers.
- You can create custom art by using various software programs as well as by scanning hand-drawn art.
- Photographs can be converted to image files via scanners, film developers, and digital cameras.

looking like

4

you know

WHAT YOU'RE DOING:
WEB PAGE AND WEBSITE DESIGN

Given an instrument and some sheet music, a musician can perform the music, modify the music by adding personal flair, or ditch the music and use the instrument and standard musical guidelines to compose an original work. Likewise, given Web page elements, you can create a Web page using a tried-and-true layout, create a modified version of a standard Web page arrangement, or use design theory guidelines to create an original piece.

Before You Design

You've read about Web text (in Chapter 2), and you've looked over Web graphics (in Chapter 3). Now you're ready for some Web page and Web site design theory. And that's what this chapter is all about—successfully blending Web text and graphics to create appealing and usable Web pages and sites. But before we dive into the mechanics of Web page and Web site design, we can't resist mentioning a couple planning issues. (Think of this section as preparation for Chapter 6, which discusses planning Web pages and sites in detail.)

Understandably, planning affects design in a couple major ways. Specifically, before you design for the Web, you should consider your audience and organize your home page's layout and Web site's structure (if you're planning to expand your home page into a Web site).

Audience Reigns Supreme

Most likely, you're creating a Web page because you have knowledge to impart, a message to pass along, a service to provide, or entertainment to offer. But before you state your piece by creating a Web page or Web site, you should answer at least four audience-related questions:

- **What is the purpose of my page?** Clearly define the goal of your Web page or Web site to yourself. For example, determine whether your site informs, entertains, serves as a Web portal (such as a search site or a directory of links), addresses a specific community (such as hobbyists, activists, employees, customers, and so on), presents an artistic expression, provides a personality profile (such as a personal page or resume), or fulfills another specific purpose. After you define the overall goal of your site, refine your site's topic. For example, let's say that you decide to create an informational site about pets. You chose an informational format—that's a start, but "pets" is a little broad. You could further refine your goal by deciding to provide information about caring for pet lizards.

- **Who is my audience?** Analyze who will be viewing your pages—corporate clients, cartoon-watching kids, artists, athletes, your extended family, and so forth. Be as specific as possible. Then think of a particular person—a real person—to represent a typical audience member that you can keep in mind while you design.

For example, let's say you're creating a fan site for a basketball team. When you design this site, you should imagine the one friend, relative, neighbor, coworker, or acquaintance who proudly owns a full spectrum of team shirts, refuses ever to miss a game, and regularly yells at the TV set throughout the season. If you don't have one of those types around (you're definitely an anomaly!), you could focus on a well-known sports analyst (Jim Rome comes to mind), a sports-driven TV sitcom character, or even a character from a novel or movie as your ideal audience member. In other words, to create a dynamic well-focused site, you would design your site with a clear picture in mind of a particular sports fan—you wouldn't want to design your site with the vague notion that you're creating a Web site for anyone who has ever watched a basketball game. (By the way, don't worry— you don't have to *tell* the person who's serving as your "ideal audience member" that you're using him or her as a design tool!) Generally, designing for a real person is much more effective (and enjoyable) than designing for a generic audience profile.

- **Who am I?** Determine how you want to present yourself to your target audience. You should consciously choose how you want to communicate to your audience—casually, formally, profession-ally, comically, creatively, seriously, and so forth. Creating a per-spective (or a persona) for yourself can keep you from straying toward inappropriate design decisions, such as including an ador-able picture of your nephew at his first birthday party on your company earnings page.

- **How will my audience view my page?** Consider the technical capa-bilities of your audience. Basically, you need to think about how a typical person within your audience will be accessing your site. If your site is targeted to on-campus university faculty members, you probably won't have to worry about bandwidth because most universities have high-bandwidth networks. On the other hand, if you're designing pages for your friends who relocated all over the country (or the world) after graduation, you should create pages that will download reasonably quickly to accommodate dial-up modem connections.

tip

Designing without an audience in mind leads to aimless design decisions. In contrast, pinpointing your audience provides recogniz-able boundaries and enables smart design choices.

lingo

As mentioned, Chapter 6 covers Web site planning and audience analyses in greater depth, but your answers to the preceding questions should give you a feel for audience considerations. And as you'll soon see, knowing your audience comes into play when you make some of your design decisions. For example, we redesigned the New Frontiers for Learning in Retirement (NFLR) Web site to serve as a case study for this chapter. The site's main audience is the retirement community, who generally access the Internet at typical (around 28.8 kilobits per second to nearly 50 kilobits per second) dial-up modem speeds (as opposed to high-speed cable modems or T1 lines). Therefore, when we redesigned the NFLR site, we kept the retirement community and their dial-up connections in mind.

Storyboarding Your Web Site

After you identify your audience but before you start to create your Web pages, you should sketch your home page's layout as well as any relationships among ancillary pages—this visual representation is called a *storyboard*. You don't have to be an artist to create storyboards for your Web pages and Web sites. In fact, one of our favorite ways to sketch a site is on napkins at a nearby Italian restaurant. As with our preceding "consider your audience" chat, storyboarding Web pages and Web sites is also covered in more detail in Chapter 6. At this point, we simply mention sketching out your pages and site (if you're creating a site) as a design step. When you were thinking about text in Chapter 2, you might've come up with some site organization ideas based on your brainstorming results. Storyboarding simply entails roughly illustrating your organizational ideas by sketching the relationships among elements on each page as well as the relationships among your Web site's pages.

Figures 4-1 and 4-2 illustrate the concept of storyboarding. Figure 4-1 shows our sketch of the redesigned version of the New Frontiers for Learning in Retirement home page (NFLR2), and Figure 4-2 displays how we thought the NFLR site should be reorganized. Later in this chapter, you'll see a couple of the storyboarded pages in the redesigned site take shape.

Now that you've at least briefly considered the concept of audience and page and site planning, let's move on to discuss how to best assimilate Web text and Web graphics into well-designed Web pages and Web sites. First we'll look at Web page design issues. Then later in this chapter, we'll address Web site design considerations.

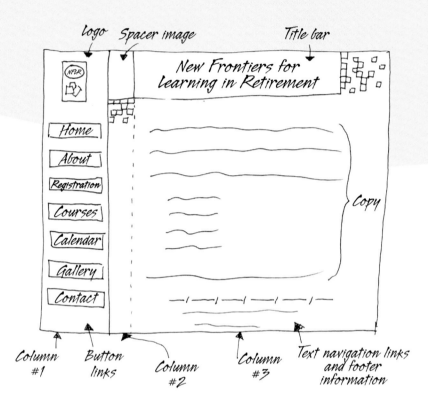

Figure 4-1
Sketch of the redesigned NFLR home page

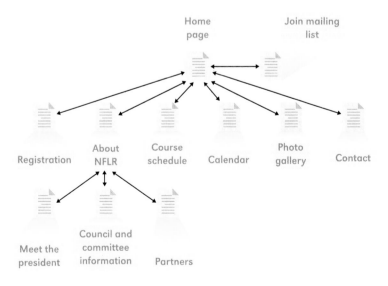

Figure 4-2
Storyboard of the redesigned NFLR Web site's page relationships

Web Page Design Rules That Won't Let You Down

Before you can create a Web site, you have to build a Web page—or maybe you're planning to build only a home page instead of a full-blown site. Either way, you can take advantage of some tried-and-true Web design tips. In this section, we address key Web page design issues and proven tactics. But we also have a small disclaimer, because first and foremost, designing Web pages (and Web sites) is a creative endeavor. We have no desire to take away a drop of your creativity—we'd much rather spark your imagination. Understand that the parameters we outline in this chapter (as well as throughout the book) are guidelines. We hope you'll experiment with your Web page designs in a number of ways not mentioned in this text. We highly encourage you to do so. The information in this chapter will provide a strong foundation for you—a good base for custom designs. If you follow the advice in this book, you'll be able to create clean, attractive, and easy-to-navigate Web pages. Then you can take the fundamentals to new creative heights (and e-mail us when you do because we'd be happy to post a link to your Web page on *www.creationguide.com*).

For discussion purposes, we've divided Web page design fundamentals into the following topics:

- Web page dimensions
- Page layout issues
- Color
- Navigation tools and hyperlinks
- Standard credibility components
- Text
- Graphics

tip

Keep in mind that most good page-design theories carry over into good site-design practices.

Web Page Dimensions

Theoretically, Web pages are infinitely long and infinitely wide because they aren't bound by the size of cut paper. Of course, designing your page with measurements such as "infinity by infinity" in mind doesn't help you or your page's visitors. So let's look at a more reasonable way to select your Web page's boundaries. The best way to narrow down your page's parameters is to consider the browser window real estate on a lowest common denominator machine. In other words, you need to think about the amount of viewable content in the browser window of the user who has the most limited browser capabilities.

For Web page design purposes, the smallest monitor out there displays 640 × 480 pixels at a time. Further, various browsers tend to show even less area than 640 × 480 pixels because of the browser's setup. For example, look at Figures 4-3 and 4-4. The two figures show Microsoft Internet Explorer 5 on Microsoft Windows and Apple Macintosh platforms along with the maximum available display area. Users running Netscape Navigator 4.7 obtain a maximum viewable area of 635 × 330 on a Windows-based system and 625 × 340 on a Macintosh.

Internet Explorer - Windows: 615 x 340

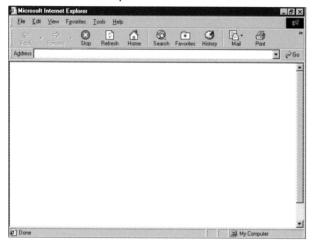

Figure 4-3
Maximum viewable area in Internet Explorer 5 on a Windows-based system using a display setting of 640 × 480

Internet Explorer - Macintosh: 600 x 340

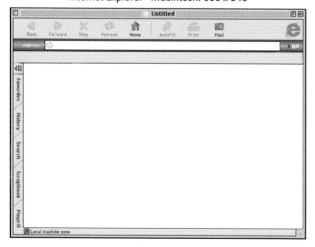

Figure 4-4
Maximum viewable area in Internet Explorer 5 on a Macintosh system using a display setting of 640 × 480

You can see that 600 × 330 is the smallest combined area when you take browser/system combinations into account—this is called the *safe area*. When you design your Web pages (particularly your home page),

try this! If you have a fairly modern (Windows 98 or later) computer system, you can see the effects of viewing Web pages at various screen sizes. To do so, follow these steps:

1 Right-click a blank area on your desktop, and choose Properties.

2 In the Display Properties dialog box, click the Settings tab.

3 On the Settings tab, drag the slider control in the Screen Area section to change the screen setting to 640 × 480, click Apply, click OK (your screen might go black for a moment or two while it readjusts the screen area), click Yes, and then click OK.

4 View *www.creationguide.com/nflr2* in your browser, and then minimize your browser window.

5 Repeat steps 1 through 3, changing the 640 × 480 setting to 1024 × 768.

6 View *www.creationguide.com/nflr2* with the new settings, and then close your browser window.

7 Repeat steps 1 through 3 using the 800 × 600 setting (the most popular screen area setting).

As you worked through the preceding process, the NFLR2 Web page's view should've gone through a metamorphosis similar to the changes shown in the accompanying figures.

640 x 480

1024 x 768

800 x 600

you should keep the safe area measurements in mind, and as we describe next, make sure that your most important information appears within the safe area's parameters.

Page Layout Issues

Now that we've pinned down a target page size, let's look at page layouts. For the record, we'd like to state that just because the Web provides almost carte blanche publishing freedom, it doesn't mean that you can get away with simply uploading text and images willy-nilly—unless you don't care whether anyone visits your page long enough to read or even glimpse your content. A more successful approach—one that we highly recommend—involves following some basic rules for laying out pages.

The number-one layout rule to follow is to apply basic template principles. A *template* (as you might know from hard-copy page design) is a grid that you can use as a guideline to lay out your page's elements. Although current limitations make it difficult for you to adhere to strict page layout rules and regulations for your Web pages as consistently as for printed text, numerous Web pages follow loosely defined templates to help contain the flow of information. For example, Figure 4-5 shows the very basic template we used to create the NFLR2 site. If you visit the NFLR2 site online (*www.creationguide.com/nflr2*) and click a few links, you'll see that every page adheres to the simple, straightforward template shown in Figure 4-5.

Using a template enables you to align elements and create consistent external and internal spacing between and around elements. When you devise templates, keep in mind that people generally scan Web pages from left to right and top to bottom; so design accordingly. Your primary design area is along the left side and top edge of the first screen that displays to users, which very nicely brings our discussion back to the "safe area" topic.

As we mentioned earlier, you can count on an area of 600 × 330 pixels as your safe area when your page loads into any browser. For the most part, users are willing to scroll down but not across. Therefore, when you create a Web page, stay within the width limitations as much as possible, but don't become overly concerned if your page flows below the safe area's height limitation.

tip

When you design Web pages, you should view your pages using various screen settings and in various browsers to ensure that your page displays correctly for the majority of people.

Figure 4-5
The NFLR2 site template

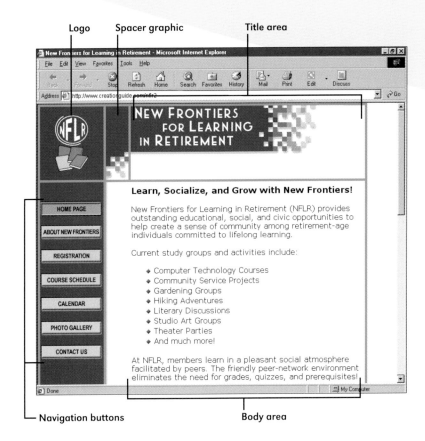

Figure 4-5
The NFLR2 site template

Now, here's an even bigger tip:

The choicest spot of all within the safe area is the upper-left corner.

Why? Because no matter how much a user resizes the browser window, the upper-left corner remains in view (or, in worst-case scenarios, it's the last area to go if window resizing gets completely out of hand). Therefore, the upper-left corner is prime property—the ideal place for you to insert your company's logo or other key information.

After the upper-left corner, the next-best area on your Web page is what journalists refer to as "above the fold." Newspapers carry the day's most notable news stories above where the paper folds so that when the paper appears on newsstands, passersby will see the top news stories and be tempted to purchase the paper. Obviously, users can't fold their monitors (not yet, at least), so your design "fold" is the bottom edge of the safe area's parameters. When you lay out your page's information, make sure that the most significant and eye-catching information appears on the opening view. Further, if your page scrolls below the fold, ensure that your design looks like it continues when viewers see the initial display. (Otherwise, users might not scroll at all.) You can indicate that a page continues by avoiding obvious page breaks (such as space between paragraphs) at the safe area's bottom limit.

Finally, you should include your site's main navigation links (such as a menu bar or buttons) within the page's safe area—preferably along the left side or top edge. The NFLR2 site uses the very common left-edge navigation setup, and Figure 4-6 shows MSN's use of top-edge navigation links.

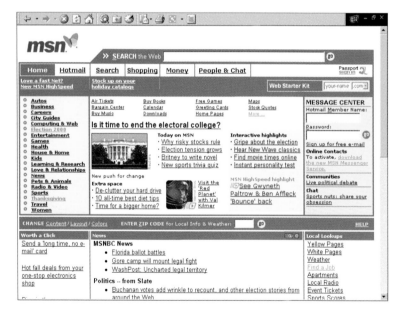

Figure 4-6
MSN's main navigational links aligned across the top of the page with secondary links aligned along the page's left edge

In addition to using templates and designing within the safe area, you should incorporate fundamental Web page elements into your page, as shown in Figure 4-7. Most pages contain a title area, logo, navigation links, body, and footer text. You'll find numerous combinations and positioning of these elements, but the basic elements generally appear on most home pages in some manner.

Figure 4-7
Incorporating basic page elements into your home page

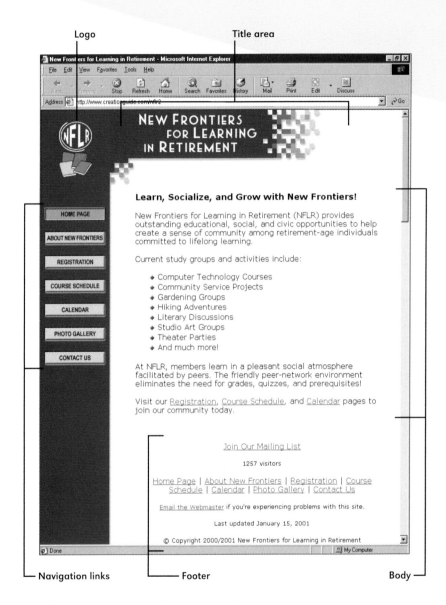

The remaining page layout considerations we want to impress on you encompass universal "good design" practices. Here are some common design principles that you should keep in mind and on-hand:

■ **Blinking text and gratuitous animation**   Avoid blinking text and unnecessary animation; many people find these effects annoying and meaningless.

- **Competition** Search similar sites to see what's out there, and then make your site unique. By viewing similar or related sites, you can also get ideas of topics that need better coverage or that you've forgotten to address on your page.

- **Content** Keep content fresh, simple, and smart. Further, aim to use at least 80 percent of your page to present your content (especially if you plan to use advertising on your page), and restrict navigation elements to 20 percent or less of your page area.

- **Cutting-edge technology** Avoid using too many high-tech features or you'll lose the majority of your viewers. Most people don't want to download a plug-in (which is a small "helper" application that works with a browser to run a specific file type) just to view a Web page.

- **Download speed** Ensure that your page downloads as quickly as possible; you have about 10 seconds before viewers itch to surf elsewhere.

- **Frames** Use frames sparingly; they're tricky to implement properly and sometimes hard for users to navigate. (Essentially, *frames* are used to divide the browser window so that users can view multiple pages at once, as we'll describe in Part Two; for now, you can view a site using a simple frames setup by visiting the Chapter 9 project site at *www.creationguide.com/resume*.)

- **Functional design** Opt for function over form—every design element should also serve a purpose. If you're not sure whether a design element is functional, temporarily remove the element from the page and analyze the page without it. If your page works as well (or better) without it, the element is more ornamental than functional and should be dropped.

- **Important elements** Size elements in proportion to their importance. Bigger means more important and draws attention quicker, whereas smaller equates to lesser importance.

- **Moderation** Avoid using too much of any element or technique, including links, colors, scrolling, and so forth.

- **Sound files**   Don't automatically enable sound files. If you must include sound, provide an option to play an audio file. Most people don't like to listen to background sounds, and extraneous audio files slow download speeds considerably.

- **The kitchen sink**   Don't get crazy and overload your home page (or any page, for that matter). If you have more than enough information for your home page, expand your page into a Web site by dividing information into logical chunks and placing each chunk on a separate subpage linked to your home page. Also, you don't have to use all your text and graphics just because you have the information on hand. Remember that Web pages are dynamic, which means you can selectively update and modify information on a regular basis, so opt to show pertinent information in a timely manner. For example, if you want to publicize the birth dates of your friends and family, consider showing just the current month's birthdays and updating the birthday listing monthly.

- **Visual appeal**   Verify that your page looks good in Internet Explorer and Navigator at various resolutions on Windows and Macintosh systems.

- **White space**   Create eye relief and visual space with strategically placed blank areas (white space), as described toward the end of the next section.

Color

After page dimensions and layout, you should consider your Web page's color scheme. A *color scheme* refers to your site's interface elements (not necessarily the colors used in images), such as title graphics, buttons, background, text, and so forth. Ideally, you should limit the number of colors used in your Web page's interface to three or four. The key is to use contrasting colors, especially if you're using a colored background. Also, keep your colors appropriate for your message. For example, if you're creating a Christmas edition of your site, use red and green (not pink and yellow), or use cool blues and purples if your site advertises a mountain ski resort. If you can't decide which colors will work best for you, you can always opt for black text on a white background—the standard black-on-white combination is pretty much bulletproof when it comes to readability and design sense.

In addition to using colors for your interface, you can use colors to call attention to certain content items on your page. For example, if you have a store site and you're running a special, you could highlight the information by placing a color background behind the text advertising your sale.

Overall, you should use your color scheme to create balance and unity throughout your site, but you should also use colors to draw attention to specific areas of the page, including links, titles, logos, key points, items of interest, and so forth.

try this! To experiment with various background and text colors, visit *www.hidaho.com/ colorcenter/cc.html*. If you find a combination you like, note the two-digit number and letter combinations along the left edge of the page. (Each color includes a separate number/letter combination for red, green, and blue.) We'll talk about RBG (red, green, blue) color values and hexadecimal color values in Part Two.

Finally, when choosing a color scheme, remember to consult the Web-safe color palette we discussed in Chapter 3. Whenever possible, opt to use Web-safe colors to avoid unnecessary dithering. For example, the NFLR2 site's purple-blue background color uses the Web-safe color that's defined as having an RGB value of 51-51-102 and a hexadecimal value of #333366. (You can find the colors used on the NFLR2 page on the Web-safe color palette shown in this book's appendix.)

try this! To compare a site that uses Web-safe colors with one that doesn't, follow these steps:

1 Right-click a blank area on your desktop, select Properties, and then click the Settings tab in the Display Properties dialog box.

2 On the Settings tab, click the Colors drop-down arrow. (Note your current setting so that you can return to it in step 5.) Select 256 Colors from the drop-down list, click Apply (your screen may go black for a moment), and then click OK.

3 Open *www.creationguide.com/nflr1* in your browser. Notice the dithering that occurs on the page's background.

4 Now open *www.creationguide.com/nflr2* in your browser. As you can see, the page's colors appear clear and crisp, without dither, because the colors used to create the page are included in the Web-safe color palette.

5 Close your browser, right-click on your desktop, and return your color display to the previous setting.

Complementary to colors is *white space*, which we've already introduced a couple times in this book. As we mentioned, white space isn't necessarily white—white space is an area without any content. The concept behind white space is to provide eye relief. You use white space to create visual space between and around images and body text. In essence, white space frames and draws attention to your content.

Navigation Tools and Hyperlinks

Navigation tools and hyperlinks include buttons, clickable logos, text links, and graphical links—basically, all the elements you provide on your Web pages that enable users to find additional information easily. Effective navigation elements tell users where they are, where they've been, and where they can go next. Therefore, all successful navigation tools and hyperlinks must use meaningful descriptors, whether the descriptors are graphical, textual, or both.

To further clarify how to effectively use navigation tools, the following sections offer some rules of thumb for designing navigation elements.

Buttons

If you create a menu bar that uses buttons, keep the buttons consistent on the current page (same dimensions, color schemes, and so forth) and display the same group of buttons on every page. You can easily confuse viewers by offering different sets of buttons on various pages. Also, ensure that buttons are named so that they clearly indicate where viewers will go after they click a particular button. Finally, consider slightly modifying buttons to display the current page's button differently—such as slightly darker—so that viewers instantly know which button points to the current page.

Logos

If you include a logo on your Web pages, ensure that your logo is a high-quality GIF graphic that uses Web-safe colors. You want your logo to look great, regardless of a user's system capabilities. Ideally, you'll want to show your logo on your home page in the upper-left corner, a little larger than the logo's display on subsequent pages. Then on all ancillary pages, link a smaller version of your logo to your home page. That way, users can easily access your home page from anywhere within your site, while you reinforce your logo identity.

tip

As we mentioned earlier in this chapter, remember to restrict your use of navigation elements so that they account for less than 20 percent of your Web page's area if possible. (At times, they might require more space, such as when you create a site or page that consists mostly of hyperlinks, or possibly you're creating a site with very little content and you want to visually balance the site.)

Text links

As mentioned in earlier chapters, you should always provide text links for all graphical links (including buttons, logos, and linked images). Doing so ensures that everyone—even those who opt to hide graphics in their browser window—can navigate within your site. Also, avoid embedding hyperlinks within paragraphs of text or linking viewers away from your page in midsentence.

Colorwise, if you don't use standard hyperlink colors (you can change link colors by using HTML code), ensure that you assign specific colors to nonvisited and visited hyperlinks and keep the colors consistent throughout your site. (Usually, sites use brighter colors for nonvisited links and darker colors for visited links—we'll talk more about formatting hyperlinks in Part Two.) Viewers frequently use visual cues to help them keep track of their online travels.

Finally, on long pages, include a "Back to the Top" or "Home" link at the base of the page. And don't forget your bottom-of-the-page Webmaster e-mail link and copyright notice.

Graphical links

On some sites, graphical elements, such as images, serve as hyperlinks. For example, a site might display thumbnails images (as explained in Chapter 3) that link to larger images. Or a site might use small icons or pictures that users can click to view additional information. If you use graphical links, ensure that users clearly understand that they can click the images for more information. Frequently, graphical links are accompanied by text links to make the association clear—we highly recommend this practice. For example, on retail sites, you might see a clickable picture of a coffee maker accompanied by hypertext (linked text) below the picture. In this setup, users can click either the linked image or the text to view detailed information about the coffee maker.

Standard Credibility Components

Often when you view a Web page, you have no idea where the page's files are located, who created the page, or where the information you're reading came from. Anyone can post a Web site, and you shouldn't automatically believe everything you find on the Web—but you already know that! You should strive to make your Web pages as credible as possible. You can do that in a number of easy ways.

tip

Above all else, avoid the cardinal Web page sin of providing dead links. To prevent this problem, check your links and run your site through an online validation service. A number of validation sites, including *validator.w3.org,* will check your Web page's links and HTML code for free. Other fee-based validation services are also available online, such as *www.websitegarage. com* and *www.netmechanic. com,* among others.

- **Attribution** Give complete attribution, credits, and references for any quotes, graphics, or statistics you use on your Web page. Not only does attribution give credit where credit is due, but it strengthens your site's trustworthiness.

- **Contact information** Make it easy for viewers to contact you and obtain more information via e-mail, mailing lists, telephone numbers, physical addresses, and so forth. One of the Web's biggest draws is its interactive appeal, so take advantage of this unique communication channel.

- **Copyright notice** Include a copyright notice on your Web site to show that you care enough about your Web pages to take ownership of your site's content.

- **Dynamic content** Keep your content up-to-date and modified regularly. If you show readers that you're serious about your page, they'll be more likely to take an interest in it.

- **Last updated** Include text that shows when the page was last updated so that viewers know they're reading current information and to reassure them that you haven't abandoned the page.

- **Personal information** Provide information about yourself or a prominent person associated with the site (such as the club president); include your name (or the prominent person's name) and possibly a picture.

- **Special interests** State your point of view if your page presents commercial interests or advocacy issues.

- **Spelling and grammar** Check your spelling and grammar religiously. Not to sound preachy or melodramatic, but typos and grammatical errors are frequently construed as highly unprofessional, and they almost instantaneously jeopardize your credibility.

- **Webmaster link** Provide an e-mail link to the Webmaster in case viewers have problems or questions.

Text

In Chapter 2, we looked at how to write effective Web text, and in Chapter 3, we reviewed how to use text in graphical elements, such as title bars and buttons. In this section, we'll review effective ways to format nongraphical text.

As you know, text is used to present content and create hyperlinks. As a Web designer, you have the power to control your text's size, color, formatting, and style. A variety of thoughts are bandied about when it comes to text rules, but for your benefit, we've consolidated the basic premises that the majority of Web designers support, including preferences for font size, font style, and font formatting.

Font size

Almost universally, Web designers recommend that you use the default font size for body text. This allows viewers to choose the font size via their browser's default settings. For special text, such as copyrights and other footer information, you can specify smaller font sizes to avoid disrupting your page's focus on the content. If you want to display larger text, such as headings, you should use the HTML default heading tags, as described in Part Two, instead of simply increasing the body text's font size.

Font style

Even though thousands of font styles exist, all font styles can be categorized as either *serif* or *sans serif*. Serif fonts, such as **Times**, use "hooks," or short lines, on the ends of letters, whereas sans serif fonts, such as **Arial**, use plain-edged letters. On the whole, the Web design community voices a mixed response to the use of serif and san serif fonts online. Personally, we generally prefer to use sans serif fonts rather than serif fonts when creating Web pages because we find sans serif fonts easier to read online as well as more visually appealing.

In the past—when monitor resolutions left much to be desired (and were generally alien-glow green)—sans serif fonts were overwhelmingly recommended for on-screen text because serifs helped only to blur the text into further illegibility. Nowadays, monitors are much improved, so accounting for the blurriness factor doesn't hold much water (unless you opt to use very small text, which we don't recommend). But you're not off the hook—you still have a number of font-related design decisions to address. For example, the NFLR2 site uses Verdana—an easy-to-read sans serif font—for the body text to present clear letters to accommodate viewers who might have vision problems. Another common serif-related design technique is to use sans serif fonts for headings and serif fonts for body text (similar to common printed-page design preferences).

tip

You should avoid displaying your text—both serif and sans serif—too small. A common (and slightly disturbing) trend seems to be emerging in which sites containing numerous links display the links in tiny font sizes. This setup can make the links illegible for users whose browsers use a small default font size or who have smaller screen resolution settings. Clarity becomes even more of an issue when a serif font is used to display the tiny text.

Regardless of your serif preferences, you should stick with cross-platform fonts to ensure that users see your text similar to how you designed your page. Cross-platform fonts include the following:

- Arial
- Arial Narrow
- Comic Sans
- Courier New
- Georgia
- Times New Roman (or Times)
- Trebuchet
- Verdana

Font formatting

Last but not least among font design issues is formatting. Basically, not to sound dull or anything, but we advocate moderation (again!). For instance, when it comes to color text, avoid overusing it—use color (within your color scheme, of course) only to draw attention to items. Plus, think before using white text because users will need to do a little finagling before they will be able to print white text from your page. Instead of simply clicking the Print button, users will have to modify their browser settings to override the Web page's color scheme (if the browser supports that functionality) or they'll have to copy the text from your page into a text editing document (such as a Microsoft Word document), select the white text, recolor the text using a darker color, and then print the text from the text document.

Another formatting technique is to use italic and boldface. When it comes to italicizing and boldfacing, however, again limit your use. Both italic and bold formats tend to make online text harder to read. Furthermore, overusing italic or boldface type waters down the emphasizing effect of the formatting technique.

Most important, do *not* underline nonlinked text. Users have become programmed to click underlined text—and there's no need to deprogram the masses starting with your site. Users can become highly annoyed if clicking underlined text doesn't take them somewhere, and nonlinked text that looks like a link ranks lower on the Web-page faux pas list than a dead link. So save everyone the hassle, and forget about underlining body text.

Finally, text alignment falls within the realm of font formatting. For the most part, use left-aligned text. For most people, left-aligned text is easy to read and readily adaptable to various browser window dimensions. Centered text is more difficult to read and creates jagged, unattractive visual lines all over your page's layout; so use centered text at your own risk or only in special circumstances (such as a poetry page). Finally, right-aligned text, while occasionally successful as an avant-garde design technique, can get lost outside the safe area or turn readers off if they find jagged left-edges too distracting. Therefore, consider using left-aligned text on most of your Web pages, and use white space to add shape to your text on the page.

try this! Many times, Web site designers will mock up sites or fill templates with default Latin text before finalizing a site. Unfortunately, some designers fail to remove the mocked-up sites after they've created their finalized pages. Just for fun, you can find hundreds of leftover, unfinished, and hastily created Web sites (in which the designer failed to delete the Latin text in a "live" site) by typing "*Lorem ipsum dolor sit amet*" (including the quotation marks) in any search engine. We're not sure what this little experiment proves, other than sloppy Web design practices, but it's fun to see what's out there.

Graphics

In Chapter 3, we took an in-depth look at Web graphics. As far as Web page design, you should adhere to the following four practices in addition to the techniques discussed in Chapter 3:

- Avoid large graphics that seem to take days to download on a 28.8-Kbps modem.

- Steer clear of meaningless graphics. If a user has to wait to see a graphic, make sure that the graphic contributes to the user's experience.

- Include an ALT tag for every graphic. (*ALT* stand for *alternative*, as in text that serves as an alternative for a graphic.) An ALT label provides the pop-up text when you move your mouse over a graphic (as shown in Figure 4-8) as well as displays in graphical placeholder areas when graphics are turned off (as shown in Figure 4-9).

- Ensure every graphical link has a text link equivalent.

Figure 4-8
An ALT label displaying image information in a pop-up window

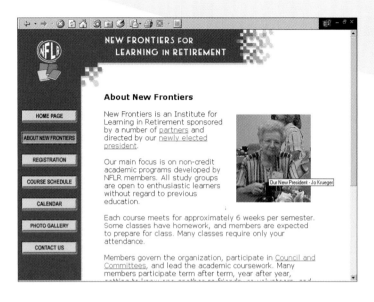

Figure 4-9
ALT labels displaying in graphic placeholders when graphics are turned off

Web Site Design Rules to Live By

Now that you've been inundated with good-Web-*page*-design tactics, let's take a quick look at good-Web-*site*-design techniques. Fortunately, good Web site design mostly involves applying good-Web-page-design tactics across the board. Therefore, make sure that you use the following two Web site design theorems in conjunction with the numerous Web page design techniques presented earlier in this chapter.

As far as Web site design goes, our goal is to have you leave this section with two main Web site design concepts painlessly emblazoned in your mind—consistency and structure.

Consistency

Web site consistency means that when viewers move from page to page throughout your site, they can visually see and intuitively grasp that they remain within your site. Viewers should recognize instantly when they've surfed to a page that's not yours. To create consistency, you use common design elements throughout your Web site, such as similar title bars, a consistent navigation bar, a universal color scheme, standard graphical text styles, consistent body text fonts, and so forth. Most important, users should be able to find your pages' navigation tools and logo in approximately the same area on every page in your site.

As you can see, if you create a solid home page, achieving site consistency is a snap; you've already taken care of all the "hard" work, such as devising color schemes, creating navigation bars, customizing title bars, and so forth. Ancillary pages simply need to mold the elements to their needs and use a complementary template.

Structure

Similar to consistency is a site's structure. And one of the most important points about site structure is to have one! In other words, you should outline your site's structure up front (as described earlier in the chapter when we discussed storyboards) and stick to your building plans so users won't get lost and turned around within your site. When creating structure, keep the following points in mind:

■ Create a clean, logical structure. Aim to keep your site three clicks (or three levels) deep or less. (For example, see the storyboard shown in Figure 4-2.)

■ Ensure that your navigation links clearly outline your site's hierarchy. On larger sites, consider including a *site map*. Frequently, we click site map links whenever we visit a new site to quickly see what's offered. We're usually pleasantly surprised at the number of treasures (cool links) we find on site maps that are otherwise hard to find on main Web pages.

lingo

A *site map* is a Web page that shows all the links in a site in hierarchical structure, enabling users to gain an overview of the Web site as well as access to every link in the site.

tip

A highly effective way to keep users informed of their location within your site's structure is to display title bars on each page that depict the page's content and to slightly modify navigation bar buttons to indicate the current page. Figures 4-12 and 4-13 in the next section show examples of modified buttons and page titles.

■ Use page titles on every page. Further, make the home page's title text larger and ancillary page's titles slightly smaller to visually indicate the page's hierarchy.

Case Study Practice

To wrap up this chapter, we present the original and redesigned versions of the New Frontiers for Learning in Retirement home pages and About New Frontiers Web pages. (You can see online versions of the sites at *www.creationguide.com/nflr1* and *www.creationguide.com/nflr2.*) Figures 4-10 and 4-11 show the original NFLR pages, and Figures 4-12 and 4-13 show the redesigned pages. Compare the four pages, and identify the Web page and Web site design issues and modifications that we've addressed in this chapter.

Figure 4-10
Original New Frontiers home page

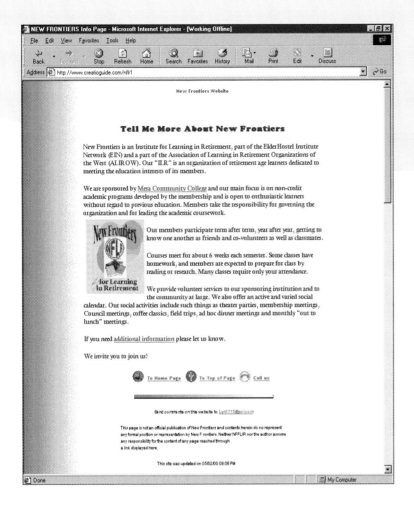

Figure 4-11
*Original About New Frontiers
Web page*

Figure 4-12
Redesigned New Frontiers home page

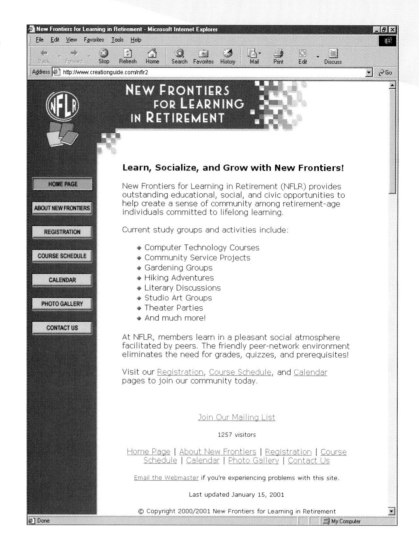

Figure 4-13
*Redesigned About New Frontiers
Web page*

key points

- Remember that the audience reigns supreme—always design with a specific audience member in mind.

- Storyboard your home page and Web site's page relationships.

- Keep the lowest common denominator computer screens in mind.

- Use templates and grids to guide your layout.

- Reserve your Web page's upper-left corner for your most important information.

- Display main concepts "above the fold."

- Include navigation links within the safe area.

- Incorporate a title area, logo, navigation links, body text, and footer text into each Web page.

- Use moderation in almost all areas of design—too much of any one element can kill a page.

- Implement a color scheme, preferably limited to three or four colors.

- Employ white space to create eye relief and draw attention to main elements on your page.

- Keep your navigation tools easily accessible, clearly defined, and consistent throughout your site.

- Link your logo to your home page throughout your site.

- Build credibility by providing contact information, clear channels of communication, and supplying attribution, credits, and references.

- Use the default font size for body text, and stick with cross-platform fonts whenever possible.

- Never underline nonlinked text.

- Include ALT tags with every graphic.

- Create consistency throughout your site by repeating your color scheme, title text, navigation tools, and other page layout elements on every page of your site.

- Ensure that users can easily identify a clear and logical structure for your site.

5

piling

THE GOODS

Picture having a scoop of ice cream for dessert. You could eat the ice cream as is, or you could spoon on some hot fudge, slice in a banana, add a dollop of whipped cream, sprinkle on a few crunchies, and top off the entire concoction with a maraschino cherry. Same ice cream; different dessert, depending on the trimmings. All you need to create a satisfying dessert—or a Web page, for that matter—are a few supplies and a little creativity.

Tools of the Trade

When you create Web pages, you need to have at least a couple (probably more) Web page creation tools on hand. Mind you, we're not talking about hardware—we're sure you've realized the importance of having a computer as well as possibly having access to a scanner, printer, and camera (digital or standard). In this chapter, our focus falls on the array of software that you can use to create, edit, and manipulate Web pages. As we'll show you in Part Two, you can create, edit, and publish Web pages by using a number of software applications and tools, and we've found that we frequently mix and match our weapons of choice. Likewise, knowing your choices will help you create a working environment that best suits your needs and personal style.

To get started, let's look at two of the most basic "tools" you'll need during your Web creation endeavors—an Internet connection and server space.

Internet Connectivity and Server Space

No matter how astounding your Web page, it will live in virtual anonymity if you can't connect to the Internet and transfer the page's files to a server. (Recall from Chapter 1 that a *server* is a powerful computer that's connected to the Internet's backbone data lines, that stores Web page files, and that responds to users' requests to view the stored Web pages.) You must be connected to the Internet or have access to an Internet connection before you can achieve an online presence. Granted, you can *create* most Web pages without an Internet connection, but you'll be dead in the water when it comes time to publish your pages online.

In addition to the basic prerequisite of Internet connectivity, you might need to purchase some space on a server for your Web files. We say *might* because in a lot of cases server space is freely given away or provided in addition to other paid services. For example, your Internet service provider (ISP) might give you 40 MB (give or take 20 MB) of free server space in addition to your Internet connection. The notion of *free server space* catches many people by surprise—but it's out there, and it's a thriving online practice. Not surprisingly, though, you'll find benefits in purchasing server space as well as using free space.

tip

If you use your computer to surf the Web, rest assured—you have an Internet connection. Using a standard dial-up Internet connection, you can copy Web page files from your computer onto a server that's connected to the Internet.

Free Space Online

It's true. You can create and display a Web site at this very moment for free, as in $0. All you need to spend is a little time and creative effort (and we'll make your task even easier by showing you how to create and display a free MSN Communities Web site in Chapter 7). You don't need any additional software or Internet accounts—nothing but your text and a few pictures, if you want to include them. Of course, you face a couple minor limitations when you take this approach (such as a long Web address and limited page-layout options), but depending on your ultimate goal, the limitations might not affect you all that much. So consider yourself informed—free Web space is readily available. As we mentioned, we've run into more than a few people who were sincerely amazed to discover this fact.

The number-one way to become the proud owner of a free Web page is to turn to an *online community*. Online communities are virtual areas on the Web where people with similar interests gather and share information. One of the benefits of joining an online community (other than the "free" factor) is that most online communities enable you to create Web pages by providing templates and wizards that you can use. Among the many free online communities, three popular ones come quickly to mind:

- MSN Web Communities (*communities.msn.com*)
- Lycos Tripod (*www.tripod.lycos.com*)
- Yahoo! GeoCities (*geocities.yahoo.com*)

As mentioned, in Chapter 7 we'll show you how to join MSN's communities and create your own free Web page. Figure 5-1 shows the MSN Communities home page. Notice that MSN offers a variety of page types you can choose from, including photo albums, family sites, personal pages, and workgroup sites. Figure 5-2 shows a sample photo album site.

The biggest drawbacks of online communities are that your Web address is usually fairly long (for example, the address for the photo album site shown in Figure 5-2 is *communities.msn.com/TonganMission2000/home.htm*), you generally have a limited amount of server space, your choices of page layouts are usually somewhat limited, and if you don't want to use a community's templates, customizing your page can sometimes be tricky.

lingo

A *wizard* is a series of dialog boxes that you fill in to complete a specific task—for example, you could provide information about yourself (such as your hobbies and interests) in a series of dialog boxes on a free Web communities site, and the wizard would create a generically styled Web page.

Figure 5-1
The MSN Web Communities home page

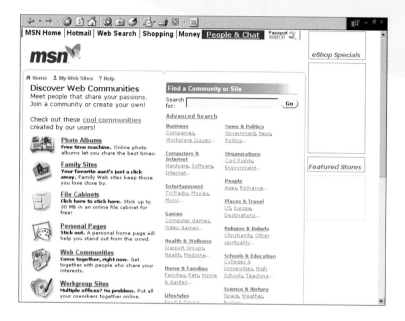

Figure 5-2
An MSN community site using the Photo Album template

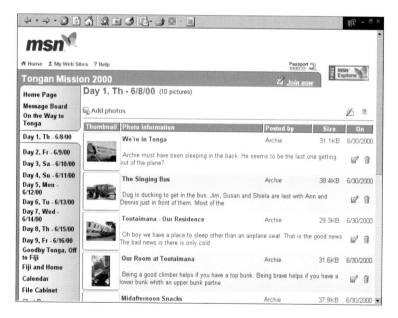

note

Most companies who sponsor online communities make their money via advertising and selling upgrades and add-on features and services.

Similar to online communities, another free way to get on the Web is to create site-specific pages. During your surfing, you might find that some Web sites offer free Web space to registered members. For example, you can create an About Me page on eBay (an online auction site located at *www.ebay.com*) if you're a registered site participant. The purpose of eBay's About Me pages is to introduce eBay users to other people who visit eBay.

Yet another type of "free" online Web space—which technically isn't free—is Web space that you get from your ISP. Because you most likely cut a check to your ISP on a regular basis, we can't exactly label ISP server space as free; it's more like prepaid, available space. When you signed up with your current ISP (assuming you have one), they probably informed you in an excited voice or a sentence ending in an exclamation point that you get "*X* megabytes of free server space!" At the time, you probably didn't know what that meant, so you might have just thought "Oh, that's nice" and moved on to the next detail. Now that you're thinking of creating a Web page, you should revisit the "free server space" component of your ISP agreement. Most likely, you'll find that you have 20 MB to 40 MB of server space at your disposal.

try this! To find free Web space, type *free "Web page"* in any search engine—you'll be rewarded with a slew of sites offering to host your page.

The upside of ISP server space is that you're already paying for it, so you might as well use it. The downside is that you'll probably have to live with a cumbersome Web address, similar to online community Web addresses. For example, a couple of our ISPs (we have several) grant "free" server space, but the Web addresses' formats are *www.primenet.com/*~username/filename.*html* and *members.home.net/*username/filename.*html*. For most people, the preceding naming formats are a little long and not easy to remember. Another advantage of ISP server space over online communities is that you have complete freedom regarding how you create and display your pages (which could be a disadvantage if you prefer to work with the preconfigured templates that seem to be standard fare on most online community sites).

All in all, the main point about free online sites is that Web space is instantly available to you. And as long as you don't mind a longish home page Web address, free space is a great way to initiate yourself on the Web.

Purchasing Server Space

In contrast to using free Web space, you can shell out a few clams for a Web page that uses the Web address of your choice as long as someone hasn't beaten you to the name. When you take this route, you have two main considerations: choosing and registering a Web address name (such as *creationguide.com*), and signing up with a provider that will host (or store) your Web pages (unless you're going to run your own server—but that topic is best saved for more advanced books). Let's look at how to register a Web address and obtain a hosting service.

Registering a Web address

Before we go any further, let's nail down some simple vocabulary. Namely, instead of *Web address*, we really should say *domain name*. Loosely speaking (very loosely), a domain name is a Web address. As you may or may not know, all Web addresses are actually groups of numbers (called *Internet Protocol*, or IP, numbers) that serve as Internet addresses. Being a human, you probably also know that, for most people, remembering a meaningful name is much easier than remembering a series of numbers divided by dots. Therefore, the *Domain Name System* (DNS) came into existence. Fundamentally, DNS simply assigns textual names (such as *creationguide.com*) to numbered Internet addresses (such as 207.155.248.5). Thus, to appear as if you know what you're doing, you should use the term *domain name* in place of *Web address*.

When you're ready to obtain your own domain name, you can pick a domain name (such as *creationguide.com*—although we can tell you right now that the name is already taken), see whether it's available, and if it is, register the domain name as your very own for a nominal annual fee. By nominal, we mean anywhere from $12 per year up to $35 or more per year.

Choosing and registering a Web domain name is straightforward after you access a legitimate registration site. Fortunately, InterNIC (which is under the umbrella of the U.S. Department of Commerce) hosts a Web page that lists all the acceptable domain name registration Web sites. Many hosting sites also offer name registration services (as we'll discuss in the next section). To see the official list of domain name registrars, visit *www.internic.net/alpha.html*.

While visiting the InterNIC site, check a few registration sites to review their pricing schedules and policies (or visit *www.creationguide.com*, and we'll link you to a couple of our favorite hosting services, which will register and host your site for you). When you've found a site you like, you can generally type your proposed domain name in a text box. Then the site will inform you whether the name is available. If it is, you work out a payment arrangement (usually by credit card) and the site registers your domain with InterNIC. Your next step is to find an ISP that will host your domain name and Web pages.

Finding space for your domain

If you don't run your own server—and most people don't—your next step is to find an ISP or hosting service that's willing to provide a home for your domain name. You can find numerous hosting services online— type *Web hosting* in any search engine and you can have a field day researching various Web hosting providers. Or better yet, visit *hostindex.com*, a comprehensive site devoted to providing information about numerous aspects of hosting services, including a monthly list of the top 25 hosts. Finally, as mentioned a moment ago, if you're feeling lazy, visit *www.creationguide.com* for links to hosting services and domain name registrars. Regardless of how you conduct your research into finding server space, remember to check a few key facts, including fees, network configuration, Microsoft FrontPage Server Extensions (as discussed in Chapter 10), and reliability. On average, basic Web hosting services run from $20 to $25 per month, with a $50 setup fee. But don't let the fees rule your decision. Before signing on with a Web hosting service, find out how the host handles the following features:

- **Bandwidth** Most hosting companies are connected to the Internet by T1 and T3 lines; anything less and you might as well choose another company. Basically, a T1 line can carry up to 1.5 megabits of data per second, and a T3 line can carry 45 megabits per second. Thus, a T3 connection provides much more bandwidth and speed. In addition to Internet connections, you should check to see how many clients are hosted on each machine. If a hosting service overloads its machines, performance will be slow despite high-speed connection lines.

■ **Space** When you sign up for Web hosting services, ISPs and hosting companies assign you a certain amount of server space (just as your computer has a certain amount of disk space that you can use to store files). Most ISPs and hosting services offer more space on their servers than you'll need (at least initially). However, you should get at least 15 MB of server space. Most hosts provide at least 25 MB.

■ **Support** Technical support is an important element when you're choosing a Web hosting company—if you run into problems, you'll want to be able to turn to someone who can help. The most basic support consideration you should look for is the number of hours per day the technical support staff is available. Many sites offer 24×7 support, so look for round-the-clock support when you're weeding out potential companies. Also see whether the site publishes its support response rate. Finally, check to see whether you can readily identify the avenues of support the company offers, including phone numbers, fax numbers, e-mail addresses, online informational reports, and a snail mail address.

■ **Extras** You might want to check to see what "extras" each company offers to entice customers. For example, most hosting services provide e-mail accounts you can use with your domain name (such as *mm@creationguide.com* or *jc@creationguide.com*). You can generally set up anywhere from 5 to 20 e-mail accounts with a single Web hosting agreement. Other features you might check out include the cost of adding space to your site, in case your site grows larger than your originally allotted space; the cost of upping your traffic quota, in case more people visit your site than you anticipated; whether FrontPage Server Extensions are supported; and available add-on services, such as adding chat groups and site search features.

Now that you've considered your domain name, hosting services, and basic Web space options, we're ready to move closer to home and talk about desktop applications. In the next section, we'll take a look at software applications you can use on your system to create, edit, and publish Web pages and Web page elements.

Web Page Creation Tools

In this section, we outline the types of tools you might need to create Web pages, name a few applications we've found helpful, and point you down the path of finding other utilities that best suit your needs. As you might imagine, because of the Web's booming popularity, lots of software vendors have busied themselves by creating Web page creation programs. In this chapter, we introduce many tools (but nowhere near all the available utilities), and in Part Two, we show you how to use some of them to create complete Web sites. Ultimately, though, we leave you with the responsibility of choosing the software packages that feel most comfortable for you.

To simplify our approach in this chapter, we've divided basic Web page development tools into the following three main categories:

- Text editors and HTML editors
- Graphics applications
- FTP (File Transfer Protocol) utilities

Text Editors and HTML Editors

Overwhelmingly, when you create Web pages, you'll be spending the greatest amount of time interacting with a text editor or an HTML editor. You use editors to create HTML files that contain display instructions for Web browsers and provide your Web pages' contents. When you use an editor, you have the option of working with basic editors, in which you enter HTML code manually, or using more advanced WYSIWYG (what you see is what you get) editors, which create HTML code for you while you type text, insert images, and drag elements around in a Web page layout view. Finally, and not surprisingly, some applications keep a foot in both camps by qualifying as an upscale basic editor but not quite an advanced WYSIWYG editing application—we'll take a quick look at all three types of editors in the next few pages.

Basic text and HTML editors

When you use a basic text editor, you type in all the HTML commands and your Web page's text into a blank document. The most basic of the basic text editors is the Notepad application that comes with the Microsoft Windows operating system. Figure 5-3 shows Notepad containing some HTML text.

tip

You can download many of the applications (or demos of the applications) mentioned in this chapter from shareware sites such as *www.tucows.com* or *www.shareware.com*. *Shareware* can be best summed up as "try before you buy." When you download a shareware program, you try it out for a while for free. If you like it, you send the developer the requested fee. Too bad all merchandising isn't so user friendly!

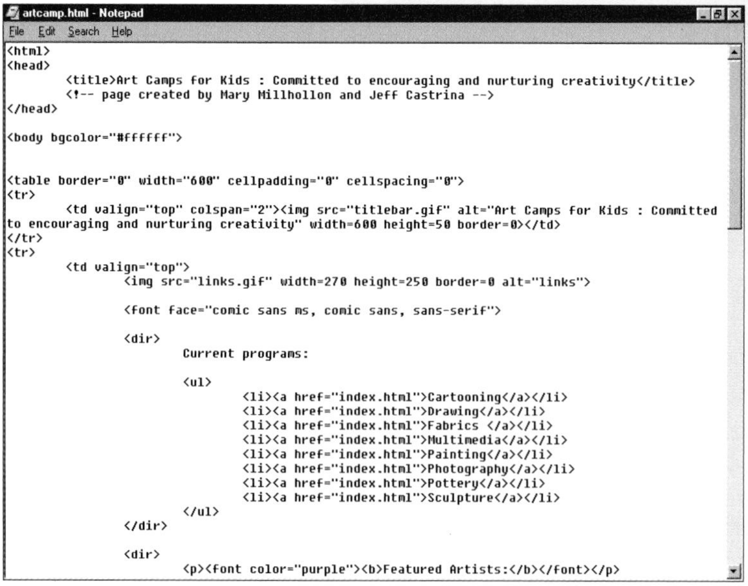


```
<html>
<head>
	<title>Art Camps for Kids : Committed to encouraging and nurturing creativity</title>
	<!-- page created by Mary Millhollon and Jeff Castrina -->
</head>

<body bgcolor="#ffffff">


<table border="0" width="600" cellpadding="0" cellspacing="0">
<tr>
	<td valign="top" colspan="2"><img src="titlebar.gif" alt="Art Camps for Kids : Committed
to encouraging and nurturing creativity" width=600 height=50 border=0></td>
</tr>
<tr>
	<td valign="top">
		<img src="links.gif" width=270 height=250 border=0 alt="links">

		<font face="comic sans ms, comic sans, sans-serif">

		<dir>
			Current programs:

			<ul>
				<li><a href="index.html">Cartooning</a></li>
				<li><a href="index.html">Drawing</a></li>
				<li><a href="index.html">Fabrics </a></li>
				<li><a href="index.html">Multimedia</a></li>
				<li><a href="index.html">Painting</a></li>
				<li><a href="index.html">Photography</a></li>
				<li><a href="index.html">Pottery</a></li>
				<li><a href="index.html">Sculpture</a></li>
			</ul>
		</dir>

		<dir>
			<p><font color="purple"><b>Featured Artists:</b></font></p>
```

Figure 5-3
Using Notepad as a basic HTML text editor

You might wonder why Web designers would opt to manually code their Web pages. The answer varies, but for the most part, Web designers hand-code their Web pages for some of the following reasons:

- **Control** Hand-coding enables you to use the codes you want instead of the codes a WYSIWYG editor inserts. For example, you might want to use two blank line breaks, but a WYSIWYG editor might insert a paragraph marker.
- **Quick fixes** Knowing how to manually create and modify HTML code enables Web designers to make quick changes to a Web page, regardless of how the Web page was initially created.
- **Code cleanup** Many advanced HTML editors (as discussed later in this chapter) add extra code to documents. If you know how to create and edit standard HTML code, you can clean out extra code and reduce the size of your HTML files. And remember—on the Web, size matters, and the smaller the better.
- **Fine-tuning** Another habit of advanced HTML editors is that they sometimes use HTML tags that not all browsers support. You can use text editors to modify HTML code so that it conforms to the capabilities of most browsers.

Of course, learning HTML is a prerequisite to creating your pages in a text editor. In Chapter 8, we walk you through the process of using HTML to create a Web page to give you an idea of HTML's form. (Don't worry— you can do it!) That chapter is just an introduction, however. You'll need to access additional resources if you really want to get serious about HTML. If you're interested in learning HTML or having an HTML reference nearby, you'll find that a generous collection of HTML books line the shelves at your local bookstore. You can also find pages and pages of helpful information online. (We've also listed some HTML references at the end of Chapter 8.)

Text editors can range from barely offering you a hand to coming fully equipped with customized HTML-specific features. To help illustrate the range, we've provided short descriptions of some of the most popular text editors in use today:

■ **Notepad**   Notepad is about as bare bones as it comes when talking about text editors. Beware, though: if you're working on a long document, you won't be able to use Notepad. For longer documents, you'll have to use WordPad (described next) instead.

try this!   Display *www.creationguide.com/artcamp* (or any other Web page of your choice) in your browser, and then click Source on your browser's View menu. A Notepad document opens that displays a text version of the Web page's HTML code.

■ **WordPad**   WordPad is a step up from Notepad. If you're running Windows, you can open WordPad by clicking Start, pointing to Programs and then Accessories, and then clicking WordPad. WordPad offers more word processing features than Notepad, and it supports longer documents. Figure 5-4 shows an HTML document in WordPad.

■ **Allair HomeSite**   HomeSite is a popular HTML design tool used by many professional Web developers. This text editor includes HTML-specific features to help you create effective, clean HTML pages. For example, it includes an HTML Tag Inspector, split-window editing, an image map utility, and more. You can download a 30-day trial version to test the product. For more information and to download a demo, visit *www.allaire.com/products/homesite*.

Figure 5-4
Using WordPad as a text editor

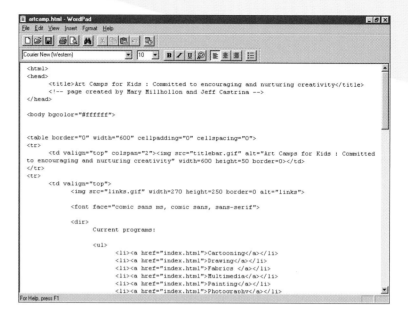

note

In addition to HotDog
Professional, Sausage
Software offers a WYSIWYG
HTML editor, called HotDog
PageWiz, and an HTML editor
for kids ages 6 and up, called
HotDog Junior. Surf around
the Sausage Software home
page to find other useful Web
page creation utilities.

■ **HotDog Professional**　Any HTML editor named HotDog Professional that's offered by a company named Sausage Software
(*www.sausage.com*) deserves mention. This editor is fairly popular
among the Web-design crowd—and not just because of its clever
name. You can download a demo for a free 30-day trial from the
Sausage Software site.

■ **BBEdit**　This HTML editor from Bare Bones Software is popular
among Macintosh Web designers. BBEdit enables you to edit,
search, transform, and manipulate text. Like the other HTML editors, BBEdit provides an array of general-purpose features as well
as many features specifically developed to meet the needs of HTML
authors. Visit the Bare Bones Software site at *www.barebones.com/
products/bbedit/bbedit.html* for more information.

Mid-range text and HTML editors

The next level of HTML editors starts to enter the realm of WYSIWYG.
We could call these editors WYSIWYG-lite applications because the applications offer text editor features along with a limited amount of advanced editor capabilities. In this category, we recommend just one main
application—Microsoft Word 2000.

note

Similar to Word 2000, other
Office 2000 programs—such
as Excel and PowerPoint—
also let you save your
documents with the .html
extension.

　　Word 2000 enables you to use a familiar word processing interface
to create HTML documents via the Save As command. When you save a

Word document as an HTML file, Word automatically creates the HTML source code for the document. Chapter 9 shows you how to use Word to create an online resume Web site. Figure 5-5 shows an HTML document in Page Layout view as well as in the HTML Source view. You can obtain Word 2000 by purchasing (or upgrading to) the Microsoft Office 2000 suite.

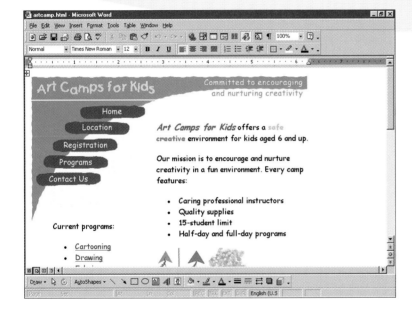

Figure 5-5
Web Layout view as well as the HTML Source view in Word 2000

Advanced HTML editors

The third group of HTML editors includes the advanced applications that enable you to create and edit Web pages by using graphical interfaces. In most advanced editors, you can also view and edit the HTML source code directly in addition to working in the WYSIWYG interface. Further, most advanced editors provide a preview feature, which enables you to view how a Web page will display online before you view the page in your browser. Web-specific features are frequently incorporated into advanced HTML editors as well. (We know that last bit sounds a little vague, but when we create a Web page in FrontPage in Chapter 10, we'll introduce you to a few high-end Web-specific tools so you'll know what we mean.) Popular advanced HTML editors are well documented online, so instead of wasting page space here summarizing online statistics, we've provided pertinent URLs for the Web sites that offer the applications appearing in our short list. Although other editors are readily available, these five are some of the most popular programs. (Check each product's Web site address to assist you in comparing features and prices.)

- Dreamweaver (*www.macromedia.com*)
- Microsoft FrontPage (*www.microsoft.com/frontpage*); also comes with Microsoft Office 2000 Premium
- NetObjects Fusion (*www.netobjects.com*)
- Adobe GoLive (*www.adobe.com*)
- HoTMetaL Pro (*www.hotmetalpro.com*)

Among the preceding applications, Dreamweaver is probably the most popular Web editor among professionals because it maintains hand-written code, enables users to preview pages in various browsers, and automatically checks for browser conflicts. On the other hand, FrontPage (shown in Figure 5-6) is the easiest advanced HTML editor for beginners to learn and provides nice clean HTML code. Further, FrontPage is also popular with the business community. As we mentioned, you'll get a feel for creating Web pages in FrontPage in Chapter 10.

note

Your Web page creation environment doesn't have to be an either/or kind of setup. At times, we find it's quicker to use an advanced WYSIWYG application (especially when resizing tables), but at other times, a quick edit in Notepad serves us best.

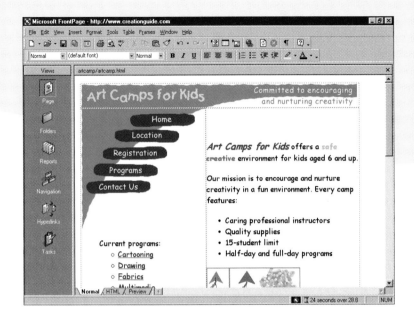

Graphics Applications

When it comes to Web page development, graphics applications come in a strong second behind the all-important text or HTML editor. After all, most pages use graphics, and you'll want to either create or tweak the graphics you use on your Web pages. Therefore, you'll need to have a graphics package installed on your system. Our personal favorites (or at least the programs we seem to use most frequently) are Jasc Paint Shop Pro and Adobe Photoshop—both appear in the graphics application list that you're about to run into after the next paragraph.

Regardless of your graphics package, the five main skills you'll need to acquire when using a graphics program are cropping, cutting, resizing, recoloring, and saving as a different file format. So check your application's help files to brush up on your technique. Now, here are six popular graphics programs along with their Web addresses. (We recommend that you visit the listed Web sites for product details and pricing.)

- **Fireworks** (*www.macromedia.com*)   This application is easy to use and especially convenient when you need to create buttons and other basic Web site graphics.

- **LView Pro** (*www.lview.com*)   LView Pro is a popular shareware graphics program.

■ **Paint**   Microsoft Paint is a graphics program that comes with Microsoft Windows. Paint is a scaled-down graphics package compared to other graphics programs, but it serves as a handy graphics tool when you're in a pinch or want to quickly make minor adjustments.

■ **Paint Shop Pro** (*www.jasc.com*)   Paint Shop Pro is an affordable, all-purpose graphics program used by many designers. Visit the Jasc Web site to download a free trial demo. Figure 5-7 shows a graphic we created using this program.

Figure 5-7
Creating a Web graphic in Paint Shop Pro

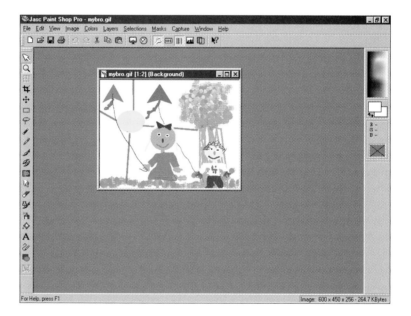

■ **PhotoDraw** (*www.microsoft.com/office/photodraw*)   This graphics and photograph editing program has a number of Web-specific features. You can obtain this program as part of the Microsoft Office 2000 Premium suite or packaged with FrontPage.

■ **Photoshop** (*www.adobe.com*)   Photoshop is probably the leading image-editing program. It can be a little tricky to use when you're first learning it, but once you get the commands mastered, you'll be highly satisfied with the application's flexibility. We frequently mock up sites using Photoshop before we create actual Web pages in an HTML editor. Figure 5-8 shows the Art Camps for Kids site mocked up in Photoshop.

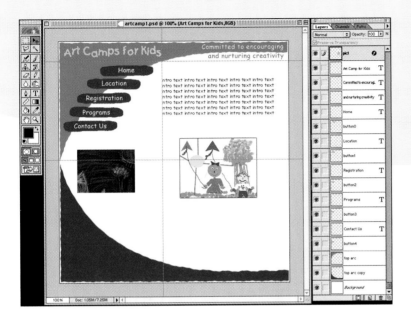

Figure 5-8
Web site mocked up in Photoshop

In addition to the preceding graphics applications, you can also use illustration programs to create *vector-based graphics*. In a vector-based graphic, you can move, resize, and otherwise manipulate an image's elements (such as moving an entire shape around within an image). Vector-based illustration programs that frequently come in handy when creating Web pages include Illustrator (*www.adobe.com/products/illustrator*), Freehand (*www.macromedia.com/software/freehand/*), and CorelDraw (*www.corel.com*).

lingo

Vector-based graphics are images made with lines and shapes instead of shaded computer pixels.

FTP Utilities

Last but not least, you might need one of those mysterious FTP utilities. Actually, FTP utilities aren't at all mysterious, but whenever we mention "FTP" to people who've never heard of it before, the color seems to drain from their faces. Basically, FTP utilities are programs that allow you to

tip

You might not need to use an FTP program if you're creating an online community Web page. Further, if you're using Microsoft's Web Publishing Wizard, Web Folders, or an advanced HTML editor's publishing utility to upload pages, you won't need to use an FTP program up front. Eventually, though, you might want to use an FTP utility to delete, copy, and otherwise manage online files. In Chapters 11 and 12, we'll fill you in on the details of online file management, where being comfortable with an FTP application can come in handy.

copy entire files from your computer to another computer across the Internet. For example, whenever we complete a chapter, we FTP the chapter's graphics to Microsoft Press in Redmond, Washington, even though we're in (overly) sunny Arizona.

You can find numerous FTP programs online, many of which are shareware programs. Popular FTP programs include the following:

- **BulletProof FTP** (*www.bpftp.com*) BulletProof provides an intuitive drag-and-drop interface, similar to other top FTP programs.

- **CoffeeCup Direct FTP** (*www.coffeecup.com*) This program serves as an FTP application that also lets you edit HTML pages online. Click the site's Download button, and you'll find that CoffeeCup Software also provides image map and animated GIF applications.

- **CuteFTP** (*www.globalscape.com/products/cuteftp*) This easy-to-use and popular FTP application has been around for a while. Using CuteFTP, you can drag-and-drop files to transfer files from your machine to a remote machine and vice versa.

GIF Animators, Image Map Applications, Banner Programs, and More

Web pages incorporate all kinds of specialty knickknacks—including elements created with "mod" sounding technologies such as Microsoft ActiveX, Java, Flash, Microsoft Visual InterDev, and so forth. In addition, you can create audio and video files for use on the Web. Although we're just as fascinated with these topics as with basic Web page design techniques, creating those elements is beyond the scope of this book. Our goal is to get you up and running on the Web. Therefore, we'll save the "fancy" stuff for another book. If you're itching to acquire some extra-credit Web page creation skills, we suggest you start by creating animated GIFs, image maps, and banners. Following are some sites you might find useful:

- **Animated GIFs** (*www.mindworkshop.com/alchemy/gifcon.html*) The GIF Construction Set Professional uses wizards to walk you through the entire process of creating an animated GIF.

- **Banners** (*www.animation.com*) The *animation.com* site enables you to instantly create advertising banners.

- **Image maps** (*www.globalscape.com/products/cutemap*) GlobalSCAPE CuteMAP is a shareware application that simplifies creating image maps. You can download a free trial version.

Keep in mind that you can find quite a few animated GIF builders, banner creation utilities, and image map creators. The preceding three applications are mentioned merely as samples to help get your search rolling.

■ **Fetch** (*www.dartmouth.edu/pages/softdev/fetch.html*)   Fetch is an older FTP client for the Macintosh (last updated in 1997 but still widely used). It was designed to make accessing FTP sites as simple as possible. Fetch is available free of charge to educational institutions and nonprofit organizations; others should pay the shareware fee.

Now that you know vaguely what FTP programs do and that you can download them from the Web, don't worry too much about them. At this point, knowing that they exist is enough—if you're really gung ho, you can download an FTP application so that you're ready to upload pages after you create them, but you don't need to do that now. We'll help you out with FTP programs and file management later in the book, in Part Three. But before we do that, we want to tackle the fun stuff in Part Two—creating your Web pages.

A Bit About Browsers

We'd be completely remiss if we wrapped up this chapter without addressing the most obvious software application tool of them all—a browser. You need to have a browser (or a few browsers) installed on your computer so that you can preview your pages before you publish them online. Remember that browsers are applications that interpret HTML pages. Unfortunately, not all browsers interpret HTML in exactly the same way. Therefore, a page you design and then view in Microsoft Internet Explorer could very easily display as a shocking mess in another browser. Even well-designed pages appear slightly differently in various browsers. To see an illustration of this phenomenon, view the various screen shots in Figure 5-9.

In Figure 5-9, you can see the following anomalies:

■ The default bullets in Netscape Navigator are bigger on both Windows-based and Macintosh machines than those in Internet Explorer.

■ The margin spacing (or *offset*) around page perimeters varies by browser. Notice that the Internet Explorer browser windows leave more margin space around the top-left graphic than do the Navigator browser windows.

■ The default font size is bigger on Windows than on the Macintosh in both Internet Explorer and Navigator. Therefore, the text wraps differently on Macintosh systems than on Windows-based systems.

tip

No two browsers (or browser versions) process HTML code in exactly the same way; therefore, when you design Web pages, view your pages in as many browsers as possible before publishing your site.

note

Although cross-platform fonts—Arial, Comic Sans, Courier, Georgia, Times New Roman, Trebuchet (MS), and Verdana—display on both Windows-based and Macintosh systems, their default sizes vary, with the fonts consistently displaying smaller on the Macintosh.

Figure 5-9
The same Web page in various browsers

Internet Explorer on Windows

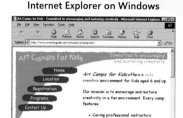

Navigator on Windows

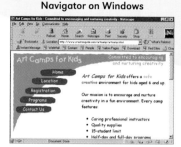

Internet Explorer on Macintosh

Navigator on Macintosh

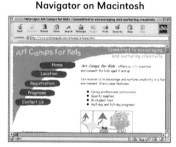

■ Because the text wraps differently, varying amounts of information appear above the Web page's "fold."

■ Browser window widths vary. Notice how the title bar graphic is slightly cut off in a couple windows and appears in its entirety in the other instances.

We designed the Arts Camps for Kids page to work cleanly in both Internet Explorer and Navigator, but you can see that slight differences remain that are beyond a designer's control.

A number of browsers exist on the Web. You may or may not want to verify that your pages display appropriately in all browsers out there. For most designers, ensuring that pages display properly in the biggies—Internet Explorer and Navigator—is plenty; combined, these two browsers account for over 90 percent of all browsers accessing the Internet. Of course, you must always consider your audience. If you *know* your viewers will be using Opera browsers, you better ensure that your page looks good in Opera. For edification purposes, here's a short list of additional browsers you can find lurking on the Web:

■ America Online uses an adapted version of Internet Explorer (*webmaster.info.aol.com*).

- Lynx is an all-text browser (*lynx.isc.org/current*).

- Opera is a small application with extremely quick download times (*www.operasoftware.com*).

You might want to download additional browsers to see how your pages display in alternate browsers. Previewing your Web pages simply entails displaying your HTML files in a browser window locally—so the process is quick and simple. Most important, though, you should ensure that you have access to at least one version (Windows or Macintosh) of Internet Explorer and Navigator for testing and previewing purposes. Don't worry—we'll remind you a few more times in Part Two about the importance of previewing your Web pages in more than one browser.

key points

- You need Internet connectivity and server space to display a Web page online.

- You'll find that free Web space is readily available online, particularly in online communities.

- You can purchase a domain name and buy server space to have full control over your Web site and Web address.

- You can use text editors to create Web pages.

- HTML editors range from all-text programs to advanced WYSIWYG interfaces.

- Graphics applications enable you to create Web graphics, edit pictures, and create mock-ups of future Web pages.

- You can find GIF animators, banner creation sites, and image map utilities online (in addition to lots of other freeware and shareware programs).

- FTP programs enable you to copy files from your computer onto a remote computer.

- Not all browsers are created equal—different browsers displays the same Web page in various ways.

- You should always view your Web pages in Internet Explorer and Navigator (at least) before publishing your Web pages online.

chment paper, scroll, treasure map

Logo / Title bar

THE CURIOSITY SHOPPE

N W E S

Featured product photo

Product icons

Contact

Home

History

Text links

Links

Up

Back

File   Edit   View   Go   Favorites   Help

Content

Copy   Paste   Undo   Delete   Properties

Address   D:\Clients\MS Press\Creation Guide Book\06Chapter\cshoppe

shoppe

Name

File Folder
3KB   Microsoft HTML Document 5.0
3KB   Microsoft HTML Document 5.0
2KB   Microsoft HTML Document 5.0
3KB   Microsoft HTML Document 5.0

Size   Type

8/12/00 4:32 PM
8/18/00 5:26 PM
8/18/00 5:26 PM
8/18/00 5:26 PM

5 object(s)

the CURIOSITY

Store Legend

Home

Products

Contact Us

Our Histor

ASPIR

6

planning

YOUR ATTACK

Let's say you decide that you're more than ready for a relaxing beach vacation. Most likely, your first thoughts turn to money—so you set a budget and figure out how much cash you'll need to save or whether your vacation money stash can cover your expenses. Next you choose a destination and reserve a beach house. Then you purchase plane tickets, line up a rental car, and promise yourself that you'll exercise more regularly. Finally, months later, you pack your bags, including at least one new bathing suit; take care of last-minute minutiae so your pets won't starve; and, as a result of your careful planning and preparation, take off to enjoy a most-deserved oceanside escape. Planning a Web site follows the same pattern (without the added workouts, of course)—you start with the "big picture" goal and work down to the details.

Building a Case for Planning

Now that you're overflowing with Web-centric knowledge from Chapters 1 through 5, we're going to walk you through a Web site planning process. You're aware of all the elements you need to consider; now it's just a matter of consolidating the information into some concrete review questions and checklists. As you've probably heard throughout your life, a little planning up front can save more than a few headaches down the road. Not surprisingly, this philosophy holds true with Web development as well—a little preparation and forethought go a long way toward smoothly achieving success on the Web.

You might've noticed that this is the final chapter in Part One. We hope that you'll see this chapter as a bridge between Web theory and practice. In Part One, we've covered a lot of Web design basics; in Part Two, you'll have a chance to apply what you've learned to the hands-on exercises we provide in which you'll be creating the overall structure of four Web sites (one per chapter).

In Part Two, you can either re-create the Web pages exactly as we describe in each chapter or use the sample Web pages as templates for custom pages. For each Web site we present in Part Two, we summarize the planning process we completed before we created the actual page. Every chapter in Part Two also includes a short planning section, so you'll know how each page evolved during the site's planning phase and where the project is taking you regarding your hands-on page-development actions. If you're going to customize any of the Web sites we've included as samples, you'll need to do some custom planning as well. Eventually, after you've graduated beyond this book (and we have every confidence you will), you'll need to conduct your own planning sessions. Therefore, we designed this chapter to clearly outline each planning stage succinctly and in an easy-to-reference format. In the future, if you're ever stumped about setting goals for your Web site, defining your audience, designing your framework, or building your Web pages, grab this book off your shelf and turn to this chapter to help jump-start your thought processes.

To help illustrate the planning process, let's look at the evolution of the Curiosity Shoppe Web site. Figure 6-1 shows the final version of the shop's home page (*www.creationguide.com/cshoppe*). In the upcoming sections, we'll address some of the issues we considered when planning the Curiosity Shoppe Web site and explain what impact our decisions about those issues had on the final design.

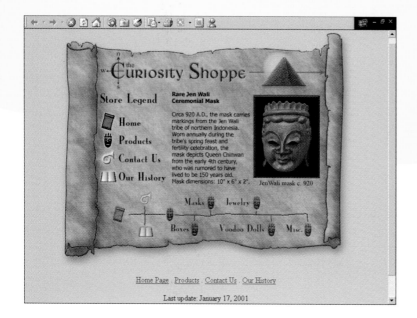

Figure 6-1
The Curiosity Shoppe home page

Defining Your Goals

Before you create a Web page or Web site, you must first address the project from a wide-angle perspective. You need to clearly consider your site's purpose and your goals for your site. Namely, you need to answer the following questions:

- Why do I want a Web page or Web site?

- What are my immediate goals for my Web site?

- What are my long-term goals for my site?

- What is my timeline?

For the Curiosity Shoppe site, the answers to the preceding questions were fairly straightforward. First, the Curiosity Shoppe owners wanted to make their shop easily accessible to more customers via an online presence. The owners' immediate goals were to inform people about the store, provide a means of contact, and advertise their products and store location. Their long-term plans are to offer their entire line of products for sale online and update the home page daily with a featured item. Finally, the owners' timeline can be summarized like this: static site online (*live*) within 2 months of the home page's inception; sales feature fully functional within 6 months after the home page has gone live; and a full line of online products available within 12 months from the date the initial home page went live.

Most likely, your goals and timeline will be less complex than those of the Curiosity Shoppe. For example, your goals might simply be to create an online résumé and have the résumé go live by next month, with updates occasionally added as necessary.

Getting to Know Your Audience

After you've outlined your goals for your site, you need to consider who's going to be visiting your Web pages. In other words, you need to think about your audience. You must have at least some perception of the people you want to visit your Web space. You need to address this planning step early in the process because (as mentioned in Chapter 4) many design and content decisions are based on your audience.

The best way to get to know your audience is to talk to them, if possible. Consider interviewing or surveying the people who will view your pages. For example, if you're making a family site, call your family members and find out what they'd like to see on the site. In addition, consider how users will be connecting to your page. Are they typical Web surfers with dial-up connections? If so, keep your page sizes small and your layouts fairly simple. Are you designing a site for online gamers? Then take advantage of high-speed connections and cutting-edge technologies. Designing for kids? Bright colors work well. You get the idea. To help analyze your audience, answer the following questions:

- **Who makes up the core of my target audience?** Your answer might include such categories as customers, students, employers, family members, kindred spirits, club members, and so on.

- **What does my audience want to find out from my site?** This question is different from asking yourself what *you* want to tell your audience—here's where you should really listen to prospective site users so you can design accordingly.

try this! Looking at Figure 6-1, you should be able to imagine how the Curiosity Shoppe's owners answered the audience questions.

■ **How experienced with the Web are the members of my audience?**
You'll need to figure out whether the bulk of your users will be
novices, casual Web surfers, or cyberspace champions. Knowing
users' level of expertise is key because while experienced users
can frequently figure out "what's going on" in complex or uniquely
designed sites, beginning users generally require a little more
guidance. For example, if you're catering to beginning surfers, you
should make it a point to clearly and consistently identify the site's
navigation elements.

■ **What types of Internet connections and bandwidth capabilities will
my users have?** Knowing whether your audience is connected via
a simple modem, an internal corporate network (called an *intranet*),
or a high-speed connection such as DSL (digital subscriber line)
will make a difference in how you design your Web site, including the types of elements you'll incorporate. For example, if you're
certain that your viewers will be accessing your Web site on high-
speed connections, you'll be freer to include video clips and numerous graphics with a minimal risk of losing viewers. If you
include video and numerous graphics on a Web site accessed by
users with dial-up connections, however, you'll risk losing those
viewers before your site displays because they'll understandably
get tired of waiting for the large elements to download.

■ **Where is my core audience located?** You'll need to determine
whether people will visit your site while at work, on campus, in
home offices, in living rooms, at cyber cafés, in your neighborhood, and so forth. This specification relates closely to the preceding question—if you know where your core audience is located,
you'll most likely get a good feel for the types of connections
they'll be using to access your site. Further, location can come into
play if you're designing a regional site versus a national site. For
example, a David Bowie site might have an international audience, whereas your Block Watch site would probably cater mostly
to your neighborhood. This differentiation is similar to the variations of information found in a newspaper's front-page section
(which would correspond to a nationally or internationally focused
Web site) compared to the local section (which would correspond
to a locally oriented Web site).

■ **What's the typical age group among my audience members?** You want to be sure that your site appeals to the age group you're targeting. This question is rooted in common sense—whether you like it or not, you can make some minor sweeping (albeit conservative) assumptions based on your audience's age, and these assumptions can help you throughout the Web page creation process. Knowing your audience's typical age ("typical" being the key word) helps you to make appropriate design decisions. For example, preteen Barbie-pink backgrounds don't work well on sport sites that target 18–40-year-old males. Further, age parameters help you to choose words (particularly slang and colloquialisms) wisely, such as whether to "dude" or not to "dude." In addition, age information enables you to create meaningful metaphors—for example, will retirees *really* know (or care) what it feels like to get kicked in the head in a mosh pit? Finally, age specifics can help you determine the types of information you'll include on your Web pages. For example, if you're creating a kid's site, you wouldn't feature AARP information, but you might seriously consider including a "Name That Pokémon" feature.

■ **How will users find out about my site?** You'll want to know whether people will hear about your site by word of mouth, from online directories, from hard-copy Web directories or phone books, via links from a "parent" page, as a result of search engines, through paid commercial advertisements on TV or radio, and so on so that you'll know best how to advertise and publicize your site.

tip

After you've interviewed, surveyed, and talked to people; listened to feedback; and summarized your data, remember to specifically visualize a *real live person* instead of a generic profile while you create your Web site and design your Web pages.

Drawing the Blueprints for Your Site

After setting your goals and defining your audience, you're ready to design your Web site's framework. If possible, your first step should always be to collect your content before you design. As we said in Chapter 2, organizing your content—or at least its main concepts—can help you organize your overall site in a logical manner.

After you gather the main types of information you want to include on your site (don't worry—your text and graphics don't have to be polished at this point), you need to figure out how best to present your information. For example, you can organize your site in any number of ways, including the following.

- Alphabetically
- Chronologically
- Graphically
- Hierarchically
- Numerically
- Randomly (not recommended—but it's out there)
- Topically

By far, most sites are organized hierarchically. A hierarchical site presents a home page that contains catchy introductory text and links to the site's main pages. This setup is widely used by designers and greatly appreciated by users (who mostly just want to use Web pages—not figure out how they're organized).

Another critical (though certainly less exciting) aspect of organizing your site involves naming your files. After all, when you boil it all down, your site is entirely made up of files—so organizing your site must include systemizing your files. Before we get to the Site Planning Checklist, let's take a look at some file-naming practices that you can mull over now and implement later.

Keeping Your Files in Line

As you now know, Web pages usually consist of a few files working together to create the appearance of a single page. Further, a Web site consists of multiple Web pages (which in turn consist of multiple files). Because of this multifile nature of Web pages and Web sites, you're going to have to come up with a plan for naming and organizing your Web site's files. (In each chapter in Part Two, we explain how we've organized each site's files, so you'll have lots of chances to get the hang of naming and organizing files before the end of this book.) For the most part, a standard Web site can consist of the following simple structure, which is shown in Figure 6-2:

- **Main directory** Contains HTML files and an images directory. You can provide any name for this directory when designing your pages on your local machine. When you upload your pages to a hosting service, you'll probably place the main directory folder's contents into an online folder named "Web" and copy the entire images folder (folder and all) into the Web folder.

■ **Images directory**   Contains GIF and JPEG (or JPG) image files used on your Web pages. This directory is usually stored within the main directory.

Figure 6-2

Directories and files for the Curiosity Shoppe Web site stored in a local directory

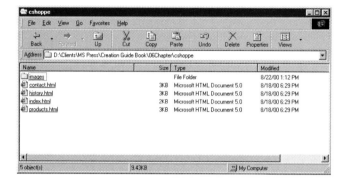

Notice in Figure 6-2 that the main directory currently holds four HTML files—contact.html, history.html, index.html, and products.html—one file for each of the Web site's main pages. Keep in mind that an HTML file's name is the name that appears in the Web page's URL address. For example, to visit the Curiosity Shoppe's Products page, you would enter *www.creationguide.com/cshoppe/products.html*. As you can see, the preceding URL consists of the domain name (*www.creationguide.com*), the directory or folder name (*cshoppe*), and a filename (*products.html*).

For most home pages, you might've noticed that you don't have to enter a filename. For example, when you visit Microsoft's home page, you simply type Microsoft's domain name: *www.microsoft.com*. If no HTML filename is indicated after a domain name, most servers will display a particularly named file by default—most likely index.html, although some servers also cater to index.htm, default.htm, or default.html. Ask your hosting service which name you should use for your home page (or test each filename online to see which one works by default); nine times out of ten (and probably more frequently than that!) index.html is the way to go when naming your home page, and it's your safest bet when you're unsure.

Because your HTML filenames will appear within your Web page's URL, you should follow a few simple rules to keep life simple for you and your users:

- **Keep filenames short, simple, and meaningful.** Users might want to access a subpage directly, so make the URL easy for them to type and remember. For example, use a file named "products.html" instead of "p1-2001m.html."

- **Avoid symbols and punctuation.** Most people find typing symbols and adding punctuation slows their typing speeds considerably and dramatically decreases their typing accuracy. Further, symbols and punctuation can create new avenues for confusion. For example, if your page is named *www.creation-guide.com*, users could easily forget the hyphen and type *www.creationguide.com* (thereby missing your page altogether and visiting ours by mistake!).

- **Use an underscore (_) to indicate a space.** Some older servers don't recognize spaces, so use underscores instead to indicate blank spaces. Further, you run into the same problem with spaces as you do with symbols and punctuation—spaces are easily forgotten and leave room for errors (lots of them).

- **Use all lowercase letters.** Once again, think "ease of use" for your Web site visitors. URLs are case-sensitive, and a randomly uppercased letter can lose more than a few visitors. All lowercase filenames are easy to type and easy to remember.

By now, you should be realizing that organization plays an important part in Web site planning. You need to streamline your thoughts as

tip

Make sure that every HTML filename has an .htm or .html extension and that every image filename has a .gif, .jpeg, or .jpg extension.

Naming Images   In addition to naming your HTML files, you'll need to name your image files. Generally, users don't access image files directly; instead, HTML pages reference image files whenever they need to be displayed. Therefore, you have more leeway when it comes to labeling your images. One handy image-naming trick that we use is to identify an image's purpose with a simple prefix incorporated into the file's name, which helps us to quickly identify and find files when we need them. Specifically, we precede image names with *p_*, *b_*, or *t_*. A *p_* image is a picture. For example, *p_mask* indicates that the image is a picture of a mask. A *b_* image is a button. For example, *b_products* indicates that the image is the navigation bar's Products button. And a *t_* image refers to a title bar. For example, *t_contacts* specifies that the image is the title bar graphic used on the Contacts page.

well as start to consider how you'll systemize your files (which, again, are basically your Web site's Web pages and graphics). You can streamline the site-organization phase by performing the tasks and addressing the issues presented in the upcoming Site Planning Checklist.

After (or while) you address the items on the Site Planning Checklist, you should storyboard your site's structure as described in Chapter 4, in the "Storyboarding Your Web Site" section. In other words, you should illustrate the relationships among your site's pages and information to ensure that you've created a clear site layout that includes all your information in an easily accessible format. Figure 6-3 shows one of the Curiosity Shoppe's initial storyboards. You can make storyboards even more detailed than the one shown in Figure 6-3 by including short descriptions of what's going to appear on each page. For example, in the storyboard shown in Figure 6-3, you could add notes such as, "The contact.html page contains an e-mail link and a map showing the shop's location."

Figure 6-3
The Curiosity Shoppe storyboard
used to show filenames used
within the initial site

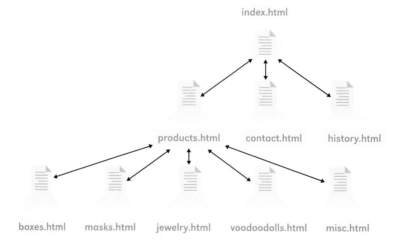

Site Planning Checklist
The items on this checklist outline the basics tasks you should perform while planning your Web site. Address each listed task and issue, and sketch your site's informational relationships as you plan.

❏ Visit similar sites to see what you like and don't like, and figure out how you can make your site unique.

❏ Be sure that your site specifies who you are and (if appropriate) your organization's identity.

❏ Pick colors that evoke an appropriate emotion for your site. Ensure that your color scheme presents a clear contrast for easy reading, analyze whether the colors work to further your site's goals, and try to use colors from the 216-color Web-safe palette. For a quick refresher on Web-safe colors, see Chapter 3 or this book's appendix.

❏ Verify that the main point of your site is clearly identified up front, not buried a page or two deep into your site. You don't want readers to visit your home page and wonder what they're supposed to do now that they've found your Web site.

❏ Classify your site to yourself so that you don't lose your focus. For design purposes, label your site as commercial, informational, educational, entertainment, navigation, community, artistic, or personal or as some other type of site.

❏ Design the site to reflect how users will most likely navigate through your pages. You can get an idea of what users want during your audience-analysis stage. Make sure that you include umbrella topics (main topics—not outdoor gear topics) on your home page, and then provide more specific links on each subpage. For example, provide a Contacts link on the home page, and provide departmental links on the Contacts page.

❏ Ensure that your site offers viewers a few ways in which they can contact you—physical address, e-mail address, phone number, carrier pigeon, and so forth.

❏ Name your files appropriately (as discussed earlier in this chapter).

❏ Create easy-to-understand button names that clearly reflect your site's structure. Cryptic buttons might look awesome, but they tend to confuse readers (especially when no explanatory text accompanies your esoteric creation).

❑   Divide your content into logical units. Don't divide one page into two just because it seems like the page is getting too long. On the other hand, if you see a logical break in a long page, by all means, divide the page (but make sure you don't lose the newly created page by burying its link deep within your site).

❑   Analyze your information, and make your most important information the most accessible.

❑   Determine ways in which you can create a unifying look or theme throughout your site. Don't forget to include a logo and use consistent navigation links on every page. Keep in mind that the nitty-gritty design aspects of your site's look and theme are addressed more thoroughly in the next planning stage, when you design your home page and subpages.

❑   Include at least one element that will encourage users to return, such as a daily or weekly updated element or a chat room.

try this!   Quick—think of three sites you've visited recently. Now analyze why those three sites made an impression on you. Are there any elements you can adopt and modify for your site? Were those sites easy to navigate? Does an element that you didn't like stand out in your mind? Use your personal experience to your benefit. After all, you know what you like when you're surfing the Web.

Laying Your Home Page's Foundation

After the site-planning dust settles, you can sweep off your slate and start to design your home page (and subpages). By now, you should have a very strong idea of what your home page should include—logo, title bar, links to your site's main pages, and so forth. For the most part, you should have taken care of the practical side of page design, such as determining a file naming structure, analyzing your audience, determining hardware limitations, and so forth. At this point, your creative juices get to take over while your organizational synapses rest and rejuvenate. In this design phase, focus your attention on how you can creatively present all the necessary home page components in a way that reflects your site's goals, optimizes your site's theme, and elicits the proper "emotional" response from users. For example, the Curiosity Shoppe wanted to convey the feeling that the store sells treasures that have been discovered throughout the world. Therefore, we came up with the treasure map theme and the N-S-E-W "C" logo for the Curiosity Shoppe's owners.

After you start to think of creative ways to present your ideas, start to sketch various layouts and ideas. You'll begin to see what works best, and ideas will breed off one another until you come up with a page design that does the trick. Figure 6-4 shows a sketch of the Curiosity Shoppe's home page. Because we designed the home page to make a unique impression, its design is notably different from the layout of the site's subpages. Therefore, we also sketched the Products page to illustrate how title bars and navigation links would display on subpages, as shown in Figure 6-5. While you're sketching your home page, refer to the Home Page Planning Checklist that starts on the following page to ensure that you've covered all your bases.

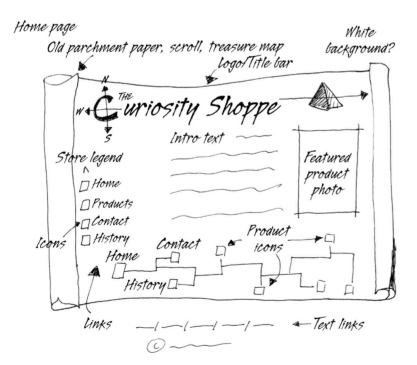

Figure 6-4
The Curiosity Shoppe home page sketch

Figure 6-5
The Curiosity Shoppe Products page sketch

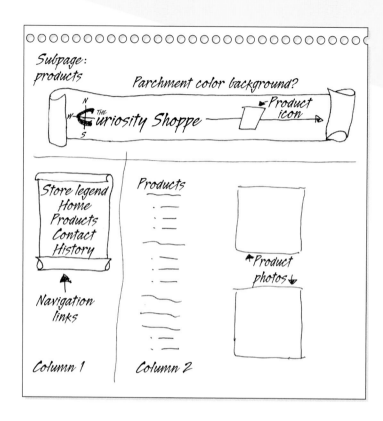

Figure 6-5
The Curiosity Shoppe Products page sketch

Home Page Planning Checklist

You need to verify that your home page includes the elements listed in the following Home Page Planning Checklist. If you purposely omit certain elements, be sure you understand why. Keep in mind that the list doesn't weight the importance of elements by order—in fact, the list is alphabetized specifically to avoid promoting any elements over others. (We're tricky like that.) Make sure that one way or another you address *all* the following elements in relation to your home page's design:

❏ Creation or revision date

❏ Easily identified and consistently displayed navigation links or buttons

❏ Home page icon or logo that can be used throughout the site

❏ Important information displayed above the fold

❏ Informative title

tip

Even though the Home Page Planning Checklist looks lengthy, your home page shouldn't. At all costs, avoid overloading your home page. You're better off adding a couple links to your navigation menu instead of cramming information into every corner (and beyond) of your users' screens.

❑ Intentional emotional effect or theme created via words, colors, layout, font, and so forth

❑ Logo or other identifying graphic, such as a family crest or departmental code

❑ Opening page "hook" to catch viewer's interest (Home pages generally vary at least slightly from subpages.)

❑ Quick loading approach (It's true—gigantic images make extremely poor backgrounds, and you really don't need to show 90 pictures on your home page.)

❑ Site's purpose is clear and viewers know what steps they can take next (beyond clicking the Back button)

❑ Subheads break up long text (if necessary)

❑ Text links display along the bottom of the page

❑ Upper-left corner is put to good use, preferably with your logo

❑ Your identity or your organization's identity

Gathering Supplies and Preparing to Build

As you might remember from Chapter 5, after you've specified your goals, met your audience, organized your site, and designed your home page's layout, one final planning component remains—rounding up your tools and supplies. This stage includes ensuring that you have well-written and edited text, appropriately sized graphics (which you might have to tweak a little when the actual page design process begins), scanned or otherwise digitized pictures, and the tools to arrange all the items on your Web pages. As you can see, the tasks in this stage are concrete and straightforward, but completing them generally takes a significant amount of

note

We're not trying to discourage you by stating that the supplies stage of the Web game can be time-consuming. It's just that gathering, creating, and modifying text and graphics almost always seems to take slightly longer than planned (at least that's been our experience—and not just because we inherently tend to enjoy creating, modifying, and playing with graphics and text!). Fortunately, you don't need to worry about "gathering supplies" types of delays at this point. Remember, our goal in this book is *easy* Web page creation. To that end, in each chapter in Part Two, we've listed the supplies necessary to create the chapter's Web pages. Then you can download the images and copy the text you'll need from the Creation Guide Web site. So never fear: the hunting and gathering stages detailed in Part Two are brief and painless.

time—so plan accordingly. Luckily, although this stage usually takes the longest, we can describe the process fairly succinctly. Basically, before you create your Web page, you need to gather the supplies listed in the following Supplies Checklist.

Supplies Checklist

Before you start to create your Web pages, you should have the following elements on hand and easily accessible—or at least in the process of being finalized.

- ❑ Text, edited and proofread
- ❑ Photographs, graphics, and illustrations (including buttons, title bars, and a high-quality logo)
- ❑ Page sketches and templates
- ❑ HTML editor, text editor, or Web page creation tool (such as an online community wizard)
- ❑ Graphics program
- ❑ Domain name, if desired
- ❑ Server space

Now that the theory and planning phases are fully covered, you're ready to get your hands dirty and tackle Part Two of this book. So roll up your sleeves—it's time to create!

tip

Remember that your domain name should be short, simple, and influenced by your Web site's purpose.

key points

- ■ **Define your Web site's goals.**
- ■ **Know your audience.**
- ■ **Outline your Web site's hierarchy, organizational flow, and overall feel.**
- ■ **Sketch your home page and subpages, if necessary.**
- ■ **Gather your supplies and tools.**
- ■ **Get ready to create Web pages and go live!**

PART

two

creating web pages

When you learned to drive a car, you probably spent some time listening to an instructor, watching defensive-driving movies, memorizing street signs, and studying driving-related facts in the Department of Motor Vehicles handbook. Sure, those learning exercises were helpful, but most likely, the art of driving truly sank in only after you got behind the wheel as a student driver and took a few spins around town with your driving instructor. Experience counts quite a bit in the real world. This sentiment isn't exactly new—Einstein summed it up pretty well when he said, "One cannot learn anything so well as by experiencing it oneself." In Part Two, we're going to put you in the driver's seat and let you put the theories you learned in Part One into practice.

In this part, you'll find four project chapters designed to help you acquire some well-rounded, hands-on experience as you test drive the Web site creation process. Throughout these chapters, we've tried to make the learning process as enjoyable, straightforward, and intuitive as possible. To that end, we've arranged the chapters progressively, from simplest to hardest, so that you can ease your way into more advanced Web page creation tasks. In addition, each Web site is created using a different tool that is either already on your computer or easy to access.

posting a

You could walk into your nearest computer-nerd store and obtain all the components necessary to build yourself a new computer—you could buy a motherboard, some RAM, a microprocessor, a tower case, a CD-ROM drive, and so forth; pack it all home; and then spend a few hours (probably more) assembling all the pieces into a working computer. Some people wouldn't upgrade their hardware in any other way. Another

Convenient

7

Fast web page
WITHIN AN HOUR (OR SO)

approach to acquiring a new computer would be to forgo leaving the comfort of your home and fire up your old computer, link to the Internet, and simply order a completely upgraded computer system directly from a manufacturer. For some, convenience is the way to go. In this chapter, we're going to show you the easiest—and fastest—way to create a basic meeting place online. Welcome to the world of MSN Communities.

To create the Web site described in this chapter, you'll need the following "supplies":

- An Internet connection.

- A browser (ideally Microsoft Internet Explorer version 4 or later).

- Figures downloaded from *www.creationguide.com/chapter7/ images*, including dad.jpg, family.jpg, mom.jpg, and vacation.jpg. To download these figures, connect to *www.creationguide.com/ chapter7/images*, right-click an image's filename, and save a copy of the file (referred to as the "Target" in Internet Explorer's shortcut menu, as shown in Figure 7-1) to a folder on your computer. Repeat the process for each image you want to save on your computer.

Figure 7-1
Downloading image files from the Internet

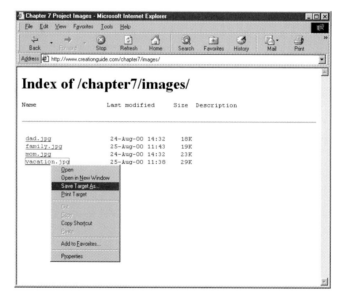

Introducing MSN and Online Communities

Here's some good news—by reading this chapter and following along with the project steps, you'll have a live Web site by the time you reach the end of the chapter. Furthermore, you won't need to partake in any deep-breathing exercises, calisthenics, or caffeine-laden drinking binges to get your Web site up and running. In other words, this is going to be easy! So let's get going.

For this chapter's purposes, let's imagine that your goal is to have some information online today. Let's also say that you'd prefer not to spend any money at this point for an online presence. Amazingly enough, this goal is realistic and easily achieved. (As we mentioned in Chapter 5, you'd be surprised at the number of people we meet who have no idea that free space is readily available online.) You can quickly create a free Web site by taking advantage of the simplest and least expensive Web publishing approach around—*online communities.*

As we explained in Chapter 5, online communities are areas on the Web where you can post Web pages for free—all you need to invest are some graphics (if desired), text, and a little time. Our tool of choice for this chapter's project is the MSN Web Communities site, which is located at *communities.msn.com.* Figure 7-2 shows the MSN Communities home page.

lingo

Online communities are areas on the Web designed to enable people to create Web pages at no charge and then share them with others who have similar interests.

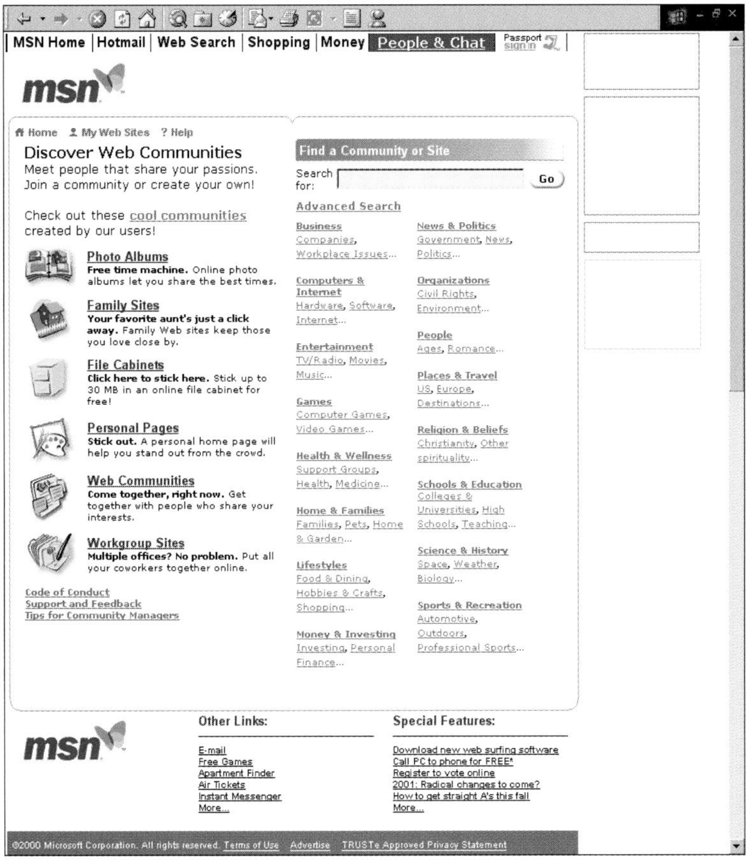

Figure 7-2
The MSN Communities home page

You can glean quite a bit of information from the MSN Communities home page. Of particular interest, notice that the MSN Communities Web sites are sorted by categories, including the following:

- Photo Albums
- Family Sites
- File Cabinets
- Personal Pages
- Web Communities
- Workgroup Sites

In this chapter, we'll show you how to create an MSN Family Site, but you can use the instructions printed here to create any site that best suits your needs. Our goal is to get you off on the right foot—where you wander from here is up to you.

As you'll soon see, all MSN templates are made up of various combinations of the following standard features:

- **Site manager**   The person who has the greatest control over a site and who is responsible for overseeing the site. Generally, the site manager is the person who originally created the site or someone the site's creator has assigned to that role. By default, you'll be the site manager of the site you create in this chapter.

- **Home page**   The first page that visitors see when they visit your site. At a minimum, MSN home pages include the name of the site, the site's description, links to the site's features, and a link to other MSN sites classified within the same category in the MSN Community Web Sites directory. (For example, if you create a Family Site, your home page will include a link to "More Families Web Sites" by default.)

- **Message board**   An area where site members can read and reply to messages and share files.

- **Photo album**   A page where members can display photos accompanied by short descriptions for other members to view.

- **Chat room**   A private space on the site where members can exchange messages in real time. In other words, members can hold online conversations as if they're on the phone, except that they type their messages instead of speak them.

- **Calendar**   A page that looks like a calendar and helps members keep track of dates and events.

- **File cabinet**   An area that members can use to store, exchange, and access files.

- **Custom lists**   Lists that members can customize for any purpose.

- **Recommendations**   An area where members can rant or rave about books, music, movies, and Web sites.

- **Member list**   An up-to-date list of the site's members, including each member's nickname, role, and join date.

- **Community settings**   A Web page that depicts the Web site's community settings, including the site's description, access and membership policies, e-mail distribution list policy, rating, and directory listing. Members can view the community settings, but only site managers can alter the settings.

- **Your member profile**   An area where a member can alter profile settings, including changing a nickname, revising a self-description, specifying an e-mail address, and canceling membership.

- **Site E-mail**   A utility that enables site managers and members to easily send messages to all members on the site's e-mail distribution list.

- **Invite Someone or Recommend To A Friend**   A tool that enables members to introduce other viewers to the sites they like and have joined.

After you create an MSN Web site, you (as the site manager) can add and remove any of the preceding elements to customize your site. Additionally, after other users sign up with your site and become members, they can participate in your site's activities by leaving messages on the message board, participating in chats, posting pictures in the picture albums, and so forth.

Now that you have an idea of where we're headed, let's get started with your first Web site creation project. As with all Web pages, this project starts with a planning phase.

Planning an MSN Community Site

Planning your site is your first task in any Web publishing endeavor—even when you're using an online community site such as MSN. Generally, online communities—MSN Communities included—simplify the planning process by providing templates, clip art, and other Web page creation resources and utilities. MSN Communities offers a number of helpful tools, most notably Web page templates. A *template* is a preformatted Web page layout that you use to plug in custom information, similar to Microsoft Word templates that you use to build formatted documents, letters, Web pages, and so forth. In contrast, a custom home page offers you a blank Web page, which you need to fill on your own.

---

see also | *In Chapter 9, we'll show you how to create a Web site based on Microsoft Word templates.*

---

tip

You can re-create the Visiting family site using the text and graphics we provide in this book, or you can choose another MSN Communities Web site template. We think a Family Site is a good place to start because it's useful and flexible to use for both family and friends. Feel free to follow this chapter's instructions verbatim or to replace the Visiting family's text and graphics with your own. You'll probably be more satisfied with your customized results. (Nothing against the Visitings, of course!)

On the MSN Communities site, you can create Web pages by using templates or creating custom pages. At this point in the book, taking advantage of the easy-to-use MSN templates is the way to go. Later, after you acquire more advanced Web page creation skills, you can return to your MSN Communities site to customize and liven up your existing Web pages. A template enables you to get online quickly and easily, plus this approach gives you a taste of how satisfying and entertaining it is to see and share your pages online.

Because we opted to take the template route, our planning process for this chapter's Web site didn't require any Web site storyboards or home page sketches. Instead, our planning process involved checking out a few of the MSN Communities templates, viewing existing pages, and determining that the Family Connections template offers the most useful set of possible MSN features for the majority of families. Also during our planning stages, we received an inside scoop that the Visiting family was anxious to have a Web site of their own. They travel quite a bit and want a place where they can easily touch base with their family and friends. So as a public service, we opted to create a family MSN Communities site for the Visiting family. You're free to use the Visiting family's pictures, which are available from *www.creationguide.com/chapter7/images*, when you practice creating your own MSN Communities site.

After selecting a flexible Family Site template and agreeing to create the Visiting family's MSN Communities Web site, our planning process entailed obtaining a few key pictures from the Visiting family and talking to them about their goals for the site.

To summarize our MSN Communities Web site planning process, we completed the following simple steps:

- Chose a site template
- Determined textual content
- Obtained a few graphics

Now that a general plan for the online community Web site is taking shape, our next step is to join the community.

Joining an Online Community

Universally, free online communities require you to join their sites. Joining usually involves filling out an online form. Being a member of an online community serves a number of purposes, including providing membership security and enabling custom settings. Having a member profile allows you to customize the Web sites you build as well as provides information to others whenever you become a member of another Web site within the community. As you'll see in a moment, obtaining MSN membership doesn't require you to divulge any retirement savings account numbers, credit card PIN passwords, or other sensitive information, so the process is hardly a scary prospect.

To join MSN Communities, you first need to obtain a Microsoft Passport. If you are the proud owner of a free Hotmail e-mail account (available at *www.hotmail.com*), you can use your Hotmail information as your Passport. If you don't have a Hotmail account, you'll need to acquire a Microsoft Passport. Obtaining a Passport entails (you guessed it) filling out an online form. Here's how you go about getting your Passport:

1 Display the Microsoft Passport home page (*www.passport.com*) in your browser.

2 If desired, click the What Is A Passport? link to read more about Microsoft Passport. Then return to the Passport home page and click the Free Passport link. Your click will earn you a chance to complete a Passport form similar to the one shown in Figure 7-3.

note

You don't necessarily need to gather graphics to get started with an online communities Web page. Using MSN Communities, you can easily add and delete graphics after you've created your Web site. Remember, you can use the Visiting family's pictures or MSN clip art for now, and then you can delete the temporary pictures and insert your own images whenever you have digitized pictures ready for online viewing.

note

You can also access a Passport registration page by clicking the Passport link on the MSN Communities home page. But because Web pages change frequently, we felt it was better to go straight to the source by visiting the Passport home page.

Figure 7-3
The Passport registration form

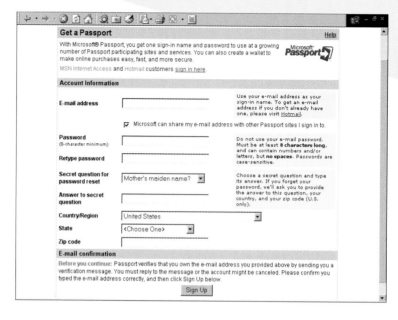

3   To complete the Passport form, you must first enter your e-mail address in the standard *username@domainname.abc* format (for example, *mm@creationguide.com*). If you don't have an e-mail address or you prefer not to use your existing e-mail address, you can click the Hotmail link to sign up for a free e-mail account (or visit *www.hotmail.com*). Whichever route you take, you must enter a legitimate e-mail address before Microsoft will grant you Passport privileges.

4   Determine whether you want to allow Microsoft to share your e-mail address with other Web sites that use the Passport technology. If you're unsure, deselect the check box below the e-mail address text box for now.

5   In the Password text box, enter a password that's at least eight characters long and doesn't include spaces. Then retype the password in the Retype Password text box. Typing your password twice ensures that you've entered your password correctly. We probably don't need to tell you this, but be nice to yourself when you choose a password—that is, choose a password you're going to remember.

6   Even though you probably just chose a password that's easy to remember, MSN provides a backup system to compensate for human nature—after all, everyone knows the feeling of instantaneously forgetting a name directly after an introduction or wandering around a bit in a parking lot before remembering where you parked the car. Therefore, MSN

tip

To view a list of sites and businesses that use the Passport technology, click the Use Your Passport link on the Microsoft Passport home page.

provides the Secret Question For Password Reset text box as a backup. Click the Secret Question For Password Reset drop-down list box arrow to select a secret question, and then type your answer to the secret question in the Answer To Secret Question dialog box. If you forget your password, MSN will ask you to supply the answer to your secret question to verify your identity. (If you've forgotten the answer too, you might be permanently locked out of your Passport. Fortunately, new Passports are cheap.)

7   Complete the Country/Region, State, and Zip Code text boxes.

8   Click the Sign Up button. In a few seconds, you'll see a Passport Confirmation page verifying that your Passport has been created.

9   You'll soon receive two e-mail notices in your e-mail application's Inbox— a welcome message and a "verify your e-mail address" message. As you'll see, the "verify your e-mail address" message contains a ridiculously long Web address that you must visit to validate your e-mail address. If the address is highlighted in your e-mail application, simply click on it; if the address isn't highlighted, copy the entire address (from *https* all the way to the end of the long string of letters and digits) and paste it into the address box of your browser. Either way, your browser will quickly display an E-mail Validated page.

Congratulations! You're officially registered as a Microsoft Passport holder, and you're ready to create an MSN Communities Web site.

Selecting an MSN Communities Template

As mentioned earlier, this project walks you through the process of creating a Family Site within the MSN Communities online arena. For the most part, using an MSN template entails filling out online forms. You've just had a taste of online forms when you registered for a Microsoft Passport; a few more text boxes and buttons won't be too taxing. To create the foundation pages for your site, follow these steps:

1   Display the MSN Communities home page (*communities.msn.com*) in your browser window. (Ideally, you should use Internet Explorer 4 or later when creating an MSN Communities Web site.)

2   On the MSN Communities home page, click the Family Sites link. The MSN Family Sites Web page displays, as shown in Figure 7-4. Notice the Passport Sign-In link.

Passport Sign-In link

Figure 7-4
The MSN Family Sites page

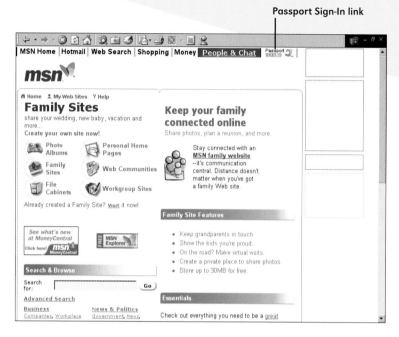

3 On the MSN Family Sites page, click the Create Your Own Site Now link
or click the Family Sites link. A Web page displays that lists and briefly
describes the available templates within the Family Sites Categories, as
shown in Figure 7-5.

Figure 7-5
*Viewing the available Family
Sites templates*

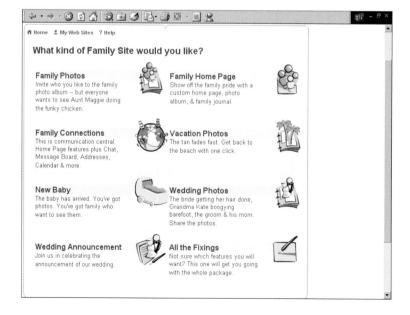

4 Click the Family Connections link. You'll be asked to sign in using your Passport information.

5 Click the Sign In With Your Passport link. The MSN Web Communities Sign In page displays.

6 Enter your Passport e-mail address and password in the text boxes, and then click the Sign-In button. You'll see the Create Your Own Web Site form requesting Web site information.

You're well on your way! In the next section, we'll describe how to complete the Create Your Own Web Site form.

Setting Up an MSN Communities Web Site

After you select a Web site template, your next task involves supplying the information you want to include within the template's parameters. MSN enables you to customize your Web site's information via the Create Your Own Web Site form, which is shown in Figure 7-6. In all, the Create Your Own Web Site form includes four steps and a smattering of Other Settings links. (Notice the numbered steps on the Create Your Own Web Site form and in Figure 7-6.) In the following procedure, the first four steps correspond to the four numbered steps on the Create Your Own Web Site form, and then steps 5 through 7 introduce the process of configuring the Other Settings options.

note

Keep in mind that because you're creating the Web site, you'll be its site manager by default.

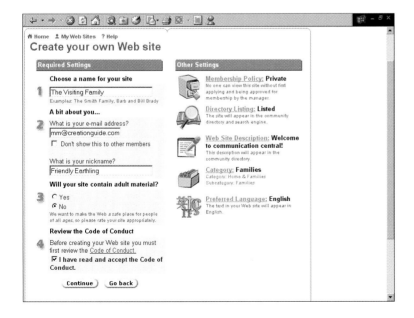

Figure 7-6
Supplying information in the Create Your Own Web Site form— steps 1 through 4

1 In step 1, enter a site name. For example, we entered *The Visiting Family*. This name will appear in your Web site's address, including the capital letters but excluding the spaces. For example, the Visiting family's Web address will be *communities.msn.com/TheVisitingFamily*. You need to use a unique name to create your site, so you'll have to enter site name text that is different than ours.

2 Supply your nickname. Because we're creating a site for the Visiting family, we kept the nickname simple; we entered *Friendly Earthling*. Notice in step 2 that your e-mail address displays by default. If prefer to hide your e-mail address from people who visit your site, you can select the Don't Show This To Other Members check box. We chose to allow our e-mail address to display to site members, so we left the check box unmarked.

3 Specify whether your site will contain adult content. We chose No.

4 This step involves reading and accepting the MSN Communities code of conduct. To view the code of conduct, click the Code Of Conduct link. A separate window opens that contains the information, as shown in Figure 7-7. After you read the code of conduct, click the Close button (found at the bottom of the Code Of Conduct page); the Code of Conduct window closes, and you're returned to the Create Your Own Web Site page. Click the I Have Read And Accept The Code Of Conduct check box.

Figure 7-7
Viewing the MSN Communities Code Of Conduct

Now notice the Other Settings links along the right side of the page. You're ready to further customize your site's settings. In the following

steps, you'll configure the Membership Policy Settings and accept the
default settings for the other options:

5 Click the Membership Policy link. The section expands, as shown in Figure 7-8. Specify whether you'd like the site to be Public, Public Restricted,
or Private. When your site is Public, anyone can view and interact with
your pages. If you select Public Restricted, anyone can view your pages
but only approved members can interact with your site. If you create a
Private site, users must apply to be members of the site and the site
manager (you) must approve users' memberships before they can participate and view your site. By default, sites are set up as Private, as
indicated by the text following the Membership Policy link. For the sake
of simplicity, we chose the Public Restricted option for the Visiting
family's Web site, as shown in Figure 7-8.

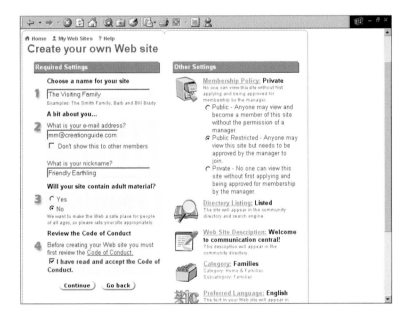

note

If you specify a Private site,
you can't change the site to a
Public site later. If you're
unsure of which option to
choose, choose Public or
Public Restricted for now. If
you want, you can later
change a Public site to a
Private site.

Figure 7-8
*Specifying a Membership Policy
for your site*

6 At this point, we chose to retain the default settings for the remaining
Other Settings options. By default, your site will be listed in MSN's
directory listing—notice that the Directory Listing link is followed by the
word *Listed*. Further, the default welcome text—*Welcome to communication central!*—will display on your home page, the site's category is
Families, and the preferred language is English. You can change any of
the default settings by clicking the corresponding link.

7 Click the Continue button. The Customize Your Web Site page then displays (providing us with a nice segue into the next section).

Customizing Your Web Site

After you supply the foundation information on the Create Your Own Web Site page, you're presented with the Customize Your Web Site page, as shown in Figure 7-9. As you can see in Figure 7-9, this page contains a preview of the selected template and four steps, which correspond to the instructions following the figure.

Template preview

Figure 7-9
The Customize Your Web Site page

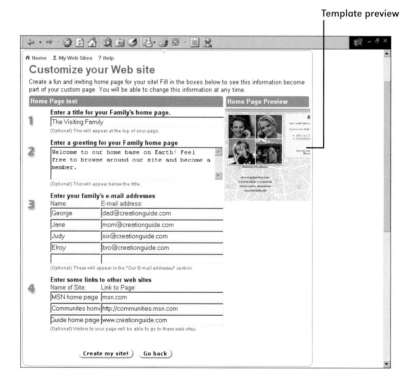

1 In this step, you provide the title text that appears at the top of your home page. By default, the text "Welcome to our web site!" appears in the text box. You can change the text to any text you want. For example, we changed the text to *The Visiting Family*.

2 You can now enter some text that will appear on your home page. You can alter the text later, so don't take this step too seriously at this point. We entered the following two sentences: *Welcome to our home base on Earth! Feel free to browse around our site and become a member*.

3 You can supply your family e-mail addresses on the Customize Your Web Site page. As you can see in Figure 7-9, you can have your family's e-mail addresses display in an Our E-mail Addresses section on your Web site's home page. As the site manager, you can add and delete e-mail addresses whenever necessary. For the Visiting family Web site, we added the following names and e-mail addresses:

- George, *dad@creationguide.com*
- Jane, *mom@creationguide.com*
- Judy, *sis@creationguide.com*
- Elroy, *bro@creationguide.com*

4 You can now add some Web site addresses that might be useful links for the site's users. The links provided in this step appear on your site's home page in the Our Favorite Web Sites section. In the Visiting family's home page, we retained the two default links and added a third link. To add the third link, we typed *Creation Guide home page* in the Name Of Site text box in the Enter Some Links To Other Web Sites section, and then we typed *www.creationguide.com* in the Link To Page text box. After completing step 4, click the Create My Site button. A Family Connections site is generated, as shown in Figure 7-10, and an e-mail message is sent to your Inbox.

tip

The names you enter in step 3 appear on your home page, but the e-mail addresses are merely associated with the names. When a user clicks a name on your home page, a blank e-mail form opens automatically.

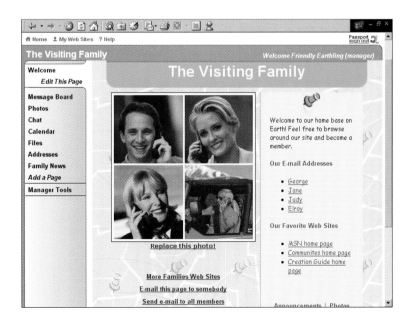

Figure 7-10
Getting a first glimpse of your MSN Communities Web page

tip

After you create a Web site, you must always sign in with your Passport information whenever you return to the MSN Communities site before you can make any changes to your Web pages. To sign in, click the Microsoft Passport icon, which appears on every MSN Communities page.

By default, MSN inserts a temporary picture on your home page as a placeholder. As the site manager, you can easily replace this picture if you have another image on hand.

Replacing the Default Photograph

Replacing the default photograph is fairly simple; most notably, it involves downloading the MSN Photo Upload Control. (Don't worry—that sounds more complicated than it is.) Before you dive into this procedure, be sure that you have a photograph stored on your computer or on a disk. Then make sure you know the path to the picture. After you have this information, follow these steps:

1 On your newly created home page, click the Replace This Photo link, which appears directly below the default photograph. You'll see the message shown in Figure 7-11, which states that you need to download the MSN Photo Upload Control before you can replace the picture.

Figure 7-11
Downloading the MSN Photo Upload Control

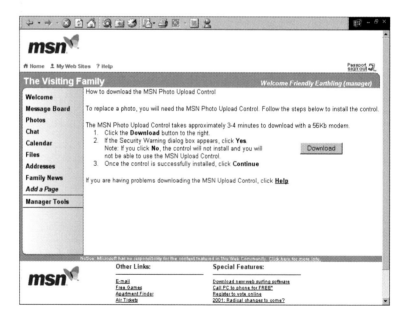

2 Read the brief instructions regarding how to download the MSN Photo Upload Control, and then click the Download button. If the Security Warning dialog box opens, click Yes to enable the control to be downloaded to your system. After the download completes, you'll see the MSN Photo Upload Control window, shown in Figure 7-12.

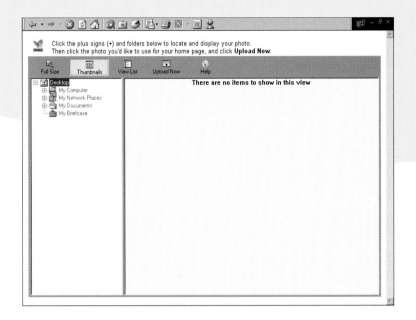

Figure 7-12
Viewing the MSN Photo Upload Control window

3 In the left pane, navigate to the folder that contains the picture you want to insert on your MSN Communities home page. As you can see in Figure 7-13, we navigated to a folder that contains the Visiting family's pictures.

Figure 7-13
Accessing pictures to be uploaded to your Web site

4   We want to feature the Visiting family's group picture on the home page, so we'll use the picture of the four family members throughout this procedure. The first step is to name the picture. Click the text below the picture you want to use, type a picture description—we typed *Cape Cod Vacation*—and then press Enter. The new name displays below the picture in the MSN Photo Upload Control, and the text you typed will display as descriptive text in a photo album. (We'll discuss photo albums in more detail a little later in this chapter.) In addition, a red check mark appears on the picture, as shown in Figure 7-14. The check mark indicates that you've selected a picture to be uploaded.

Figure 7-14
Selecting a picture for your home page

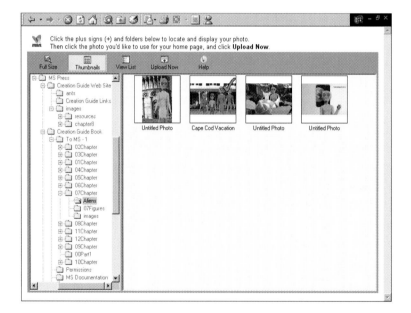

5   In the MSN Photo Upload Control, click the Upload Now button. You'll receive a message that the picture is uploading. After the uploading completes, your home page displays with your custom picture. At this point, the Visiting family's home page displays as shown in Figure 7-15. As you can see, the Visiting family is a typical alien family, and they're trying their best to blend in on Earth.

As mentioned, the home page picture is also added to your site's Photos page in a photo album named Shoebox. You can add additional pictures and photo albums on your site's Photos page.

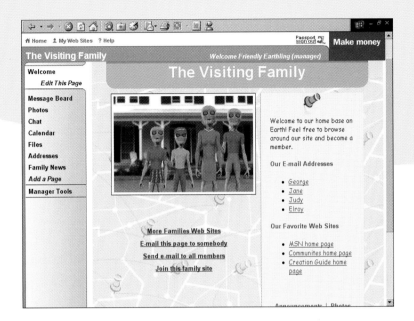

Figure 7-15
Viewing the Visiting family's home page with a custom picture

Adding Pictures to Your Site's Photos Page

First, take a look at your site's Photo Albums page. To do so, click the Photos link in your site's navigation bar. (Your site's navigation bar appears along the left side of your site; the MSN Communities menu bar consists of three small links—Home, My Web Sites, and Help—and it appears along the top of your Web site.) Then click the Shoebox link. You can see that the Cape Cod picture displays along with the picture's title text, Cape Code Vacation, on the Visiting family's Shoebox page, as shown in Figure 7-16. To create another photo album and add additional photos, follow these steps:

note

You can add photos to the Shoebox photo album, or you can create a new photo album. In this exercise, we show you how to create a new album.

1 After viewing the contents of the Shoebox photo album, click the Albums link to return to the Photo Albums main page.

2 On the Photo Albums main page, click the Create A New Album link to access the Create A New Photo Album page shown in Figure 7-17.

3 As you can see in Figure 7-17, creating a photo album involves two steps— naming the photo album and determining who can add and modify photo album pictures. For the Visiting family's site, we created a photo album named Vacation Pictures and specified that members can add, edit, and delete their own pictures. After you set the photo album's parameters, click the Create Album button.

Figure 7-16
Photos page containing the home page's picture

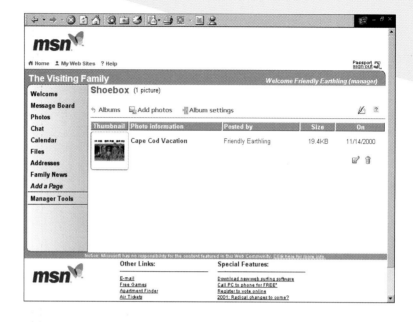

Figure 7-17
Creating a new photo album

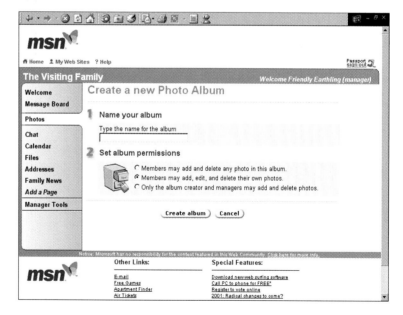

4   Now that you've created a new photo album, you're ready to add pic-
    tures. To do so, click the Add Photos link, which appears within your
    photo album's window, near the top. Clicking the Add Photos link reopens
    the MSN Photo Upload Control window.

5 Display the picture you want to upload in the MSN Photo Upload Control window, rename the pictures you want to upload, ensure that all the pictures you want to upload display with a red check mark (you can add and remove selection check marks by clicking the pictures), and then click Upload Now. After the uploading process completes, the photos display as thumbnail pictures in your photo album. We uploaded the three remaining Visiting family pictures to the Vacation Pictures photo album, as you can see in Figure 7-18.

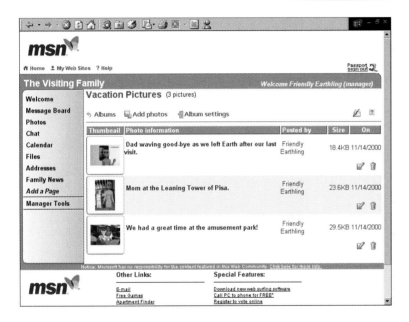

Figure 7-18
Viewing the contents of the Vacation Pictures photo album

6 To view larger versions of the pictures, click the thumbnails.

Editing Your Site's Text

In addition to adding pictures, you can add and edit your Web site's text at any time. As the site manager, you have full control over your site's text. In this section, we'll show you how you can add some text below the home page picture.

note

You must be signed in before you can modify your Web site's text.

lingo

A *thumbnail* is a smaller version of a full-sized picture. Thumbnails download faster than large pictures. Generally, you can view a larger version of a thumbnail image by clicking the thumbnail. To refresh your memory about using thumbnails, see the section "Using thumbnails" in Chapter 3.

1 In the menu bar, click the Welcome link to display your Web site's home page. As the site manager, when you're signed in and on the Welcome page, an Edit This Page link displays under the Welcome menu item.

2 Click the Edit This Page link. Your page opens in MSN's Page Builder utility, as shown in Figure 7-19.

Figure 7-19
Displaying your Web site in MSN Page Builder

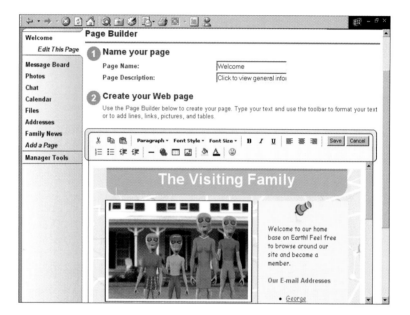

3 Notice that your window has two scroll bars—a window scroll bar and a Page Builder scroll bar. Using both scroll bars if necessary, scroll down until you can see a space below the home page picture. Click on your Web page below the picture, and type some figure caption text. We typed, *We always have fun when we visit Earth!,* selected the text, and then clicked the Bold toolbar button to create boldface caption text, as shown in Figure 7-20.

4 After you finish making changes to your home page, click the Save button, which displays in the upper-right area of the Page Builder. Your changes are saved, and then your home page redisplays with your modifications.

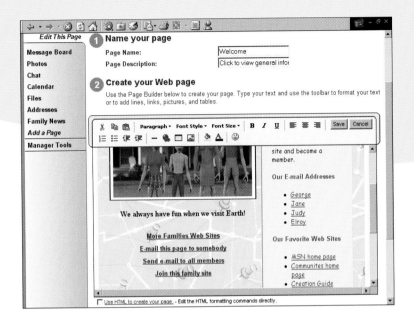

Figure 7-20
Adding text to your Web site using MSN Page Builder

Viewing the HTML Behind Your Page

The next element we want to introduce to you in this chapter is your Web page's HTML (Hypertext Markup Language) code. Remember from Chapter 1 that HTML is the code that instructs browsers regarding how a Web page's text and images should display. In Chapter 8, you'll see how to create a custom page by using HTML. After you're comfortable using HTML, you can modify your MSN Communities page by tweaking the HTML code. In this chapter, you get a small introduction to HTML as we show you how to remove the background image on your home page and add a color.

1 To display your home page's HTML code, ensure that you're signed in, display the Welcome page, and click the Edit This Page link below the Welcome link.

2 After the Page Builder displays, scroll to the bottom of your page and click the Use HTML To Create Your Page link. The HTML code used to create your Web page displays.

3 In the HTML Editor, select the following text (which instructs browsers to show a background picture):

```
background=/content/templates/familynews/background.jpg
```

Figure 7-21 shows the HTML code with the background image information selected.

Figure 7-21
Viewing your home page in MSN's HTML Editor

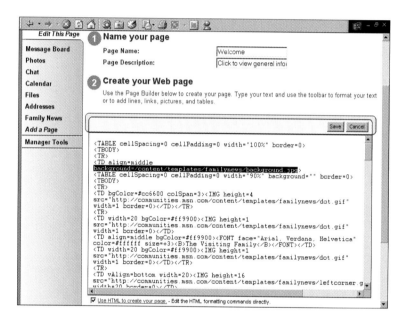

4 To remove the background image and add a background color, type the following HTML code in place of the selected background image text:

```
bgColor=#6495ED
```

The *bgColor* stands for background color, and *#6495ED* specifies a hexadecimal color code. Basically, the hex system is a base-16 numbering system that uses the numbers 0 through 9 and the letters *A* through *F*. (See this book's appendix for a chart of colors and their hexidecimal equivalents.)

tip

Ensure that you don't delete the ">" mark when you replace the background image name with the color code.

note

If you used a different template to create your Web site, the background filename and path will be different than the filename and path shown in Figure 7-21.

5   Click Save. Your Web page will now display with a blue background, as shown in Figure 7-22. To experiment with various colors, redisplay your home page's HTML code and replace *#6495ED* with other color codes found in the hexadecimal color chart in this book's appendix.

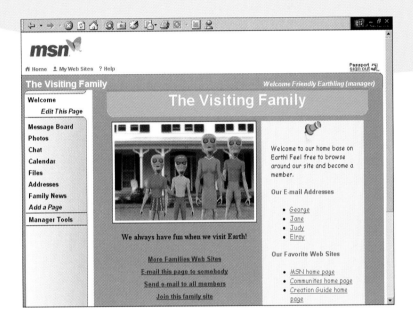

Figure 7-22
Viewing your home page with a modified background

Deleting Your Web Site

Last but not least, you should know how to delete your Web community. Deleting unused communities is good practice; not only does a deletion prevent a site from being associated with your profile, but it also removes the contents from the MSN servers, thereby conserving MSN server space. (MSN provides and maintains online space for free, so the least we can do is ensure that we don't waste the space.) To delete a Web community, follow these steps:

1   Ensure that you're signed in, and click Manager Tools in your site's menu bar.

2   On the Tools pages, click Adjust Your Site Settings.

3   Scroll to the bottom of the Site Settings page.

4   Under Current Status, click Delete Site.

5   In the dialog box that pops up, click OK.

Expanding Your Web Site

In this chapter, we've provided the foundation for you to create an MSN Communities Web site. You've created a home page, inserted a custom home page picture, created a photo album, added some text, and modified the HTML code. Not surprisingly, a number of features exist that we didn't touch on here. For example, you can click the Add New Page link in your site's menu bar to add additional calendars and specialty lists. (Take a look at the lists—you'll find some intriguing options.) You'll want to browse through the pages and options on your site. Further, you should peruse the MSN Communities Help and FAQ pages to see what other capabilities you can include in your site. Adding additional pages and features follows procedures similar to those we outlined in this chapter. At times, you'll need to fill in forms, download special tools (similar to downloading the MSN Photo Upload Control described earlier in this chapter), and provide various settings. After you've created your master-piece, visit us at the Visiting's family home page (*communities.msn.com/ TheVisitingFamily*) and leave us a message. We'd enjoy seeing your site!

Additional Resources

As with all Web creation projects, you'll find that you can benefit from accessing design and troubleshooting resources. For MSN Communities sites, your best troubleshooting resources can be found on the MSN Communities Help pages. To access the Help pages, click Help in the MSN Communities top menu bar. If you're interested in HTML resources, refer to the section "Additional Resources" near the end of Chapter 8.

tip

You can easily return to your Web site (as well as to any Web site you're a member of) by clicking the My Web Sites option in MSN's top menu bar. The My Web Sites link displays a linked list of the sites you've created and joined.

key points

■ Online communities enable you to create Web sites quickly and easily.

■ Planning an online community site general entails choosing a template for your site, gathering pictures, and thinking about the textual content of the site.

■ Generally, you must join an online community before you can create a Web page. To join the MSN Communities site, you must have a Microsoft Passport.

■ Initially, setting up an MSN Communities site involves completing online forms.

■ By default, you're the site manager of the sites you create.

■ As a site manager, you control your Web site's content and activity.

■ To customize the Text on your MSN Communities page, click the Edit This Page link.

■ You can add images to your MSN Communities Web page by using the MSN Photo Upload Control.

■ You can use the MSN Photo Upload Control to store pictures in your site's Photo Albums.

■ You can edit text, add e-mail addresses, change background colors, edit HTML code, and manage other Web page properties within MSN's Page Builder utility.

■ To delete your MSN Communities site, click the Delete Site link on the Site Settings page.

■ The MSN Communities site offers numerous tools that you can use to customize the pages and content you present on your Web site. Browse MSN to find the tools that will best serve the purpose of your site.

■ Help is never far away on the MSN Communities site. Whenever you're feeling a little lost, simply click MSN's Help link.

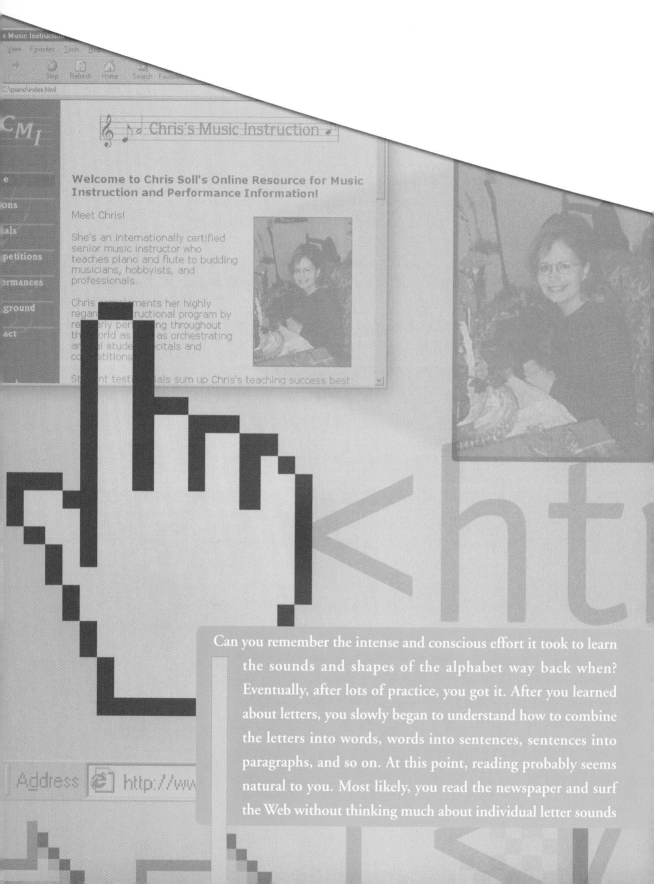

Chris's Music Instruction

Welcome to Chris Soll's Online Resource for Music Instruction and Performance Information!

Meet Chris!

She's an internationally certified senior music instructor who teaches piano and flute to budding musicians, hobbyists, and professionals.

Chris complements her highly regarded instructional program by regularly performing throughout the world as well as orchestrating annual student recitals and competitions.

Student testimonials sum up Chris's teaching success best:

Address http://ww

Can you remember the intense and conscious effort it took to learn the sounds and shapes of the alphabet way back when? Eventually, after lots of practice, you got it. After you learned about letters, you slowly began to understand how to combine the letters into words, words into sentences, sentences into paragraphs, and so on. At this point, reading probably seems natural to you. Most likely, you read the newspaper and surf the Web without thinking much about individual letter sounds

demystifying

BASIC HTML

and shapes. That's because over the years you've developed your foundation in letters and words into a seemingly innate ability to read. Learning how to create HTML documents from scratch—by using HTML tags and understanding how HTML works—is a lot like learning to read. The process might take some patience and lots of practice at the beginning, but if you take the time to learn about HTML now, you'll eventually be able to use HTML to create Web pages as naturally as you read.

To create the Web pages described in this chapter, you'll need the following "supplies":

■ A basic text editor, such as Notepad or WordPad (applications that are included with Microsoft Windows) or SimpleText (which comes with Apple Macintosh)

■ A browser and an Internet connection (An Internet connection is necessary only to download the sample project's graphics from this book's companion Web site.)

■ The following figures downloaded from *www.creationguide.com/ chapter8/images*:

b_background.gif	b_lessons2.gif	picture.gif
b_background2.gif	b_performances.gif	sendnote.gif
b_competitions.gif	b_performances2.gif	t_background.gif
b_competitions2.gif	b_recitals.gif	t_competitions.gif
b_contact.gif	b_recitals2.gif	t_contact.gif
b_contact2.gif	bg.gif	t_home.gif
b_home.gif	footer.gif	t_lessons.gif
b_home2.gif	logo.gif	t_performances.gif
b_lessons.gif	p_chris.jpg	t_recitals.gif

To obtain the figures to use with this chapter's project, display *www.creationguide.com/chapter8/images*, as shown in Figure 8-1, right-click an image's filename, and save a copy of the file to a folder named C:\piano\images on your computer. For detailed downloading steps, see the section "Getting Your Folders and Graphics in Place" later in this chapter.

tip

If you're Zip savvy, you can download just the zip_images8.zip file and extract the images locally.

Figure 8-1
Downloading image files from the Internet

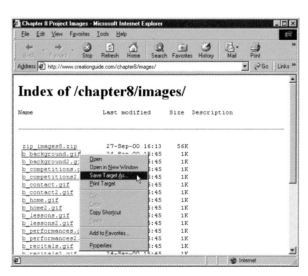

Why HTML?

In Chapters 1, 3, and 7, we briefly introduced you to Hypertext Markup Language (HTML). Basically, we explained that you construct Web page documents by including HTML commands (also called HTML *tags*) within the text of a basic document. Although other technologies (such as XML, or Extensible Markup Language) are beginning to have a significant impact on Web page development, HTML is the foundation of most Web pages today—and if you're going to create Web pages, you need to know about HTML.

Now we understand that you might not feel ready to create a Web page from scratch using only a blank document and a vaguely familiar-sounding technology named HTML. But believe it or not, you're ready—so for now, just go for it. We're having you use HTML in the first major Web page project in this book because you'll find that understanding HTML's basics will come in extremely handy whenever you create Web pages in the future—no matter how you create those pages. Therefore, we're taking a baptism-by-fire approach in this chapter, which means that you'll be writing your own HTML documents before long.

In some ways, you might find that the project in this chapter is the most important project in all of Part Two. If you're going to create Web pages, you'll be well ahead of the game if you master some basic HTML commands and concepts. Someday, when you're much more comfortable with Web page creation, knowing at least some HTML will enable you to modify and tweak pages to suit your preferences, even if the pages you're modifying have been generated by an HTML editor. Further, knowing HTML means that you'll be able to remove unnecessary (and sometimes proprietary) HTML commands that many HTML editors tend to add to Web page documents. Removing unnecessary code can make your HTML documents smaller, which in turn means that your pages will load faster. Finally, as you become more proficient using HTML commands, you might find that you can make changes more quickly and precisely by adding, deleting, or modifying HTML code instead of modifying a Web page in an HTML editor.

We're now ready to get started. The first order of business, before we commence creating a Web site, is to briefly (very briefly) go over some basic HTML theory. By the way, when we say *theory*, we're talking clear, helpful information—not complex rhetoric. Think of the upcoming theory discussion as spreading a blanket before picnicking—you might as well get somewhat comfortable and discourage at least a few of the pests up front.

HTML Basics

Fundamentally, HTML commands serve as instructions that tell a browser how to display a Web page's content. In other words, HTML commands provide format information that controls the display of your Web page's text and graphics. Keep the purpose of HTML commands in mind. You'll see later how HTML commands weave their way in and around your Web page's content in an HTML document, but basically, an HTML document contains two types of information:

- Content information, including text and pointers to graphics
- HTML commands, which are used to manipulate how content displays

In this chapter, we'll show you how to enter HTML commands and page contents into a plain-text document to create Web pages. Further, you'll link the pages you create so that they can work together to create a Web site. To accomplish this feat, you'll need to use Notepad or WordPad (if you're running Windows) or SimpleText (if you're using a Macintosh). Figure 8-2 shows how fully coded HTML documents appear in SimpleText, WordPad, and Notepad, respectively. When you start this chapter's project, you'll start with a blank page. To open Notepad, click Start, point to Programs, point to Accessories, and then click Notepad. To open WordPad, click Start, point to Programs, point to Accessories, and then click WordPad. To open SimpleText, double-click the SimpleText icon on your hard drive.

As we mentioned, HTML tags take care of formatting your page. In contrast, your content is the information that displays on your page (text, graphics, headings, and so forth). In other words, HTML takes care of *how* information displays (bold, italic, left-aligned, and so forth), and content specifies *what* is displayed. Knowing how to incorporate the proper HTML tags throughout a Web page's content is the key to making a Web page in a text editor. So let's look at how to use HTML tags.

Using HTML Tags

In this section, we introduce the basic rules of HTML along with a few common tags. Keep in mind that this section does *not* define every HTML tag out there; quite a few HTML tags exist, and plenty of books devoted to HTML provide comprehensive command lists. (If you want to find out more about HTML than what we cover here, check out any of our favorite

note

Don't be alarmed at the seemingly incomprehensible conglomeration of HTML commands shown in Figure 8-2. HTML can look complex, but it really consists only of combinations of letters, numbers, and symbols with a little organization thrown in. You're obviously familiar with letters, numbers, and symbols, so rest assured that learning to use HTML commands is well within your skill set.

Figure 8-2
*Viewing an HTML document
in SimpleText, WordPad,
and Notepad*

HTML references, which are listed in the section "Additional Resources" near the end of this chapter). Our philosophy is that if you learn the basic rules of using HTML tags, you'll be able to use any of the tags you discover online or in HTML books.

Let's start our discussion of HTML tags with a simple rule:

HTML tags consist of commands that appear within angle brackets (<>).

For example, the first tag in a Web page's source code is typically <HTML>. This tag tells a browser right off the bat that the text document is an HTML document. The browser knows that any text within angle brackets (<>) is an HTML command that needs processing and that all text outside angle brackets (<>) is content that needs to be displayed.

lingo

Source code refers to the contents of the HTML document that creates a Web page. Most browsers enable you to view a Web page's source code. For example, to display a Web page's source code in Microsoft Internet Explorer, display a Web page, click the View menu, and click Source.

Here's the second rule you need to remember:

HTML tags are not case-sensitive.

This rule isn't earth shattering, but it's convenient to know. It means that browsers don't care whether the text between the angle brackets is capitalized or lowercased. Therefore, `<B>` and `<b>` are essentially the same tag (which, incidentally, is a tag that instructs the browser to display the text following the tag in boldface). Similarly, `<HTML>`, `<html>`, `<HtMl>`, and any other combination of capital and lowercase letters represents the same tag.

Here's rule number three:

HTML tags frequently come in pairs.

Because most HTML tags are used primarily for formatting purposes, HTML tags often come in twos: a *starting tag* and an *ending tag* (also referred to as an *opening tag* and a *closing tag*). This pairing enables you to tell browsers where a particular formatting attribute (such as boldfacing) should start and where it should end. It's kind of like when you go to the movies with a few friends and two friends go in to save seats while the rest of the group goes to the concessions counter. The two people saving the seats sit separately to mark a span of seats that will contain the friends. If the seat-savers were HTML tags, they'd tell the browser that all the seats between them should be formatted as their friends' seats.

Starting tags and ending tags have slightly different purposes—namely, a start tag indicates when an action should start, and an ending tag indicates when an action should stop. (See, we're not talking rocket science here!) Therefore, these tags are similar but with a minor, albeit critical, difference. Ending tags are differentiated from starting tags by the inclusion of a forward slash just after the left bracket, like this: `</HTML>`. The last element in HTML documents is usually the `</HTML>` command, which indicates the end of the Web page's display. Going back to the movie theater example, let's say that one seat-saver is sitting in an aisle seat and the other seat-saver is sitting in the middle of the row. The seat-saver sitting in the middle of the row is wearing a red shirt. Suddenly, a new arrival asks the seat-saver sitting in the aisle seat whether the seats are taken. The aisle-side seat-saver would say something like, "Yes—all the seats down to the person in the red shirt are taken." That's the role of a starting tag; the red-shirted seat-saver serves as an ending tag. For example, a `<B>` tag tells a browser, "Please boldface all the text between me and that `</B>` tag over there."

For further illustration, let's look at an example of text that uses HTML tag pairs. The following sentence includes HTML starting and ending tags that format the sentence as a paragraph (`<P></P>`), display the phrase *butter flavoring* in italic (`<I></I>`), and format the word *popcorn* in boldface (`<B></B>`), as shown in Figure 8-3:

```
<P>Do you want <I>butter flavoring</I> on your <B>popcorn</B>
or do you like it plain?</P>
```

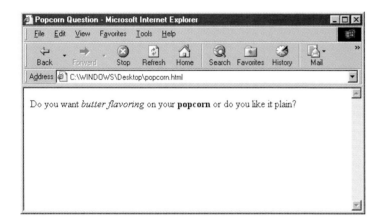

Figure 8-3
Viewing the popcorn question in a browser (if the popcorn question were included in an HTML document)

The popcorn sentence also illustrates an interesting concept called *nesting*. In HTML documents, nesting has nothing to do with twigs and feathers and everything to do with the order in which HTML tags appear. In the popcorn sentence, the italic tag set (`<I></I>`) and the boldface tag set (`<B></B>`) are nested within the paragraph tag set (`<P></P>`). Here's a key rule you should follow when you're nesting HTML tags:

Nested HTML tags should close in the reverse order in which they open.

That rule might seem a little confusing, so let's look at an example. Basically, opening and closing HTML tags shouldn't get their lines crossed. Here's a correct pattern:

```
<HTML>  <P>  <B>  </B>  </P>  </HTML>
```

In this example, the `<B>` (boldface) tags are nested within the `<P>` (paragraph) tags, which are nested within the `<HTML>` (document identifier) tags. This setup would result in bold text within a paragraph within an HTML document. The following setup would also work:

```
<HTML>  <P>  <I>  </I>  <B>  </B>  </P>  </HTML>
```

Notice that this nesting example uses the same pattern as the pop-corn sentence. In this example, the italic tag set and the boldface tag set aren't nested inside each other, but both tag sets are nested within the paragraph tag set.

Now let's lighten up the discussion a bit and look at a more clear-cut rule:

> By default, HTML documents display a single space between text elements.

This rule might seem odd to mention, but spacing issues are a great concern on the Web for a number of reasons (mostly because designers have had to deal with content that resizes and reflows—issues that are nonexistent in printed documents). In an HTML document, adding any number of spaces within your code by using the spacebar, Tab key, or Enter key results in a single space. Therefore, typing:

```
<I>Music Instruction</I>
```

in a Web page displays the same as

```
<I>Music                    Instruction</I>
```

which displays the same as

```
<I>        Music Instruction            </I>
```

which displays the same as

```
<I>
Music Instruction
</I>
```

When the four preceding examples are used as separate paragraphs in an HTML page, the text appears as shown in Figure 8-4.

Now you're ready for the next rule, which adds some spice to HTML tags:

> Some opening HTML tags can contain *properties* (also called *at-tributes*), which further refine an HTML tag's instructions.

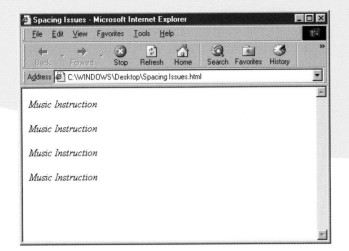

Figure 8-4
Text displaying with single spaces between words, even though extra space is added in the HTML document

In other words, you can frequently customize the instructions related to an HTML formatting command. For example, you can add a `COLOR` attribute to the `<FONT>` command to change the display color of text, like this:

```
They say the <FONT COLOR="green">grass</FONT> is greener.
```

If you inserted the preceding sentence into an HTML document, the text would display as shown in Figure 8-5.

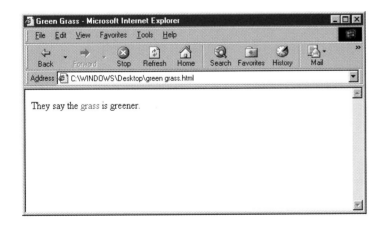

Figure 8-5
Viewing the green grass statement in a browser (if the statement was included in an HTML document)

Finally, here's the last rule in this section:

Numerous variations exist when it comes to the HTML nesting theme, properties, and use of tag sets.

As with all rules, you'll find that although most of HTML is predictable, the technology is as consistent as spelling rules are, which means that you'll frequently find exceptions to the rules. For example, if you want to add a line break in HTML, you enter <BR>. There's no closing tag for a line break—you either have a line break or you don't. Similarly, you insert a horizontal rule with the <HR> tag; again, no closing tag is required.

Don't worry if you're feeling slightly confused. You'll start to get a feel for HTML as you work on the Web site project in this chapter. There's nothing like hands-on experience to gain knowledge. We'll introduce you to additional HTML tags and concepts in the project as we go. For added assistance, you might want to keep Table 8-1 handy while you work.

table 8-1

HTML tags used in the HTML project

Tags	Function
`<A HREF="xxx.xxx"></A>`	Marks the anchor portion of a hyperlink. The HREF attribute points to the information that should be displayed after the anchor's content is clicked. Anchor content is specified between the anchor tags (`<A></A>`) and can include text and images.
`<B></B>`	Indicates to display text between the `<B>` and `</B>` tags in boldface.
`<BLOCKQUOTE></BLOCKQUOTE>`	Offsets a paragraph from the regular body text, usually by indenting the paragraph's left and right margins.
`<BODY></BODY>`	Marks the start and end of the Web page's displayable content.
` `	Inserts a line break. The ` ` tag doesn't have a closing tag, and this tag is frequently used consecutively to create white space on a Web page.
`<CENTER></CENTER>`	Centers the enclosed information on the page or within a table cell.
`<FONT></FONT>`	Enables you to specify the enclosed text's font color, face, and size.

HTML tags used in the HTML project *continued*

Tags	Function
`<H1></H1>`	Specifies heading text. Heading sizes range from `H1` through `H6`, with `H1` being the largest heading size.
`<HEAD></HEAD>`	Provides an area in which you can display your Web page's title, include search engine information, add advanced formatting information, and write scripts. Other than the text within the embedded `<TITLE></TITLE>` tags, most head information doesn't display directly to viewers.
`<HTML></HTML>`	Delineates the start and end of an HTML document.
`<I></I>`	Indicates to italicize the text appearing between the `<I>` and `</I>` tags.
`<IMG SRC="xxx.xxx">`	Displays an image on a Web page. The `SRC` attribute points to the particular image that should be displayed.
`<LI></LI>`	Identifies a list item within an unnumbered (bulleted) list `<UL>` or an ordered (numbered) list `<OL>`.
`<OL></OL>`	Specifies an ordered (numbered) list.
`<P></P>`	Indicates the start and end of a paragraph. By default, paragraphs display left-aligned. The closing `</P>` tag is optional. (In other words, you can simply insert the `<P>` tag at the start of each new paragraph to format your HTML contents without typing `</P>` at the end of each paragraph.) We've included the closing `</P>` tag throughout this chapter for added clarity. Browsers typically insert a blank line (plus a little extra space) before starting a paragraph.
`<TABLE></TABLE>`	Delineates the start and end of a table.
`<TD></TD>`	Defines the start and end of a cell within a table. `<TD>` tags are nested within `<TR>` tag sets.
`<TITLE></TITLE>`	Enables you to insert the Web page's title text that should display in the browser's title bar.
`<TR></TR>`	Indicates a table row. `<TR>` tags are nested within a `<TABLE>` tag set.
`<UL></UL>`	Specifies an unnumbered (bulleted) list.

Just as a last note in this section, we want to make a minor disclaimer. While we're confident that you can create an HTML document from scratch, please keep in mind that this chapter serves only as an introduction to creating Web pages in HTML. Unfortunately, covering all the available HTML commands in a single chapter is unrealistic, but this chapter is packed with helpful coding tips and you'll find some leads on good HTML references in the "Additional Resources" section near the end of the chapter. If you create the Web site described in this chapter's project, you'll gain a strong foundation in HTML coding as well as have a template that you can customize to create unique Web pages. (We even tell you how to use the site as a template later in this chapter.)

see also | Chapter 11 describes how you can upload the Web pages you create to the Internet.

Handling HTML Documents and Web Graphics

When you create Web pages, you usually work with multiple files. You'll have your home page HTML file (generally named index.html or index.htm), a graphics file for each graphical element on your page, and additional HTML files for linked pages. Therefore, before you start creating, you have to think of an organizational scheme so that you don't drive yourself crazy later. We highly recommend that you create a folder to contain all the HTML files used in your Web site, and within the main folder, create a subfolder named *images*. Then you can store all your HTML documents in the main folder and place your graphics in the *images* folder. To illustrate, see Figure 8-6, which shows the HTML documents and images necessary to create this chapter's project site.

Keeping your files organized is imperative when you're adding graphics and creating hyperlinks because you must include instructions in your HTML document regarding where the browser should look for a particular graphic or linked page. Further, being organized can greatly simplify the file uploading process when you're ready to go "live" by transferring your local files to a Web server. Your best bet is to create a folder that you can use consistently throughout the Web page and Web site creation process.

Along with being organized, you should religiously save and preview your Web pages throughout the development process.

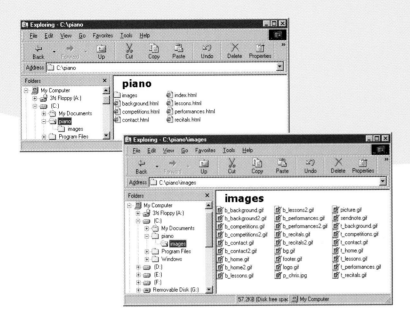

Figure 8-6
Organizing a Web site's files and folders

Saving and Previewing HTML Documents

When you create Web pages—especially when you're hand-coding HTML—you should save and preview with abandon. Speaking from firsthand "We can't believe we just lost all that data" experiences, we can recommend without reservation saving your work frequently—that pretty much goes without saying whenever you're working on any file on any computer. (If monitors grew grass, our mice would wear out a well-worn diagonal path to the Save button; of course, we also know people who slowly erode the text off their Ctrl and S keys by pressing Ctrl+S every so often.)

In addition to frequently saving your files, you should preview the Web pages you build numerous times throughout the creation process. Previewing an HTML page simply means looking at your HTML document in a browser as opposed to staring at the text and HTML code version of the document in a text editor. Performing this exercise, you can see how the HTML is formatting your content and you can troubleshoot display problems early. We'll often alter a site's layout simply because what looks good on paper doesn't transpose well to an online page.

To preview a Web page in your browser, use any of the following procedures after you've created an HTML file.

tip

"Save, save, save!" should be one of your mantras when you're working with computers.

- Display the contents of the folder containing the HTML document, and double-click the HTML document's icon.

- Open your browser application (such as Internet Explorer), and type in the HTML file's location.

- Open your browser application, open the folder containing the HTML document, and drag the HTML file's icon from its folder into the browser window in the brower's Address bar.

We've covered a good bit of theory; now it's the witching hour. If you've read the previous few pages, you're ready to tackle the HTML Web page creation project. You should have a workable knowledge of basic HTML tags, realize that you should save your HTML documents and images in designated folders, and recognize the importance of frequently saving and previewing your Web pages throughout the creation process. We're satisfied that you're ready, so let's get the project rolling.

Planning the HTML Site

For the HTML project, we decided to create a Web page for Chris Soll, a professional musician and music instructor. Our first planning step involved meeting with Chris and finding out what types of information she wanted to include on her Web site. In our initial consultation, we found that she had a number of student-specific as well as professional-specific topics she wanted to incorporate into her site. Based on this information, we initially attempted to design a two-tier navigation bar, but the design started to look too cluttered. We determined that we could make a cleaner site by using specifically named buttons and providing a quick Site Overview section on the home page. The final design resulted in a clean, flexible layout.

After you create Chris Soll's Web site—which we quickly began to refer to as "the piano site" during our consultation, based on the overwhelming presence of her baby grand piano in her music studio—you can use your HTML document as a template to create similar Web sites that have a completely different look and feel. (Don't worry—we describe how to use the piano site's code as a template later in this chapter.) Figure 8-7 shows the storyboard we came up with to illustrate the pages we wanted to include in the piano site. Figure 8-8 shows a finalized sketch of the piano site's home page.

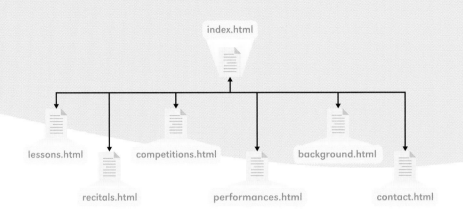

Figure 8-7
Outlining the piano site's pages

Figure 8-8
Sketching the piano site's home page design

note

Notice in Figure 8-8 that we initially planned to insert the address information below the site's text links along the bottom of the page. Later, during the design process, we realized that placing the address above the links made better design sense. The links were already listed in the navigation bar on the left, so we wanted to present the "new" and more important address information before repeating the text link information.

Getting Your Folders and Graphics in Place

As we mentioned earlier in this chapter, your first task is to create a folder for your Web files and organize your graphics. Here's the process we suggest you follow (though feel free to change the folder location and name to suit your preferences):

1 Create a folder on your C:\ drive, and name the folder *piano*.

2 Open the *piano* folder, and create a subfolder named *images*.

3 Open your browser, and display *www.creationguide.com/chapter8/images*.

4 Right-click the b_backgound.gif image (or right-click the Zip file, if you're familiar with Zip files and your system can extract them), and select Save Target As (if you're using Internet Explorer). The Save As dialog box opens.

5 In the Save As dialog box, browse to the C:\piano\images folder, as shown in Figure 8-9, and then click Save.

Figure 8-9
Saving graphics from the Web to your computer

6 Right-click the next graphic, and save the file to the *images* folder.

7 Repeat step 6 until you've saved all the graphics files to your computer.

As you download the graphics for the piano site, notice the naming scheme we've used to label images:

tip

After you're done experimenting with the piano Web site, you can delete the C:\piano folder if you like.

■ **b_*xxx*** Specifies that the image is a button. A b_ graphic appended with the number 2 (for example, b_background2.gif) indicates a second version of the button that displays whenever the associated page is displayed. (You'll see what we mean later.)

Therefore, b_background.gif is the Background button, and b_background2.gif is the "current page" version of the Background button, as shown in Figure 8-10.

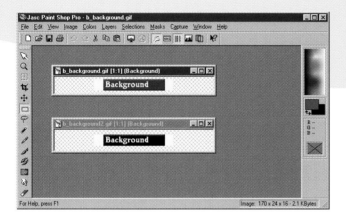

- **bg.gif** Specifies the background graphic. The piano site uses the same background graphic throughout the site, so only one bg.gif file is required.

- **footer.gif** Identifies the graphic as a running footer graphic used at the bottom of the site's pages.

- **logo.gif** Identifies the logo graphic. The piano site uses the same logo graphic throughout the site, but it's possible that you'd have a few versions of a logo graphic (especially if you're using a smaller or modified version of the logo on subpages).

- **p_xxx** Specifies that the graphic is a picture. The piano site has only one photograph, and it's on the home page.

- **sendnote.gif** Identifies the graphic as the "send mail" icon. Later, we'll link this icon on the piano site so that users can click the sendnote.gif graphic to open a preaddressed e-mail message when they want to send a message to Chris Soll.

- **t_xxx** Specifies that the image is a title bar banner graphic. For example, t_background.gif is the Background page's title bar banner graphic (which displays the word *Background* and is placed at the top of the page that presents background information about Chris Soll), as shown in Figure 8-11.

note

The picture.gif file is a placeholder graphic used on the template discussed later in the chapter. You won't use the picture.gif file in the piano site.

Figure 8-11
Viewing the graphic file used to create a title bar banner graphic on the piano site's Background page

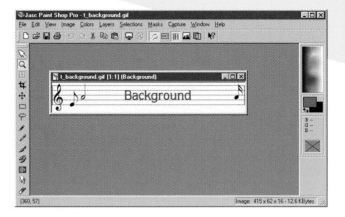

When you create your own Web pages and Web graphics, you'll probably devise your own naming scheme. We've shown you the method we used to name our graphics to give you an idea of how helpful having a naming system can be. You'll see the benefit of a well-planned graphics-naming scheme as you start to insert HTML code in a few moments.

Preparing Your Home Page File

After you have your folders and graphic files in place, you're ready to begin creating your site's home page. To begin the creation process, you need to create an HTML document that contains the standard tags that appear in all HTML documents. The standard tags are listed in Table 8-2.

table 8-2

Standard HTML tags

Tags	Function
`<HTML></HTML>`	Delineates the start and end of the HTML document.
`<HEAD></HEAD>`	Provides an area in which you can display your Web page's title, include search engine information, add advanced formatting information, and write scripts. Other than the text within the embedded `<TITLE></TITLE>` tags, most head information doesn't display directly to viewers.
`<TITLE></TITLE>`	Enables you to insert the Web page's title text that displays in the browser's title bar.
`<BODY></BODY>`	Marks the start and end of the Web page's displayable content.

Figure 8-12 shows the proper way to nest the standard HTML tags in an HTML document and shows how to insert title text. (In Figure 8-13, shown later in this section, you'll see how the empty HTML tags with the title would display in a browser.) After you type the standard HTML tags in a text document, you need to save the text document as an HTML document, as described in the upcoming procedure.

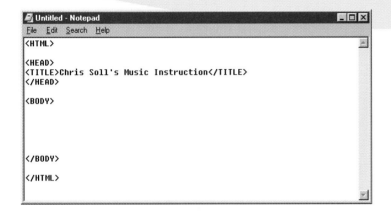

Figure 8-12
Viewing HTML standard tags with title text inserted between the <TITLE> *tags*

To begin creating the piano site's home page and save it as an HTML file, follow these steps:

1 Open Notepad, WordPad, or SimpleText. We used Notepad throughout this project.

2 Click in a new blank document, type <HTML>, and then press Enter twice.

3 Type <HEAD>, and press Enter.

4 Type <TITLE>Chris Soll's Music Instruction</TITLE>, and then press Enter.

5 Type </HEAD>, and press Enter twice.

6 Type <BODY>, press Enter a few times (to give you some breathing room when you enter your Web page's content information), type </BODY>, and press Enter twice.

note

Content text—text that displays between and outside HTML tags—displays in the same case as it is entered in the text document. Thus, if you type *chris soll's* instead of *Chris Soll's* in step 4, Chris's name will appear in all lowercase letters on your Web page. Also, remember that you don't have to worry about putting too many spaces (including blank lines) between content text and HTML tags. When a browser displays the document, it ignores the extra spaces.

7 Type </HTML> to complete the standard HTML tag setup.

You're now ready to name and save the file to your C:\piano folder:

8 On the File menu, click Save. The Save As dialog box opens.

9 In the Save As dialog box, type *index* in the File Name box and ensure that Text Documents is selected in the Save As Type drop-down list. (If necessary, click the arrow to select the Text Documents option.)

10 Use the Save In drop-down list and navigate to the C:\piano folder on your computer.

11 Click Save.

12 Close Notepad.

Finally, you need to rename the index.txt file so that it has an .html extension in place of the .txt extension:

13 Open Windows Explorer, and display the contents of C:\piano. You should see the file index.txt stored in the *piano* folder. If you see *index* (without the *.txt* extension), you'll need to adjust the folder's options to display filename extensions. To display filename extensions in the *piano* folder, first open the Folder Options dialog box in Windows Explorer. (In Windows 98, click Folder Options on the View menu. In Windows Me, click Folder Options on the Tools menu.) In the Folder Options dialog box, click the View tab. On the View tab, ensure that the Hide File Extensions For Known File Types check box is cleared. Click OK.

14 After you spot the index.txt file in the *piano* folder, right-click the filename, click Rename on the shortcut menu, click after the .txt extension, press Backspace three times to delete the *txt*, type *html*, and press Enter. When asked to confirm the rename, click Yes.

The file should now display as *index.html*, and the icon should change. You can now view the file in your browser. To view your newly created HTML file, follow this step:

15 Double-click index.html. The file should open in your Web browser, as shown in Figure 8-13. Notice that the only content is the Web page's title text, which displays in your browser's title bar.

Now that the Web page's title and standard HTML tags are in place, let's add the page's background image and default link colors.

Title text

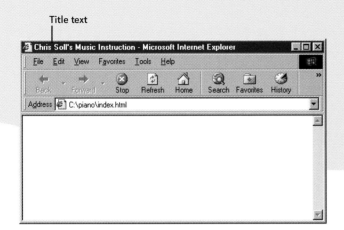

Figure 8-13
Viewing an HTML document that only contains standard HTML tags and title text

Specifying the Background and Link Colors

You can include attributes in the <BODY> tag to add background colors, background images, default text link colors, and so forth, as described in the following steps:

1 Open Notepad, WordPad, or SimpleText, and then open the C:\piano\ index.html file from within the text editor. If you don't see the file index.html listed in the Open dialog box, ensure that the Files Of Type list box displays All Files (*.*).

2 In the <BODY> tag, click after the Y and before the >, press the spacebar, and then enter the following attributes and values, including the quotation marks:

```
BGCOLOR="#ffffff" BACKGROUND="images/bg.gif"
LINK="blue" VLINK="purple" ALINK="red"
```

The <BODY> attributes you just added are defined as follows:

■ **BGCOLOR**   Defines a background color. Although the piano site uses an image for the background, we defined a white background for folks who view the site with images turned off. In the color chart in this book's appendix, you can see that #ffffff is a hexadecimal number that equates to white.

■ **BACKGROUND**   Enables you to specify a graphics file to use as a background image. Remember that browsers automatically tile background images to fill the browser window. The piano page uses the bg.gif file, which is stored in the *images* subfolder

tip

You must open your HTML file by using the text editor's Open command or by dragging the document's icon into the text editor's window. If you double-click an HTML file, you'll display the HTML document in your Web browser.

lingo

Tiling refers to repeating an image across a window's area and down until the entire window is filled with the repeating image.

tip

Whenever you enter HTML code, always verify that you've included all angle brackets (**<>**) and quotation marks (**""**) in your HTML code as well as spelled the HTML command properly. Missing small elements or misspelling commands can cause your Web page to display incorrectly or not at all. We've included screen shots of the code you're creating throughout this chapter so that you can easily check your work.

of the *piano* folder, as a background image. Because both the index.html document and the *images* folder reside in the *piano* folder, you don't have to indicate the image's complete address. If your image was saved elsewhere (that is, not within a subfolder of the folder that contains the index.html document), you'd have to enter the entire address that points to the image.

■ **LINK** Enables you to specify the color in which unvisited text hyperlinks display.

■ **VLINK** Enables you to specify the color in which visited hyperlinks display. In other words, after a user visits a site's Contacts page, any text links pointing to the Contacts page will display in the visited link color.

■ **ALINK** Enables you to specify the color in which links display while users click the links. Showing a different color while the users click links clearly indicates to users that they are activating a hyperlink.

Your HTML code should now display as shown in Figure 8-14.

Figure 8-14
Adding attributes to the <BODY> *tag (The newly added code is shown in red.)*

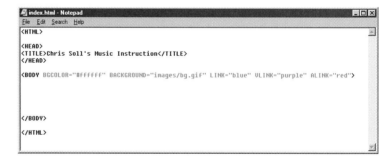

tip

If the changes you make in your HTML document don't show up on the preview page in your browser, click the Refresh button to update your view.

3 Save your HTML document, open your browser, and view index.html in your browser window. (You don't have to close your text document, but you do have to ensure that you've saved your most recent changes.) The index.html file should now display the background image in your browser window, as shown in Figure 8-15.

Now that the standard HTML tags, default background image, and link colors are in place, the next step is to begin to format your Web page's <BODY> area.

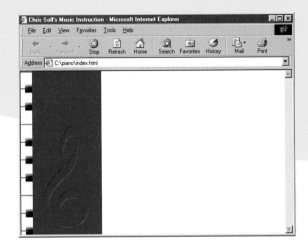

Figure 8-15
*Previewing the Web page's back-
ground image*

Creating a Table

In this section, we're going to show you how to create a table that will
contain all the elements of your Web page. Controlling elements on a Web
page is a little tricky because of the variable nature of browsers and browser
windows, so many sites are designed using tables with hidden borders
to help lay out Web pages. Not every Web page uses a table, but you'll
find tables to be an extremely useful tool.

Basically, tables use three tags:

- ◼ **<TABLE></TABLE>** Delineates the start and end of a table.

- ◼ **<TR></TR>** Indicates a table row. <TR> tags are nested within a
  <TABLE> tag set.

- ◼ **<TD></TD>** Defines the start and end of a cell within a table. <TD>
  tags are nested within a <TR> tag set.

In the piano site, you'll create a two-column, three-row table:

1 If necessary, open Notepad, WordPad, or SimpleText, and then open
   C:\piano\index.html from within the text editor.

2 In the index.html file, click below the opening <BODY> tag (the <BODY>
   tag should now have attributes within it), type <TABLE BORDER="1"
   WIDTH="100%" CELLPADDING="5" CELLSPACING="0">, and press
   Enter. Notice the quotation marks around the attribute's values. Make
   sure you include beginning and ending quotation marks throughout.

Here's the purpose of each of the attributes included in the opening
<TABLE> tag:

- **BORDER**   Defines the width of the table's outline in pixels. For now,
  we're showing a 1-pixel border to aid in seeing the table while you design. After the page design is complete, you'll change BORDER="1"
  to BORDER="0".

- **WIDTH**   Defines the table's exact pixel width or specifies the percentage of the browser's window that the table should fill. We're
  using a table to format the entire page, so the table is sized to fill
  100 percent of the browser's window space.

- **CELLPADDING**   Creates a space (measured in pixels) between the
  cell contents and the table border. After sampling a few spacing
  parameters, we found that adding a CELLPADDING value of 5 did
  the trick. This type of setting exemplifies the value of testing
  settings, saving, and previewing your HTML page during the
  creation process.

- **CELLSPACING**   Specifies the amount of space (in pixels) between
  cells. In the piano site, we didn't need to specify any spacing
  between cells, so we set the attribute to 0.

tip

For added assistance, you
can refer to Figure 8-16 on
page 200 while you work
through the table creation
process.

3   Type <TR> to start the first table row.

4   Press Enter, press Tab to make reading your code easier, and type
    <TD VALIGN="top"> to begin the first cell in the first row. The
    VALIGN="top" attribute indicates that you want to align the cell con-
    tents to the top of the cell (by default, cell contents align to the middle).
    You can align cell contents using the values *top, middle, bottom*, or *base-
    line*. Also, by default, cell contents align at the left. (Later we'll show you
    how to change the default alignment by centering contents within a cell.)

5   Press Enter twice, press Tab, and type </TD> to mark the end of the first
    cell in the first row.

6   Press Enter, press Tab, and type <TD VALIGN="top"> to create the sec-
    ond cell in the first row.

7 Press Enter twice, press Tab, and type `</TD>` to mark the end of the second cell in the first row.

8 Press Enter, and type `</TR>` to complete the first row of your table.

9 Press Enter and repeat steps 3 through 8 to create the second table row.

10 Press Enter after creating the second table row, and then create a third row by retyping the commands in steps 3 through 8.

11 After entering the third table row, press Enter and type `</TABLE>` to complete the table tags.

Finally, you'll add a WIDTH attribute to the two cell tags (`<TD>`) in the first row of the table. You can assign column width by percentage (for example, the left column could be assigned to take up 50% of the browser window), or you can insert an exact pixel measurement. By default, if you don't include the WIDTH attribute in table cells, the table sizes the columns based on the size of the cell content and the size of the browser window. You need to add the WIDTH attribute to only one cell in a column (and if you have conflicting measurements in cells in the same column, the browser will use the largest setting by default). To keep our setup orderly, we'll add the WIDTH attribute to the cells in the first row:

12 In the first cell in the first row, click after `"top"`, press the spacebar, and type `WIDTH="170"` to set the first column to 170 pixels wide.

13 In the second cell in the first row, click after `"top"`, press the spacebar, and type `WIDTH="*"`. The asterisk in place of a pixel number indicates that the browser should allow the second column to be as wide as necessary to fill the remaining table width. Because this table is formatted as 100% of the browser window, the asterisk instructs browsers to expand the second column to fill the remainder of the browser window area.

14 Save your HTML document. Your HTML code should look like the code shown in Figure 8-16.

Now that your table is in place, you're ready to enter content into the table. The first order of business is to insert the logo into the top-left corner.

tip

If you prefer not to retype the table row commands when creating the second and third table rows, click before the first row's `<TR>` command and drag to select all the text up to and including the `</TR>` closing command. Then press Ctrl+C to copy the selected code. Click after the `</TR>` command, press Enter, and press Ctrl+V to paste the copied HTML code into your text document. Press Ctrl+V again to create the third table row.

note

If you don't define column widths in tables by adding the WIDTH attribute to `<TD>` tags, browsers automatically size the columns based on each column's widest item and the browser window size.

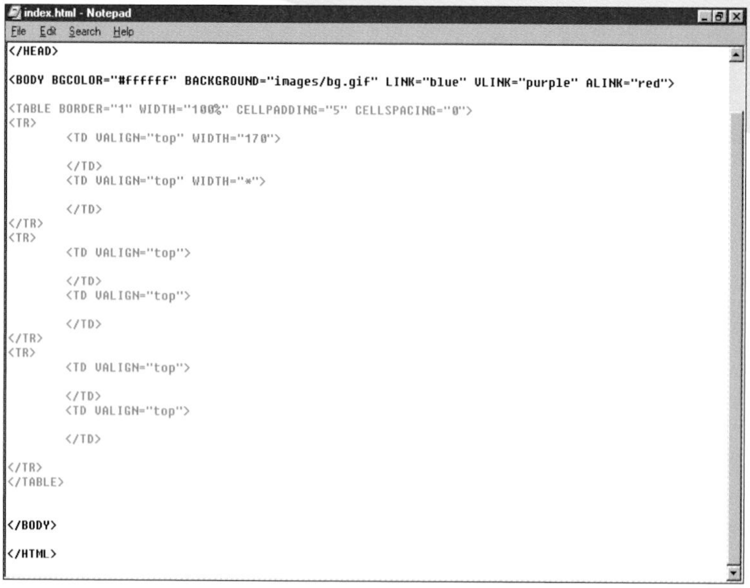

Figure 8-16
Viewing the table code in the HTML document (The added table code is shown in red.)

Inserting and Linking the Logo

We're creating a standard page design, so we opted to insert the logo in the top-left (prime real estate) corner. We plan to use the home page as a template for all subpages, so we're going to link the logo to the home page. That way, when you use the home page as a template, all subpages will automatically include a logo that links to the site's index.html home page.

When you insert a logo, you're basically inserting an image. To insert an image in an HTML document, you use the `<IMG>` tag with the `SRC` attribute, which points to a particular graphic. For example, to specify the piano site's logo, you'd type `<IMG SRC="images/logo.gif">`. Similarly, when you insert your logo and format it as a hyperlink, you use the same HTML codes that you use to link any graphic. So pay attention to the following steps—you'll find yourself using these commands quite a bit. First let's insert the logo graphic. (We'll take care of linking the graphic in just a bit.)

1 If necessary, open your text editor and open index.html.

2 In the first cell in the first row, click after the `<TD VALIGN="top" WIDTH="170">` tag, press Enter, press Tab, and type the following HTML tag, which points to the logo image:

```
<IMG SRC="images/logo.gif"
ALT="logo: Chris's Music Instruction"
WIDTH="170" HEIGHT="68" BORDER="0">
```

With the exception of the SRC attribute, the <IMG> tag's attributes used in the piano site are optional (but very useful) and defined as follows:

- **SRC**   Specifies the filename of the image (the *source* of the image) to be displayed.

- **ALT**   Enables you to provide descriptive text that displays when the cursor is placed over the image area.

- **WIDTH and HEIGHT**   Specify the image's width and height. You should specify the sizes of your images because doing so helps browsers display your Web page's layout faster. Keep in mind that any actual image resizing (as in making an image larger or smaller) should be done in your image editing program and not by using WIDTH and HEIGHT attributes in your HTML document—ideally, you want your images to be sized as closely as possible to the size you'll display the images on your Web pages.

- **BORDER**   Specifies the thickness of the border around the image. By default, a 1-pixel border appears around graphics that are formatted as hyperlinks. Generally, designers change the default by setting the BORDER attribute to "0".

Next you'll format the logo.gif image to serve as a hyperlink to the home page. Basically, creating a hyperlink entails marking some text or a graphic as an *anchor* by using the <A></A> tag set and then specifying to the browser what should be displayed after the anchor element is clicked. To make the logo a hyperlink, follow these steps:

3   Click before the <IMG> tag, and type <A HREF="index.html"> to specify that when users click the logo they will be taken to the home page. (As mentioned earlier, this linking information will come in handy when we copy the home page to create subpages.)

4   Click after the closing > of the <IMG> tag, and type </A> to specify the end of the anchor's contents.

5   Save index.html. Your HTML code should look similar to the code shown in Figure 8-17.

tip

Adding spaces and returns in your HTML code won't affect your Web page's appearance, so you don't need to add returns in your HTML document to match the examples in the text. Our text examples had to be shortened to fit properly within the book's page design. Your code can be entered as shown in the project's HTML reference figures included throughout this chapter.

lingo

An *anchor* is either the clickable text or graphic component of a hyperlink or a specified target area within a document. Most notably, anchor text is surrounded by the <A></A> tag set in HTML documents.

Figure 8-17

Inserting a linked logo image on the home page

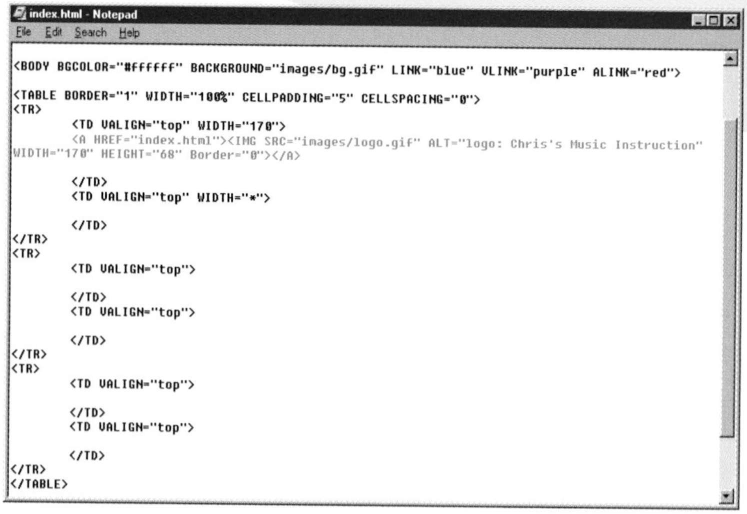

```
index.html - Notepad
File  Edit  Search  Help

<BODY BGCOLOR="#ffffff" BACKGROUND="images/bg.gif" LINK="blue" VLINK="purple" ALINK="red">

<TABLE BORDER="1" WIDTH="100%" CELLPADDING="5" CELLSPACING="0">
<TR>
        <TD VALIGN="top" WIDTH="170">
        <A HREF="index.html"><IMG SRC="images/logo.gif" ALT="logo: Chris's Music Instruction"
WIDTH="170" HEIGHT="68" Border="0"></A>

        </TD>
        <TD VALIGN="top" WIDTH="*">

        </TD>
</TR>
<TR>
        <TD VALIGN="top">

        </TD>
        <TD VALIGN="top">

        </TD>
</TR>
<TR>
        <TD VALIGN="top">

        </TD>
        <TD VALIGN="top">

        </TD>
</TR>
</TABLE>
```

Inserting the Home Page Banner Graphic

After inserting the logo, inserting the home page's banner graphic will be a piece of cake. This step entails inserting an image in the second cell of the first table row. You won't have to link this graphic, so the procedure is fairly straightforward. The only twist to inserting the banner graphic is that you'll want to center the graphic within the table cell by nesting the <IMG> tag within the <CENTER></CENTER> tag set. To insert a banner graphic on the home page, perform the following steps:

1 If necessary, open your text editor and open index.html.

2 In the second cell of the first row, click after the <TD VALIGN="top" WIDTH="*"> tag, press Enter, press Tab, and then type the following:

```
<CENTER><IMG SRC="images/t_home.gif" ALT="title: Chris
Soll's Music Instruction" WIDTH="415" HEIGHT="62"
BORDER="0" ALIGN="middle"></CENTER>
```

3 Save index.html. Your HTML code should display as shown in Figure 8-18.

tip

You must save your HTML document before you can view the document's changes in a browser window. If your most recent changes aren't displaying in your browser, ensure that you've saved your HTML document. If you still aren't seeing the changes, click the Refresh button in your browser to ensure that you're viewing the most up-to-date version of your page.

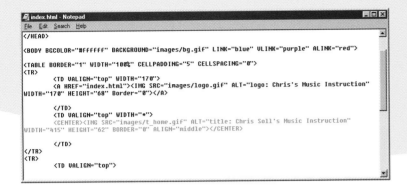

Figure 8-18
Viewing the banner image code in index.html

4 Open index.html in your browser. (If index.html is already open in your browser, click the Refresh button to update your view.) The browser should display your version of index.html as shown in Figure 8-19. In the figure, notice that the table borders for the first row display around the inserted graphics. Hold your cursor over the logo or banner graphic to display the image's ALT text.

Figure 8-19
Viewing index.html in a browser with the linked logo and home page banner graphic, which were positioned using a table

In the next section, you'll see how to create a navigation bar that you can use throughout the piano site.

Adding Navigation Links

Creating a navigation bar for the piano site entails inserting button graphics and linking each graphic to a Web page. You've already inserted the logo and banner graphics, so you know how to use the <IMG> tag. Further, you've linked the logo, so you're also familiar with the <A></A> anchor tags. The only slightly tricky part about using navigation buttons in the piano site is that each page shows a custom button for the current page. For example, whenever a user visits the home page, the black version of the Home button displays, and whenever a user visits another page in the site, the standard maroon Home button displays. This setup will become clearer as you progress through this section. To create a navigation bar on the home page, follow these steps:

1 If necessary, open your text editor and open index.html. We'll place the navigation bar in the first column of the table's second row, which will cause it to display on the left side of the page.

2 After the second <TR> tag, click after the first <TD VALIGN="top"> tag, press Enter, press Tab, and type <BR> to insert a blank line between the logo graphic and the upcoming navigation bar.

In the next few steps, we'll embed each button's image tag within an anchor tag that links the button to an appropriately named Web page. We haven't created the subpages yet, so take note of the filenames provided in the anchor tags. The subpage's filenames will have to match the filenames in the anchor references. In all, you need to add seven buttons. You'll start by adding the current-page version of the Home button. (Recall that you downloaded two versions of each button—the current-page version of each button has a "2" at the end of the button's filename.)

3 Press Enter, press Tab, and type the following:

```
<A HREF="index.html"><IMG SRC="images/b_home2.gif"
ALT="btn: Home Page" WIDTH="170" HEIGHT="24"
BORDER="0"></A>
```

4 Type

 to add two line spaces, press Enter, and press Tab.

You're now set up to enter the next button link and graphic.

5 Type the following:

```
<A HREF="lessons.html"><IMG SRC="images/b_lessons.gif"
ALT="btn: Lessons" WIDTH="170" HEIGHT="24" BORDER="0">
</A><BR><BR>
```

tip

You can repeatedly type the HTML code with varied HREF file references, SRC filenames, and ALT information, or you can copy the code you typed in steps 3 and 4 and paste the copied code into the table cell six times. Then replace the HREF file references, SRC filenames, and ALT text definitions in each entry, as shown in Figure 8-20 on page 206.

6 Press Enter, press Tab, and type:

```
<A HREF="recitals.html"><IMG SRC="images/b_recitals.gif"
ALT="btn: Recitals" WIDTH="170" HEIGHT="24"
BORDER="0"></A><BR><BR>
```

7 Press Enter, press Tab, and type:

```
<A HREF="competitions.html">
<IMG SRC="images/b_competitions.gif"
ALT="btn: Competitions" WIDTH="170" HEIGHT="24"
BORDER="0"></A><BR><BR>
```

8 Press Enter, press Tab, and type:

```
<A HREF="performances.html">
<IMG SRC="images/b_performances.gif"
ALT="btn: Performances" WIDTH="170" HEIGHT="24"
BORDER="0"></A><BR><BR>
```

9 Press Enter, press Tab, and type:

```
<A HREF="background.html">
<IMG SRC="images/b_background.gif"
ALT="btn: Background" WIDTH="170" HEIGHT="24"
BORDER="0"></A><BR><BR>
```

10 Press Enter, press Tab, and type:

```
<A HREF="contact.html"><IMG SRC="images/b_contact.gif"
ALT="btn: Contact" WIDTH="170" HEIGHT="24"
BORDER="0"></A><BR><BR><BR><BR>
```

Notice that there are four <BR> tags at the end of step 10. The extra line spaces are included because we also want to insert the Send Us A Note icon to give users an easy way to send e-mail messages to Chris. When you create an e-mail link, you use a special HREF format in the anchor tag, as follows:

11 Press Enter a couple times to separate the Send Us A Note icon from the main navigation bar, press Tab, and then type

```
<A HREF="mailto:mm@creationguide.com">
```

except replace *mm@creationguide.com* with your own e-mail address so that users will open a blank e-mail message addressed to you when they click the Send Us A Note icon.

12 Insert the Send Us A Note icon, and close the anchor reference by typing:

```
<IMG SRC="images/sendnote.gif" ALT="btn: E-mail Chris"
WIDTH="170" HEIGHT="77" BORDER="0"></A>
```

13 Save index.html. Your HTML code should look similar to the code shown in Figure 8-20.

Figure 8-20
Viewing the navigation bar HTML code

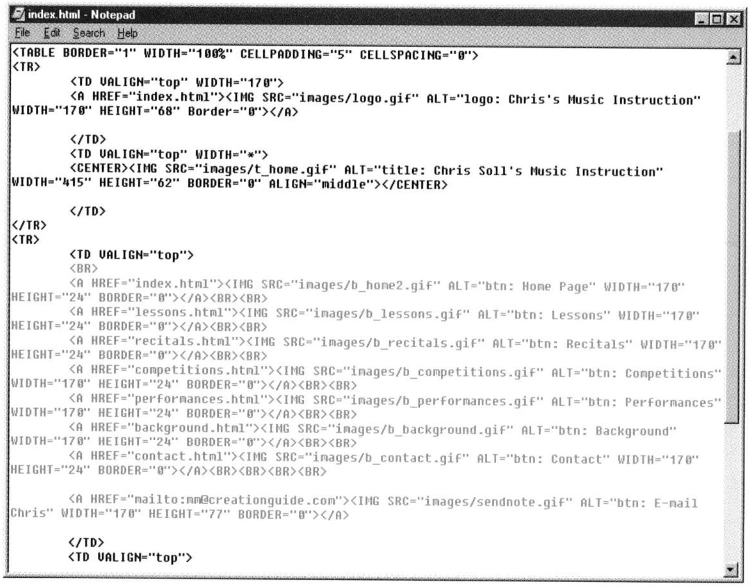

```
index.html - Notepad
File  Edit  Search  Help
<TABLE BORDER="1" WIDTH="100%" CELLPADDING="5" CELLSPACING="0">
<TR>

        <TD VALIGN="top" WIDTH="170">
        <A HREF="index.html"><IMG SRC="images/logo.gif" ALT="logo: Chris's Music Instruction"
WIDTH="170" HEIGHT="68" Border="0"></A>

        </TD>
        <TD VALIGN="top" WIDTH="*">
        <CENTER><IMG SRC="images/t_home.gif" ALT="title: Chris Soll's Music Instruction"
WIDTH="415" HEIGHT="62" BORDER="0" ALIGN="middle"></CENTER>

        </TD>
</TR>
<TR>
        <TD VALIGN="top">
        <BR>
        <A HREF="index.html"><IMG SRC="images/b_home2.gif" ALT="btn: Home Page" WIDTH="170"
HEIGHT="24" BORDER="0"></A><BR><BR>
        <A HREF="lessons.html"><IMG SRC="images/b_lessons.gif" ALT="btn: Lessons" WIDTH="170"
HEIGHT="24" BORDER="0"></A><BR><BR>
        <A HREF="recitals.html"><IMG SRC="images/b_recitals.gif" ALT="btn: Recitals" WIDTH="170"
HEIGHT="24" BORDER="0"></A><BR><BR>
        <A HREF="competitions.html"><IMG SRC="images/b_competitions.gif" ALT="btn: Competitions"
WIDTH="170" HEIGHT="24" BORDER="0"></A><BR><BR>
        <A HREF="performances.html"><IMG SRC="images/b_performances.gif" ALT="btn: Performances"
WIDTH="170" HEIGHT="24" BORDER="0"></A><BR><BR>
        <A HREF="background.html"><IMG SRC="images/b_background.gif" ALT="btn: Background"
WIDTH="170" HEIGHT="24" BORDER="0"></A><BR><BR>
        <A HREF="contact.html"><IMG SRC="images/b_contact.gif" ALT="btn: Contact" WIDTH="170"
HEIGHT="24" BORDER="0"></A><BR><BR><BR>

        <A HREF="mailto:mm@creationguide.com"><IMG SRC="images/sendnote.gif" ALT="btn: E-mail
Chris" WIDTH="170" HEIGHT="77" BORDER="0"></A>

        </TD>
        <TD VALIGN="top">
```

14 Open index.html in your browser. Your home page should now include a navigation bar on the left, as shown in Figure 8-21. Notice that the Home button displays differently than the other buttons in the navigation bar to indicate that users are currently viewing the home page. Click the logo and Home button to make sure that the home page redisplays. (Clicking any other button in the navigation bar will display an error because you haven't created those pages yet.) Hover your cursor over each button to ensure that the ALT text is correct throughout. Click the Send Us A Note icon to ensure that a blank e-mail message opens and is addressed to you.

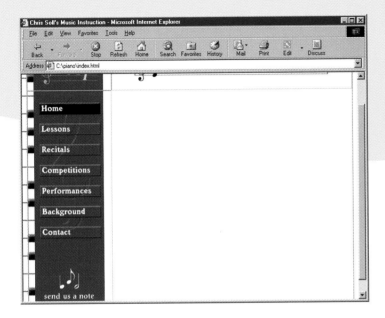

Figure 8-21
Viewing the navigation bar and Send Us A Note element in a browser

Inserting Footer Information

You next need to add the footer information. The piano site's footer includes a footer graphic, the address and phone number information, text links that correspond to the navigation bar links, and some copyright text.

The process of inserting a footer graphic is similar to the process of inserting the header graphic described earlier in this chapter. The main difference in the footer area is that you're going to place the footer graphic in the second cell in the third row, and you're going to insert some additional information in the cell along with the graphic (as described in the next section). Because we're going to include other information below the footer graphic, we'll nest the footer graphic within paragraph tags (`<P></P>`) to ensure that space will be included above the graphic. Let's start to create the footer element by inserting the footer graphic:

1 If necessary, open your text editor and open index.html.

2 In the third row of the table, click after the second `<TD VALIGN="top">` tag, press Enter, press Tab, and then type `<P ALIGN="CENTER">` to indicate the start of a paragraph and to specify to center align the paragraph's contents. (By default, paragraphs are left-aligned.)

tip

For added assistance, refer to Figure 8-22 on page 210 as you insert the Web site's footer information.

3 Specify the footer image's information by inserting the image tag with the following attributes:

```
<IMG SRC="images/footer.gif" ALT="footer: Chris's Music
Instruction" WIDTH="415" HEIGHT="62"
BORDER="0" ALIGN="middle">
```

4 Type `</P>` to indicate the end of the paragraph section. The closing `</P>` is optional, but adding it makes the code clearer.

Next you'll insert a second paragraph that centers the address and phone number information:

5 Press Enter twice, press Tab, and type:

```
<P ALIGN="CENTER">1234 Songbird Alley, Mesa, AZ 85201<BR>
555 555-5555</P>
```

Notice the `<BR>` tag in the preceding HTML code between the address text and the phone number. Adding the `<BR>` tag displays the phone number below the address on the next line.

Now you'll add some text links in the footer area that correspond to the navigation bar's buttons—that way, if any users have graphics turned off, they can still navigate around your site. To add text links, you follow a procedure similar to creating graphic links. The difference between the two tasks is that you enclose text between anchor links instead of enclosing an IMG tag, as shown in the following steps. First we'll center the paragraph that will contain the text links:

6 Press Enter twice, press Tab, and type `<P ALIGN="CENTER">`.

7 Press Enter, press Tab, and type:

```
<A HREF="index.html">Home Page</A> |
```

In the preceding link, the words *Home Page* will display as hypertext on the Web page. If users click the words *Home Page*, the index.html file will display. Also notice the pipe symbol (|). You include this symbol between each text link to make differentiating the links easier. The symbol is optional but popular. You're now ready to add the remaining text links:

8 Press Enter, press Tab, and type:

```
<A HREF="lessons.html">Lessons</A> |
```

note

You don't *have* to press Enter and Tab between each of the text link entries in steps 8 through 14. Browsers will show the links in a row regardless of the space you add in the HTML document. We chose to format our text links in the described way to make working with the information easier.

9 Press Enter, press Tab, and type:

```
<A HREF="recitals.html">Recitals</A> |
```

10 Press Enter, press Tab, and type:

```
<A HREF="competitions.html">Competitions<A> |
```

11 Press Enter, press Tab, and type:

```
<A HREF="performances.html">Performances</A> |
```

12 Press Enter, press Tab, and type:

```
<A HREF="background.html">Background</A> |
```

13 Press Enter, press Tab, and type:

```
<A HREF="contact.html">Contact Information</A> |
```

The final text link entry is the text equivalent of the Send Us A Note icon you inserted earlier. Thus, this text link uses the `mailto:` component in the HREF attribute. Remember to replace *mm@creationguide.com* with your own e-mail address in the following step:

14 Press Enter, press Tab, and type:

```
<A HREF="mailto:mm@creationguide.com">E-mail Chris</A>
```

15 To complete the text link paragraph, press Enter, press Tab, and type `</P>`.

The final component of the footer is the copyright information. In this section, you create a centered paragraph and enter the copyright information. One interesting twist here is that you can use a special character entity reference to create a copyright symbol:

16 Press Enter twice, press Tab, and type:

```
<P ALIGN="CENTER">&copy 2001 Chris Soll.
All Rights Reserved</P>
```

17 Save index.html. Your HTML code should look similar to the code shown in Figure 8-22.

18 Open index.html in your browser. The footer in the index.html file should look similar to the page shown in Figure 8-23.

lingo

A *character entity reference* is a special key combination that includes the ampersand (&) symbol and enables you to display nonstandard characters—such as accent marks, registered trademarks, and so forth—in Web pages. For a list of common character entity references, see the appendix of this book.

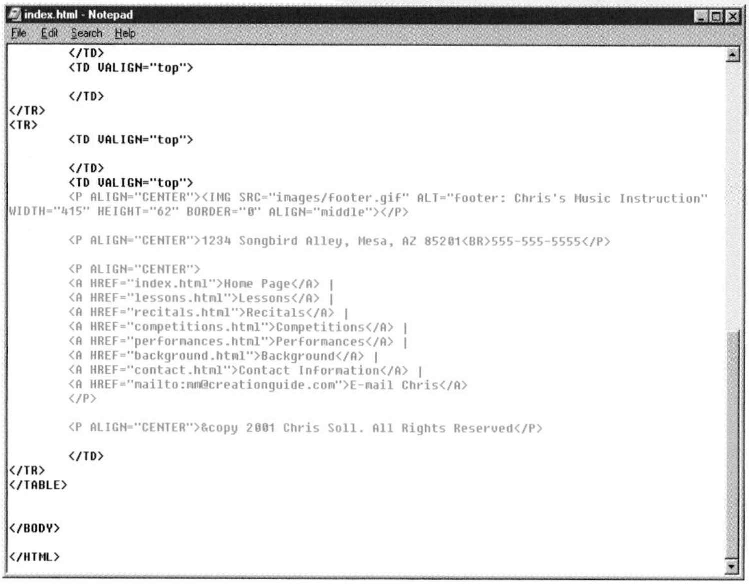

Figure 8-22
Adding footer information into the HTML document

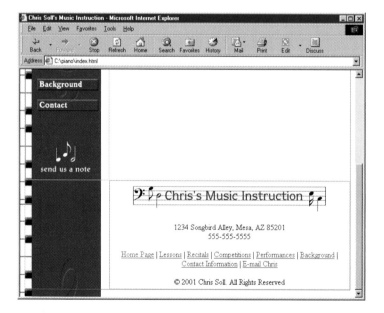

Figure 8-23
Viewing the footer for the piano site's Web pages

You might have noticed that we've designed everything on the home page except the main content. You'll be happy to hear that there's a method to our madness. Now that we have the basic structure of the home page created, and because we're planning to mimic the home page structure on the subpages, we can use the index.html file to quickly create the foundation pages for the subpages, as described in the next section.

Copying the Home Page Framework to Subpages

By now you've probably realized that we need to make some pages for the navigation bar and text links to link to. Namely, the piano site calls for the following pages:

- index.html (which we're already in the process of creating)
- lessons.html
- recitals.html
- competitions.html
- performances.html
- background.html
- contact.html

In this section, you're going to create the six additional HTML pages that make up the piano site. You *could* copy all the code from index.html, paste it into a blank text document, and then save the text document as an HTML file, but we're much lazier than that! Here's how we went about creating most of the code for the subpages:

1 Open the C:\piano folder.

2 Right-click the index.html file, and click Copy on the shortcut menu.

3 Click the Paste button in the toolbar six times. Your *piano* folder should display as shown in Figure 8-24.

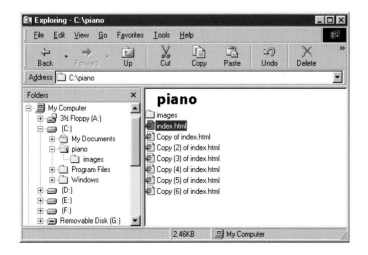

Figure 8-24
Copying index.html six times to serve as a template for subpages

4 Right-click the first copy of index.html, click Rename on the shortcut menu, type *lessons.html*, and press Enter.

5 Using the procedure described in step 4, rename the subsequent files *recitals.html*, *competitions.html*, *performances.html*, *background.html*, and *contact.html*.

6 Open your text editor, open the lessons.html file, and then perform the following six changes, which are highlighted in red in Figure 8-25:

■ In the <TITLE> tag, click after the word *Instruction* and type *: Lessons*.

■ In the <TABLE> tag, change the BORDER attribute to "0".

■ In the second cell of the first table row, change *t_home.gif* to *t_lessons.gif*.

■ Also in the second cell of the first table row, replace the text ALT="title: Chris Soll's Music Instruction" with the text ALT="title: Lessons".

■ In the navigation bar HTML code, change the *b_home2.gif* Home button text to *b_home.gif*.

■ Also in the navigation bar HTML code, change the *b_lessons.gif* Lessons button text to *b_lessons2.gif*.

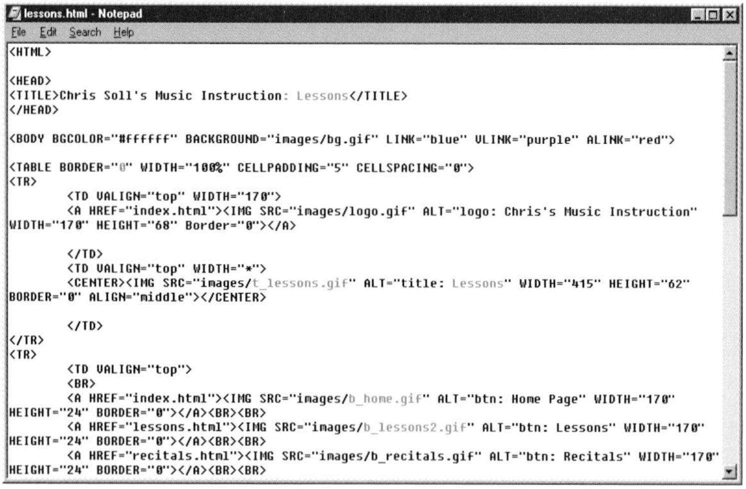

Figure 8-25
Modifying the copied HTML code
to create the lessons.html page

```
lessons.html - Notepad
File  Edit  Search  Help
<HTML>

<HEAD>
<TITLE>Chris Soll's Music Instruction: Lessons</TITLE>
</HEAD>

<BODY BGCOLOR="#ffffff" BACKGROUND="images/bg.gif" LINK="blue" VLINK="purple" ALINK="red">

<TABLE BORDER="0" WIDTH="100%" CELLPADDING="5" CELLSPACING="0">
<TR>
        <TD VALIGN="top" WIDTH="170">
        <A HREF="index.html"><IMG SRC="images/logo.gif" ALT="logo: Chris's Music Instruction"
WIDTH="170" HEIGHT="68" Border="0"></A>

        </TD>
        <TD VALIGN="top" WIDTH="*">
        <CENTER><IMG SRC="images/t_lessons.gif" ALT="title: Lessons" WIDTH="415" HEIGHT="62"
BORDER="0" ALIGN="middle"></CENTER>

        </TD>
</TR>
<TR>
        <TD VALIGN="top">
        <BR>
        <A HREF="index.html"><IMG SRC="images/b_home.gif" ALT="btn: Home Page" WIDTH="170"
HEIGHT="24" BORDER="0"></A><BR><BR>
        <A HREF="lessons.html"><IMG SRC="images/b_lessons2.gif" ALT="btn: Lessons" WIDTH="170"
HEIGHT="24" BORDER="0"></A><BR><BR>
        <A HREF="recitals.html"><IMG SRC="images/b_recitals.gif" ALT="btn: Recitals" WIDTH="170"
HEIGHT="24" BORDER="0"></A><BR><BR>
```

7 Save lessons.html.

You've just completed the foundation document for the Lessons page. Pretty easy! You now have to repeat this short customization process in the remaining subpage documents.

8 Open recitals.html in your text editor, and make the following changes:

- In the <TITLE> tag, click after the word *Instruction* and type : *Recitals*.

- In the <TABLE> tag, change the BORDER attribute to "0".

- In the second cell of the first table row, change *t_home.gif* to *t_recitals.gif*.

- Also in the second cell of the first table row, replace the text ALT="title: Chris Soll's Music Instruction" with the text ALT="title: Recitals".

- In the navigation bar HTML code, change the *b_home2.gif* Home button text to *b_home.gif*.

- Also in the navigation bar HTML code, change the *b_recitals.gif* Lessons button text to *b_recitals2.gif*.

9 Save recitals.html.

10 Open competitions.html in your text editor, and make the following changes:

- In the <TITLE> tag, click after the word *Instruction* and type : *Competitions*.

- In the <TABLE> tag, change the BORDER attribute to "0".

- In the second cell of the first table row, change *t_home.gif* to *t_competitions.gif*.

- Also in the second cell of the first table row, replace the text ALT="title: Chris Soll's Music Instruction" with the text ALT="title: Competitions".

- In the navigation bar HTML code, change the *b_home2.gif* Home button text to *b_home.gif*.

- Also in the navigation bar HTML code, change the *b_competitions.gif* Lessons button text to *b_competitions2.gif*.

11 Save competitions.html.

note

Using a completed foundation page to create subpages is fast and promotes consistency throughout your site.

12 Open performances.html in your text editor, and make the following changes:

- In the `<TITLE>` tag, click after the word *Instruction* and type *: Performances*.

- In the `<TABLE>` tag, change the `BORDER` attribute to `"0"`.

- In the second cell of the first table row, change *t_home.gif* to *t_performances.gif*.

- Also in the second cell of the first table row, replace the text `ALT="title: Chris Soll's Music Instruction"` with the text `ALT="title: Performances"`.

- In the navigation bar HTML code, change the *b_home2.gif* Home button text to *b_home.gif*.

- Also in the navigation bar HTML code, change the *b_performances.gif* Lessons button text to *b_performances2.gif*.

13 Save performances.html.

14 Open background.html in your text editor, and make the following changes:

- In the `<TITLE>` tag, click after the word *Instruction* and type *: Background*.

- In the `<TABLE>` tag, change the `BORDER` attribute to `"0"`.

- In the second cell of the first table row, change *t_home.gif* to *t_background.gif*.

- Also in the second cell of the first table row, replace the text `ALT="title: Chris Soll's Music Instruction"` with the text `ALT="title: Background"`.

- In the navigation bar HTML code, change the *b_home2.gif* Home button text to *b_home.gif*.

- Also in the navigation bar HTML code, change the *b_background.gif* Lessons button text to *b_background2.gif*.

15 Save background.html.

16 Open contact.html in your text editor, and make the following changes:

- In the `<TITLE>` tag, click after the word *Instruction* and type *: Contact*.

- In the `<TABLE>` tag, change the BORDER attribute to "0".
- In the second cell of the first table row, change *t_home.gif* to *t_contact.gif*.
- Also in the second cell of the first table row, replace the text `ALT="title: Chris Soll's Music Instruction"` with the text `ALT="title: Contact"`.
- In the navigation bar HTML code, change the *b_home2.gif* Home button text to *b_home.gif*.
- Also in the navigation bar HTML code, change the *b_contact.gif* Lessons button text to *b_contact2.gif*.

17 Save contact.html.

18 Open index.html in your browser. Click each navigation bar button to check your work. A foundation page should display after you click each button; each subpage should include a custom title bar graphic and a current page (black) navigation bar button that corresponds to the displayed page. Also, the table border lines shouldn't display on the subpages. Figure 8-26 shows how the Lessons page should display in your browser window.

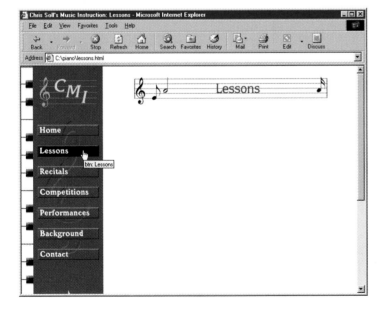

Figure 8-26
Displaying the Lessons subpage

Congratulations! You've created the structure for the entire piano site. Now we'll insert some content on the home page.

Inserting Body Text on the Home Page

In this section, you're going to insert some body text into the piano site's home page. What this endeavor actually boils down to is practice in formatting text. The main content of the home page consists of a couple headings, paragraph text, colored block quotes, and a linked unnumbered list. So as you can imagine, we'll be discussing how to create these types of elements over the next couple pages.

Creating Headings

In HTML coding, you can define six heading levels by using `<H1></H1>`, `<H2></H2>`, and so on through `<H6></H6>` tag sets, with the size 1 heading being the largest and size 6 being the smallest. Figure 8-27 shows a sample of the various heading sizes.

Figure 8-27

Testing out the various heading sizes

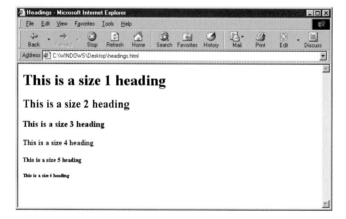

The piano site uses one heading tag on the home page, which formats the welcome message at the top of the page:

1 Open your text editor, and then open C:\piano\index.html.

2 In the second row and second cell of the table (the cell after the navigation bar information), click after `<TD VALIGN="top">`, press Enter, and press Tab.

First you'll define the font style for the cell's body text:

3 Type the following:

```
<FONT FACE="verdana, arial, sans-serif">
```

Notice in step 3 the three font names in the FACE attribute. Because you never know what fonts users will have installed on their systems, you should provide a backup plan when you define font styles. In step 3, if a user's computer has the Verdana font installed, the browser will display upcoming body text in the Verdana font style. If Verdana isn't installed on the user's computer, the browser will look for the Arial font family. If neither Verdana nor Arial is installed on the user's system, the browser will display the body text in a sans serif style. If fonts listed in the font tag can't be found on the user's computer, the browser will display the text in the browser's default font style.

Next you'll add a line break and insert a "welcome" heading on the piano home page:

4 Press Enter, press Tab, type `<BR>` to add a line break, press Enter, press Tab, and then type the following size 3 heading information:

```
<H3>Welcome to Chris Soll's Online Resource for Music
Instruction and Performance Information!</H3>
```

5 Save index.html. Your code should appear as shown in Figure 8-28.

Figure 8-28
Specifying a font style and inserting a size 3 heading

Adding Paragraph Text

Below the welcome heading you created in the previous section, you'll add some body text. The `<P></P>` tags are the main tags you'll use when entering paragraph text, which you'll do next.

1 Click after the </H3> tag you created in the previous section, press Enter, press Tab, and type <P>Meet Chris!</P>.

2 Press Enter, press Tab, and type the following:

<P>She's an internationally certified senior music instructor who teaches piano and flute to budding musicians, hobbyists, and professionals.</P>

3 Press Enter, press Tab, and type the following:

<P>Chris complements her highly regarded instructional program by regularly performing throughout the world as well as orchestrating annual student recitals and competitions.</P>

4 Finally, press Enter, press Tab, and type the following:

<P>Student testimonials sum up Chris's teaching success best:</P>

5 Save index.html.

Your HTML code should appear as shown in Figure 8-29. Further, if you preview index.html in your browser, your home page should look similar to the page shown in Figure 8-30. Your page is all set up except for adding a block quote or two, which is the topic of the next section.

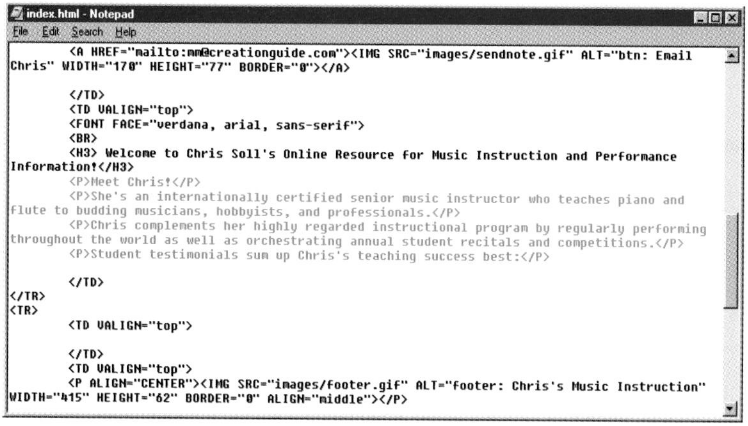

Figure 8-29
Adding paragraph text to the piano site's home page

```
index.html - Notepad
File  Edit  Search  Help
        <A HREF="mailto:mm@creationguide.com"><IMG SRC="images/sendnote.gif" ALT="btn: Email
Chris" WIDTH="170" HEIGHT="77" BORDER="0"></A>

        </TD>
        <TD VALIGN="top">
        <FONT FACE="verdana, arial, sans-serif">
        <BR>
        <H3> Welcome to Chris Soll's Online Resource for Music Instruction and Performance
Information!</H3>
            <P>Meet Chris!</P>
            <P>She's an internationally certified senior music instructor who teaches piano and
flute to budding musicians, hobbyists, and professionals.</P>
            <P>Chris complements her highly regarded instructional program by regularly performing
throughout the world as well as orchestrating annual student recitals and competitions.</P>
            <P>Student testimonials sum up Chris's teaching success best:</P>

        </TD>
</TR>
<TR>
        <TD VALIGN="top">

        </TD>
        <TD VALIGN="top">
        <P ALIGN="CENTER"><IMG SRC="images/footer.gif" ALT="footer: Chris's Music Instruction"
WIDTH="415" HEIGHT="62" BORDER="0" ALIGN="middle"></P>
```

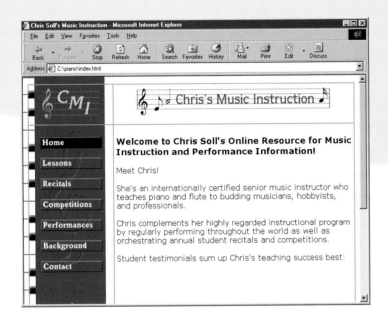

Figure 8-30
*Viewing a heading and para-
graph text inserted into the
home page*

Formatting Block Quotes and Colored Text

You can format text as a block quote to set off the text from the surrounding body text. Generally, browsers interpret the <BLOCKQUOTE>
</BLOCKQUOTE> tag set by indenting the enclosed text's left and right mar-
gins. If you really want to indent your paragraph, you can nest block quote
commands inside one another, as here: <BLOCKQUOTE><BLOCKQUOTE>
</BLOCKQUOTE></BLOCKQUOTE>. In this section, you'll create block quotes with
maroon text:

1 Open index.html in a text editor if necessary, click after best:</P> in
the second cell of the table's second row, press Enter twice, and press Tab.

2 Type <BLOCKQUOTE><BLOCKQUOTE> to create a block quote nested within
a block quote.

3 Press Enter, press Tab, and type the following:

```
<FONT COLOR="maroon"><P><I>Chris is by far the best
music teacher I've ever had! She taught me more
than I could have learned in a lifetime from Viktor
McTonedeaf, "the Royal Music Instructor!</I></P>
```

Notice that the COLOR attribute in the FONT tag is used to modify
the color of the paragraph text.

4 Press Enter twice, press Tab, and type the following:

```
<P ALIGN="RIGHT"><I>- Moe Zart</I></P>
```

Step 4 inserts a right-aligned, italicized name, which is associated with the block quote entered in step 3.

5 Press Enter twice, press Tab, and type the following:

```
<P><I>Chris Soll is the best teacher I had before "the
incident" that ended my professional music career--
she's a true master!</I></P>
```

6 Press Enter twice, press Tab, and type:

```
<P ALIGN="RIGHT"><I>- Vincent Vanngo</I></P>
```

7 Press Enter, press tab, and type </FONT> to end the maroon font color formatting.

8 Press Enter twice, press Tab, and type </BLOCKQUOTE></BLOCKQUOTE> to end the block quote formatting setting.

9 Save index.html.

Your block quote text should display in your HTML document as shown in Figure 8-31. Figure 8-32 shows the block quote text when it's viewed in a browser.

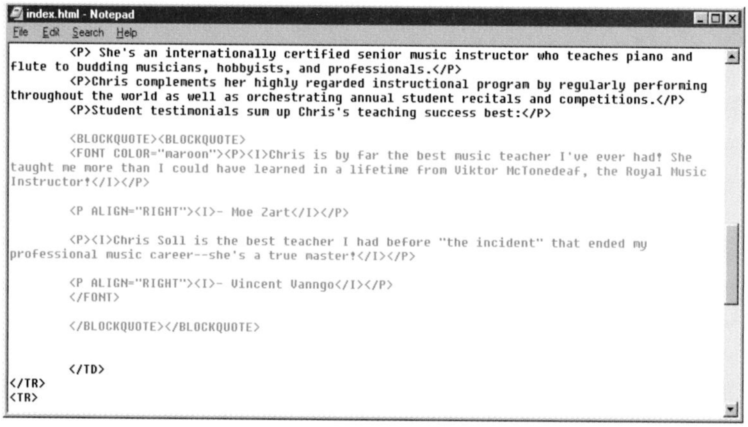

Figure 8-31
Adding block quotes to the piano site's home page

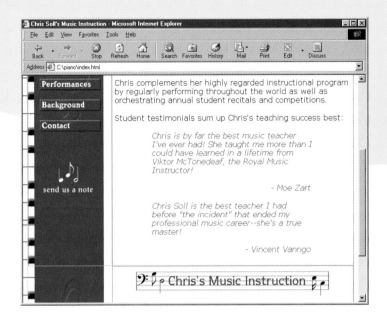

Figure 8-32
Viewing block quotes

Creating a Linked Unnumbered List

The final type of body text you'll create on the piano home page is an unnumbered list. An unnumbered list appears as a bulleted list on a Web page, as shown in Figure 8-33.

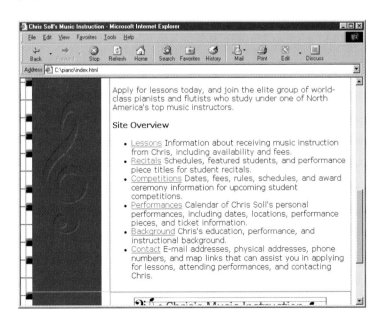

Figure 8-33
Viewing an unnumbered list

note

You can use <OL></OL> HTML commands to create numbered (ordered) lists, or you can use <UL></UL> commands to create unnumbered (bulleted) lists. Each list item within either type of list is identified by the <LI></LI> tag set.

In this section, you'll first add a small amount of text that introduces the unnumbered list, and then you'll create the list (which includes links to appropriate pages):

1 Open index.html in a text editor if necessary, click after the final </BLOCKQUOTE> in the second cell in the second table row, press Enter twice, press Tab, and then enter the following paragraph:

```
<P>Apply for lessons today, and join the elite group of
world-class pianists and flutists who study under
one of North America's top music instructors.</P>
```

2 Press Enter twice, press Tab, and then type the following:

```
<P><B>Site Overview</B></P>.
```

In step 3, you'll begin the unnumbered list by inserting the <UL> tag:

3 Press Enter twice, press Tab, and type <UL>.

In steps 4 through 9, you'll create list items by surrounding each list item with the <LI></LI> tag set. Further, you'll format the first word of each list entry as a hyperlink to another page in the site:

4 Press Enter, press Tab, and type the following:

```
<LI><A HREF="lessons.html">Lessons</A> Information
about receiving music instruction from Chris,
including availability and fees. </LI>
```

5 Press Enter, press Tab, and type the following:

```
<LI><A HREF="recitals.html">Recitals</A> Schedules,
featured students,and performance piece titles
for student recitals. </LI>
```

6 Press Enter, press Tab, and type the following:

```
<LI><A HREF="competitions.html">Competitions</A> Dates,
fees, rules, schedules, and award ceremony
information for upcoming student competitions.</LI>
```

7 Press Enter, press Tab, and type the following:

```
<LI><A HREF="performances.html">Performances<A>
Calendar of Chris Soll's personal performances,
including dates, locations, performance pieces, and
ticket information.</LI>
```

8 Press Enter, press Tab, and type the following:

```
<LI><A HREF="background.html">Background</A> Chris's
education, performance, and instructional
background.</LI>
```

9 Press Enter, press Tab, and type the following:

```
<LI><A HREF="contact.html">Contact</A> E-mail
addresses, physical addresses, phone numbers, and
map links that can assist you in applying for
lessons, attending performances, and contacting
Chris.</LI>
```

10 Press Enter, press Tab, and type `</UL>` to end the unnumbered list.

11 Press Enter, press Tab, and type `</FONT>` to complete the body text and end the font family specification.

12 Save index.html.

Your unnumbered list code should display as shown in Figure 8-34.

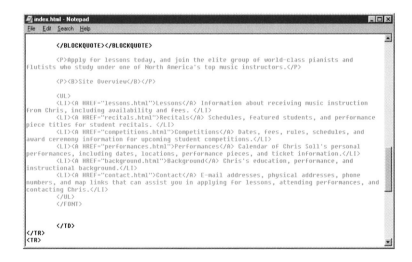

Figure 8-34
Viewing HTML code that includes paragraph text and an unnumbered list

Last but not least, you'll insert a linked photograph into the body area of the piano site's home page.

Inserting and Linking a Picture

By now, you should be very comfortable with inserting and linking graphics. (You had a lot of practice just a little while ago when you were creating the navigation bar!) For this page, we opted to display the picture below the size 3 heading and along the right side of the page. Further, because the photograph is a picture of Chris, we linked the photograph to the Background page.

To insert a linked picture within your page's body text, follow these steps:

1 Open index.html in a text editor if necessary, click after the </H3> tag in the second cell in the second row of the table, press Enter, and press Tab.

2 Type the following link and image information:

```
<A HREF="background.html"><IMG SRC="images/p_chris.jpg"
ALT="pic: Chris Soll" WIDTH="170" HEIGHT="250"
BORDER="0" HSPACE="25" VSPACE="10" ALIGN="right"></A>
```

In step 2, you can see some added attributes to the <IMG> tag, which are defined as follows:

- **HSPACE**   Enables you to specify extra space (in pixels) between the image and text on the left and right sides of the image.

- **VSPACE**   Enables you to specify extra space (in pixels) between the image and text above and below the image.

- **ALIGN**   Indicates to align the picture on the page. In our example, the picture is aligned to the right side of the page.

3 Save index.html.

Finalizing the Home Page

Finally, you need to remove the table borders on the home page before you can proclaim your project complete. In addition, you should check your links and view all your pages to ensure that you've entered accurate HTML code. First let's get rid of those borders on the home page:

1 Open index.html in a text editor.

2 In the <TABLE> tag, change the BORDER attribute from "1" to "0".

3 Save index.html.

Now let's click around and check your links, graphics, ALT text, and other page elements. For example, we need to make sure that none of your pages display with two black buttons.

4 Open your browser, display index.html (or if the document is already open in your browser, click Refresh), and then click every link (including the linked picture, logo, Send Us A Note icon, and text links) to verify that your links work properly and your pages display correctly. If any links don't respond as expected, open the proper HTML document in your text editor and check the HTML code carefully. Check your banner graphics and button graphics to ensure that you've included the proper graphics on each page.

Your completed home page should display as shown in Figure 8-35. If you'd like to visit a sample online version of the piano site, connect to the Internet and display *www.creationguide.com/piano*. You can use the Source command on the View menu in your browser to display the online Web site's source code. The source code might come in handy if you want to check your own code or if you need some assistance.

Figure 8-35
The completed home page

note

You might have noticed that we provided content only for the home page. At this point, we think you're well enough prepared to enter content into the other pages if you desire more practice using HTML.

Using the Piano Site's Framework as a Template

After all your hard work creating the piano site, we wanted you to have a useful HTML template that you can easily customize. Therefore, we're going to let you in on a little secret. You can create a Web site using the piano template even if you don't have any graphics. You don't have to have a background image, banner graphics, or buttons. Instead, you can create an entire Web site using text links and color backgrounds by replacing the content elements in the piano site's Web pages. Figure 8-36 illustrates a Web page that uses the piano Web site without graphics. You can visit the sample site at *www.creationguide.com/chapter8/sample*.

Figure 8-36

Creating a text-based Web site that uses the piano site as a template

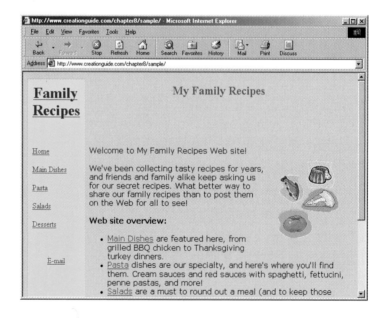

tip

The small graphics on the sample page in Figure 8-36 are clip-art images downloaded for free from *www.free-clip-art.to* and pasted together to create a simple picture. If you prefer not to include a graphic on your page, simply delete the <IMG> tag in your HTML document.

After you surf around the sample text site for a bit, visit the template page we created and posted at *www.creationguide.com/chapter8/sample/template.html*. Figure 8-37 shows the template page, and Figure 8-38 shows some of the template's source code. To speed along your progress when using the template to build a custom page, display the template's source code by clicking the View menu and then Source. Then in the source code window, click the File menu, click Save As, and save the source code to your computer. At that point, you're free to modify your local version of the template by replacing the placeholder text with your custom content. After you're finished creating a page using the template, turn to Chapter 11 to see how you go about uploading your pages to the Internet.

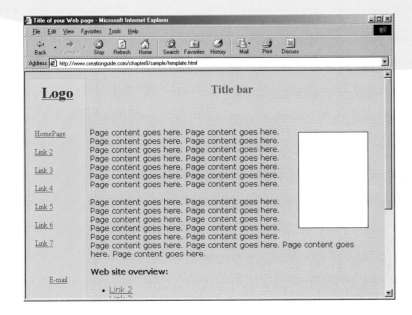

Figure 8-37
Accessing the text-based template

```
<HTML>
<HEAD>
<TITLE>Title of your Web page</TITLE>
</HAD>

<!-- Body tag sets background color to white, loads background image and sets link colors -->

<body bgcolor="#ccccff" link="blue" vlink="purple" alink="red">

<!-- Table used to control the alignment of the navigation and body elements -->

<TABLE BORDER="0" WIDTH="100%" CELLPADDING="10" CELLSPACING="0">
<TR>
        <TD VALIGN="top" BGCOLOR="#ffcc00" WIDTH="100">

        <!-- logo -->
        <H1 ALIGN="center"><A HREF="index.html">Logo</A></H1>
        </TD>

        <TD VALIGN="top" WIDTH="*">
        <!-- title bar -->
        <H2 ALIGN="center"><FONT COLOR="#990000">Title bar</H2>
        </TD>
</TR>
<TR>
        <TD VALIGN="top" BGCOLOR="#ffcc00">
        <BR>

        <!-- start navigation links -->
        <A HREF="index.html">HomePage</A><BR><BR>
        <A HREF="link2.html">Link 2</A><BR><BR>
        <A HREF="link3.html">Link 3</A><BR><BR>
```

Figure 8-38
Viewing the template's source code

tip

In Figure 8-38, you can see HTML code entries that begin with an exclamation point and two dashes: `<!-- logo -->`. These types of entries are called *comments*. Comments don't display on a Web page; they are used as notes to developers to help label parts of the HTML document. Comments have been added to the sample template to help you identify HTML components when you customize the source code.

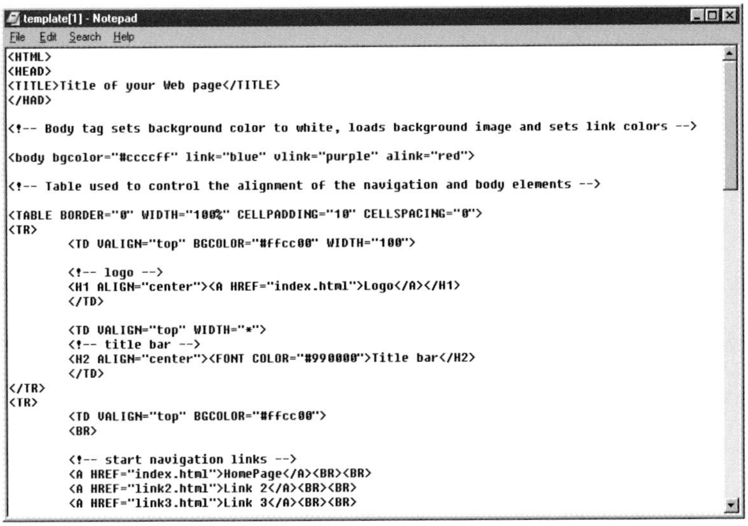

Finally, notice in Figure 8-38 that the `<BODY>` tag's `BGCOLOR` attribute has been changed from white (`#ffffff`) to purple (`#ccccff`), and that the first `<TD>` tag in each table row contains a `BGCOLOR` attribute set to gold (`#ffcc00`). You can use the `BGCOLOR` attribute to color your page's background as well as to color your table's cells if you're not using a background image. You can get fairly creative with color by coloring the background one color and then selectively coloring table cells various other colors. (You don't have to color all your table cells the same color.) Refer to the hexadecimal color chart in this book's appendix if you'd like to experiment with various colors on your Web page.

Additional Resources

As we mentioned, HTML books and Web pages abound. Here are a few of our favorite HTML resources:

- Morrison, Michael. *HTML and XML for Beginners*. Redmond, WA: Microsoft Press, forthcoming. (ISBN: 0-7356-1189-0) This book targets interested but inexperienced users who want to develop Web pages by using HTML. A nice feature of this book is that it offers numerous opportunities for hands-on learning.

- Castro, Elizabeth. *HTML for the World Wide Web*. 4th ed. Berkeley, CA: Peachpit Press, 2000. (ISBN: 0-201-35493-4) This book does a nice job of visually showing how to use most HTML commands. The textual explanations are brief yet helpful when used in conjunction with the visual references.

- Musciano, Chuck, and Bill Kennedy. *HTML & XHTML: The Definitive Guide*. 4th ed. Sebastopol, CA: O'Reilly, 2000. (ISBN: 0-596-00026-X) This book serves as a good HTML dictionary of HTML tags and attributes as well as serves as a resource for other common Web page creation tools, such as XML. The explanations are clear, concise, and comprehensive.

- *www.creationguide.com/resources*   We'll continually update the Creation Guide's Resource page to include current Web development resources.

- *www.stars.com*   The Web Developer's Virtual Library provides resources, sample code, and tutorials for Web developers.

■ ***www.w3.org/TR/html401*** The W3C (World Wide Web Consortium) Web site is the online home for the official most current HTML specifications. As of this writing, HTML 4.01 is the currently accepted specification. Use the Table of Contents, Elements, and Attributes links along the top of the page to find HTML commands and command descriptions.

■ ***www.webmonkey.com*** This site provides numerous resources for online developers.

key points

■ HTML commands serve as instructions that tell a browser how to display a Web page's content.

■ HTML commands appear between < > marks, usually come in pairs, and are not case-sensitive.

■ Opening HTML tags frequently contain attributes to further refine the tag's instructions.

■ The standard tags for HTML documents consist of the following:

```
<HTML>
<HEAD>
<TITLE></TITLE>
</HEAD>
<BODY>
</BODY>
</HTML>
```

■ If possible, store all your Web site documents and graphics within the same master folder. Create an images folder for your Web site's images within the master folder.

■ To make life easier, devise a graphics naming system to help differentiate various image types, such as buttons, banners, pictures, and so forth.

■ When creating Web pages, save your HTML documents and preview your pages in a browser frequently.

■ Always verify that you've included all angle brackets (<>) and quotation marks ("") in your code. Missing small elements or misspelling HTML commands can cause your page to display incorrectly (or not at all) in a browser.

swimming

Most of us are creatures of habit—we like to eat at favorite restaurants, hang out with customary friends, and so on. Sometimes, life is more enjoyable (and easier) when we're surrounded by the familiar. Thus, you might feel most comfortable creating Web pages in an "old" standby application such as Microsoft Word. Most people have used Word to create standard documents, so this application easily serves as a widely recognized comfort-zone interface. If you're among the at-least-slightly-familiar-with-Word users, you'll be pleased to find that

9

deeper

INTO WEB WATERS: CREATING WEB PAGES WITH MICROSOFT WORD

creating Web pages in Word is very similar to creating standard documents. In this chapter, you'll be able to put all your Word and word processing knowledge to work as well as pick up a few Word tricks. By the way, if you generally use another word processing application, don't be overly concerned at this point; you'll soon see that Word offers the standard fare of word processing features and commands, so following along in this chapter won't take you much more than knee-deep into new waters.

To create the Web pages described in this chapter, you'll need the following "supplies":

- Microsoft Word 2000 or later

- A browser and an Internet connection (An Internet connection is necessary only to download the sample project's text file from the Creation Guide Web site.)

- The resume.doc text file, which you will download from *www.creationguide.com/chapter9/text*. To obtain this text file, create a folder named *resume* on your computer's hard drive. (For convenience, we'll refer to your hard drive as the C:\ drive throughout this chapter.) Connect to the Internet, open your browser, display *www.creationguide.com/chapter9/text*, right-click the resume.doc filename, and save a copy of the file to the C:\resume folder on your computer, as shown in Figure 9-1.

Figure 9-1
Downloading the resume.doc text file from the Internet

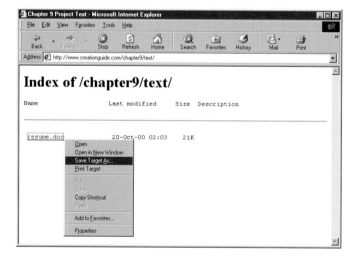

Introducing the Web Capabilities of Word 2000

In Chapter 7, we described how to create an online presence using free online resources (such as MSN Communities). Then in Chapter 8, we showed you how to use a text editor and some HTML commands to create Web pages from scratch. In this chapter, we'll explain how you can create a Web site using an application that many people already have installed on their computers—Microsoft Word 2000.

Over the past few years, we've been watching as Word has evolved, with each version incorporating increasing levels of Internet and networking functionality. Word 2000 continues the networking-integration trend of Word by supplying you with a number of ways in which you can interact with the Internet:

- **View Web pages** You can click View, choose Toolbars, and then click Web to display the Web toolbar. The Web toolbar provides basic Web navigation buttons similar to the toolbar buttons found in Microsoft Internet Explorer. Figure 9-2 shows the Web toolbar in Word 2000.

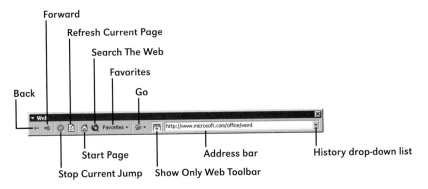

Figure 9-2
The Web toolbar in Word 2000

- **E-mail messages** To create an e-mail interface within Word, you can click the E-mail button on Word's Standard toolbar. Clicking the E-mail button opens the E-mail header pane within the current document view. After the E-mail pane displays, you can enter e-mail addresses in the address text boxes, add text in the Subject text box, and then click Send to send the currently displayed Word document to another person connected to your network or the Internet. Figure 9-3 shows Word with the E-mail pane open and ready to send a document.

- **Create Web pages** Using the Save As feature, Web page templates, or the Web Page Wizard, you can convert any Word document to a Web page or create Web pages from scratch. When you create a Web page in Word, Word automatically generates the HTML source code necessary to display your document as a Web page.

tip

To close the E-mail pane without sending an e-mail message, simply click the E-mail button in the Standard toolbar.

In essence, Word acts as a midrange HTML editor. Keep in mind that although Word isn't a bare-bones HTML editor like Notepad, it isn't nearly as comprehensive as a full-scale HTML editor like Microsoft FrontPage.

Figure 9-3
The E-mail pane in Word 2000

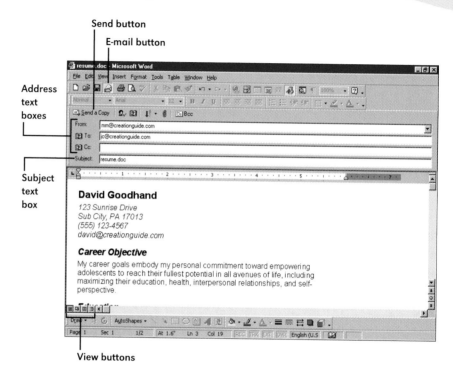

Send button

E-mail button

Address text boxes

Subject text box

View buttons

If you're interested in learning more about the e-mail features and Web browsing capabilities of Word 2000, thumb through one or two of the resources mentioned near the end of this chapter in the section "Additional Resources."

Because this book is all about creating Web pages, our focus in this chapter is on creating Web pages using the Web page creation features of Word. As we just mentioned, you can create Web pages in Word in three ways:

- Execute the Save As command to save a document as an HTML file

- Create a Web page using Web page templates

- Create a Web site using the Web Page Wizard in Word

In the next few pages, we'll take a brief look at the preceding three ways of creating Web pages. Then in this chapter's project, we'll focus on how you can use the Web Page Wizard in Word 2000 to create a Web site. We'll also provide hints, instructions, and pointers regarding formatting any HTML document while you're in Word. Throughout the project, we'll explain how to tweak Word-generated Web pages as well as create and add design elements—such as WordArt and clip art. That's our preamble. Now let's look at how to use Word to create Web pages. First, let's use the quickest method of converting a Word document into a Web page—using the Save As command.

Saving a File as an HTML Document

As you might know, you can save Word documents in various file formats (with various filename extensions, such as .txt, .doc, .rtf, and so forth). Among the file-type options, Word includes an option to save your Word document as a Web page (with an .htm extension). You can save any Word document as an HTML document via the Save As dialog box. When you save a Word document as an HTML document, Word generates the Web page's HTML source code automatically.

try this! Before you save a document as a Web page, you should preview how the document will display as a Web page. To preview a document as a Web page, open any Word document (such as the C:\resume\resume.doc file, if you downloaded it for this chapter's project) and then use the following steps to try various methods of previewing Web documents:

1 After opening a Word document, click View on the menu bar and then click Web Layout. The view changes to Web Layout view within the Word application.

2 Click View, and then click Normal to revert to Normal view.

3 Click the Web Layout View button, located in the lower-left corner of the document window (as shown earlier in Figure 9-3). Word's view changes to Web Layout view within the Word application.

4 Click the Normal View button in the lower-left corner of the window.

5 Click File, and then click Web Page Preview. When you use the Web Page Preview command, Word displays the current document in your browser (instead of within Word).

6 Close your browser. Your Word document should still be displayed within Word in Normal view.

After you preview your Word document as a Web page, you're ready to save the document as a Web page. To do so, you access the Save As dialog box, as described here:

1 Open an existing Word document (such as the C:\resume\resume.doc file you downloaded for this chapter's project), or create a new document and enter some miscellaneous text. Then click File, and click Save As. The Save As dialog box opens.

2 In the Save As dialog box, click the Save As Type drop-down list and choose Web Page. After you specify the Web Page file type, notice that the Save As dialog box changes to include a Change Title button, as shown in Figure 9-4.

Figure 9-4
Saving a Word document as a Web page

Change Title button

3 Click the Change Title button. The Set Page Title dialog box opens. You can use the Set Page Title dialog box to provide custom text, as shown in Figure 9-5, that displays in a browser's title bar.

Figure 9-5
Adding title text to a Web page generated in Word

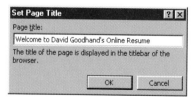

4 In the Set Page Title dialog box, enter some text that you want to display in the title bar of the viewer's browser whenever your Web page is viewed, and then click OK.

tip

The Save In pane of the Save As dialog box includes a Web Folders icon (in Microsoft Windows 98) or a My Network Places icon (in Windows Me or Windows 2000). Using the Web Folders feature in Microsoft Office 2000, you can save Web pages directly to your server if it supports Web Folders. See Chapter 11 for details about creating and using Web Folders to upload and manage Web pages.

5 Click the Save button to save the document as an HTML document (with an .htm extension).

After you save a document as a Web page, you'll see that the file is saved with an .htm filename extension instead of .doc. You can now edit and upload the Web page document just as you would any HTML file you created using a text editor or another HTML editing program.

Viewing a Document's HTML Source Code

After you save a Word document as a Web page, you can view the Web page's HTML source code in Word. You can freely edit a document's source code within the Word interface. Keep in mind, however, that the auto-generated code in Word is more complex than the basic HTML commands you worked with in Chapter 8. To view a Web document's HTML source code in Word, follow these steps:

1 Open the .htm document in Word. For the sake of simplicity, you'll want to open Word, click File, and then click Open to open your .htm document, or you'll need to drag the .htm document from a folder view into Word. If you double-click an .htm icon name in a folder, you'll open the document in your browser window.

2 After you open an .htm document in Word, click View and then choose HTML Source. The Microsoft Development Environment window opens and displays the page's source code, as shown in Figure 9-6.

Notice in Figure 9-6 that you can see a document's title text in the document's source code. The title text should match the text you entered in the Set Page Title dialog box. You can modify the Web page's title text directly in the source code within the Microsoft Development Environment window by using standard editing techniques (deleting, inserting text, and so forth).

tip

If you click the filename of a Word document saved as a Web page and the page opens in Internet Explorer, you can quickly open the document in Word by clicking the Edit button in Internet Explorer. To do so, click the Edit button's drop-down list and then select the Edit With Microsoft Word For Windows command. Selecting this option opens the .htm document in Word.

try this! You can add or change an HTML document's title text by adding or modifying the title text in the document's Properties dialog box. To do so, follow these steps:

1 Open an HTML document in Word.

2 Click File, click Properties, and then click the Summary tab.

3 Type the title text in the Title text box, and click OK.

Figure 9-6
An .htm page's source code in the Microsoft Development Environment

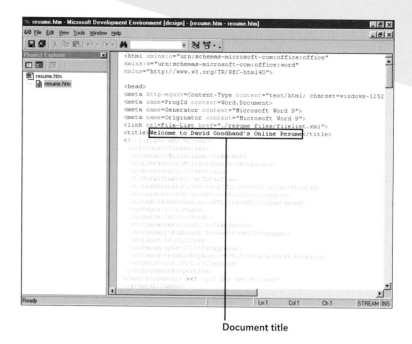

Document title

After you peruse the source code, close the development window as well as the Word document to prepare for the next section. As you can see, you can create fairly advanced Web pages by simply creating a Word document and then saving the document as a Web page. Further, you can also easily modify Web pages by using standard Word tools and procedures. Finally, you can really get your hands dirty by editing a Word document's HTML source code directly in the Microsoft Development Environment.

Later in this chapter, as we get into the project, we'll show you some ways in which you can edit and modify Web pages by using other tools and features in Word. We don't want to spoil any surprises at this point, but you'll be happy to see that editing Web pages in Word is a whole lot like editing regular documents in Word.

Now let's take a look at some Web page templates that Word provides to assist you in your Web page creation endeavors.

Creating a Web Page with a Template

As you just saw, saving a Word document as a Web page is pretty easy, so you might be wondering why you'd want to bother with Web page templates. After all, the word *template* tends to teeter on the edge of "overly complex" for more than a few people. But as you'll soon see firsthand, templates provide a few advantages and shortcuts over the save-a-Word-document-as-a-Web-page technique.

Templates can speed up your Web page creation process if you plan to use any of the following elements:

- Headings
- Columns
- Frames
- Hyperlinks that point to areas on the same page
- Common Web page layouts, such as Frequently Asked Questions (FAQ) pages

The biggest advantage of using a Web page template is that it enables you to jump-start your Web page creation process. When you use a Web page template, you can almost instantaneously add and arrange quite a few elements on your Web page with just a couple clicks. For example, using a template, you can quickly format a two-column Web page containing placeholder headers, hyperlinks, and body text as well as a graphics placeholder. To experiment with Web page templates, perform the following four simple steps:

1 Open Word.

2 Click File, and choose New.

3 In the New dialog box, click the Web Pages tab. The default templates available in Word 2000 are shown in Figure 9-7.

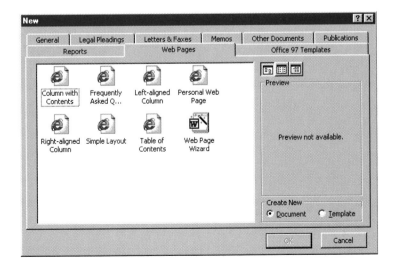

Figure 9-7
Templates available in the Web Pages tab of the New dialog box

4 Click a template, ensure that the Document option is selected (it's selected by default), and click OK. A new document is created with preformatted elements you can customize to create your Web page. For example, Figure 9-8 shows the result of selecting the Right-Aligned Column Web page template in Word 2000.

Figure 9-8
A page created with the Right-Aligned Column Web page template

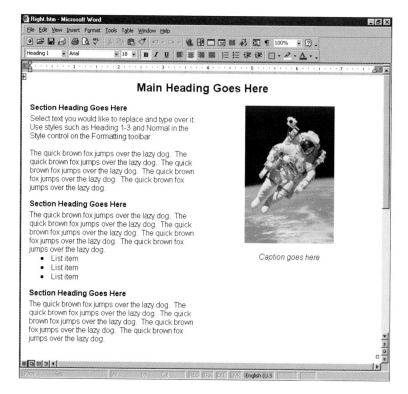

After you create a document based on a Web page template, you can modify the page's text, layout, background, formatting, hyperlink properties, and so forth just as if you were editing any other Word document. You can use the page editing procedures we describe in the project for this chapter on template pages as well as on the pages the Web Page Wizard creates.

When you save a document based on a Web page template, the Save As dialog box automatically selects the Web Page file-type format for you. Before you click the Save button, don't forget to add a title to your Web page by clicking the Change Title button and entering custom title text.

Deleting Files and Folders Generated by Templates If you practice creating and saving Web pages using templates, you'll want to delete the documents that you created during your practice session. So be sure that you remember where you save the template documents before you click the Save button. Then ensure that you delete the .htm document as well as the associated folder that's automatically generated to hold the figures used on the template.

When you save a Web page based on a template that includes a graphic (such as the Right-Aligned Column Web page template), Word saves the .htm file and automatically creates a similarly named subfolder without even telling you. The subfolder contains the graphic images used on the Web page. For example, if you save the Right-Aligned Column Web page template with its default filename to your C:\resume folder, your C:\resume folder will contain a file named Right.htm along with a folder named Right_files, as shown below. To delete all the practice files, delete both the Right.htm file and the Right_files folder.

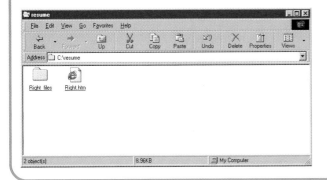

Building a Web Page with the Web Page Wizard

In addition to the Save As feature and Web page templates, Word 2000 comes equipped with a Web Page Wizard tool. (You might've noticed the Web Page Wizard icon in Figure 9-7.) The Web Page Wizard enables you to generate a foundation Web site by working through a series of dialog boxes. For example, you can use the wizard to generate a home page along with any number of additional pages. After you run the wizard, you can customize each page to create an entire Web site—the wizard gets you started by linking your subpages to your home page. One of the most useful benefits of the Web Page Wizard is that you can apply Web templates to existing documents, as we'll show you in the upcoming project.

If you plan to follow along in the upcoming project—and we strongly recommend that you do—you're about to become very familiar with the Web Page Wizard. So we won't dillydally here with an overly long description of the tool—you'll see it in action in just a moment.

Planning Your Word 2000 Web Page

In this chapter's project, you'll learn how to create an online resume, which is a handy resource to have available these days. Like most people, we're pretty familiar with resumes. Therefore, the planning stage merely required us to consider the typical types of information to include on our fictitious resume as well as how we wanted to organize the resume's information. For this project, we chose to create a resume for a social worker. Therefore, we anticipated that the site should be professional (without being overly formal), easy to navigate, and straightforward. Of course, if we were creating a resume for a graphic designer or an interior decorator, we'd have taken a different approach altogether (but creating an avant-garde online resume didn't seem to be the most useful approach for this book).

At this point in the planning process, we knew the type of information we wanted to include (typical resume data) and the stylistic approach we wanted to take (simple and fairly conservative). We were also planning to use the Web Page Wizard in Word. Therefore, our next step was to streamline the process by entering the resume's information into a single Word document. (We'll talk about creating a foundation document in just a bit.) As you'll soon see, the Web Page Wizard can automatically format headings and text in your Web site if you format your Word document using the default styles in Word. So we formatted the resume information by using the default styles in Word, as described later.

Next we made a rough sketch of how we wanted to display the resume's home page and a simple site map indicating the various pages we wanted to include. Figure 9-9 shows the resume's home page sketch, and Figure 9-10 shows the site map.

After we created the Word document resume, snooped around the formatting options in Word, sketched our home page, and outlined the site's structure, we were ready to proceed with the Web Page Wizard. But before we start creating the Web page, let's take a few moments to go over our document preparation steps.

lingo

A *style* is a set of formats (such as Arial, Bold, 24 point) saved as a group and given a name (such as Heading 1) that can be applied to text or paragraphs.

tip

Notice on the sketch that we planned to include a Print Version link. Although online resumes are convenient, many employers also request a printable version of a resume so that they can "pass it around the table" during the hiring process.

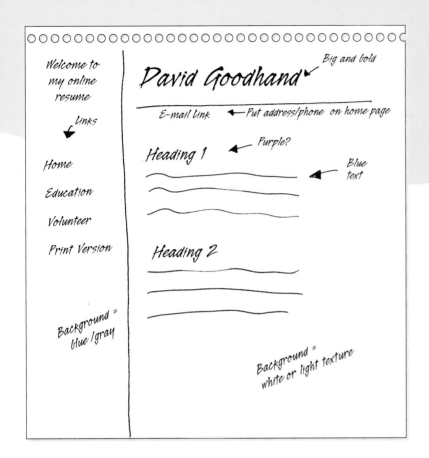

Figure 9-9
Sketch of the resume site's home page

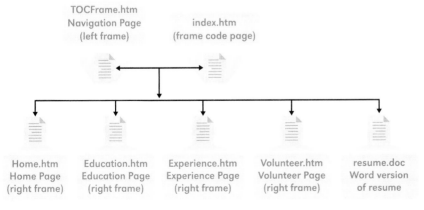

Figure 9-10
Storyboard depicting the resume site structure

Formatting a Text Document

As we mentioned, before we clicked our way into the Web Page Wizard, we created a Word document containing the site's main information to use as our foundation document (which is resume.doc). You don't have to create a foundation document, but the Web page creation process can be greatly simplified with just a little foresight and planning. The key to preparing a document that the Web Page Wizard can easily format is to enter text in a Word document and then apply standard Word styles to page elements.

Whether or not you know it, you use styles every time you create a Word document. Every time you create a new Word document, you open a blank document based on the Normal template, which includes style definitions, such as Normal (for normal text), Heading 1, Heading 2, and so forth. When you click within text in a document, the applied style name displays in the Style drop-down list in the Formatting toolbar, as shown in the following Try This!

You can apply styles to text while you're entering it by selecting the style you want to use in the Style drop-down list box on the Formatting toolbar before you type. Or you can format text after you've entered it by selecting existing text and then choosing a style in the Style drop-down list on the Formatting toolbar.

Styles are handy tools—you can use them to create custom styles, including your own naming schemes and formatting preferences. But for our purposes—using the Web Page Wizard—you just need to know the bare essentials of the Styles feature in Word. Simply knowing how to format your future Web page's text using Word's basic three or four default styles is a good start. If you're interested in a more complete discussion of Word styles, refer to the references listed in the "Additional Resources" section near the end of this chapter.

If you preformat your text document, the Web Page Wizard will format your text based on the typical styles included in the default Normal template in Word. You'll see what we mean after you work through the wizard. If you're working on your own resume instead of the sample resume, we suggest that as you enter your information, you style your Word document using the Normal, Heading 1, Heading 2, Heading 3, and possibly the Bull List styles for now. (You can apply the Bull List style by selecting text and clicking the Bullets button in the Formatting toolbar.) After you work through the Web Page Wizard, you'll have additional styles available that you can use to format your Web page's text manually.

At this point, you can close the resume.doc file if it's open. As mentioned earlier, the upcoming project assumes that you created the C:\resume directory on your computer and you've download the resume.doc file to the directory. But if you'd like, you can use your own resume document in place of David Goodhand's resume.doc throughout the upcoming procedures. Regardless of which foundation resume document you use, ensure that your folder and file are properly set up.

try this! To view all the styles used in the C:\resume\resume.doc file, follow these steps:

1 Open C:\resume\resume.doc.
2 Click Tools on the menu bar, click Options, and then click the View tab.
3 On the View tab, type 1 in the Style Area Width text box, and then click OK. The view will change to include a Style Area pane that shows the name of each style applied to each element in the document, as shown here:

Style drop-down list

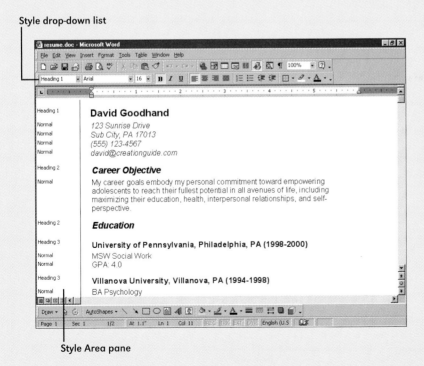

Style Area pane

4 You can resize or hide the Style Area pane by dragging the pane's right-side rule line or by replacing the 1 with a 0 or another measurement in the Style Area Width text box on the View tab of the Options dialog box.

try this! To practice applying styles, try reformatting David Goodhand's name using the Heading 2 style instead of Heading 1. To do so, take these steps:

1 Open C:\resume\resume.doc.
2 Select the David Goodhand text.
3 Click the Style drop-down list on the Formatting toolbar, and then click Heading 2.
4 To change the text back to the Heading 1 style, reselect the David Goodhand text, click the Style drop-down list, and click Heading 1.

Following the Wizard's Lead

Finally, we've arrived at the fun part—creating a Web site using the Web Page Wizard. So let's not spend any more time philosophizing; let's get started:

1 Open Word, click File, and then click New. The New dialog box opens.
2 In the New dialog box, click the Web Pages tab and then choose the Web Page Wizard icon.
3 Ensure that the Document option is selected, and then click OK. The first Web Page Wizard dialog box opens, as shown in Figure 9-11.

Figure 9-11
The Web Page Wizard's opening dialog box, which briefly outlines the upcoming steps

4 Click Next. The Title And Location dialog box displays. In the Web Site Title text box, type *Welcome to David Goodhand's Online Resume* and display (or type) *c:\resume* in the Web Site Location text box.
5 Click Next. The Navigation dialog box displays, as shown in Figure 9-12.

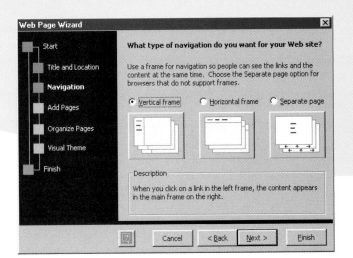

Figure 9-12
Selecting where you want to display your Web site's navigation links

6 In the Navigation dialog box, ensure the Vertical Frame option is selected and then click Next. The Add Pages dialog box displays, as shown in Figure 9-13.

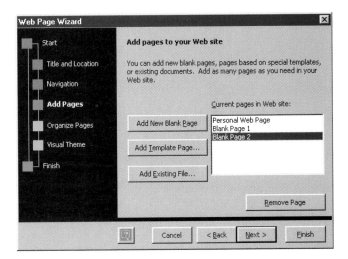

Figure 9-13
Viewing the Add Pages dialog box before customizing your site's setup.

David Goodhand's resume site includes a home page and pages for Education, Experience, and Volunteer Activities. Thus his site incorporates four pages. You use the Add Pages dialog box to create the number of pages you want to include in your Web site.

7 In the Add Pages dialog box in the Current Pages In Web Site list box, select the Personal Web Page entry and click the Remove Page button. The Personal Web Page item is removed.

8   Click the Add Existing File button. The Open dialog box displays. Here's where you specify that you want to use the resume.doc file as your home page.

9   In the Open dialog box, navigate to C:\resume and then double-click the resume.doc file. The resume file is added to the Current Pages In Web Site list box on the Add Pages screen.

At this point, you should have the resume file and two blank pages listed in the Current Pages In Web Site list box. We determined earlier that David's site needs four pages. Therefore, we need to add one more page to the Web site.

10 On the Add Pages dialog box, click Add New Blank Page. Your modified Add Pages dialog box should look similar to Figure 9-14.

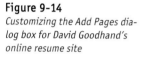

Figure 9-14
Customizing the Add Pages dialog box for David Goodhand's online resume site

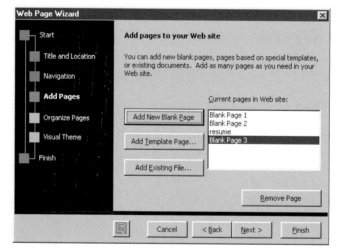

11 Click Next. The Organize Pages dialog box displays. You can use this dialog box to create a hierarchy for your Web pages and to rename the blank pages. The names you supply here are also the hyperlinks that display on your home page that link to the subpages.

12 In the list box, select *resume* and then click Move Up twice to position the file at the top of the list and specify that the resume file will serve as your home page.

13 With *resume* still selected, click the Rename button. The Rename Hyperlink dialog box displays.

14 Type *Home*, as shown in Figure 9-15, and then click OK.

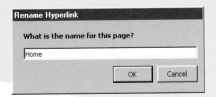

Figure 9-15
Renaming a page and specifying the hyperlink text in the navigation bar that will be associated with the page

15 Select Blank Page 1, click Rename, type *Education*, and then click OK.

16 Select Blank Page 2, click Rename, type *Experience*, and then click OK.

17 Select Blank Page 3, click Rename, type *Volunteer*, and then click OK. Your modified Organize Pages dialog box should look similar to the dialog box shown in Figure 9-16.

note

Be careful when using spaces in page names. Some servers don't support filenames and folder names with spaces.

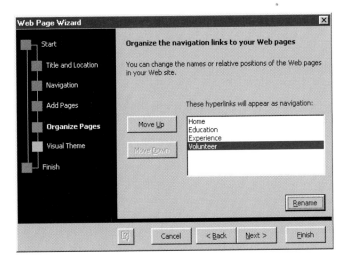

Figure 9-16
The modified Organize Pages dialog box

18 Click Next to access the Visual Theme dialog box.

At this point, you can pick from a variety of formatting themes to automatically style your Web pages. You can also choose not to use a theme. In this project, we'll select a theme so that you can experiment with the types of formatting offered by the Visual Theme feature.

19 On the Visual Theme dialog box, click the Browse Themes button. The Theme dialog box opens.

lingo

A *theme* is a coordinated set of fonts, colors, and graphics that are used to add visual appeal to a page or group of pages.

20 In the Theme dialog box, scroll down and select the Sumi Painting theme. Then ensure that the Vivid Colors and Background Image check boxes are selected, as shown in Figure 9-17.

Figure 9-17
Selecting Sumi Painting in the Theme dialog box

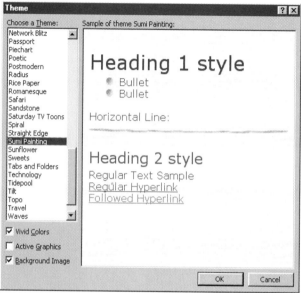

21 Click OK. The Visual Theme dialog box reappears. Your screen should look similar to the dialog box shown in Figure 9-18.

Figure 9-18
Completing the Visual Theme dialog box

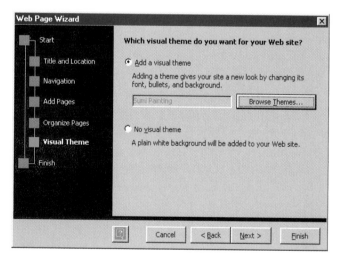

22 Click Next, and then click Finish.

After a few seconds, Word generates your Web site and displays your home page. At this point, your home page should look similar to the home page shown in Figure 9-19.

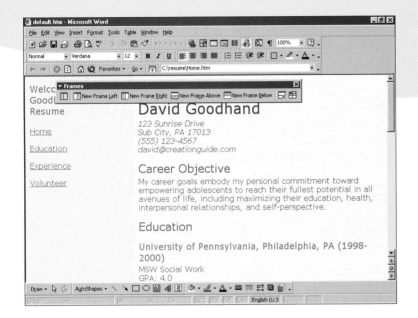

Figure 9-19
The final product of the Web Page Wizard

Notice that the Frames toolbar opens automatically because the page is divided into two frames (one frame for the navigator bar and the other for page content). Also notice that when you click the hyperlinks in the navigation bar, they will automatically display the page created to serve as each hyperlink's target page.

At this point, the job of the Web Page Wizard is done—you're now fully in charge of formatting the remainder of your Web page. We won't leave you hanging, though. In the remainder of the chapter, we'll explain various ways that you can customize, format, clean up, smooth out, and generally add a more professional look to your Web pages.

Tweaking the Navigation Bar Settings

In this section, you'll perform a couple small tweaks to modify the navigation bar. When we initially created David's resume site, we weren't too happy with the width and yellow hue of the navigation pane, so we adjusted those elements. In addition, we played with the Welcome text a little to clean up its appearance. You can follow the next few steps to modify the navigation bar.

note

After Word generates your Web site, you can close the Frames toolbar. You won't need it in this project to customize your Web site.

1 To make the navigation bar narrower, click the right edge of the yellow area and drag the frame's edge left to the 2-inch mark.

2 Select the *Welcome to David Goodhand's Online Resume* text, click the Font Color button on the Formatting toolbar in Word, and then click the White color square. Don't worry if the text is hard to read at this point—you're going to change the yellow background next.

3 Click a portion of the navigation bar's yellow background. (Clicking anywhere within the navigation bar ensures that the next procedure applies to the navigation frame and not the content frame of your Web page.)

4 On the menu bar, click Format, click Background, and then click the Blue-Gray color square (second row from the top, second-to-the-last color square in the row). You can view each color square's name by positioning your cursor over the square; after a couple seconds, the color's name will display.

5 To clean up the welcome text, click directly before the *D* in *David* and press Enter. Click directly before the *O* in *Online* and press Enter. (Adding hard returns helps to control how the text will display within the navigation bar.)

Your home page should now look more professional, as shown in Figure 9-20.

Figure 9-20
Modifying text and background colors to enhance the look of David's resume

Adding Text to Subpages

At this point, we should start to pay some attention to the Web site's subpages. Our plan is to move the appropriate text from the home page to an associated subpage. In other words, we're going to cut and paste text from the home page to subpages. We could've initially created a number of files and automatically included the information on each subpage (by adding existing files instead of blank pages in the Web Page Wizard), but we also want to include a hyperlink to a printable resume. Therefore, it made more sense in this project to create a single document that we'll link to later as a printable document. Cutting and pasting information is quick and easy—especially because the wizard has already set up hyperlinks to the site's subpages, so our plan of attack makes sense. To reorganize David Goodhand's text, follow these steps:

1   On the home page, select David's education information—heading and all—as shown in Figure 9-21.

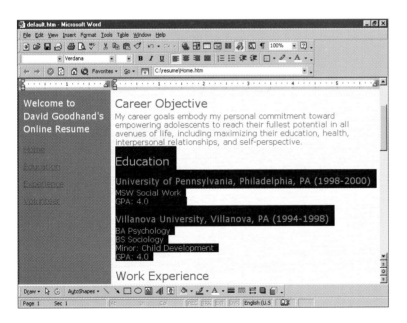

Figure 9-21
Selecting text to cut and paste

2   Press Ctrl+X, or click the Cut button on the Standard toolbar.

3   In the navigation bar, double-click the Education link. The Education page displays in the right-hand frame.

4 Select the This Page Is Education text on the Education page, and then press Ctrl+V or click the Paste button on the Standard toolbar. The education text displays on the Education page.

5 Double-click the Home link.

6 Select the Work Experience text, press Ctrl+X, and then double-click the Experience link in the navigation bar.

7 Select the This Page Is Experience text on the Experience page, and press Ctrl+V.

8 Double-click the Home link.

9 Select the Volunteer Activities text, press Ctrl+X, and then double-click the Volunteer link in the navigation bar.

10 Select the This Page Is Volunteer text on the Experience page, and press Ctrl+V.

11 Double-click the Home link.

You should now be able to double-click each link in the navigation bar to see the appropriate text on each linked page. Figure 9-22 shows thumbnail views of the Web site's pages at this point in development.

Figure 9-22
Thumbnails of the Web site's four pages

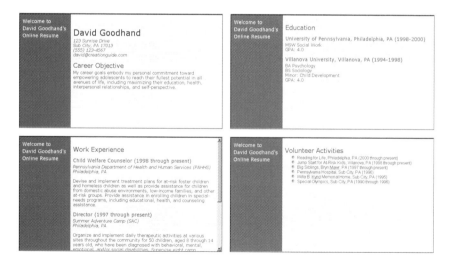

Saving and Closing Your Site

Now that you have the foundation of your Web site in place, we think it's a good time to save and close your files. When you create a Web site using the Web Page Wizard in Word, you'll find that you have quite a few open files in your taskbar. Therefore, just to streamline activities and to ensure that you'll know how to save, quit, and reopen your Web site files, we're interrupting your regularly scheduled formatting tasks with some mundane workaday tasks:

1 Click the Save button in the Standard toolbar. Then close all the windows associated with your Web site, and click Yes in each dialog box that asks if you want to save changes.

2 After all your files are saved and closed, you can reopen your home page in Word by opening Word, clicking File, clicking Open, navigating to C:\resume, selecting default.htm, and then clicking the Open button. Keep in mind that if you click default.htm within the resume folder view, you'll display the .htm file in your browser window.

Granted, the saving, closing, and reopening tasks aren't that thrilling, but following this routine is smart, especially if you decide to spread out this project over a couple days. Plus, by closing the wizard-created pages, you'll reduce the number of windows you have open while you work.

Creating and Inserting WordArt

You might recall in Part One of this book that we promised to show you how to use the WordArt tool in Word to create text graphics for your Web pages. Well, WordArt time is upon us. When we created David's online resume, we felt it needed some spicing up graphically. We thought the best way to incorporate some graphical elements would be to add some WordArt and a small amount of clip art (namely, a horizontal rule). In this section, we'll show you how to use WordArt. Then in the next section, we'll talk about clip art.

An obvious way to use WordArt on David's resume was to create a graphical image out of his name, which we did. Just follow these steps to get a result similar to ours:

1 Open C:\resume\default.htm in Word.

2 Click in the right frame, and ensure that paragraph marks are showing. (If they aren't showing, click the Show/Hide ¶ button in the Standard toolbar.) Then select the David Goodhand text along with the text's paragraph marker, as shown in Figure 9-23.

note

The Web Page Wizard saves your home page as default.htm instead of index.htm. Most servers will recognize either filename as a home page. Verify with your hosting service (if you have one) that the server recognizes default.htm as the page it will show if no filename is specified in a Web address. (For example, when you type *www.domain-name.com* in your browser's address bar, the domain's server assumes that you want to see the default.htm page.) Most likely, *default.htm* will work fine. In our case, as if to illustrate our point, the *www.creationguide.com* hosting service required us to rename the default.htm page to index.html.

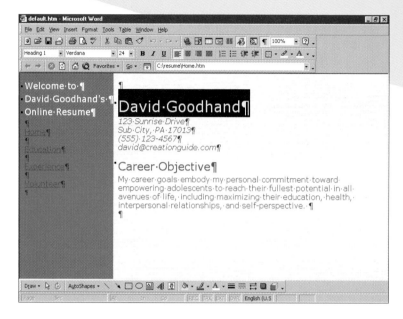

3   Press Delete, and then click the Show/Hide ¶ button to hide the paragraph markers.

4   On the menu bar, click Insert, point to Picture, and then click WordArt. The WordArt Gallery dialog box opens, as shown in Figure 9-24.

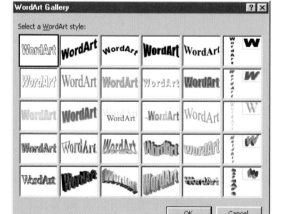

For this project, we'll use the first WordArt style, which is selected by default. If you want to choose another style, simply click on the square within the WordArt Gallery dialog box.

5 Ensure that the first WordArt sample is selected, and then click OK. The Edit WordArt Text dialog box displays.

6 Type *David Goodhand*, as shown in Figure 9-25, and ensure that the font is Arial Black and the size is 36. Then click OK. The WordArt displays on your home page as shown in Figure 9-26—but clearly, the graphic needs some added attention. Notice that the WordArt toolbar opens automatically. You'll see that the WordArt toolbar comes and goes depending on whether the WordArt element is selected.

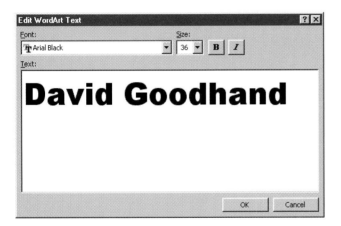

Figure 9-25
Adding text in the Edit WordArt Text dialog box

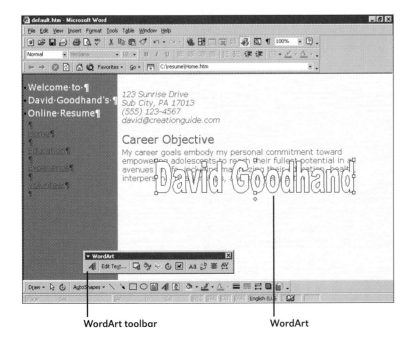

WordArt toolbar   WordArt

Figure 9-26
The first phase of adding WordArt

tip

You can also open the Format WordArt dialog box by clicking the Format WordArt button in the WordArt toolbar.

Figure 9-27
The Colors And Lines tab in the Format WordArt dialog box

7 Click in the center of the WordArt element (somewhere around the middle of the *G* would work nicely), and drag the element to the top-left area of the frame. It's OK if the WordArt overlays the address information— we're going to fix that in a moment.

8 After you've positioned the WordArt, right-click the WordArt element, and then select Format WordArt to access the Format WordArt dialog box.

9 On the Colors And Lines tab, click the Color drop-down list and then select the Blue-Gray color square (second row, second-to-the-last color square), as shown in Figure 9-27.

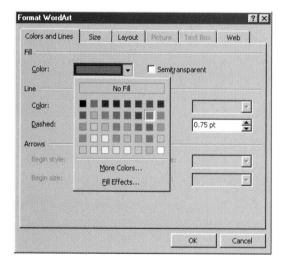

10 Click the Layout tab.

11 On the Layout tab, set the Wrapping Style to In Line With Text, as shown in Figure 9-28.

12 Click OK, and then click in a blank area on your Web page. Your WordArt element should now display as shown in Figure 9-29.

13 Click the Save button on the Standard toolbar to save your Web page with the WordArt element.

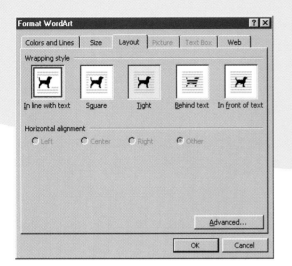

Figure 9-28
Specifying how text should wrap around the WordArt image

Figure 9-29
Viewing the WordArt image after specifying how surrounding text should wrap

Adding Clip Art

Now let's add a horizontal rule below the newly added WordArt on David's home page. You can find a number of Web page clip art items on the Microsoft Office 2000 CD. To insert a horizontal rule graphic in a Web page, follow the steps on the next page.

1 If necessary, click slightly to the left of the *1* in *123 Sunrise Drive*.

2 On the menu bar, click Insert, point to Picture, and then click Clip Art. The Insert ClipArt window opens.

3 Scroll to the bottom of the Categories window to view the Web categories, as shown in Figure 9-30.

Figure 9-30
The Web categories available in the Insert ClipArt window in Word

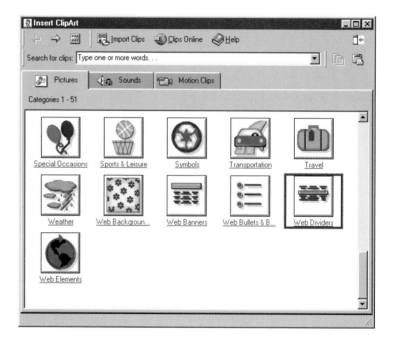

4 Click the Web Dividers category to access the horizontal rule graphics that you can insert into your Web pages.

5 Click the first item in the Web Dividers category, as shown in Figure 9-31, and then click the Insert Clip button (the top button) on the pop-up menu.

6 Close the Insert ClipArt window.

7 Right-click the horizontal rule, and select Format Horizontal Line. The Format Horizontal Line dialog box opens.

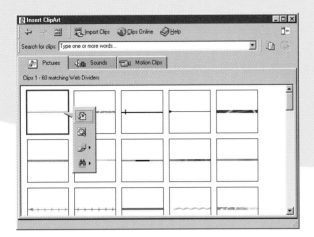

Figure 9-31
Choosing a Web divider graphic

8 Click the Measure In drop-down list box, and select Percent. When you assign a percentage to a horizontal rule line, the line will adjust to fit within the user's window.

9 In the Width text box, enter *100%*.

10 In the Alignment area, click the Left alignment box, as shown in Figure 9-32, and then click OK.

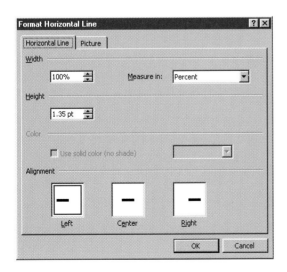

Figure 9-32
Setting a horizontal line's properties

11 Click in a blank area on your Web page, and then click the Save button. Your home page should look similar to the page shown in Figure 9-33.

Figure 9-33
David's home page with WordArt and a Web divider graphic

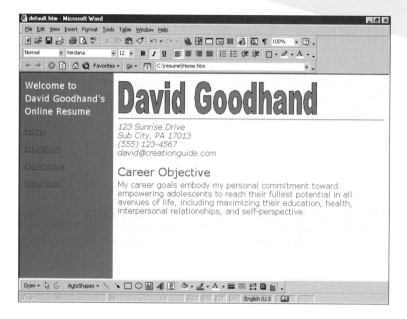

Copying Graphics to Subpages

Now that David's home page is shaping up, let's turn to the subpages once again. To visually tie the subpages to the home page, you can copy the WordArt and clip art on the home page to each subpage. Here's how you can accomplish this simple feat:

1 On the home page, click slightly to the left of the David Goodhand WordArt element, press and hold Shift, and then press the down arrow twice. The WordArt and clip art elements should be selected as shown in Figure 9-34.

2 Press Ctrl+C or the Copy button on the Standard toolbar.

3 Double-click the Education link in the navigation bar.

4 Ensure that your cursor is located in the upper-left corner of the right frame (it should be blinking there by default), and then press Ctrl+V or click the Paste button in the Standard toolbar.

Now let's reduce the size of the WordArt element on the subpage so that it isn't as large as the graphic on the home page. This little design trick helps visually cue viewers that they're on a subpage.

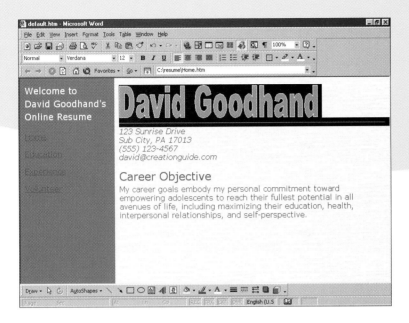

Figure 9-34
Selecting the WordArt and clip art

5 Right-click the freshly pasted WordArt element, and select the option Format WordArt.

6 In the Format WordArt dialog box, click the Size tab.

7 On the Size tab, click the Lock Aspect Ratio check box, and then type *80* in the Height text box. Click in the Width text box. The Width text box automatically adjusts to 80% as well, as shown in Figure 9-35.

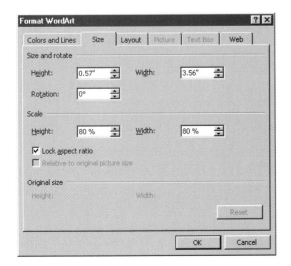

Figure 9-35
Resizing a WordArt element

8 Click OK, and then click in a blank area on the Education page to dese-lect the WordArt element. The Education Web page should now display as shown in Figure 9-36.

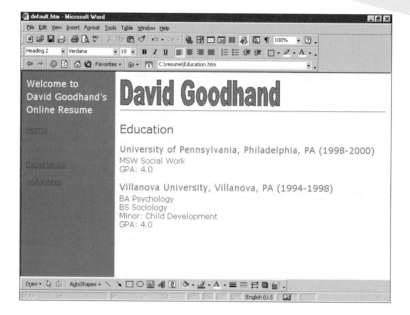

9 Select the newly resized WordArt element and horizontal rule, press Ctrl+C or click Copy in the Standard toolbar, double-click the Experience link in the navigation bar, ensure that the cursor displays in the up-per-left corner of the right-hand frame, and then press Ctrl+V or the Paste button in the Standard toolbar to paste the items into the Ex-perience page.

10 Double-click the Volunteer link, ensure that the cursor displays in the upper-left corner of the right-hand frame, and press Ctrl+V to paste the graphical elements into the Volunteer Activities page.

11 Save and close your Web site.

Working with Hyperlinks

Last but not least, we're going to show you how to work a little magic with hyperlinks. Namely, you're going to undertake the following hyperlink-related tasks to help finalize David's online resume site:

- Recolor existing hyperlinks so that they stand out more against the navigation bar's blue-gray background.

- Add a Print Version hyperlink so that viewers can print the entire resume on one page.

- Customize the ScreenTip text associated with each hyperlink in the navigation bar.

- Reformat the e-mail address as a Mail To hyperlink, and add the Mail To hyperlink to the subpages.

- Link the WordArt graphics to the home page.

Knowing how to accomplish the preceding tasks will give you a good grounding in mastering the art of working with hyperlinks. You'll need to know how to work with hyperlinks when you create your own custom Web pages. As usual, we'll start you off with the most basic task and work toward more complex tasks (although rest assured, none of this gets too convoluted). Our first hyperlinking escapade entails simply selecting a new color for the existing hyperlink style.

Modifying Hyperlink Styles

As discussed earlier, Word uses styles and templates to create pages. While you were working through the Web Page Wizard to create your template-based Web pages, you applied the Sumi Painting theme to your Web site's templates. (That's how the headings in your text document ended up being blue and purple on your Web pages.) The template the Web Page Wizard applied includes Hyperlink and FollowedHyperlink styles. So if you want to change the properties of all hyperlinks within a frame, you're better off changing the Hyperlink and FollowedHyperlink styles instead of formatting each hyperlink individually. In this section, we'll show you how to edit the Hyperlink and FollowedHyperlink styles so that you can change the purple hypertext links to yellow and the visited hyperlink text to lime green:

1 Open Word, and then open C:\resume\default.htm.

2 Click on a clear area of the navigation bar to select the frame.

3 On the menu bar, click Format, and then click Style. The Style dialog box opens.

4 In the Styles list, select Hyperlink, as shown in Figure 9-37.

Figure 9-37
Accessing the frame's Hyperlink style settings

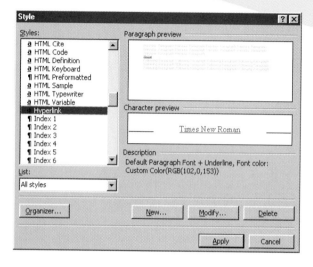

5 Click the Modify button. The Modify Style dialog box opens.

6 In the Modify Style dialog box, click the Format button, and then click Font on the pop-up menu, as shown in Figure 9-38. The Font dialog box displays.

Figure 9-38
Modifying a style's font properties

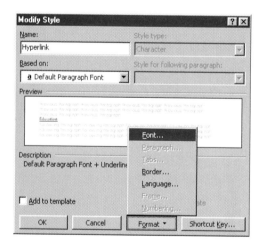

7 In the Font dialog box, click the Font Color drop-down list and click the Yellow color box (second-to-the-last row, third color from the left), as shown in Figure 9-39.

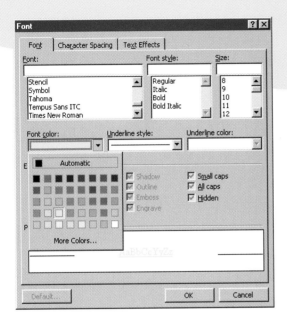

Figure 9-39
Selecting a new color for the Hyperlink style

8 Click OK twice.

9 In the Style dialog box, select FollowedHyperlink in the Styles list.

10 Click the Modify button.

11 In the Modify Style dialog box, click the Format button and then click Font on the pop-up menu.

12 In the Font dialog box, click the Font Color drop-down list and click the Lime color box (third row down, third color from the left).

13 Click OK twice, and then click Apply.

14 Click Save in the Standard toolbar, right-click the Home link, and select Update Field on the shortcut menu. The hyperlink is reset to the unvisited color (yellow).

15 Right-click the Education link, click Update Field, right-click Experience, click Update Field, right-click Volunteer, and click Update Field. The links should all be refreshed and display in yellow text.

16 Double-click the Education link, and then double-click the Home link. Figure 9-40 shows the Web site's new and improved hyperlink colors.

Figure 9-40
Hyperlinks after modifying the Hyperlink and FollowedHyperlink styles

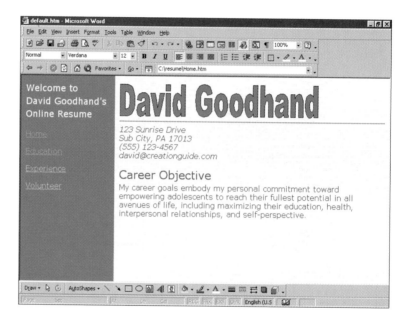

Adding Hyperlinks

Our next task is to add a hyperlink that provides a link to a text version of David's resume to the navigation bar. Basically, we'll add a pointer to the resume.doc file that's stored in the C:\resume folder. When you upload your Web pages, you'll also need to upload the text file to the server so viewers can access the text file online. To create a link pointing to resume.doc, follow these steps:

1 Click directly after the *r* in *Volunteer*, and then press Enter twice to position your cursor where you want to insert the Print Version hyperlink.

2 In the menu bar, click Insert and then click Hyperlink. The Insert Hyperlink dialog box displays. Figure 9-41 shows the Insert Hyperlink dialog box after the proper information is inserted.

tip

You can also press Ctrl+K to display the Insert Hyperlink dialog box.

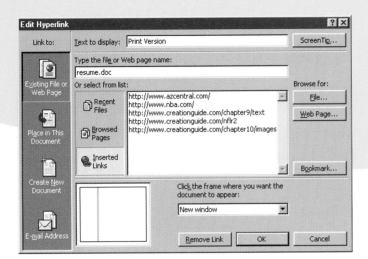

Figure 9-41
Creating a hyperlink

3 In the Text To Display text box, type *Print Version*. This text will display in your navigation bar.

4 In the Type The File Or Web Page Name text box, enter *resume.doc*. You don't have to indicate a path for the file because default.htm is stored in the same folder as resume.doc.

5 In the Click The Frame Where You Want The Document To Appear drop-down list, select New Window. Selecting New Window means that when viewers click the Print Version hyperlink, resume.doc will open as a Word file in a separate window.

6 Click the ScreenTip button. The Set Hyperlink ScreenTip dialog box opens. In the ScreenTip Text box, type *Click to open a Print Version of David's resume*, as shown in Figure 9-42.

7 Click OK to close the Set Hyperlink ScreenTip dialog box.

tip

Keep in mind that whenever you create hyperlinks, you must enter uppercase and lowercase letters in filenames accurately. Some servers are case-sensitive. If you enter the name of a linked page inaccurately, you'll end up with broken links on your Web site. For future reference, the Web Page Wizard capitalizes the first letter of automatically generated filenames by default.

lingo

A *ScreenTip* is descriptive text that pops up when the mouse cursor hovers over a hyperlink.

Figure 9-42
Adding ScreenTip text to the Print Version hyperlink

8 Click OK in the Insert Hyperlink dialog box. Then save the Web page. The navigation bar should now include the newly added Print Version hyperlink, as shown in Figure 9-43.

Figure 9-43
The new Print Version hyperlink

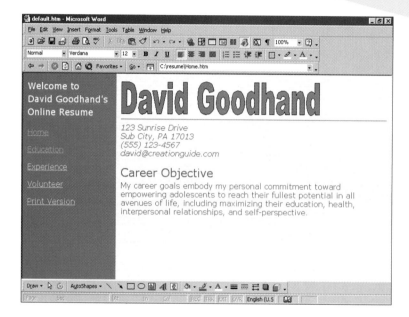

9 Click the Print Version hyperlink to see how the text document opens in a new window. Then close the text document.

Adding ScreenTips to Existing Hyperlinks

As you just saw, you can customize the text that pops up when viewers hold their mouse cursor over a hyperlink. By default, the Web Page Wizard displays the associated Web page's filename as the ScreenTip. You should change the default ScreenTip text to more user-friendly (or at least more entertaining) text. To do so, follow these steps:

1 Right-click the Home hyperlink in the navigation bar, click Hyperlink, and then click Edit Hyperlink. The Edit Hyperlink text box opens, which looks very much like the Insert Hyperlink text box shown in Figure 9-41.

2 Click the ScreenTip button, type *Home Page* in the Set Hyperlink ScreenTip dialog box, and then click OK twice.

3 Right-click the Education hyperlink in the navigation bar, click Hyperlink, and then click Edit Hyperlink.

4   Click the ScreenTip button, type *Educational Background* in the Set Hyperlink ScreenTip dialog box, and then click OK twice.

5   Right-click the Experience hyperlink in the navigation bar, click Hyperlink, and then click Edit Hyperlink.

6   Click the ScreenTip button, type *Work Experience* in the Set Hyperlink ScreenTip dialog box, and then click OK twice.

7   Right-click the Volunteer hyperlink in the navigation bar, click Hyperlink, and then click Edit Hyperlink.

8   Click the ScreenTip button, type *Recent Volunteer Activities* in the Set Hyperlink ScreenTip dialog box, and then click OK. Let's also modify this hyperlink's display text.

9   In the Text To Display text box, click after the *r* in *Volunteer*, press the spacebar, type *Activities*, and then click OK.

10   Click Save in the Standard toolbar, and then place your cursor over each hyperlink to view each link's ScreenTip text.

Creating a Mail To Hyperlink

Next on our agenda is to show you how to format David's e-mail address as a Mail To hyperlink. You can then copy the Mail To link to each subpage so the link is easily accessible to viewers.

Formatting a Mail To hyperlink is very similar to inserting a hyperlink. If you already have the e-mail address typed into the body of your Web page, the process is even easier:

1   On David Goodhand's home page, select the *david@creationguide.com* e-mail address, right-click the selected text, and click Hyperlink. The Insert Hyperlink dialog box opens with the e-mail address information already inserted.

2   In the Link To pane, click the E-mail Address icon. The Insert Hyperlink dialog box alters its contents so that you can specify e-mail settings, as shown in Figure 9-44. Notice that the Mail To options enable you to automatically provide Subject line text in the message as well as your e-mail address.

lingo

A *Mail To* hyperlink is a link that automatically opens a preaddressed blank e-mail message form when a user clicks the link.

Figure 9-44
The Mail To options in the Insert Hyperlink dialog box

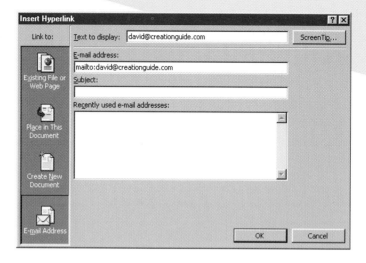

note

Notice that the Mail To hyperlink displays in purple instead of yellow. The hyperlink displays in the theme's default color scheme because earlier in this chapter, you customized the Hyperlink and FollowedHyperlink styles only in the navigation bar frame, not in the main fame.

tip

Always check hyperlinks after you create them to ensure that you formatted the hyperlink's properties properly and that the hyperlink responds in the way you intended.

3 Click the ScreenTip button, and add the following text in the Set Hyperlink ScreenTip dialog box: *Please send your comments to David Goodhand.*

4 Click OK to close the ScreenTip dialog box, and then click OK to close the Insert Hyperlinks dialog box. The e-mail address now displays as a hyperlink.

Word precedes a newly created Mail To hyperlink with the text *mailto:* if you don't modify the text entered in the Text To Display text box in the Insert Hyperlink dialog box. You can remove the superfluous text by editing the Mail To hyperlink.

5 Right-click the *mailto:david@creationguide.com* hyperlink, click Hyperlink, and then click Edit Hyperlink. The Edit Hyperlink dialog box opens.

6 In the Text To Display text box, delete the *mailto:* text that displays be-fore the *david@creationguide.com* text and then click OK.

7 Click the link to ensure that a blank e-mail message form opens when the Mail To link is clicked. Close the message form after it opens.

Finally, to simplify the process for anyone who wants to send an e-mail message to David, you can copy the e-mail address hyperlink to each subpage.

8 Select the linked e-mail address, press Ctrl+C to copy the link, and then double-click the Education hyperlink in the navigation bar.

9 Click to the right of the horizontal rule, press Enter, and then press Ctrl+V to paste the Mail To hyperlink onto the page, as shown in Figure 9-45.

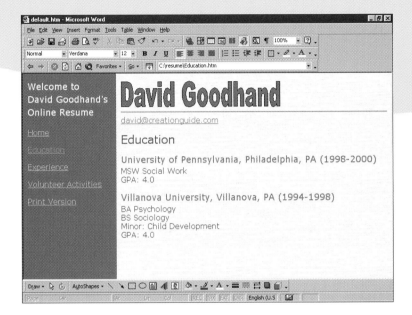

Figure 9-45
Copying the Mail To link to subpages

10 Double-click the Experience hyperlink in the navigation bar, click to the right of the horizontal rule, press Enter, and then press Ctrl+V to paste the Mail To hyperlink onto the page.

11 Double-click the Volunteer Activities hyperlink in the navigation bar, click to the right of the horizontal rule, press Enter, and then press Ctrl+V to paste the Mail To hyperlink onto the page.

12 Click Save in the Standard toolbar to save your changes, and then close all open documents.

Linking Graphics

Our last task will be to format graphical elements as hyperlinks. (Remember this technique when you want to link graphical buttons to subpages.) For David's online resume, you can link the WordArt elements on David's subpages to the site's home page, as follows:

1 Open Word, open C:\resume\default.htm, and then double-click the Education hyperlink to display the Education page.

tip

After you copy the email hyperlink onto a page, you might have to delete an extra line space between the e-mail hyperlink and the following heading.

2 Click the WordArt component and click the Hyperlink button in the Standard toolbar, or right-click the WordArt component and click Hyperlink. The Insert Hyperlink dialog box opens.

3 Click the ScreenTip button, add the following ScreenTip text: *Click to return to the Home Page*, and click OK.

4 In the Link To area, ensure that the Existing File Or Web Page icon is selected.

5 In the Type The File Or Web Page Name text box, enter *C:\resume\ Home.htm*.

6 In the lower portion of the dialog box, click the right frame in the page layout image (to the left of the Click The Frame Where You Want The Document To Appear text), as shown in Figure 9-46.

Figure 9-46
Formatting the WordArt graphic as a hyperlink

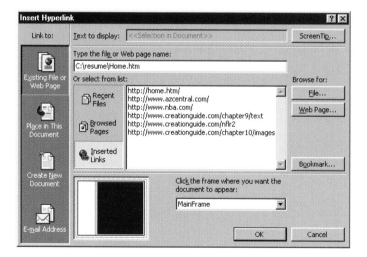

7 Click OK, and then click the WordArt component to ensure that the home page text displays in the main frame.

8 Double-click the Experience hyperlink in the navigation bar.

9 Click the WordArt component, click the Hyperlink button in the Standard toolbar, and then repeat steps 3 through 7.

10 Double-click the Volunteer Activities hyperlink.

11 Click the WordArt component, click the Hyperlink button in the Standard toolbar, and then repeat steps 3 through 7.

12 Save your changes, and then close the Web documents.

Previewing Your Word-Generated Web Page

Congratulations! You've completed the online resume project. In the process, you've learned how to use the Web Page Wizard and you've gotten quite a bit of hands-on experience in modifying Web pages, including adding components and working with hyperlinks, WordArt, and styles. Now you can preview all your hard work.

As mentioned toward the beginning of this chapter, you can preview your Web pages in a number of ways. At this point, you might as well look at the pages in your Web browser so that you can see how the pages will display and how well your hyperlinks work. To view your Web site in your browser, simply display the contents of C:\resume and then click default.htm to open the HTML document in a browser window. Figure 9-47 shows thumbnails of the completed Web site's pages. As a finalization step, remember to click your hyperlinks to ensure that your Web page responds properly to users' requests and to test the Print Version link and the linked WordArt features.

note

If you opted to read through this chapter without creating the Web site or if you want to compare your site to the Web pages we developed for this project, you can view David Goodhand's completed online resume at *www.creationguide.com/ resume.*

Figure 9-47
Previewing David Goodhand's completed online resume Web site

After you preview and test your Web site on your computer, your site will be ready for uploading to a server.

see also Chapter 11 describes how you can go about uploading your Web site to a server when you're ready to make your site live.

Additional Resources

As you might know, numerous Word 2000 books and resources exist, and they all cover much more than Web page creation features. To help narrow down the field, we've listed four of our favorite Word 2000 resources:

- Camarda, Bill. *Special Edition Using Word 2000*. Indianapolis, IN: Que, 1999. ISBN: 0-7897-1852-9. This book covers Word 2000 features in depth for intermediate-level readers.

- Glenn, Walter. *Word 2000 in a Nutshell*. Sebastopol, CA: O'Reilly, 2000. ISBN: 1-56592-489-4. This book serves as a good feature-by-feature review of the menus and tools in Word 2000.

- Rubin, Charles. *Running Microsoft Word 2000*. Redmond, WA: Microsoft Press, 1999. ISBN: 1-57231-943-7. This book provides comprehensive coverage of the features in Word and serves as a good Word 2000 documentation guide.

- ***www.microsoft.com/office/word*** Microsoft's official home page for Word users. Visit this site often to learn new tricks, access support, and stay on top of possible software updates.

key points

■ You can use Word 2000 to create Web pages by using the Save As feature, Web page templates, or the Web Page Wizard.

■ After you save a document as an HTML page in Word, you can edit the Web page in Word view or you can access the HTML source code to edit the HTML commands directly.

■ Word 2000 provides a number of Web page templates on the Web Pages tab of the New dialog box.

■ Templates help you to quickly add headings, hyperlinks, columns, frames, and other Web page features to a blank document.

■ The Web Page Wizard can assist you in formulating entire Web sites, including home pages, subpages, themes, and other common Web site components.

■ Applying styles to your text simplifies your task when you apply themes to your Web pages.

■ After you create Web pages, you can customize and modify Web page text and components using many of the standard features and tools in Word.

NEPT

JUPITER

MARS

EARTH

MERCURY

VENUS

going

When you watch the news on TV, the only "equipment" you need is the TV, a place to sit, and a basic remote control. But what about when you rent a video or order a pay-per-view movie that's filled with cool special effects and has an awesome soundtrack? Instead of turning to grandma's 15-inch hand-me-down TV, you'd probably prefer the ultimate in home entertainment systems: you know, the rare setup that can be easily controlled by a *single* remote control and that has an ultra-clear big-screen TV, digital cable, Dolby stereo, and a full range of audio equipment artfully blending into the shadows—

all out:
CREATING WEB SITES WITH FRONTPAGE

all strategically placed for optimal viewing and listening pleasure from the comfortable folds of an enormous leather couch. Granted, these "extras" aren't strictly necessary, but they sure can make a big difference sometimes. The same can be said of HTML editors. Notepad (a basic text editor) can be likened to the "TV, seat, and remote control" way of creating Web pages, whereas FrontPage provides the luxury-home-entertainment-system approach to Web site development. In this chapter, we're going for the "extras."

To create the Web pages described in this chapter, you'll need the following "supplies":

- Microsoft FrontPage 2000 or later

- An Internet connection (An Internet connection is necessary to download the sample project's graphics and text files from the Creation Guide Web site.)

- The mars.doc and thankyou.htm text documents downloaded from *www.creationguide.com/chapter10/text*. To download these files, create a folder named "astronomy" on your computer's hard drive. (For convenience, we'll refer to your hard drive as the C:\ drive throughout this chapter.) Then connect to *www.creationguide.com/chapter10/text*, right-click mars.doc, and save the file to the C:\astronomy folder on your computer. Repeat the process to save thankyou.htm to your C:\astronomy folder.

- The following figures downloaded from *www.creationguide.com/chapter10/images*:

b_aboutus.gif	bg.gif	neptune.jpg
b_aboutus2.gif	bigdip1.gif	saturn.jpg
b_contact.gif	bigdip2.gif	solarsystem.gif
b_contact2.gif	bigdip3.gif	t_aboutus.gif
b_gallery.gif	bigdip4.gif	t_contact.gif
b_gallery2.gif	bigdip5.gif	t_gallery.gif
b_links.gif	corner_botm_left.gif	t_links.gif
b_links2.gif	corner_botm_right.gif	t_meetings.gif
b_meetings.gif	corner_top_left.gif	t_skyguide.gif
b_meetings2.gif	corner_top_right.gif	titlebar-home.gif
b_skyguide.gif	logo.gif	titlebar.gif
b_skyguide2.gif	mars.jpg	

To obtain these figures, first create an images folder in C:\astronomy. Then connect to *www.creationguide.com/chapter10/images*, right-click an image's filename (or the Zip file if your computer is set up to open Zip files), and save a copy of the file to the C:\astronomy\images folder on your computer, as shown in Figure 10-1. Repeat the process for each image.

tip

If you're Zip savvy, you can download the file ZIP_images10.zip and extract the images locally.

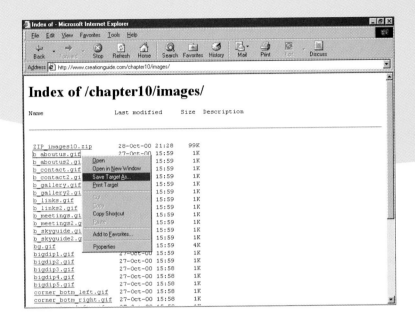

Figure 10-1
Downloading image files from the Internet

Introducing FrontPage:
A Full-Featured HTML Editor

For this book's final project, we're going to show you how to use Microsoft FrontPage to create a fairly advanced Web site. FrontPage is a full-featured HTML editor that you can purchase as a stand-alone application or as part of Microsoft Office Premium. As you'll see in this chapter, using a true HTML editor such as FrontPage opens numerous doors to Web page design for beginning designers. Full-scale HTML editors also provide some handy shortcuts for more seasoned designers. Our goal is to give you firsthand experience in creating a Web site that uses a number of Web page elements that are easily implemented using full-fledged HTML editors. These elements include (but are not limited to) the following:

■ **Button rollover effects**   Buttons that seem to glow or change appearance in other ways when users place their cursors over the buttons. (By the way, when a user places a mouse cursor over a button or hyperlink, this action is called *hovering*.)

■ **Image map**   A picture with clickable areas that link to related pages or other areas on the current page. The image serves as a directory, and users access information by clicking an area of the picture, such as clicking New York on a U.S. map to display a Web page about New York.

■ **Marquee text**   Text that slides in from the edge of the page (left or right) like tickertape. You can create marquee text that slides in once and then stays put, repeats a specified number of times, or repeats continuously.

■ **Thumbnails**   Small images that link to larger images. Thumbnails enable users to decide whether they want to view a larger version of an image (which might take extra time to download).

■ **Counter**   A component that displays the number of times users have accessed the Web page. The counter number increments (increases) by 1 each time a visitor accesses the page.

Before you see how easily you can use FrontPage to create all the preceding elements, let's give the FrontPage interface a quick once-over to preview where you're headed.

Strolling Past the FrontPage Window

Much of the FrontPage interface is similar to that of other Office applications. In other words, when you first open FrontPage, you'll probably feel that it looks quite familiar—that is, if you're used to working in Office. In fact, at first glance, you'll see the Standard and Formatting toolbars across the top, menu bar options, a workspace area, and a status bar along the bottom. But in addition to the standard fare, FrontPage offers a couple key interface options to assist you in creating Web pages. Namely, the FrontPage interface includes a Views bar and three view tabs—Normal, HTML, and Preview—as shown in Figure 10-2. These elements will help you track the multiple files and folders of your Web site, preview Web pages during development, edit HTML source code, manage hyperlinks, and more. For example, you can use the HTML tab to access a Web page's source code, as shown in Figure 10-3, and the Preview tab to preview Web pages as you build them, as shown in Figure 10-4. You'll be using all three views in this chapter's project.

As you'll soon see, taking advantage of many of the features in FrontPage requires you merely to select menu options, click toolbar buttons, and complete dialog boxes—activities you should be accustomed to if you're a veteran of other Office programs, such as Microsoft Word. Therefore, although FrontPage is considered a high-end HTML editor with advanced Web development capabilities, you should feel comfortable working within its interface pretty quickly—even if you've never composed so much as a single text-based Web page in an HTML editor. Regardless of any predevelopment jitters, we're confident that if you work through this chapter's project, you'll have a strong grasp of the capabilities of FrontPage.

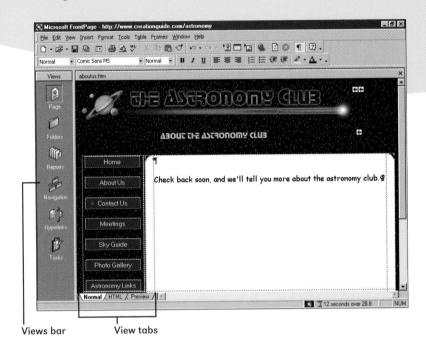

Figure 10-2
Designing a FrontPage Web page in Normal view

Views bar   View tabs

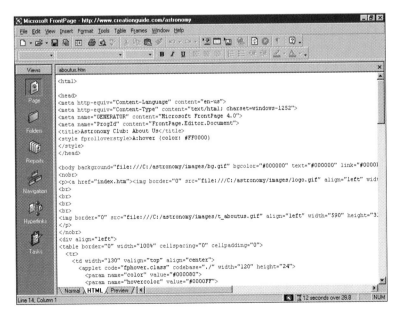

Figure 10-3
Viewing a FrontPage Web page's source code in HTML view

Figure 10-4
Using Preview view to see how a FrontPage Web page in progress will appear online

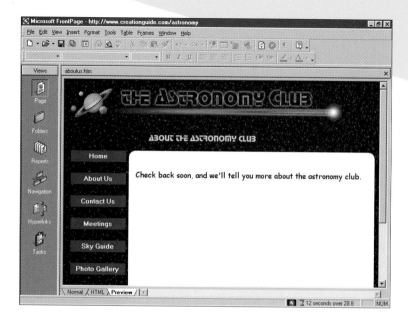

The Advantages of Using FrontPage

Like all full-service HTML editors, FrontPage sports some definite advantages. FrontPage is fairly easy to use (once you know where to look and what you're looking for), it provides many advanced design features, and it creates HTML code automatically. Using FrontPage, you can easily create professional-looking Web pages with just a few clicks. Throughout the project in this chapter, we're going to highlight a lot of the functionality in FrontPage. Our reasoning for covering a wide range of FrontPage capabilities also includes a hidden benefit:

> Not only will you learn how to create Web pages in FrontPage, but you'll also learn about HTML editors in general.

The key to mastering HTML editors (or any type of application) is to learn the types of functionalities commonly available within most HTML editors. For example, you know that most word processing applications have a Find feature. Thus, regardless of the word processing application you're using, if you need to find text, you probably look automatically for the application's Find or Search tool. Similarly, with HTML editors, if you learn some of the capabilities of FrontPage—and it has a lot of them—you can benefit from that knowledge when you work in similar environments. So using FrontPage as a model, you'll be introduced to a selection of tasks that most HTML editors offer. That way, if you later decide to design Web pages using another HTML editor, you'll have a good idea of the types of features to look for. Or if you decide to design your Web pages in FrontPage, you'll be way ahead of the game.

FrontPage Server Extensions

The final issue we need to touch on before we get going on the chapter project is *FrontPage Server Extensions*, which are specific to FrontPage. Before the onset of advanced HTML editors, developers had to write, buy, or copy code to enable certain Web page features, such as forms, counters, Java programs, and so forth. FrontPage provides the code for many of these features, enabling designers to easily include functionality that requires some coding—without having to code themselves or acquire the code in some other way. The catch is that your server (or your hosting service) needs to support FrontPage Server Extensions. So before you go crazy using the advanced design features of FrontPage, check with your Web hosting service to verify that they support FrontPage Server Extensions.

lingo

FrontPage Server Extensions are installed on servers to enable additional functionality in Web pages created or imported in FrontPage.

Editing Existing FrontPage Sites
One of the convenient features of FrontPage is its online editing capabilities. When you install FrontPage, the Edit With Microsoft FrontPage command is automatically added to the Microsoft Internet Explorer toolbar, via the Edit button, as shown here:

You can quickly edit your online Web pages by displaying your Web page in Internet Explorer and clicking the Edit button. After you click Edit, FrontPage opens automatically, asks for your user ID and password, and then displays the page for editing.

After you're satisfied with your changes, you can click Save in FrontPage to automatically save and upload the changed version of your Web page to your server. This quick-access editing feature is great for making small tweaks and fixing typos. But be careful when you're making major changes to your Web page. By default, after you've made changes to a downloaded Web page, clicking Save in FrontPage overwrites your existing online Web page; reverting to your "old" Web page might be tricky or nearly impossible after you save the modified version online.

In this day and age, most hosting services support FrontPage Server Extensions. You'll definitely find some exceptions, including hosting services that support some but not all of the FrontPage Server Extensions. So if you're shopping for a hosting service and think you'll be using FrontPage extensively (and you might appreciate the benefit of that approach by the time you've reached the end of the chapter project), you'll want to ensure that your hosting service supports FrontPage Server Extensions fairly extensively before you plunk down any cash and commit to the hosting service's plan. For our purposes in this chapter, however, you don't need to have server space to create the project. For the most part, you build the site locally on your computer, so you won't need to worry about server space and FrontPage Server Extensions until you're ready to publish your Web site online (that is, go live) or if you want to test the publishing feature in FrontPage by publishing the project site. We'll talk a little about publishing FrontPage sites later in this chapter, but you'll need to consult one of the references in the section "Additional Resources" for a full discussion of this topic.

At this point, you know enough to get started on the project. So let's forge our final frontier in this book's Web-site-development section and have some fun creating a Web site in FrontPage!

Planning Your FrontPage Web Site

When we initially planned this chapter's project site, we intended to create a team page featuring a fictitious softball team. Unfortunately, we couldn't bribe enough of our friends to pose for the team picture, so we opted to create a Web site for an astronomy club instead. (By the way, this site has nothing to do with the Visiting family we created an MSN Communities site for in Chapter 7 and a lot to do with the fact that we recently bought a new telescope!) We ended up incorporating many of the functionalities we had originally planned for the softball site into the astronomy site. For example, instead of making an image map out of a team picture, in which you could click each person's head to access a stats or personal page, we used a solar system image map in which you can click each planet to access a page of information about that planet. We hope that as you experiment with the techniques we present in this project, you'll begin to think of ways you can vary them to create custom Web sites.

After determining that an astronomy club site would suit our purposes, we decided that the site should consist of a custom home page linking to standard-format subpages. Using a nonstandard home page is a common Web site design technique used to make the home page stand out from the subpages. Because FrontPage offers so many options, we felt that showing a nonstandard home page made good design sense and would also enable us to show you a few additional features of FrontPage. To see our planning process, take a look at Figures 10-5 through 10-7. Figure 10-5 shows a sketch of the Big Dipper design we came up with for the home page. Figure 10-6 shows the sketch of the standard subpage layout. And finally, Figure 10-7 shows the astronomy club site's storyboard.

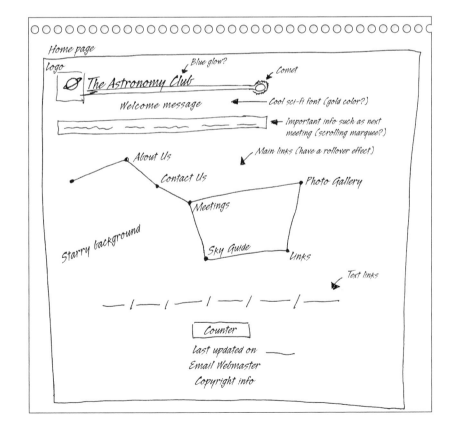

Figure 10-5
Sketching the astronomy club's home page

Figure 10-6
Sketching the astronomy club's subpages

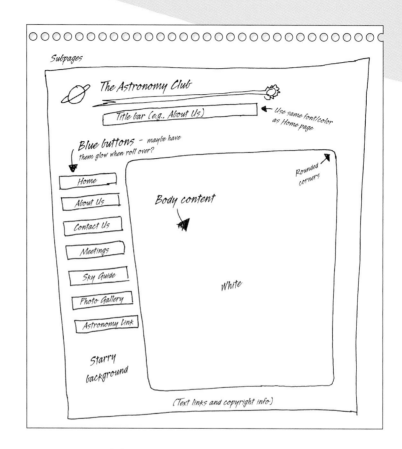

Because of the relative complexity of the home page, we're going to create that page last. In this project, we'll start the design process by solidifying the site's standard layout for subpages by creating a subpage.htm document that you can use as a template to create the site's pages. But first, before you begin building Web pages, you need to tell FrontPage that you want to create a new Web.

Creating a New Web

As we just mentioned, the first step to designing a Web site is to express your Web-page-building intentions to FrontPage by creating a new Web. To do so, follow the simple steps that start on the next page.

note

FrontPage refers to Web sites as *Webs*.

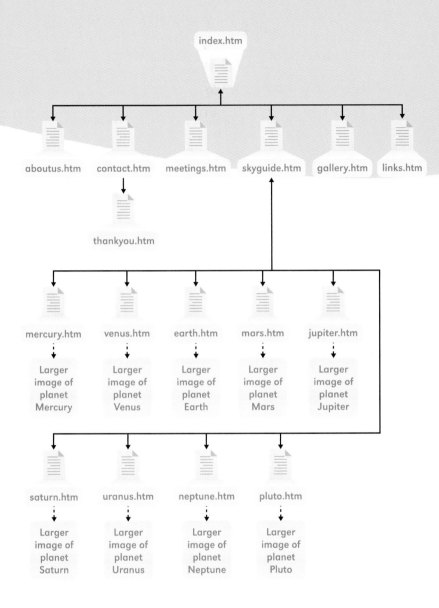

Figure 10-7
Storyboarding the astronomy club's Web site

1 Ensure that you've created a folder named C:\astronomy\images in which you've stored the images you downloaded from *www.creationguide.com/ chapter10/images*. Also be sure that you've downloaded mars.doc and thankyou.htm from *www.creationguide.com/chapter10/text* and stored the files in C:\astronomy.

2 Open FrontPage.

3 On the File menu, select New and then click Web. The New dialog box opens, as shown in Figure 10-8.

Figure 10-8
Creating a new Web

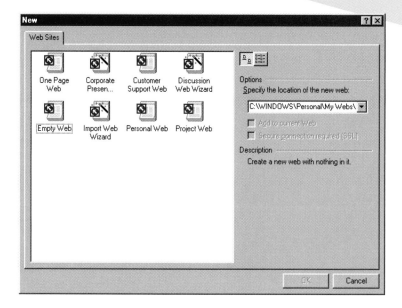

4 Click the Empty Web icon, click in the Specify The Location Of The New Web text box, highlight the existing text, type *C:\astronomy*, and then click OK. After a moment, FrontPage displays a message box that asks if you want to convert the specified folder to a Web.

5 In the message box, click Yes. After some brief processing in which FrontPage adds FrontPage Server Extensions to your Web folder (C:\astronomy), you'll see a blank page ready for action.

6 In the Views bar, click the Reports icon. A site summary like the one shown in Figure 10-9 appears. This report displays because you have graphics stored in C:\astronomy\images and mars.doc and thankyou.htm stored in C:\astronomy. Notice in Figure 10-9 (and in your own FrontPage window) that C:\astronomy now displays in the FrontPage title bar.

note

Although having all the images you plan to use on your Web site ready up front is convenient, it's not necessary. But because the astronomy club's graphics are readily available (and because this book is about creating Web pages, not Web graphics), you can simplify creating the Web in this project (or any project for that matter) by organizing the graphics for the site before you start creating it.

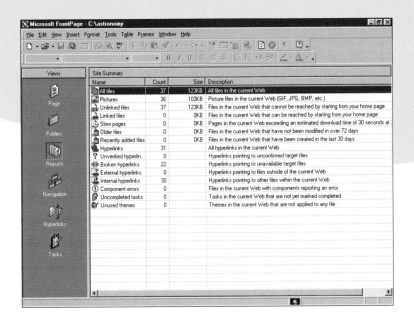

Figure 10-9
The astronomy Web's summary report

7 Click the Page icon in the Views bar to return to the blank page.

You're now ready to create a standard subpage that you can use as a template for the astronomy club's Web site.

Creating the Subpage Layout

In this section, you'll create a standard subpage layout that you'll be able to copy and use to create foundation pages for each subpage in the site. First you'll set the subpage's page properties.

Setting Page Properties

To begin, ensure that you have a blank workspace displaying in FrontPage. If you followed the steps in the preceding section, you should be set. Here are the steps to create a basic subpage:

1 Right-click a blank area on the page, and select Page Properties. The Page Properties dialog box opens.

2 In the Title text box, type *The Astronomy Club*, as shown in Figure 10-10.

3 Click the Background tab, select the Background Picture check box to specify that you want the page to use a background picture, and then click Browse. The Select Background Picture dialog box opens.

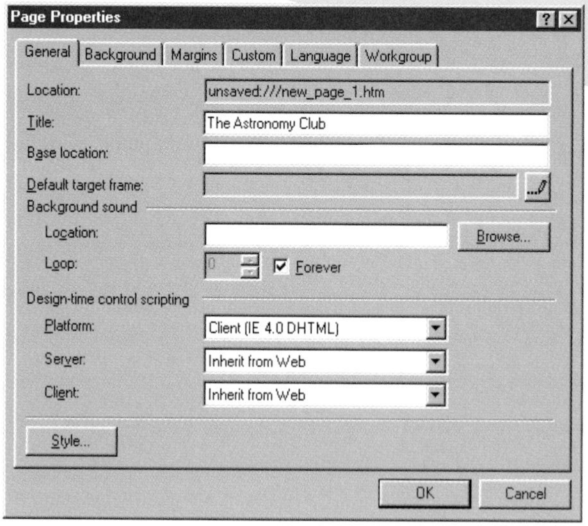

Figure 10-10

Entering Title text in the Page Properties dialog box

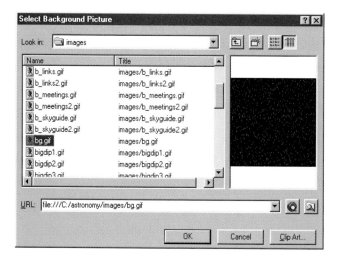

4   In the Select Background Picture dialog box, double-click the images folder in C:\astronomy and then click bg.gif, as shown in Figure 10-11. Notice that a thumbnail of the selected image displays in the right portion of the dialog box.

Figure 10-11

Selecting the bg.gif background image

note

Step 6 doesn't contain a mistake—you *should* set both the background and the text colors to black. For this project, most of the text you enter will display in white table cells, so to save yourself time later on, you should set the default text color to black at this point even though the background is set to black as well.

5   Click OK to select the background image and return to the Page Properties dialog box.

6   Continuing on the Background tab, click the Background drop-down arrow and click the Black color box; then click the Text drop-down arrow and click the Black color box.

7 Click the Hyperlink drop-down arrow and click the Blue color box; click the Visited Hyperlink drop-down arrow and click the Purple color box; then click the Active Hyperlink drop-down arrow and click the Red color box.

Even though the project uses the default hyperlink colors, you should click each component's color boxes in steps 7 and 8 and replace the "automatic" color setting for each element. If you don't replace the automatic colors with specified colors, some browsers might insert custom hyperlink colors that might not work well with your site—for example, if a user's "visiting" hyperlinks are set to black, the links will disappear into the black background after the user clicks them.

8 Click the Enable Hyperlink Rollover Effects check box, and then click the Rollover Style button. The Font dialog box opens. In the Font area, retain the (Default Font) selection, and in the Font Style text box, select Regular.

9 Click the Color drop-down box, click the Red color square, and click OK. This setting specifies to display text links in red whenever a user's mouse cursor hovers over the text link. The Background tab should now look like the one shown in Figure 10-12.

lingo

An *active hyperlink* refers to a hyperlink that's being clicked. If you set an active hyperlink color property to red, the hyperlink will appear red while the user clicks the link.

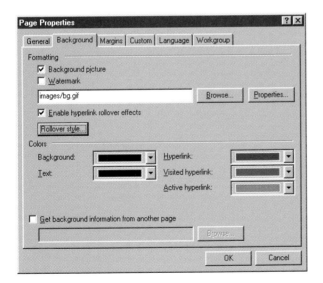

Figure 10-12
Completed Background tab

10 Click OK to implement the Page Property settings and close the Page Properties dialog box.

Saving Your Work

Before you get too far along, you should save your work. You'll be able to use the same basic settings for all subpages, so you'll save the page you're currently creating as a generic subpage that you can copy to create all the site's subpages. To save the current file, follow these steps:

1 On the File menu, click Save. The Save As dialog box opens.

2 Click the Change button (located in the lower-right portion of the dialog box) to open the Set Page Title dialog box, and enter *The Astronomy Club: Generic Page*, as shown in Figure 10-13. Then click OK.

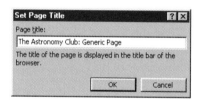

3 In the File Name text box, type *subpage*, as shown in Figure 10-14, and then click Save.

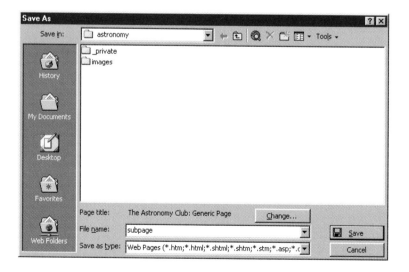

Adding the Logo and the Title Bar Graphic

In this section, you'll continue to configure the subpage template by inserting the astronomy club's logo and title bar graphic, which appears along the top of every page.

1 In the C:\astronomy\subpage.htm document (which should be opened in FrontPage if you're continuing the project from the previous section), click the Insert menu, point to Picture, and then choose From File. The Picture dialog box opens.

2 In the Picture dialog box, display the contents of the images folder in the C:\astronomy folder, select the logo.gif file, and click OK. The logo (which is simply Saturn and a few miscellaneous moons) displays on the page.

3 Click the Insert menu, point to Picture, choose From File, select the titlebar.gif file, and click OK. The title bar image is inserted next to the logo.

4 Right-click the logo.gif image, select Picture Properties, type *Astronomy Club Logo* in the Alternative Representations text box, and then click OK.

5 Right-click the titlebar.gif image, select Picture Properties, type *Astronomy Club* in the Alternative Representations text box, and then click OK.

6 Right-click the logo image again, select Hyperlink, type index.htm in the URL text box, and then click OK.

At this point, the logo is linked to the (future) home page, and both graphics are inserted and left-aligned by default. In most browsers, the left alignment will help keep the graphics side by side, but because two images span the top of your page, the title bar could feasibly wrap to the next line in some browsers if users resized their browser windows to a very small size (in which case the logo would display on the top line and the title bar would display flush-left below the logo graphic on the next line—not the effect you're after for this Web site). Just to be safe, you can add the "no break" (`<NOBR></NOBR>`) HTML tags to your page's source code to specify that the two graphics should be kept together regardless of the browser's window size.

7 In FrontPage, click the HTML view tab. The HTML source code displays in FrontPage's workspace window.

8 In the source code, click in the line above the image tag containing a pointer to logo.gif, type `<NOBR>`, click in the line below the image tag containing a pointer to titlebar.gif, and type `</NOBR>`. Figure 10-15 shows the newly added HTML tags (in red) that will ensure that the graphics will always display next to each other.

tip

If you closed subpage.htm, you can reopen the document by opening FrontPage, clicking the Open icon (or clicking Open on the File menu), navigating to C:\astronomy in the Open dialog box, and double-clicking subpage.htm.

Figure 10-15
Adding <NOBR> and </NOBR> to the page's source code

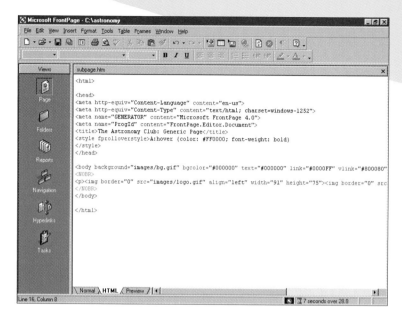

9 Click the Normal view tab to redisplay the graphical representation of subpage.htm in your working area, and click the Save button. Your page should display as shown in Figure 10-16.

Figure 10-16
Viewing the progress of subpage.htm

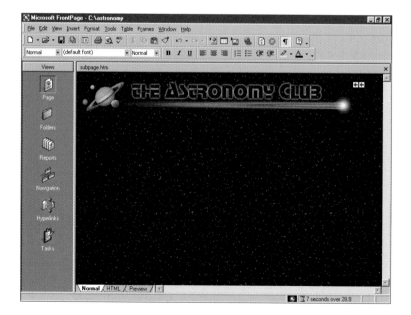

Inserting a Table

In this section, you'll create the foundation table used to contain the body text of each subpage in the astronomy club's Web site. Take your time going through the upcoming steps—it's easier to configure your table correctly the first time around instead of trying to find an erroneous setting. Further, although this section might seem to include a few too many steps, the steps throughout are fairly repetitive, so the process isn't overly complex. (In other words, don't let the number of steps get to you.) When you create your own tables, you'll probably have to experiment with a few settings before you get your table just right. Don't worry—that's what we do, too. To create your table for this project, follow these steps:

1   Click to the right of the title bar graphic, and press Shift+Enter three times to position your cursor where you want to insert the table.

2   In the Standard toolbar, click the Table button, drag to select two rows and five columns worth of boxes on the pop-up window, and then release to insert the table into your page. Figure 10-17 illustrates the table creation process. As you can see, the table borders display when you first insert a table. In effect, the table's borders are set to display as 1 pixel wide. Later, after you fill the table with content, you'll change the table's borders setting to 0 to hide the table's lines.

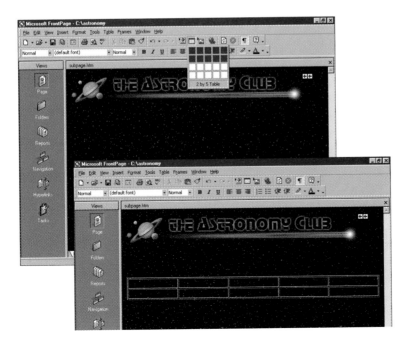

Figure 10-17
Creating a table

3 Right-click anywhere on the table, choose Table Properties, set Cell Padding to 0, set Cell Spacing to 0, ensure that the Specify Width setting is set to 100 percent, and click OK.

4 Right-click the cell in row 1, column 1. On the shortcut menu, select Cell Properties. The Cell Properties dialog box opens.

5 Set the Horizontal Alignment option to Center, set Vertical Alignment to Top, ensure that the Specify Width check box is selected, enter *130* in the Specify Width text box, and ensure that the In Pixels option is selected, as shown in Figure 10-18.

Figure 10-18
Configuring cell properties

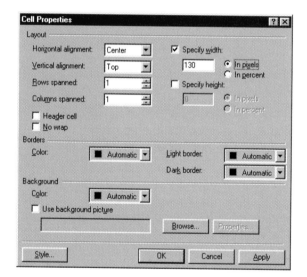

6 Click OK to activate the settings.

7 Right-click the cell in row 2, column 1. On the shortcut menu, select Cell Properties.

8 In the Cell Properties dialog box, set the Horizontal Alignment Option to Center, set Vertical Alignment to Bottom, set the Specify Width setting to 130 pixels, select the Specify Height checkbox, set the Specify Height setting to 15 pixels, and click OK.

9 Right-click the cell in row 1, column 2. Select Cell Properties. Set the Horizontal Alignment Option to Left, set Vertical Alignment to Top, set the Specify Width setting to 1 pixel, and click OK.

10 Right-click the cell in row 2, column 2. Select Cell Properties. Set the Horizontal Alignment Option to Left, set Vertical Alignment to Bottom, set the Specify Width setting to 1 pixel, select the Specify Height check box, set the Specify Height setting to 15 pixels, and click OK.

11 Right-click the cell in row 1, column 3. On the shortcut menu, select Cell Properties, set Horizontal Alignment to Left, set Vertical Alignment to Top, set the Specify Width setting to 15 pixels, specify the Background Color as White, and click OK.

12 Right-click the cell in row 2, column 3. On the shortcut menu, select Cell Properties, set Horizontal Alignment to Left, set Vertical Alignment to Bottom, set the Specify Width setting to 15 pixels, click the Specify Height check box, set the Specify Height setting to 15 pixels, specify the Background Color as White, and click OK.

13 Right-click the cell in row 1, column 4. On the shortcut menu, select Cell Properties, set Horizontal Alignment to Left, set Vertical Alignment to Top, deselect the Specify Width check box (don't set a width for this column because you'll want it to resize to fit each user's browser window), specify the Background Color as White, and click OK.

14 Right-click the cell in row 2, column 4. On the shortcut menu, select Cell Properties, set Horizontal Alignment to Left, set Vertical Alignment to Bottom, deselect the Specify Width check box, select the Specify Height check box, set the Specify Height settings to 15 pixels, specify the Background Color as White, and click OK.

15 Right-click the cell in row 1, column 5. On the shortcut menu, select Cell Properties, set Horizontal Alignment to Right, set Vertical Alignment to Top, set the Specify Width setting to 15 pixels, specify the Background Color as White, and click OK.

16 Right-click the cell in row 2, column 5. On the shortcut menu, select Cell Properties, set Horizontal Alignment to Right, set Vertical Alignment to Bottom, set the Specify Width setting to 15 pixels, set the Specify Height setting to 15 pixels, specify the Background Color as White, and click OK. Your table should now display as shown in Figure 10-19.

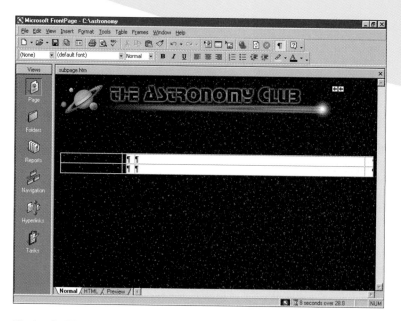

Notice in Figure 10-19 that the right set of table cells displays as a white rectangular area. You're now going to add small graphics to the white area's corner cells to create the illusion that the table has rounded corners.

17 Click in the cell in row 1, column 3. On the Insert menu, point to Picture and choose From File. Select the corner_top_left.gif image in the C:\astronomy\images folder, note the graphic in the Picture dialog box's preview window (you can probably guess how the small curved graphic will create the illusion of a rounded corner), and then click OK.

18 Click in the cell in row 2, column 3. On the Insert menu, point to Picture and choose From File. Select the corner_botm_left.gif image in the C:\astronomy\images folder, and then click OK.

19 Right-click the newly inserted corner_botm_left.gif image. On the shortcut menu, click Picture Properties, click the Appearance tab, select Bottom in the Alignment drop-down list, and click OK.

20 Click in the cell in row 1, column 5. On the Insert menu, point to Picture and choose From File. Select the corner_top_right.gif image in the C:\astronomy\images folder, and then click OK.

21 Click in the cell in row 2, column 5. On the Insert menu, point to Picture and choose From File. Select the corner_botm_right.gif image in the C:\astronomy\images folder, and then click OK.

22 Right-click the newly inserted corner_botm_right.gif image. On the shortcut menu, click Picture Properties, click the Appearance tab, select Bottom in the Alignment drop-down list, and click OK.

23 Click Save in the toolbar. At this point, your table should display as shown in Figure 10-20.

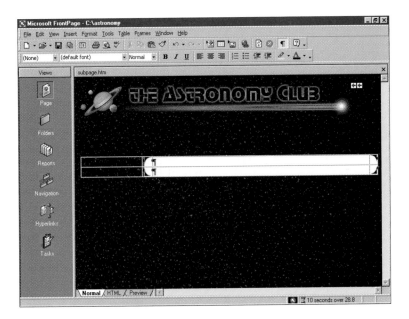

Figure 10-20
Table with modified cells

Adding Navigation Buttons

Now that the table is created, you're ready to start filling the table's cells. First on the agenda is to add some navigation buttons to the first column in the table. FrontPage offers some nice special-effects buttons, which you'll use in this project.

1 Click in the cell in row 1, column 1.

2 On the Insert menu, point to Component and then choose Hover Button. The Hover Button Properties dialog box displays.

3 Configure the Hover Button Properties dialog box as shown in Figure 10-21, using the following settings:

Option	Setting
Button Text	Home
Link To	index.htm
Button Color	Navy
Effect	Glow
Width	120
Background Color	Automatic
Effect Color	Blue
Height	24

Figure 10-21
Creating navigation buttons

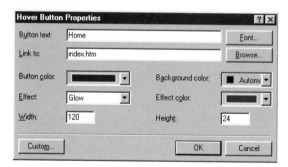

4 Click OK.

5 Press Enter. On the Insert menu, point to Component and choose Hover Button. Type *About Us* in the Button Text text box, type *aboutus.htm* in the Link To text box, specify the remaining settings as outlined in step 3, and then click OK.

6 Press Enter. On the Insert menu, point to Component and choose Hover Button. Type *Contact Us* in the Button Text text box, type *contact.htm* in the Link To text box, specify the remaining settings as outlined in step 3, and then click OK.

7 Press Enter. On the Insert menu, point to Component and choose Hover Button. Type *Meetings* in the Button Text text box, type *meetings.htm* in the Link To text box, specify the remaining settings as outlined in step 3, and then click OK.

8 Press Enter. On the Insert menu, point to Component and choose Hover Button. Type *Sky Guide* in the Button Text text box, type *skyguide.htm* in the Link To text box, specify the remaining settings as outlined in step 3, and then click OK.

9 Press Enter. On the Insert menu, point to Component and choose Hover Button. Type *Photo Gallery* in the Button Text text box, type *gallery.htm* in the Link To text box, specify the remaining settings as outlined in step 3, and then click OK.

10 Press Enter. On the Insert menu, point to Component and choose Hover Button. Type *Astronomy Links* in the Button Text text box, type *links.htm* in the Link To text box, specify the remaining settings as outlined in step 3, and then click OK.

11 Click Save. Your subpage should display in Normal view and Preview view as shown in Figure 10-22.

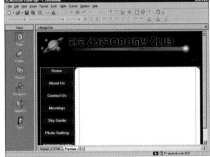

Figure 10-22
Table and navigation buttons in Normal and Preview views

Adding Footer Information Below the Table

The final components you'll add to the subpage template before you begin to create actual site pages are the bottom-of-the-page elements: a text-based navigation bar and copyright information. As we've discussed earlier in the book, your Web pages should include text-based navigation links for users who turn off graphics or access the Web with nongraphical browsers. Further, you should include copyright information to protect your creation. To add bottom-of-the-page information to the astronomy club's Web, follow these steps:

1 In Normal view, click in the area below the table, click the drop-down arrow on the Font Color button in the Formatting toolbar, and click the White color box.

2 Type the following (including the pipe symbols):

Home | About Us | Contact Us | Meetings | Sky Guide |
Photo Gallery | Links

3 Select the line of text you just typed, display the font drop-down list in the Formatting toolbar, and choose Comic Sans (or Comic Sans MS).

4 Click the Center button on the Formatting toolbar to center the text.

5 Click at the end of the line of text, press Enter a couple times, and then type the following:

```
Questions or comments about the Web site? Email the
Webmaster.
```

6 Press Enter, display the Font Size drop-down list in the Formatting toolbar, choose 1 (8 pt), and then type the following:

```
Copyright 2001 - [your name or organization's name]
```

You're now ready to link the navigation bar's text and add a Mail To link to the "Email the Webmaster" text.

7 Select Home in the text-based navigation bar, right-click the selected text, and click Hyperlink. The Create Hyperlink dialog box opens.

8 Ensure that the Look In drop-down list shows C:\astronomy, type *index.htm* in the URL text box (be sure to delete the http://), as shown in Figure 10-23, and then click OK.

tip

You can press Ctrl+K to open the Create Hyperlink dialog box.

Figure 10-23
Linking text to a Web page

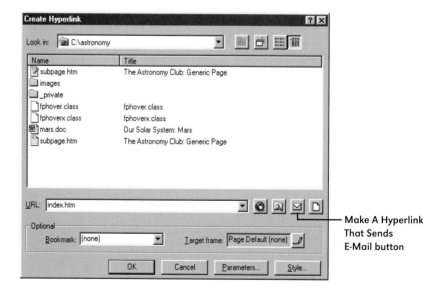

Make A Hyperlink
That Sends
E-Mail button

9 Repeat steps 7 and 8 using the following parameters:

Select	Enter in the URL Text Box
About Us	aboutus.htm
Contact Us	contact.htm
Meetings	meetings.htm
Sky Guide	skyguide.htm
Photo Gallery	gallery.htm
Links	links.htm

10 Select the Email The Webmaster text, right-click the selected text, and click Hyperlink to open the Create Hyperlink dialog box.

11 In the Create Hyperlink dialog box, click the Make A Hyperlink That Sends E-mail button, as shown earlier in Figure 10-23. The Create E-mail Hyperlink dialog box opens.

12 Enter your e-mail address, click OK, click OK again to close the Create Hyperlink dialog box, and then click Save. The lower portion of your subpage template should appear as shown in Figure 10-24, which shows the Preview view.

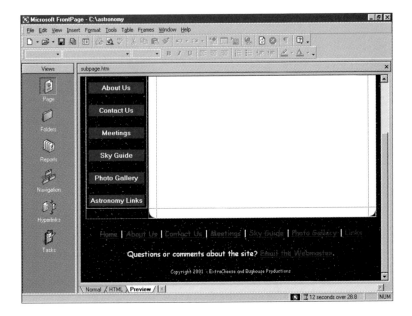

Figure 10-24
Previewing the subpage's footer information

13 Close subpage.htm.

You now have a subpage template ready for use.

Using the Subpage Layout to Build Web Pages

Now you're going to use subpage.htm to create a couple subpages for the astronomy club's Web. The site requires six main subpages:

- aboutus.htm
- contact.htm
- meetings.htm
- skyguide.htm
- gallery.htm
- links.htm

In this section, you'll create contact.htm and skyguide.htm as well as a subpage (mars.htm) of the skyguide.htm page. Although we don't walk you through the creation of all the subpages, the images you downloaded from *www.creationguide.com/chapter10/images* include title bar text graphics so that you can complete all the subpages on your own if you want to. We chose to show you how to create mars.htm, skyguide.htm, and contact.htm because creating each of those pages includes information on how to add particular functionality to your Web pages, as follows:

- **mars.htm**   Shows you how to use the thumbnail feature in Front-Page as well as copy text from a Word document. Further, this page links to the Sky Guide page (skyguide.htm).
- **skyguide.htm**   Teaches you how to create an image map in Front-Page.
- **contact.htm**   Provides a quick overview of how to create a working form in FrontPage.

After you create the three subpages described in this project, you'll be fully prepared to create the remaining subpages on your own.

Preparing to Create Subpages

Preparing to create subpages is straightforward now that you've laid such a solid groundwork by creating a template. To use the template, you simply rename copies of the subpage.htm file, as follows:

1   Open C:\astronomy in Windows Explorer.

2   Right-click subpage.htm, and choose Copy.

3 Click the Paste button in the toolbar three times, to create three copies of subpage.htm. The copies should be named as follows:

- Copy of subpage.htm
- Copy (2) of subpage.htm
- Copy (3) of subpage.htm

4 Right-click Copy of subpage.htm, select Rename, type *mars.htm*, and press Enter.

5 Right-click Copy (2) of subpage.htm, select Rename, type *skyguide.htm*, and press Enter.

6 Right-click Copy (3) of subpage.htm, select Rename, type *contact.htm*, and press Enter.

7 Close Windows Explorer.

Adding Text and a Thumbnail Image

After you create new files based on the subpage.htm file, you can open the new documents in FrontPage and customize the files' contents. The first subpage you'll create is an informational page about the planet Mars.

1 Open FrontPage, click the Open button on the toolbar, display the contents of C:\astronomy in the Open dialog box, and double-click the mars.htm file.

2 Click Properties on the File menu, change the Title text to *Astronomy Club: Mars Informational Page*, and then click OK.

3 Click below the title bar, point to Picture on the Insert menu, choose From File, display the contents of C:\astronomy\images, and double-click t_skyguide.gif. The mars.htm page is a subpage of the Sky Guide, so it should display the Sky Guide subtitle bar.

4 Right-click the t_skyguide.gif image, select Picture Properties, type *Sky Guide* in the Alternative Representations text box, and click OK.

Now you'll add some text to the Web page's table.

5 Open C:\astronomy, and then double-click mars.doc (*not* mars.htm) to open the Word document.

6 Arrange your desktop so that you can see some portion of the Word document's text as well as mars.htm in FrontPage, similar to the layout shown in Figure 10-25.

tip

You need to name the subpages in the same way they were referenced when you linked the navigation buttons and hypertext link. For example, the About Us subpage needs to be saved with the name aboutus.htm.

tip

You can copy and rename subpage.htm to create the aboutus.htm, meetings.htm, gallery.htm, and links.htm files as well.

Figure 10-25
*Preparing to copy text from a Word
document into a Web document*

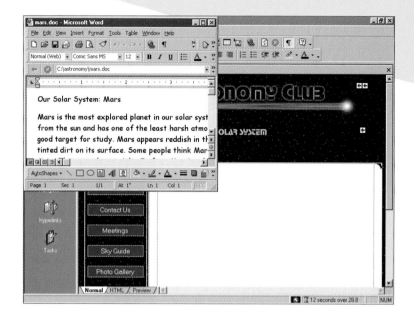

note

You can type text directly
into the table (as you'll see
later in this project), but we
provided text for this page so
that you wouldn't have to
retype the information. You
can also copy and paste
information into FrontPage
or use the File command on
the Insert menu.

Figure 10-26
Text inserted into mars.htm

7   Click within the Word document, and press Ctrl+A to select the entire
contents of the Word document.

8   Drag the selected text in the Word document into the white portion of
the table in mars.htm. The text should fill the table cell, as shown in
Figure 10-26.

9   Close the Word document.

10 In FrontPage, click to the left of Our Solar Sytem: Mars (the top line of the inserted text), point to Picture on the Insert menu, choose File, and double-click the mars.jpg image from the C:\astronomy\images folder. A very large picture of Mars takes over your view in FrontPage.

11 Click Mars to display the Pictures toolbar, which appears automatically when you select a picture, as shown in Figure 10-27.

Auto Thumbnail button

Figure 10-27
Creating a thumbnail image of Mars

12 Click the Auto Thumbnail button in the Pictures toolbar. A 100-by-100-pixel version of Mars is created from the larger version of mars.jpg. The smaller graphic is automatically named mars_small.jpg and stored in the C:\astronomy folder.

13 Right-click the thumbnail picture of Mars, choose Picture Properties, select the Appearance tab, and configure the properties as follows:

Option	Setting
Alignment	Right
Border Thickness	0
Horizontal Spacing	15
Vertical Spacing	10
Specify Size	Selected
Width	200 pixels
Height	200 pixels
Keep Aspect Ratio	Selected

tip

To test the thumbnail link, click the Preview view tab and then click the thumbnail picture of Mars. Click the Normal view tab to return to working view.

Figure 10-28

Viewing a page with a thumbnail graphic

14 Click OK, and then click in the text to deselect the graphic.

15 Right-click anywhere on the table, and choose Table Properties. The Table Properties dialog box opens.

16 In the Borders section, type *0* in the Size text box, and then click OK.

17 Click Save, and then click the Preview view tab. Your mars.htm page should now look similar to Figure 10-28, and the small graphic is automatically linked to mars.jpg.

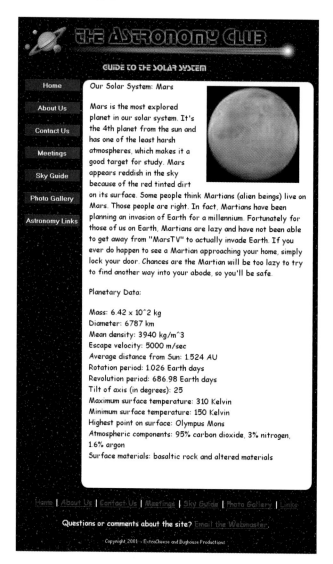

18 Close mars.htm.

Congratulations! You've completed your first subpage for the astronomy club's Web site. No reason to stop now—in the next section, you'll learn how to add an image map.

Creating an Image Map

In this section, you'll create an image map on the Sky Guide's main subpage. You'll create the image map from a picture of the solar system. You'll format the solar system image so that when users click the picture of Mars, the mars.htm page you created in the preceding section will display. To accomplish this (it's easier than it sounds), follow these steps:

1 Open FrontPage, click the Open button on the toolbar, display the contents of C:\astronomy in the Open dialog box, and double-click the skyguide.htm file.

2 Click Properties on the File menu, change the Title text to *Astronomy Club: Sky Guide*, and then click OK.

3 Click below the title bar, point to Picture on the Insert menu, choose From File, display the contents of C:\astronomy\images, and double-click t_skyguide.gif.

4 Right-click the t_skyguide.gif image, select Picture Properties, type *Sky Guide* in the Alternative Representations text box, and click OK.

Now you'll add some content to the Web page's table:

5 Click in the large table cell to the right of the Home button, and type *This Month's Featured Item: Our Solar System*.

6 Select the text, click the Center icon on the Formatting toolbar, and select Comic Sans (or Comic Sans MS) in the Font drop-down list.

7 Click after the word *System*, and press Shift+Enter twice.

8 Type the following:

```
Click a planet to go to the planet's information page.
Note: Only Mars is active at this time.
```

9 Click in the blank area between the two text components you added in steps 5 and 8.

10 On the Insert menu, point to Picture, choose From File, navigate to the C:\astronomy\images folder if necessary, and double-click solarsystem.gif.

11 Right-click anywhere on the table, choose Table Properties, set the Border Size to 0 in the Table Properties dialog box, and then click OK.

tip

The project image files you downloaded from *www.creationguide.com/chapter10/images* include neptune.jpg and saturn.jpg, which are pictures of Neptune and Saturn (respectively) that you can use if you'd like to create additional planet informational pages for extra practice.

12 Click Save on the toolbar. Then click the Preview view tab. Your table should appear similar to the table shown in Figure 10-29.

Figure 10-29
Viewing the picture that will be used to create an image map

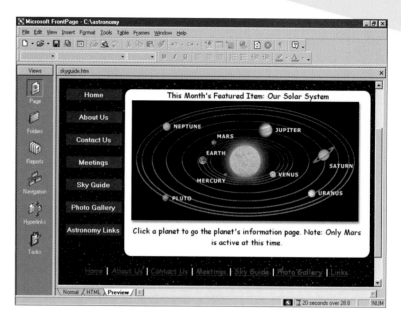

13 Return to Normal view.

14 Click the solar system image. The Pictures toolbar opens automatically. Notice the Rectangular Hotspot, Circular Hotspot, and Polygonal Hotspot tools located toward the right end of the Pictures toolbar.

lingo

A *hotspot* is a clickable area on an image that's linked to another Web page or another area on the current page.

15 Click the Polygonal Hotspot tool, and then click multiple points around Mars and the Mars label in the solar system graphic to create a polygon, as shown in Figure 10-30. When you complete the polygon, the Create Hyperlink dialog box opens automatically.

Figure 10-30
Drawing a clickable polygonal hotspot on an image

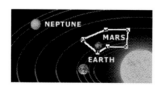

tip

If you create a line that you don't want to use, right-click to remove the existing lines, and start over.

16 In the Create Hyperlink dialog box, double-click mars.htm in the C:\astronomy file list.

17 Create shapes around the remaining planets (if desired) that point to future pages, such as mercury.htm, venus.htm, earth.htm, jupiter.htm, saturn.htm, uranus.htm, neptune.htm, and pluto.htm.

18 Save skyguide.htm, preview the page in Preview view, move your cursor over Mars (notice that the cursor changes to a hand), and click Mars to see whether your link works.

19 Click the Normal view tab, and then close skyguide.htm.

You're well on your way to creating the astronomy club's Web site. The final subpage you'll create is a form within the contact.htm page.

Creating Forms

At this point, you should be getting used to adding elements and configuring settings in FrontPage. As we mentioned at the beginning of the chapter, the trick is in knowing where to find tools and configuration menus. In this section, you'll create an online form. As you might recall from Chapter 2, an online form enables users to enter information into text boxes. Then when users click the form's Submit button, the results will be sent to your e-mail address.

Preparing the Contacts page

The first step to creating a form on the Contacts page is to prepare the page by adding a title bar and inserting title text, as described in the following steps:

1 Open FrontPage, click the Open button on the toolbar, display the contents of C:\astronomy in the Open dialog box, and double-click the contact.htm file.

2 Click Properties on the File menu, change the Title text to *Astronomy Club: Contact Page*, and then click OK.

3 Click below the title bar, point to Picture on the Insert menu, choose From File, display the contents of C:\astronomy\images, and double-click t_contact.gif.

4 Right-click the t_contact.gif image, select Picture Properties, type *Contact Page* in the Alternative Representations text box, and click OK.

note

When you use Forms on your Web site, your server must support FrontPage Server Extensions and you must publish the form using the publishing tool in FrontPage or Web Folders.

Inserting a form area and adding labels

Now that the Contacts page is ready for action, you're set to create an online form. First you'll insert the standard form box and then enter labels for the form's text boxes, option buttons, and selection boxes:

1 Click in the large table cell to the right of the Home button, point to Form on the Insert menu, and choose Form. An outlined area displays within the table that contains Submit and Reset buttons, as shown in Figure 10-31.

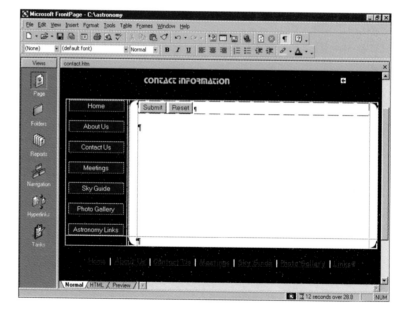

2 With the cursor positioned to the left of the Submit button, type *Name:*, and then press Shift+Enter.

3 Type *Email Address:*, and press Enter.

4 Type *Are you currently a club member?* and then press Enter.

5 Type *If so, how often do you attend our monthly meetings?* and then press Enter.

6 Type *Please let us know how you found our Web site (check all that apply):*, press Shift+Enter, type *I attended a meeting.*, press Shift+Enter, type *I found it in a search engine.*, press Shift+Enter, type *A friend told me.*, and then press Enter.

7 Type *Please enter comments or questions here:*, press Shift+Enter, and then press Enter. Your form should appear similar to the form in progress shown in Figure 10-32.

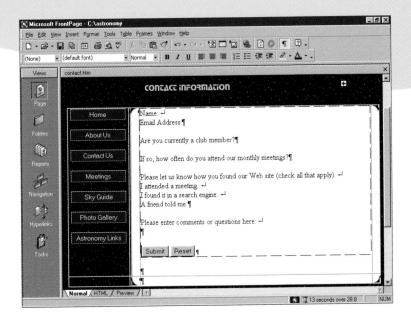

Figure 10-32
The form in progress

Creating form fields

You're now ready to enter the form fields, the areas in which viewers select or enter text so that they can submit information.

1 Click after Name:, press the spacebar, point to Form on the Insert menu, and choose One-Line Text box.

2 Click after Email Address:, press the spacebar, point to Form on the Insert menu, and choose One-Line Text box.

3 Click after Are You Currently A Club Member?, point to Form on the Insert menu, choose Radio Button, type *Yes*, press your spacebar, point to Form on the Insert menu, choose Radio Button, and then type *No*.

4 Click after If So, How Often Do You Attend Our Monthly Meetings?, press the spacebar, point to Form on the Insert menu, and choose Drop-Down Menu.

5 Click before I Attended A Meeting, point to Form on the Insert menu, and choose Check Box.

note

We'll format the form fields in a moment—so don't be concerned if the form fields don't look quite right at this point.

6 Click before I Found It In A Search Engine, point to Form on the Insert menu, and choose Check Box.

7 Click before A Friend Told Me, point to Form on the Insert menu, and choose Check Box.

8 Click below Please Enter Comments Or Questions Here, point to Form on the Insert menu, and choose Scrolling Text Box.

9 Click Save. Your form should now display as shown in Figure 10-33.

Figure 10-33
A form with labels and unformatted form fields

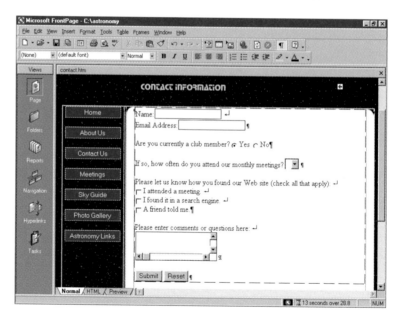

Configuring form field properties

You now have the bulk of the form created. The next step is to configure the properties for each form field and specify the form's overall properties. So get your right-click finger ready—you're about to configure some property forms.

1 Right-click the field next to Name, and select Form Field Properties. The Text Box Properties dialog box opens.

2 In the Name field, type *Name*, set the Width In Characters to 25 (as shown in Figure 10-34), and then click OK.

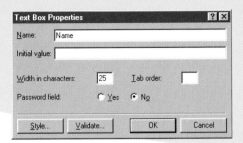

Figure 10-34
Setting the properties for a one-line text box

3 Right-click the field next to Email Address, select Form Field Properties, type *Email*, set the Width In Characters to 30, and then click OK.

4 Right-click the Yes button, choose Form Field Properties, type *Member* in the Group Name text box, type *Yes* in the Value text box, and click OK.

5 Right-click the No button, choose Form Field Properties, type *Member* in the Group Name text box, type *No* in the Value text box, and click OK.

6 Right-click the If So, How Often Do You Attend Our Monthly Meetings? drop-down list box, and choose Form Field Properties. The Drop-Down Menu Properties dialog box opens.

7 Type *Attendance* in the Name text box, and then click Add. The Add Choice dialog box opens.

8 In the Add Choice dialog box, enter *I attend every meeting*, choose the Selected option as shown in Figure 10-35, and click OK.

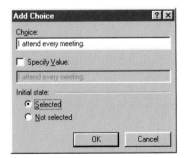

Figure 10-35
Adding an entry to a drop-down list

9 Click Add, type *Every other month*, and click OK.

10 Click Add, type *Couple times a year*, and click OK.

Naming Your Fields
Generally, you should supply a name for every form field. Field names help identify information after it's submitted to you as well as enable browsers to differentiate like elements. You can configure your form to display each field's name along with the submitted data. This setup will help you to quickly see what information was submitted in response to which form field entries. For example, here's what a filled-in online form might look like:

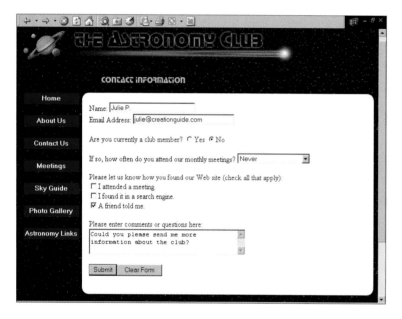

After the user clicked the Submit button, a confirmation page like this would display to the user:

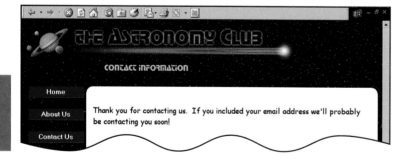

You would receive an e-mail message containing the submitted information similar to the following message.

(continued)

Naming Your Fields (continued)

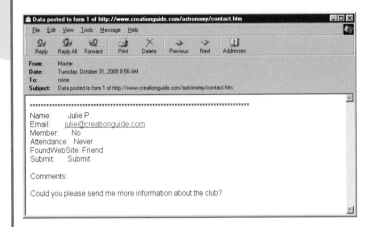

The images displayed here show how the form you're creating in this project will display after you publish the contact form to a Web server.

11 Click Add, type *Never*, and click OK. Your Drop-Down Menu Properties dialog box should look like the one shown in Figure 10-36.

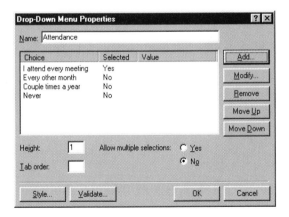

Figure 10-36
The completed Drop-Down Menu Properties dialog box

12 Click OK.

13 Right-click the first check box, choose Form Field Properties, enter *FoundWebSite* in the Name text box, enter *Attended a meeting* in the Value text box, and click OK.

14 Right-click the second check box, choose Form Field Properties, enter *FoundWebSite* in the Name text box, enter *Search engine* in the Value text box, and click OK.

15 Right-click the third check box, choose Form Field Properties, enter *FoundWebSite* in the Name text box, enter *Friend* in the Value text box, and click OK.

16 Right-click the scrolling text box, choose Form Field Properties, type *Comments* in the Name text box, enter *40* in the Width In Characters text box, enter *3* in the Number Of Lines text box, and click OK.

17 Right-click the Submit button, choose Form Field Properties, enter *Submit* in the Name text box, and click OK.

18 Right-click the Reset button, choose Form Field Properties, enter *Clear Form* in the Value/Label text box, and click OK.

19 Click before the Name label at the top of the form, and press Shift+Enter. Then save your work.

Completing the Contacts page

To complete the Contacts page, you need to hide the table's borders and set the form's properties.

1 Right-click anywhere on the table, choose Table Properties, enter *0* in the Size text box in the Borders area, and click OK.

2 Right-click the form, and choose Form Properties. The Form Properties dialog box opens.

3 In the Form Properties dialog box, ensure that the Send To option is selected, enter your own e-mail address in the E-mail Address text box, and enter *Astronomy Contact Form* in the Form Name text box, as shown in Figure 10-37.

4 In the Form Properties dialog box, click Options, click the E-mail Results tab, and select the Include Field Names check box. Selecting the Include Field Names option specifies that the field names should accompany the submitted information.

5 Click the Confirmation Page tab, type *thankyou.htm* in the URL Of Confirmation Page text box (we created a simple thankyou.htm file for you, which you should've downloaded to the C:\astronomy folder from *www.creationguide.com/chapter10/text*), click OK twice, and then click No.

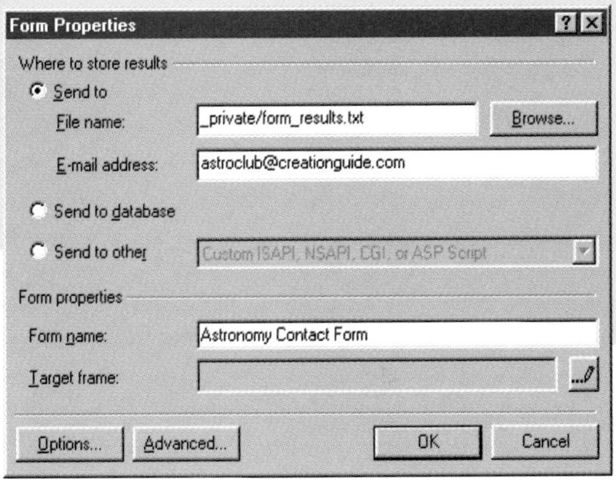

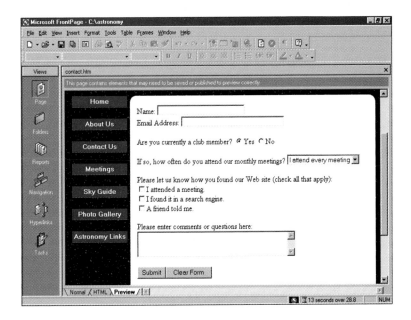

Figure 10-37
Specifying where to send form information

6 Save contact.htm, and then click the Preview view tab. Your newly created form should look similar to the form shown in Figure 10-38.

Figure 10-38
The final form

7 Close contact.htm, and close FrontPage.

That's it for your subpage experimentation for this project. You've worked through a number of FrontPage features that you should be able to use when you create your own Web site. But before we wrap up this project, we need to create the astronomy club's home page.

Creating a Home Page in FrontPage

Last but not least, you're ready to create the home page. Creating this page might seem a little tricky at moments (especially for a book with "easy" in its title), and we'll readily admit that it's probably the most advanced procedure we describe in this book. However challenging, though, we want to give you an inkling of where you can go from here if we've inspired you to continue designing Web sites. (And we hope you do!) Further, we thought you might be interested in seeing how tables and graphics are sometimes used to create advanced page layout designs. Anyway, let's start by setting up the home page's framework.

Setting Up the Home Page Framework

To begin, follow these steps:

1 In Windows Explorer, open C:\astronomy, right-click subpage.htm, choose Copy, click Paste in the toolbar, and rename Copy of subpage.htm to index.htm. Close Windows Explorer.

2 Open FrontPage, click the Open button on the toolbar, display the contents of C:\astronomy in the Open dialog box, and double-click index.htm.

3 Click Properties on the File menu, change the Title text to *Astronomy Club's Official Web Site*, and click OK.

4 Right-click a blank area of the page, click Page Properties, click the Background tab, click the Text Color box, choose White, and click OK.

5 Place your cursor before the Home link in the text-based navigation bar, drag to select everything above the text-based navigation bar, right-click the selected elements, and click Cut.

6 Press Enter, and then press the Up arrow button (or click in the space above the text-based navigation bar).

7 Point to Picture on the Insert menu, choose From File, and display the contents of C:\astronomy\images if necessary. Then double-click titlebar-home.gif and press Enter.

8 Point to Component on the Insert menu, and choose Marquee. The Marquee Properties dialog box opens.

9 In the Marquee Properties Dialog box, type *Our Next Meeting is February 21. Reserve your space today!* in the Text text box—this is the message that will scroll across the page.

10 Choose the Slide option in the Behavior section, choose Middle in the Align With Text section, deselect Continuously in the Repeat section, and enter *1* in the Repeat text box, as shown in Figure 10-39.

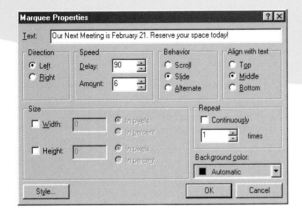

Figure 10-39
Configuring the marquee's properties

11 Click OK.

12 Press Enter, click the Table button in the toolbar, and create a 1-row, 5-column table. Your index.htm page should look similar to the page shown in Figure 10-40.

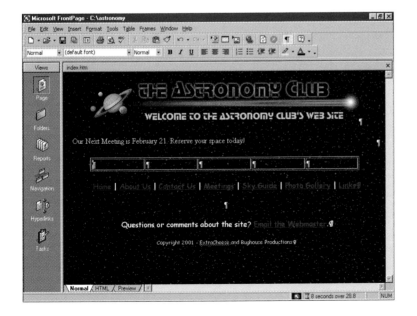

Figure 10-40
Creating a table on the astronomy club's home page

13 Right-click the table, choose Table Properties, click the Alignment drop-down list, select Center, ensure the Specify Width check box is selected, enter *580* in the Specify Width text box, choose the In Pixels option, set Cell Spacing to 0, set Cell Padding to 0, and click OK.

14 Select all five table cells, right-click the selected cells, choose Cell Properties, set Vertical Alignment to Top, and then click OK.

15 Right-click the titlebar-home.gif graphic, choose Picture Properties, type *Welcome to the Astronomy Club Web Site* in the Alternative Representations text box, and click OK.

16 Click Save.

Assembling the Main Graphic

lingo

DHTML (Dynamic HTML) is a technology that provides Web pages with the capability to change and update automatically in response to a user's actions, such as displaying a graphic or additional information in response to a user's mouse movement.

You're now going to insert pieces of an image that has been cut to fit into the table. The image, before we chopped it into pieces, is shown in Figure 10-41. The reason we divided the image into separate graphics is that we wanted to use Dynamic HTML (DHTML) to create a glowing rollover effect whenever users place their cursor over a hyperlinked area. If we hadn't wanted to show the rollover effect (and demonstrate how you can chop up and reassemble pictures when necessary), we could've created an image map similar to the solar system image map you created on the Sky Guide page earlier in this chapter.

Figure 10-41
Original Big Dipper image

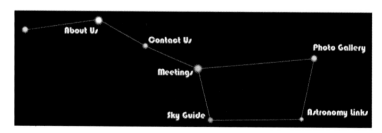

1 In index.htm, click in cell 1, point to Picture on the Insert menu, choose From File, display the contents of C:\astronomy\images, and double-click bigdip1.gif.

2 Click in cell 2, and insert b_aboutus.gif.

3 Click in cell 3, insert bigdip2.gif (a transparent graphic that will help to align the other graphics), press Shift+Enter, insert b_contact.gif, press Shift+Enter, insert b_meetings.gif, press Shift+Enter, and insert b_skyguide.gif.

4 Click in cell 4, and insert bigdip3.gif.

5 Click in cell 5, and insert bigdip4.gif (another transparent image), press Shift+Enter, insert b_gallery.gif, press Shift+Enter, insert bigdip5.gif, press Shift+Enter, and insert b_links.gif. Your index.htm page should display as shown in Figure 10-42.

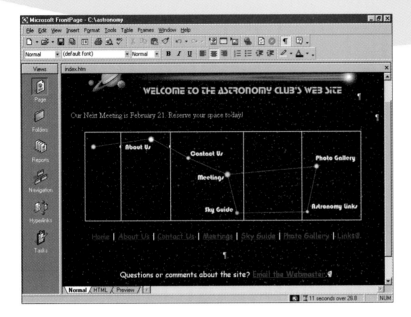

Figure 10-42
Piecing the Big Dipper back into shape

Creating Links Within the Main Graphic

The next step is to link each image that contains a button name in the Big Dipper graphic to the appropriate subpage:

1 Right-click the About Us text, choose Hyperlink, type *aboutus.htm* in the URL text box (or select the aboutus.htm file if you created it earlier in the project), as shown in Figure 10-43. Then click OK.

2 Link the remaining graphics as follows:

Graphic	Link To
Contact Us	contact.htm
Meetings	meetings.htm
Sky Guide	skyguide.htm
Photo Gallery	gallery.htm
Astronomy Links	links.htm

Figure 10-43
Linking to the aboutus.htm document

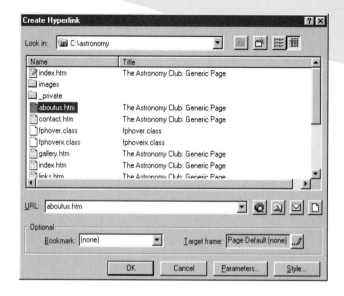

Adding Dynamic HTML to the Main Graphic

Next you'll add the rollover effect to each hyperlinked area in the table by using the FrontPage DHTML toolbar:

1 Select the About Us button, and choose Dynamic HTML Effects on the Format menu. The DHTML Effects toolbar displays. You'll configure the toolbar to display as shown in Figure 10-44.

Figure 10-44
Configuring the DHTML Effects toolbar

2 In the On drop-down list, choose Mouse Over.

3 In the Apply drop-down list, choose Swap Picture, click the Choose Settings drop-down list, select Choose Picture, and then double-click b_aboutus2.gif.

4 Repeat steps 1 through 3 for each linked area, linking the secondary graphics as follows:

Link	Picture File
Contact Us	b_contact2.gif
Meetings	b_meetings2.gif
Sky Guide	b_skyguide2.gif
Photo Gallery	b_gallery2.gif
Astronomy Links	b_links2.gif

5 Close the DHTML Effects toolbar.

6 Right-click the table, choose Table Properties, enter 0 in the Size text box in the Borders section, click Apply, and then click OK.

7 Click Save, and then click the Preview tab to check your work.

8 Click the Normal view tab to return to your working area.

Adding Finishing Touches to the Home Page

Finally, to complete the home page, you'll insert counter and last-modified date elements. To insert a counter, follow these steps:

1 On index.htm, click below the text navigation links, point to Component on the Insert menu, and select Hit Counter. The Hit Counter Properties dialog box displays.

2 Select the green digital number style, choose the Fixed Number Of Digits check box, accept the default setting of 5 digits, as shown in Figure 10-45, and click OK.

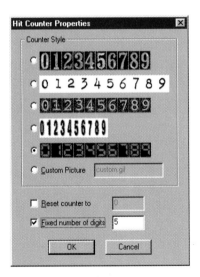

note

Counter elements won't display until you publish your FrontPage Web.

Figure 10-45
Inserting a counter

3 Press Enter, choose Date And Time on the Insert menu, and click OK on the Date And Time dialog box. The date will automatically update each time you edit the page.

4 Save index.htm, and then click Preview. Your page should look similar to the page shown in Figure 10-46.

Figure 10-46
Previewing the completed index.htm file

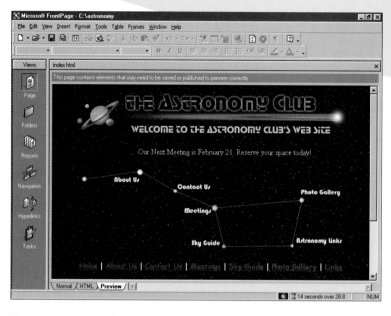

tip

To see a live version of the astronomy club Web site created in this project, visit *www.creationguide.com/ astronomy*.

You've completed the home page and most of the subpages for the astronomy club's Web site. Great work! You should now understand some of the cool capabilities of FrontPage. We hope this newfound knowledge will help you as you design and create your own Web sites.

As far as the astronomy club's site, the only remaining step is to publish the C:\astronomy Web by using the Publish feature in FrontPage. Be sure to read the following section before you upload your astronomy club Web site to your server space.

A Word About Publishing

When you create Webs in FrontPage, your best bet is to upload the pages using the FrontPage Publish feature, especially if you've inserted items that rely on FrontPage Server Extensions (such as forms and counters). To publish your site, select the Publish Web option on the File menu. You should have your server space and address already lined up. Further, you should have ensured with your hosting service that FrontPage Server Extensions are supported. For more information about publishing FrontPage Webs and using FrontPage Server Extensions, contact your ISP, review any of the resources listed in the following section, and refer to the help files in FrontPage.

Additional Resources

Here are some FrontPage references we've found helpful:

- Buyens, Jim. *Running FrontPage 2000*. Redmond, WA: Microsoft Press, 2000. This book is a complete FrontPage documentation source.

- London, Sherry. *FrontPage 2000: Get Professional Results*. Berkeley, CA: Osborne/McGraw-Hill, 2000. This book provides clear information in a friendly manner.

- Matthews, Martin S., and Erik B. Poulsen. *FrontPage 2000: The Complete Reference*. Berkeley, CA: Osborne/McGraw-Hill, 1999. Although this book is long, it includes a good discussion of publishing FrontPage Webs and files.

- *www.microsoft.com/frontpage* is the definitive online resource for FrontPage.

key points

- **FrontPage is a full-featured HTML editing program.**

- **You can use FrontPage to easily create advanced Web page features such as button rollover effects, image maps, thumbnails, forms, counters, and other Web page components.**

- **The FrontPage interface enables you to display your Web pages in Normal (working) view, HTML view, and Preview view.**

- **Learning FrontPage opens doors to using other full-service HTML editors because it exemplifies the types of capabilities HTML editors can provide.**

- **Before you create your Web pages using FrontPage, you should ensure that your Web hosting service supports FrontPage Server Extensions. (These days, most servers support extensions.)**

- **Before you start creating Web pages in FrontPage, you should set up a Web, which provides special formatting to a selected folder.**

- **You can simplify the process of building a Web site by creating a standard template that you can copy to create linked pages.**

- **The key to creating Webs in FrontPage is keeping your files organized, knowing where to find FrontPage tools and menu options, and experimenting with various settings.**

- **For best results, upload FrontPage files using the Publishing feature.**

PART
three

THE REST: GOING LIVE
and moving on

Ten years ago, a couple friends of ours hatched a plan to build a cabin in the White Mountains. It all started one day when they were chatting over coffee. Their conversation turned to vacations and getaways, and soon they were half-jokingly sketching "dream" blueprints for a mountain cabin. Not long after their initial conversation, they found themselves talking to an architect to see whether their dream cabin could be turned into a reality. In a few weeks, the blueprints were solidified, and before they knew it, they were gathering supplies and laying the cabin's foundation. Within the year, the cabin was built. But they didn't stop there. Ever since that first year, they've been improving their cabin. They regularly take on "big jobs" (such as building cabinetry, installing window seats, and building a stone fireplace) as well as undertake "not-so-big" tasks (such as creating a rock garden and hand-sewing drapes). As a result of our friends' hard work, attention to detail, and dedication, even the most casual passerby can see that although the other cabins in the area are nice, our friends' cabin is a unique and well-loved mountain escape.

You might be wondering, How in the world does this little story relate to Web site development? Fortunately, the answer's simple, and it serves as a foundation for Part Three. Specifically, after you post your Web site (as described in Chapter 11), you should count on providing at least a small dose of continuing attention to your Web pages (as discussed in Chapter 12). Sure, you could slap any old Web page onto the Web and leave it unattended, but you'd hardly be the proud owner of a successful site. To have a successful Web site, you need to tend your Web pages regularly. In the chapters in this part, we'll show you how to both go live (get your pages online) and keep your site alive and well.

sending your

11

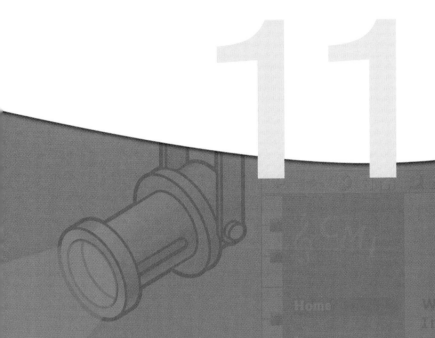

home page
INTO THE REAL WORLD

The troupe is well rehearsed, and the set is a work of art. It's time to put the name up in lights, meet for a last-minute dress rehearsal, hand out the flyers, and let the show begin.

Now That Your Pages Have Taken Shape

When you create Web pages, you'll eventually be ready to display your pages online. That's what this chapter is all about—moving your pages off the "for your eyes only" desktop and onto the "for everyone to see" Internet. Most likely, you've built Web pages so that you can create a Web presence—not just as an intellectual exercise—so we'll go with that assumption.

The key to going "live" and getting your pages onto the Web is to copy your HTML documents and image files onto a server. In Chapter 5, we went over server space, domain names, and Internet service providers (ISPs) in detail, so we won't rehash those subjects here. If you need an in-depth refresher on those topics, refer to Chapter 5. If you feel comfortable with just a summarization of requirements, here's a short list of items you'll need to gather before your Web pages can go live:

- HTML and image files, properly named and organized

- Server space (You can pay a monthly fee to a hosting service for server space, or you can use server space your ISP provides as part of your Internet connection account.)

- A software application that enables you to transfer files from your computer to a server (We'll discuss this requirement later in the chapter.)

- A Web address (You need to purchase a domain name and register it with a hosting service, or you need to obtain your Web address from your ISP—free server space is usually based on the ISP's domain name followed by your username.)

At this point in the book, the preceding list shouldn't sound too daunting. Further, in just a bit, we'll describe exactly which file transfer applications you can use and how you can copy files onto a server. So even if you have a few questions about these requirements, hang on—we'll likely address most of them shortly.

In addition to transferring your files to a server, you have a couple other tasks to attend to. Namely, you'll need to check your Web pages after you transfer your files to a server, and you'll need to let others know that your site is available for viewing.

These three "after production" tasks—transferring files, checking live Web pages, and getting the word out—are the main points we'll touch on in this chapter. If you have all your files, an Internet connection, and some server space on hand, your site can be available online by the end of this chapter.

Transferring Your Files to the Internet

Having HTML and image files as well as some server space and an Internet connection means that you're ready to post your Web pages. You can transfer files across the Internet in several ways. Here are some of the methods you can use to transfer files:

- FTP (File Transfer Protocol) programs
- Web Folders
- Web publishing wizards
- ISP interfaces and HTML editors
- Browsers

There's really no way around it—you're going to have to use some method to post your pages. After all, one of the most common transactions a Web designer has with a server is to *upload* HTML documents, images, and media files. Therefore, read on. Uploading is pretty straightforward as long as you keep in mind the process's main goal, which is moving files in an organized manner.

Whenever you upload files from your desktop to the Internet, you use FTP. The trick to transferring files via FTP is to use an application or interface that's designed specifically to serve as an FTP agent. Although that "trick" doesn't seem too profound, stating the obvious is well worth the space necessary to clarify what it means to use FTP. We've seen people's eyes glaze over as soon as we've uttered those three mysterious letters—*F-T-P*. Fortunately, as with many other Web page creation technologies, using FTP to upload Web page files isn't at all intimidating after you've gotten up to speed on a few basics.

FTP Applications

We think FTP applications provide one of the easiest and most straightforward methods of uploading files to the Internet. Apparently we're not alone in this thinking because zillions of FTP applications are available

lingo

Uploading refers to the process of copying files from your computer to a server. *Downloading* refers to copying files from a server to your computer (such as when you downloaded graphics from the Creation Guide Web site to complete the projects in Part Two of this book).

lingo

FTP is a client/server protocol that enables you to use a computer to transfer files between computers over the Internet.

tip

You should be able to buy a good FTP program for $30 or less. Generally, purchasing an FTP application means you'll have added functionality compared to most barebones freeware and shareware utilities. Keep in mind that you probably received an FTP application from your ISP with your startup package. If so, contact your provider or leaf through your ISP documentation for application-specific instructions.

as freeware, shareware, and commercial software. For the most part, we use a program named CuteFTP for Windows-based PCs and Fetch for the Apple Macintosh. But you can find numerous other FTP applications online (free for download as well as available for purchase) and at computer software retailers.

Figure 11-1 shows the interface of CuteFTP, which is a fairly typical FTP application interface.

Figure 11-1
The CuteFTP interface

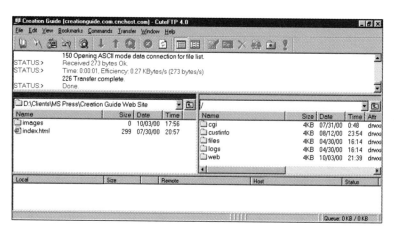

note

Beware—if you're using a shareware program and your allotted trial time runs out, you risk losing the configuration information for your FTP connections. If this happens, you have two options: you can purchase a full-fledged copy of the shareware program or (in some cases) you can temporarily backdate your system clock so that you can open the shareware application and retrieve your configuration information.

The beauty of most newer FTP applications is that you can drag and drop the files you want to upload from one window into another. For example, in CuteFTP, you can display a local folder in the left pane and display your server space in the right pane. To upload your Web page files, you simply click and drag the files or folders from the left pane into the right pane.

We've heard from a number of users that the most intimidating part of using an FTP application is configuring the initial connection. Fortunately, after you initially configure a connection, most FTP applications keep the connection data "on file" for future use.

Even though every FTP application has a custom interface for gathering account information, you'll need to provide a few basic types of

try this! Visit *www.tucows.com* or *www.shareware.com* to find listings of available FTP programs. Download and install an FTP program of your choice, and then put the application through its paces. You can always uninstall the FTP program you downloaded and try some others if the one you chose doesn't suit your working style. If you do find a shareware program that you like, be sure to register it.

information to establish an FTP connection to a server no matter which application you use:

■ **FTP site label**   A name you provide for the FTP account you're creating. The sole purpose of the site label is to help you remember which FTP account goes with which server. So be sure to name your connections logically.

■ **FTP host address**   The address of your server space. For example, the Creation Guide site's host address is *creationguide.com*.

■ **FTP site username**   The username you use to access your server space. An FTP site username is generally the same as your e-mail address, such as *mm@creationguide.com*. Some providers allow you to enter your username without the *@domain.com* portion, in which case only *mm* would be necessary in the preceding example.

■ **FTP site password**   A password associated with your username that enables you to access your server space.

Figure 11-2 shows an example of a completed FTP connection form. On many forms, you'll also be asked whether you want to transfer information in ASCII, binary, or auto-detect. The default is usually auto-detect (or some variation of that terminology), and we recommend that you retain the default setting.

tip

You might want to write down your password and store it somewhere safe. When you enter your password in FTP applications or the Web Publishing Wizard, it displays as asterisks.

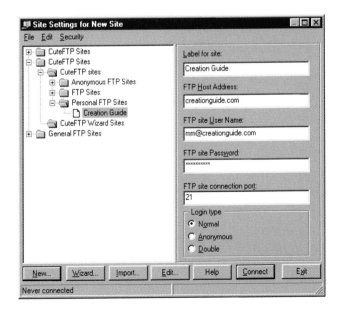

Figure 11-2
Configuring an FTP connection

tip

HTML files should be transferred in ASCII, text, or DOS text mode. All other files, including images, sounds, and videos must be transferred in binary mode. Ensuring that the Auto, Auto-Detect, All Files, or Raw Data option is selected in your FTP application's options generally means that the application can differentiate between the common file types, so you won't have to worry about specifying between images and HTML files. By default, CuteFTP (as well as most other FTP applications) is configured to auto-detect common file types.

To create an FTP connection, you insert the proper information into the respective fields (in CuteFTP, in the Site Settings For New Site dialog box) and finalize the configuration by clicking OK, Finish, or Connect (depending on your application). After you configure an FTP connection to your server space, you can connect to the Internet, activate the FTP connection, and upload your pages. (Call your ISP or visit your ISP's help pages if you have trouble connecting.)

At this point, we want to mention a couple uploading rules you need to follow religiously when you copy your Web page files to a server. You can't copy files and folders willy-nilly—you have to keep the process orderly; otherwise, you'll risk creating broken links and erroneously overwriting files that have the same name. (For example, most subfolders contain a file named index.html—if you don't upload your files into the proper folders, you might inadvertently replace one index.html file with another, nonrelated index.html file.) Here's the key point to remember when you're actively uploading Web pages:

Retain the file and folder structure of your Web pages.

In other words, if your Web page consists of one index.html document and a folder named *images*, make sure that you upload the index.html file and then create an images folder in your server space and copy the graphics stored in your local images folder into the online images folder. Retaining your site's structure is crucial to avoiding broken links on your pages.

Here's another extremely important point:

Name your online folders with exactly the same names as your local folders.

Don't rename any folders or files when you're uploading—especially don't rename any folders that contain Web page images. (By the way, accidentally creating a folder named *image* when it should be *images* constitutes renaming a folder; further, altering capitalization within file and folder names also qualifies as an unacceptable renaming practice.) The reason for retaining your existing naming structure is simple—your HTML document probably contains HTML commands that tell browsers where to look for graphics. The instructions (contained within the <IMG> tag, if you worked through the HTML project in Chapter 8) specifically point to images stored in a particularly named folder. If you change a folder's name without changing the HTML commands, browsers won't know where to find your Web page's graphics and the graphics won't display on your Web page. To reiterate, uploading is *not* the time to rename your Web page folders and files. In fact, the opposite is true:

Uploading is the time to replicate your local Web page file setup onto a server in as exact a manner as possible.

After you've successfully copied your Web page files onto a server, terminate your FTP connection, open your browser, and enter your Web page's URL. Your Web page's URL is the same as the FTP host address we mentioned earlier. If you've uploaded an index.htm or index.html HTML document, you should be able to access your new home page by entering your URL in your browser's Address bar without having to type a filename. For example, you can simply type *www.creationguide.com* instead of *www.creationguide.com/index.html* to view the Creation Guide home page.

As you can see, most FTP applications serve the sole purpose of providing a means to transfer and manipulate (rename, delete, move, and so forth) files across a network. If you're looking for other file transfer options or a more automated approach, you'll find that more than a few applications have built-in FTP capabilities, as you'll discover in the next section.

Web Folders

Microsoft Web Folders provide another method of uploading and managing a Web site's files and folders. Before you can use Web Folders, you must be running Microsoft Office 2000 (or later), and you need to check with your hosting service's or ISP's administrator to ensure that the server you'll be using supports Microsoft Web Folders. If your server supports Web Folders, you're in luck! You'll be able to use Web Folders to simplify the file and folder management tasks necessary for you to create and maintain your Web site.

Basically, Web Folders are special folders you create on your computer that link to the files and folders stored on your Web space. Manipulating the contents of a Web Folder is similar to manipulating local files and folders—the difference is that changes made to files in a Web Folder are made to the online files. In short, a Web Folder serves as a shortcut to your server space.

tip

ISPs generally tell you where you should store your Web page files within your server space. On our server space for the Creation Guide site, we copy all our information into the ISP-generated folder named web. Check with your ISP to see whether you must work within similar parameters. Some ISPs simply provide you with the top-level folder that you can use to store your Web page files.

lingo

Web Folders provide shortcuts on your desktop to files and folders located on an Internet or intranet server.

You can create Web Folders in a couple ways: accessing the Web Folders feature directly in My Computer (in Windows 98) or in My Network Places (in Windows Me and Windows 2000), or creating a Web Folder from within Microsoft Word when you save a Word document as an HTML file. Regardless of how you create a Web Folder, you can view your Web Folders by opening the Web Folders directory, shown in Figure 11-3. Notice that the Web Folders directory automatically includes an item named *Add Web Folder*. (You can probably guess the purpose of that small gem!)

Figure 11-3
Accessing the Web Folders folder

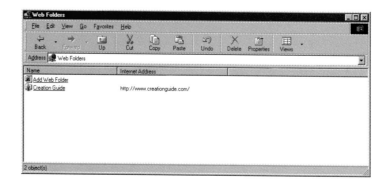

When you open a Web Folder within the Web Folders directory and view its contents, you'll see a list of online folders and files, along with their associated Web addresses (URLs), as shown in Figure 11-4. Within the Web Folder, you can move, copy, rename, and delete folders and files as well as view folder and file properties. You can also drag files between Web servers (if you have multiple Web sites) and between a Web server and your hard disk or other storage device (such as a floppy disk). In other words, Web Folders make Web site file management as straightforward as local file management.

Figure 11-4
Viewing the contents of a Web Folder

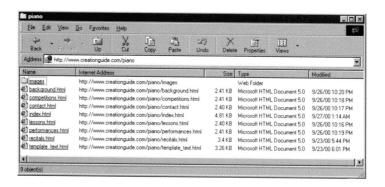

Now let's take a quick look at two ways you can create Web Folders on your system. In both instances, you'll need the following information:

- Domain information, which is your Web site's Internet address (such as *www.creationguide.com*)

- The password to access your server space

Creating a Web Folder by using My Computer

To create a Web Folder by using My Computer, follow these steps:

1 On the Microsoft Windows 98 desktop, open My Computer, and then open Web Folders. (If your computer is running Windows 2000 or Windows Me, open My Network Places.)

2 Double-click the Add Web Folder icon. (In Windows 2000 or Windows Me, double-click Add Network Place.) The Add Web Folder wizard opens, as shown in Figure 11-5.

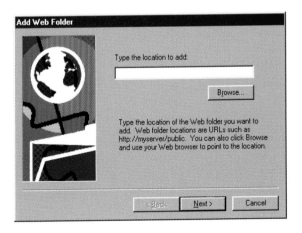

Figure 11-5
Accessing the Add Web Folder wizard

3 In the Type The Location To Add field, enter your Web site's address (such as *www.creationguide.com*) and then click Next.

4 In the Enter Network Password dialog box, type your username and password and then click OK.

5 In the Add Web Folder dialog box, type a name for the Web Folder (for example, *Creation Guide*). The name you enter here displays in the Web Folders list.

6 Click Finish to complete the process.

Now that you've created your Web Folder, you can transfer files to your Web site by dragging them into your newly created Web Folder or by saving files directly from any Office 2000 program. Later, you can right-click filenames to rename the files, select and delete files, and otherwise modify your Web page documents and directories.

Creating a Web Folder from within Word

To create a Web Folder while you're working within Word, follow these steps:

1 In Word, click File and then click Save As. The Save As dialog box displays.

2 In the Save As dialog box, click the Web Folders or the My Network Places icon in the Save In pane to display the contents of the Web Folders or My Network Places directory, as shown in Figure 11-6.

Figure 11-6
Using the Save As dialog box to create a Web Folder

Create New Folder button

Web Folders icon

3 In the Save As dialog box, click the Create New Folder button (shown in Figure 11-6). The Add Web Folder wizard opens (as shown earlier in Figure 11-5).

4 In the wizard, enter your Web site's address (such as *www.creationguide .com*) and then click Next.

5   In the Enter Network Password dialog box, type your username and password and then click OK.

6   In the Add Web Folder dialog box, type a name for the Web Folder and then click Finish.

At this point, you can save your Word document in the Web Folder (thereby uploading your Web page) in the same way that you save other Word documents.

7   In the Save As Type drop-down list box, specify Web Page, specify the document's name in the File Name text box, click the Change Title button if you want to specify the Web page's title text, click the Web Folder in which you want to post the HTML document, and then click Save.

After you save an HTML document in a Web Folder, you can view the page online by entering the Web page's address in your browser's Address bar.

Other FTP Options

If you don't want to install an FTP program on your computer or if your server doesn't support Web Folders, all hope is not lost. You can copy files to a Web server in other ways as well. Namely, you can use the FTP functions built into any of the following types of applications:

- Web publishing wizards, such as the Web Publishing Wizard that comes with Windows

- ISP online services and HTML editors, such as Microsoft FrontPage

- Browsers, such as Microsoft Internet Explorer

Web publishing wizards

You can easily upload Web documents by using the Web Publishing Wizard in Windows. The Web Publishing Wizard works in the same way as other wizards: it provides a series of dialog boxes that you complete to upload a page. The wizard's dialog boxes gather the same types of information that you enter into an FTP connection form. Like FTP programs, the wizard stores FTP connection information after you initially configure a connection. In this way, the wizard provides an easy-to-use alternative to FTP applications. If you become a "power" Web designer, however, you'll quickly crave the greater flexibility that FTP applications offer.

note

You'll need to establish an Internet connection before you can save a Web document in a Web Folder.

note

If you're running an older version of Windows, the Web Publishing Wizard might not be available since it wasn't added until the OSR2.5 release of Windows 95.

Regardless of what your future needs might be, consider the Web Publishing Wizard as a viable option when it comes time to publish your first Web site.

The best way to understand how the Web Publishing Wizard works is to walk through the process. Because the process comes in wizard form, there's no reason for us to show you the pages you can see on your computer. We will give you a head start, though. Before you start the Web Publishing Wizard, gather the following bits of data so that you'll have it handy when the wizard asks for the information:

- **Path and name of the file or folder you want to upload**   You need to be able to locate the file you want to upload.

- **Name you want to use to refer to the connection**   This element is similar to the site label attribute provided in an FTP application's connection form. The name you provide is for your benefit only, so give the connection a logical name. That way, you'll know which connection to reuse the next time you work through the wizard.

- **Path and directory to which you want to upload your Web page files**   This element is the same as the FTP host address, which is a fancy way to refer to your future site's URL. For example, we'd upload the index.html file to *www.creationguide.com* and we'd upload images to *www.creationguide.com/images*.

- **Internet connection account you want to use to upload the files**   If you have multiple Internet connections, you'll have to specify which connection you want the wizard to use to upload the file. (Hint: Use your fastest connection!)

- **Username**   Generally, your username is formatted in the same manner as your e-mail address—for example, *jc@creationguide.com*. Some providers allow you to enter your username without the *@domain.com* portion, in which case only *jc* would be necessary in the preceding example.

- **User password**   You'll need to provide the password that's associated with your username.

After you've gathered the appropriate information, you're ready to work through the Web Publishing Wizard. To access the wizard, use either of the following procedures.

- Click Start, click Programs, click Accessories, click Internet Tools, and then click Web Publishing Wizard.

- Click Start, click Programs, click Internet Explorer, and then click Web Publishing Wizard.

To kick off the wizard, click the Next button. Then work your way through each page, providing the proper information. When you've completed all the wizard forms, you'll need to click Finish to upload your files. If you have the correct information on hand, the process should flow smoothly without incident. Make sure you check your typing—a simple typo can throw off the entire process. The initial page of the wizard is shown in Figure 11-7.

tip
You can create a desktop shortcut to the Web Publishing Wizard and then drag files and folders onto the shortcut to automatically activate the wizard.

Figure 11-7
Getting started with the Web Publishing Wizard

try this! Copy any existing HTML document stored on your computer, and name the copied file test.html. Then work through the Web Publishing Wizard to practice uploading the test.html file. After you successfully upload the test document (don't forget to view the test page online to verify your success), you'll have to delete the test.html file from your server space via an FTP application or Internet Explorer (as described later in this chapter). Unfortunately, the Web Publishing Wizard doesn't offer a way to delete existing files on your server space.

ISP interfaces and HTML editor features

Other resources for transferring files include ISP interfaces and HTML editors. Basically, these tools are variations or hybrids of FTP applications and the Web Publishing Wizard. The main benefits are that the tools are easily accessible. For example, some ISPs offer online forms you can use to upload files from your computer to the server. In fact, the Creation Guide host provides a form, but we've found it to be cumbersome, so we never use it to manage the site's files. If you're shopping for a hosting service, look into the file management services the hosting service offers. Our hosting service provides a number of quality features—such as logging statistics (including tracking the number of page hits and visitor traffic) and lots of space—so we overlooked the file manager feature because we knew full well that we can whip a few pages across an FTP application interface pretty quickly. In our opinion, if you're planning to use an ISP file transfer interface, make sure that the online tool is at least as intuitive as an FTP application or the Web Publishing Wizard.

Similar to an ISP's online FTP forms, a number of HTML editors, including FrontPage, offer automatic file uploading features (as discussed in Chapter 10). Using an HTML editor to upload files can be extremely convenient. The main concern is that you should be keenly aware of which files are uploading and where they're going. Further, know when you're replacing existing online files; otherwise, you might not be able to backtrack to a previous page if you decide you don't want to keep your most recent modifications. To illustrate, if you're using Internet Explorer and you have FrontPage installed, you can visit your Web site and then click the Edit button in the Internet Explorer toolbar to open a local version of your Web page in FrontPage. You can then make modifications to the page and click Save to save the modified page directly to the server. When you do this, if you don't rename the newly modified page, the existing page is replaced with the updated page. As you'll see in Chapter 12, you should archive your unused Web pages in case you need to revert to older pages or borrow elements from past publications. When you modify and save a page using the online access feature in FrontPage, you overwrite your existing HTML document. That's definitely something to keep in mind.

To learn how to use ISP forms or an HTML editor's uploading features, refer to the application's help files or published documentation. Too many variations exist among systems to adequately provide procedural descriptions in this chapter.

Browsers as FTP Clients

Last but not least, you can use some browsers as FTP clients. Most people know that you can download files from within a browser window, but

tip

Using the FrontPage Publish Web command to initially upload Web pages you've created in FrontPage ensures that FrontPage features that rely on FrontPage Server Extensions are properly implemented. If you've added advanced capability to your FrontPage Web pages, we highly recommend that you use the Publish Web command to upload your Web site.

few people know that you can also upload files and folders in some browser applications, Internet Explorer included. Keep in mind that your hosting service must support this feature—we've found that some sites work with browser uploads better than others. If your hosting service works well with this feature, the methodology is simple: you use the Address bar to display the contents of your server folder, and then you can drag files from local folders into the server folders displayed in your browser window. Further, you can right-click existing online files and folders to access a shortcut menu that allows you to rename, move, and delete online files. To display your online folders, you enter the following information in the Internet Explorer Address bar:

ftp://username:password@ftp.domain.com

For example, an entry might look like the following:

ftp://mmail:coffee2@ftp.primenet.com

After your server space displays, open the folder containing your Web page files and drag the files and folders into your browser window to copy the Web page components. Figure 11-8 shows FTP access to a Web folder. You can upload, delete, and rename your Web files within Internet Explorer.

tip

To access AOL's file uploading feature, use the "myplace" or "myftpspace" keyword. If you're creating a page on AOL, your Web page's URL will be *members.aol.com/ screenname/filename.*

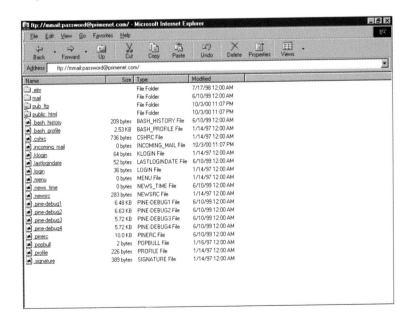

Figure 11-8
Using Internet Explorer as an FTP client to transfer Web files

In this chapter, we've introduced a number of tools that you can use to transfer your local Web page files to a server. Try a few of the options, and see which works best for you. Because many variations exist within each category, we'd be embarking on an unrealistic task if we tried to describe every aspect of every means of transferring files to the Internet. Your best bet is to choose which uploading style you want to attempt and then give it a try. If you have questions, visit the application's help files or printed documentation. If you're uncomfortable with one process, try another approach. We're confident that if you gather the appropriate connection information and enter the information properly, you'll be able to connect to your Web space and get your pages online.

try this! If you used the Web Publishing Wizard to upload a test file, display the contents of your server space in Internet Explorer, right-click the test.html file, and click Delete on the shortcut menu to remove the test document from your server space.

Reviewing Your Work

After you upload your Web pages, the first order of action is to surf to your pages and check your Web site's presentation. As we discussed in Part Two, you should preview your Web pages throughout the creation process—and we consider uploading part of the creation process. So check your live pages. If you've been careful, you shouldn't find too many surprises after your pages go live. Nevertheless, before you start calling all your friends and directing people to your Web site, you should view your Web pages. After you display the home page, check for the following details:

- Ensure that all images display properly. You don't want any broken image markers on your page, as shown in Figure 11-9.

- Click your links to ensure that they work, including the buttons on your navigation bar, linked logo graphics, text links, and image maps, if those appear on your page.

- Verify whether the page and its elements fit within the standard browser window. Remember—users report that having to scroll left and right to view a Web page is highly annoying.

- Complete and submit a test form to yourself if your site uses forms.

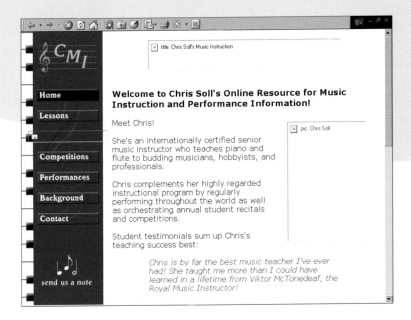

Figure 11-9
Viewing the piano site from Chapter 8 with three broken image links

- Read each page title in the title bar for accuracy.
- Verify that text and text links are easy to read against the Web pages' backgrounds.

Basically, take the time to scrutinize your site. Click everywhere, test each interactive element, and employ your critical eye. Better to take a little extra time after uploading to check your work than to have a viewer send you an e-mail message to tell you that your Web site is lame because it doesn't display properly or respond as expected.

The last postproduction task we'll cover is getting the word out that your Web site exists. The most common way to begin publicizing your site is to ensure that your Web page is readily recognizable by search engines and search directories.

Registering with Search Engines and Directories

After you upload your site and your Web pages satisfy your error-checking critical eye, you're ready to start publicizing your Web site's existence. The most popular way to start the process is to register your site with search engines and directories. You've probably used search engines, such as Lycos, Yahoo!, and AltaVista, to find Web pages in the past. Now you need to approach search services from the opposite angle—instead of searching for other people's sites, you want to enable others to find your site. But first, a little background information.

The term *search engine* has come to encompass true search engines, such as HotBot, as well as directory setups, such as Yahoo! Distinct differences exist between the two major types of information retrieval systems (although after the following brief explanation, we'll go with the crowd on this one and continue to refer to both of the following setups as search engines).

lingo

Spiders are automated programs that search (or *crawl*) the Internet for new Web documents. The spiders then index all the addresses they find along with content-related information in a database that search engines can use.

- **Search engines** Search engines create listings automatically or with a little assistance (such as a URL submission) and via spiders that crawl the Web. Whenever you post or change Web pages, search engines will eventually find your pages. Page titles, body copy, and other page elements can affect how your Web page is categorized. Generally, you don't need to supply any specific information to a search engine, although sometimes you might be required to submit your URL.

- **Directories** Directories rely on human input. To be listed in a directory, you must submit a short description of your site. Directory editors also write brief descriptions of the sites they review. When users run a directory search, the process looks for matches in the descriptions (not for matches within the Web pages' titles, body text, or other elements).

Popular search engines that don't require any input from you—which means they'll find your site automatically—include the following:

- AltaVista (*www.altavista.com*)
- Excite (*www.excite.com*)
- Go.com (*www.go.com*)
- Google (*www.google.com*)
- HotBot (*www.hotbot.com*)
- Lycos (*www.lycos.com*)
- Magellan (*magellan.excite.com*)
- NorthernLight (*www.northernlight.com*)
- WebCrawler (*www.webcrawler.com*)

Some search engines that require you to provide additional information or that pick and choose which sites get listed in their directories include the following:

- **AOL Netfind** *(search.aol.com)*   Requires you to choose a category for your site to be listed and then fill out a submission form.

- **Ask Jeeves** *(www.askjeeves.com)*   Requires you to e-mail your URL and a description of your site to the site registration address. Then the site managers decide whether and where your site gets listed.

- **LookSmart** *(www.looksmart.com)*   Requires you to choose a category for your site and fill out a submission form.

- **MSN** *(search.msn.com)*   Requires you to complete a form by providing your e-mail address, Web page's title, and a description of your site.

- **Netscape** *(search.netscape.com)*   Requires you to complete a form by providing your e-mail address, Web page's title, and a description of your site.

- **Yahoo!** *(www.yahoo.com)*   Requires you to choose a category and fill out a submission form. Yahoo! administrators decide whether and where your site gets listed.

Some sites, such as AltaVista, will list your site within a day or two after submission, but others, such as Yahoo!, can take months (many, many months) to list your site, if they choose to list your site at all.

In addition to registering your sites with search engines and directories, you can use HTML code within your HTML documents to help search engines properly classify your Web pages or ignore your Web pages altogether. The key to assisting search engines is to add META tags within your HTML document's header section.

META Tags

To some extent, you can control how search engines "see" the contents of a Web page. To do this, you can add META tags to your HTML documents that specify keywords and descriptions that should be associated with your pages. META tags are especially helpful if you want to classify a page that contains little textual content (like a corporate splash page).

To use META tags, you include them within the `<HEAD></HEAD>` tag set in an HTML document. (See Chapter 8 for an explanation of the

tip

Some search engines query other search engines to get results from multiple sources. A prime example is the DogPile *(www.dogpile.com)* site. You can click the Add URL link on the DogPile home page to access hyperlinks to the submission pages of a number of popular search engines.

tip

Limit your META *keyword* tags to 10 to 20 keywords, with the most important keywords listed first. Likewise, some search engines will catalog only the first dozen or so words in META *description* tags, so keep your descriptions short and place the most important information up front.

`<HEAD></HEAD>` tag set.) You can use *keyword* or *description* META tag attributes, or both. For example, to include keywords and a description in your Web page that search engines can access, you could enter information similar to the following:

```
<HEAD>
<META NAME="keywords" CONTENT="extracheese, web design,
    multimedia design, Jeff Castrina, resort gifts, cd-rom,
    animation, website, web, design, macromedia flash,
    graphic design, illustration, arizona, cheese,
    tempe, phoenix">
<META NAME="description" CONTENT="ExtraCheese is a multimedia
    design firm specializing in Web and interactive media.
    We create Web sites, interactive CD-ROMs, Web animation,
    and other interactive media that utilize the latest
    technologies to deliver the most effective message to your
    clients.">
</HEAD>
```

You can also instruct search engines not to catalog your site. In other words, you can display a virtual "Do Not Enter" sign for search engines by including the following tag within your HTML document's `<HEAD>` `</HEAD>` section:

```
<HEAD>
<META NAME="robots" CONTENT="noindex, nofollow">
</HEAD>
```

Calling Attention to Your Site
Other ways you can attract attention to your site include participating in any of the following activities:

- Telling others about your site via word of mouth, e-mail messages, newsgroups, or list servers.

- Participating in reciprocal programs in which you display links on your page to other sites and vice versa (if possible).

- Displaying banner ads for other Web sites on your Web pages as well as submitting banner ads for your site on other sites.

- Getting your site publicly reviewed by a third party.

- Putting your Web site address on your printed and marketing material, including business cards, stationery, brochures, and advertisements.

If you don't include META tag information in your Web pages, search engines will catalog your site according to the text information on your home page, which can work for or against your site.

After copying your Web files to a server, checking your online pages, and publicizing your site, you're ready to sit back and enjoy the fruits of your creative endeavor—at least for a little while. But don't get too comfortable. It won't be long before you're ready to update, archive, and modify your existing pages. In Chapter 12 (the final chapter in this book), we'll provide you with a few pointers that you can use to keep your site alive and dust-free.

key points

- You can use FTP applications to copy files from your computer to a server.

- You can transfer files and folders by using FTP applications, Web Folders, the Web Publishing Wizard, ISP online forms, HTML editors, and browsers such as Internet Explorer.

- If your server supports Web Folders and you're using Windows 98, Windows 2000, or Windows Me, you can use the Web Folders feature to easily upload and manipulate your Web site's files and folders in the same manner you manage local folders.

- When uploading Web files to a server, retain your Web site's file and folder structure, including using the exact naming and organizational parameters as the files and folders on your local computer.

- After you upload Web pages, always view them online to check for errors and broken links.

- To publicize your Web site, register with search engines.

- Consider adding META tags to your HTML documents to somewhat control how search engines categorize your site.

- Finally, let others know that your site is live—via word of mouth and other typical communication channels—and start the exchange of online information!

index.htm

updating,

onClick

Dark Red   Dark Slate Gray   Moccasin

<script language

12

archiving,
AND MOVING ON

Most people would gladly accept the opportunity to drive around in a new Porsche. But even an expensive sports car loses its appeal if it's never tuned up or if it's allowed to gather dust, rust, and cobwebs. Similarly, Web pages can quickly lose their glow if they're neglected and left to fend for themselves on the Internet.

After the "Going Live" Dust Settles

By the time you've reached this point in the book, you've probably posted your Web pages online and you're enjoying a little breather. Congratulations! Soon, though, you'll want to explore ways in which you can modify and improve your site's visual appeal and content. In this chapter, we give you some practical instructions for post-Web-site-production tasks as well as provide you with a few pointers for additional Web-site-creation opportunities that will arise now that you've passed the "beginner" stage of Web development.

Updating Your Web Pages

One of the beauties of Web sites is that they're never really "done." Just as most self-actualized people never stop learning, effective Web pages are evolving works-in-progress. So after a few days away from your Web pages, you might want to think about ways you can update your Web site to make it more interesting and useful for visitors.

Reasons to Update

A few reasons exist that bolster the argument for updating your Web pages regularly. The following list includes some of the reasons we've run across. Pick and choose whichever seem relevant for your needs, or feel free to concoct some custom reasons for keeping your Web site fresh.

- To supply new and updated information
- To show viewers that you're just as interested in your Web site as you want them to be (This one's a biggie.)
- To encourage people to return to your site (not to bore them with the same old stuff)
- To provide additional features for visitors that you didn't address when you first created the site
- To remove features that visitors find distracting or confusing
- To promote special causes
- To celebrate an upcoming holiday or event
- To reflect changes in the site's parent entity (such as a company that might want to incorporate a new logo, slogan, or color scheme)

Keep in mind that the overriding reason you update pages should be to *benefit your viewers*. You shouldn't update your site just to provide a forum for your experimentation with Web page gimmicks. Likewise, if you have a popular item on your Web page, resist the urge to remove it just because you're tired of it. If viewers find an item useful and they voice their opinions via your guest book, feedback page, or other avenues, keep the component or upgrade it to make them even happier. Just as you had a reason for adding each element when you first created your Web pages, make sure you have reasons for adding and removing items when you modify your site. In other words, think before you act.

Easily Updateable Elements

Certain page elements lend themselves to being updated easily. For the most part, you'll probably want to maintain your Web site's overall structure, navigation bars, logos, color schemes, and contact information. Occasionally, though, such as when a company revamps its image or embarks on a new marketing campaign, the preceding elements are changed intentionally. But you shouldn't make arbitrary changes, say, just because you get tired of blue and want to try purple. Here are the four Web site elements that change most often:

- Graphics
- Text
- Last-updated date
- Recommended links

The reason the preceding elements are easy to change and are changed more frequently than others is because they generally convey a Web site's content. Most viewers can appreciate a well-styled Web site, but they return to and use sites that contain dynamic (as opposed to static) information.

Updating Tip and Tricks

Now that we've briefly outlined why you might want to update your site in the future as well as the types of elements you might want to change, let's look at some guidelines you should follow when you're updating your Web pages. Most of these guidelines are based on common sense, but they're worth noting here anyway.

Above all, avoid taking your perfectly good page and rendering it useless via unnecessarily complex design or coding modifications. We've actually seen clean, once-working sites "updated" with the latest and greatest Web features that were ultimately rendered unviewable by the majority of browsers. Here's a motto to keep in mind:

Aim for "better," not "deader."

And because change is inevitable, consider the next guideline as well:

Create a regular schedule for updates.

A regular schedule forces you to clearly plan how you want to up-date your Web site as well as provides a target date for completing fu-ture changes. For example, let's say you decide that you'll update your site every third Monday of each month. Throughout the month, you can jot down update notes to yourself or create local versions of live pages. When the third Monday rolls around, commit yourself to implementing any planned changes and uploading modified pages. Then start taking notes for the next month's update. Of course, in some instances, a quick nonscheduled update might be in order—for example, if a phone num-ber needs to be corrected, a typo needs to be fixed, or a broken graphic link needs to be redirected. But for more routine changes, you should try to stick to some regular schedule. Randomly updating your site can lead to slovenly or chaotic practices, in which your Web page can either gather too much dust or change too frequently (which can cause regular visi-tors to miss some of the updates).

Here's the next rule of thumb:

Avoid updating a live site.

Some HTML editors (Microsoft FrontPage included) enable you to edit live sites. This feature can be useful for emergency fixes, such as the in-correct information, typos, and broken links just mentioned. In most cases, though, you should follow these steps when beginning your update:

1 Download the most recent version of the page you want to update.

2 Redesign the page locally.

3 Preview the page in a browser.

4 Upload the modified page only after you've ensured that the page runs and displays properly.

Updating a live site might result in users seeing half-completed changes as you work on the page. Further, you might be hard pressed to revert to an earlier version of your site if you need to recover from disastrous or undesirable changes. (Later in the chapter, we talk about archiving to avoid losing "old" data.)

Finally, as part of your routine maintenance on your site, you should follow this practice:

Regularly check the hyperlinks on your pages.

As you know, the Web is extremely fluid; pages come and go. So check your links frequently—nothing signals a neglected page as clearly as hyperlinks to nonexistent pages.

Archiving Web Page Elements

Updating your Web site goes hand in hand with saving past versions of your Web pages. This practice is referred to as *archiving*. The underlying concept of archiving is this:

When you update your site, don't throw away your old Web page elements!

At least not right away.

Best practices dictate that you let your has-been Web pages and graphics hang around for a while (at least six months in most cases and possibly a year, if you can foresee any chance that you'll need the "old" information or graphics, especially if you can't easily re-create the information). The most notable reason for archiving instead of deleting is that you never know when you might need old text, graphics, JavaScript, and so forth. Many times, you can use old pages as templates or reuse old graphics in new ways. You'll find it's much easier to create an Archive folder to store past page elements than it is to re-create graphics and data after you've obliterated them.

You can store archived information in several ways. The easiest way is to create a folder named *Archive* and copy past Web page elements into subfolders within that folder. You can store an Archive folder and its subfolders in several places:

- Local computer
- Removable storage device, such as floppy disks, Zip disks, or writable CDs

lingo

Archiving refers to copying files onto a tape or disk for long-term storage.

- Web site's hosting service (You'll probably have more than enough server space for a while.)

- Online storage cabinet (such as the storage cabinets available on the MSN Communities site)

Another way to think of archiving is as a method to copy and store Web pages before you choose to stop displaying them for viewers. For example, let's say you created a new home page. Your updating and archiving procedures might take the following form:

note

When archiving HTML documents, remember also to archive the associated graphics files and folders. Store the graphics in a folder with the same name as the original graphics folder so that your archived page's links will work properly.

1 You've named the new page *index2.html* and uploaded it to the Internet, and the page checked out. You're now ready to display the new home page in place of the existing home page.

2 Before you rename *index2.html* to *index.html* and replace the existing *index.html* page, you create a subfolder within the Archive folder. You give the folder an informative name, such as *Old Home Page-Sept-15-2000*, and then you copy the existing index.html page into the Archive folder's subfolder.

3 After copying index.html to the Archive folder, you delete the existing index.html file in your Web site's main directory.

4 You then rename *index2.html* to *index.html* and place the new index.html file into your Web site's main directory.

In the preceding steps, the old index.html file is safely stowed away for possible future use and the new page displays. Creating an organized archiving storage system and directory-naming scheme can make finding "old" information a snap.

After you master updating and archiving—and it shouldn't take you long—and you've worked your way through this book, you can safely say that you've covered all the basics of Web page creation. The only direction to go now is beyond "easy" and into the realm of advanced Web page development.

Moving Beyond Easy Web Pages

As we wrap up this book, we hope you've found that you've gained a strong foundation for Web page creation. Although we could go on for a few hundred more pages describing more advanced Web page creation techniques (and we really wouldn't mind doing that, either!), we realize that we've had to pick and choose what's most helpful when it comes to creating Web pages the *easy* way. We want to point out, though, that while we've covered quite a bit of information in this book, we haven't explained everything: many more advanced techniques for creating Web pages are available to you as well. At some point in the future, you'll probably want to incorporate multimedia elements such as video, animation, and audio. Or maybe you'll want to add security features to your Web site by employing encryption algorithms or password protection schemes. At this point in the book, we're confident that your understanding of the Web should enable you to move on to more complex issues if you so desire. In the meantime, because you've stuck with us this long, we'll give you a couple bonus JavaScripts to play with to give you a taste of more advanced techniques.

Bonus JavaScript Components

One simple way you can add pizzazz to your sites is to incorporate JavaScript into your HTML pages. JavaScript is a lightweight programming language that enables you to add Web page functionality by inserting JavaScript code into an HTML document.

Typically, JavaScript enables effects such as fading backgrounds, button rollover effects, cursor animations, multicolored text, banner displays, stylized text, password protection, games, and other creative design elements. Fortunately, you don't have to be a programmer to use JavaScript. A number of sites offer free JavaScript code samples that you can copy and paste into your HTML documents. For example, check out the sites *www.wsabstract.com/cutpastejava.shtml* and *www.creationguide.com/javascript* to find some clever, free-for-your-use JavaScripts. Other links to JavaScript codes are listed on the Creation Guide Web site's Resources page.

Just for fun, we've included two scripts that you can play with at home and use on your Web pages—a countdown component and a background color selection feature. To use JavaScript samples, simply type the JavaScript code into a text document or an existing HTML document. Save the document as an HTML file (remember, you might have to right-click the filename and change the *.txt* extension to *.html*), and then view the document in your browser.

If you prefer not to manually enter the code necessary to create the countdown element and the background color selection feature (or if you want to see the JavaScript in action without actually creating HTML documents), visit the *www.creationguide.com/javascript/countdown* and *www.creationguide.com/javascript/bgcolors* Web pages. Display the source code on either page, and then copy and paste the code into a locally stored HTML document.

Adding a countdown element to a Web page

You can add a couple lines of JavaScript code to create an automated countdown component on your Web page. Figure 12-1 shows the code necessary to create the countdown component. The countdown component automatically counts down to the date of your choice. You can change the *January 1, 2002* date to any date, and you can customize the countdown message by modifying the *days until the year 2002!* text. (The elements you can customize display in red in Figure 12-1.) Figure 12-2 shows the countdown component in action.

Figure 12-1
Adding a countdown component to an HTML document

```
countdown.html - Notepad
File  Edit  Search  Help
<HTML>
<HEAD>
<TITLE>Countdown to the New Year!
</TITLE>
</HEAD>
<BODY>

<SCRIPT LANGUAGE="JavaScript">
var now = new Date();
var then = new Date("January 1, 2002");
var gap = then.getTime() - now.getTime();
gap = Math.floor(gap / (1000 * 60 * 60 * 24));
document.write("Only " + gap + " days until the year 2002!");
</SCRIPT>


</BODY>
</HTML>
```

Figure 12-2
Viewing the countdown component in action

Countdown to the New Year! - Microsoft Internet Explorer
File Edit View Favorites Tools Help
Back Forward Stop Refresh Home Search Favorites History Mail Print Edit
Address http://www.creationguide.com/javascript/countdown/

Only 348 days until the year 2002!

Providing the background color selection feature

Using JavaScript, you can display background color selection buttons on your Web page so that users can display your page with the background color of their choice. This feature is mostly just for fun, but it's a nice practice in inserting JavaScript and sampling the effect JavaScript can have in Web page development endeavors.

Figure 12-3 shows the code necessary to create the background color selection component. You can use any color names or hexadecimal numbers (refer to this book's appendix) when providing color selections. Remember, if you change an *onclick* value (the color you want to display after a user clicks a button), you should also change the button's name by modifying the button's *value* parameter. In Figure 12-3, *onclick* values and *button value* parameters display in red. Figure 12-4 shows the background color selection buttons in action.

Figure 12-3
Providing background selection buttons in an HTML document

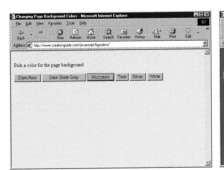 

Figure 12-4
Viewing the background selection buttons in action, with Moccasin selected in the left image and Teal selected in the right

If you search the Web using the term *JavaScript*, you'll find all sorts of free JavaScripts. When you find free JavaScript online, you can copy the code and paste it directly into your HTML documents—no typing required! So keep those Ctrl+C (copy) and Ctrl+V (paste) keyboard commands in mind when you want to quickly and efficiently add JavaScript features to your Web pages.

Whenever you copy JavaScript to a document, ensure that you test your pages in various popular browsers to verify that your pages display properly for the greatest number of visitors. JavaScript (as well as most other advanced features) can be a little touchy sometimes.

key points

- Consider updating your Web pages regularly to keep visitors happy and Web site content fresh.

- Archive old pages and graphics (at least for a while) in case you need to reuse elements.

- Don't fear the unknown! Have fun—move beyond easy creation techniques and try your hand at various advanced procedures. You might be surprised to find how much you've learned.

- Finally—our last key point in this book. We hope you've enjoyed learning about Web page creation as much as we've enjoyed creating this book and the companion site. Feel free to use all the resources incorporated into the companion site and drop us a line (*mm@creationguide.com* and *jc@creationguide.com*) if you ever have a question or want to share your Web page creation results. We'd certainly enjoy hearing from you, and we'll do our best to respond to your queries as quickly as possible. Best wishes for success on the Web!

Appendix

web-safe colors and html special characters

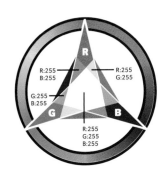

As discussed throughout this book, many factors come into play when you use colors on Web pages. These factors—including bit-depth settings on users' monitors and whether your pages are displayed on a PC running Microsoft Windows or on a Macintosh—can alter how pages display. Fortunately, you can ensure that the colors on your Web pages look fairly consistent regardless of computer platforms or setups. The trick to using colors effectively is to design your Web pages using the colors available on the Web-safe color palette. This appendix includes the 216 Web-safe colors along with their hexadecimal and RGB color values, arranged into three charts: bright colors, neutral colors, and grays. (Remember that you use hexadecimal values to define colors in your HTML documents, as described in Chapter 8, and RGB color values to create graphics in most graphics programs.)

On this page, you can see the red, green, and blue (RGB) color model, which represents the visible color spectrum. Computer monitors use the RGB model to create color. By mixing red, green, and blue values (in which 0 equates to none and 255 equates to the full color value), you can create any color you need. In the diagram, the outer circle represents the full RGB color spectrum. The triangular shape shows the colors you can achieve by mixing full RGB color values (that is, by combining only 255 color values of red, green, and blue in various combinations). RGB colors are also known as *additive colors* because when mixing all colors in full intensity (255), they create white, as represented by the center of the diagram. The table on this page shows a few examples of how Web-safe colors, RGB values, hexadecimal values, and browser-recognized color names (color names that can be used in place of hexadecimal numbers in HTML source code) correspond to each other.

Web-safe RGB values and their hexadecimal equivalents	
RGB value	Hexadecimal value
0	00
51	33
102	66
153	99
204	CC
255	FF

RGB color values and the hexadecimal equivalents for the eight named colors that are Web-safe

white	black
RGB: 255, 255, 255	RGB: 0, 0, 0
Hex: #FF0000	Hex: #FFFF00

red	yellow
RGB: 255, 0, 0	RGB: 255, 255, 0
Hex: #FF0000	Hex: #FFFF00

lime	cyan
RGB: 0, 255, 0	RGB: 0, 255, 255
Hex: #00FF00	Hex: #00FFFF

blue	magenta
RGB: 0, 0, 255	RGB: 255, 0, 255
Hex: #0000FF	Hex: #FF00FF

Bright Web-safe colors

				255, 0, 0 #FF0000	204, 0, 0 #CC0000	153, 0, 0 #990000	102, 0, 0 #660000	51, 0, 0 #330000
				255, 0, 51 #FF0033	204, 0, 51 #CC0033	153, 0, 51 #990033	102, 0, 51 #660033	51, 0, 51 #330033
			255, 51, 102 #FF3366	255, 0, 102 #FF0066	204, 0, 102 #CC0066	153, 0, 102 #990066	102, 0, 102 #660066	
		255, 102, 153 #FF6699	255, 51, 153 #FF3399	255, 0, 153 #FF0099	204, 0, 153 #CC0099	153, 0, 153 #990099		
	255, 153, 204 #FF99CC	255, 102, 204 #FF66CC	255, 51, 204 #FF33CC	255, 0, 204 #FF00CC	204, 0, 204 #CC00CC			
255, 204, 255 #FFCCFF	255, 153, 255 #FF99FF	255, 102, 255 #FF66FF	255, 51, 255 #FF33FF	255, 0, 255 #FF00FF				
204, 204, 255 #CCCCFF	204, 153, 255 #CC99FF	204, 102, 255 #CC66FF	204, 51, 255 #CC33FF	204, 0, 255 #CC00FF				
	153, 153, 255 #9999FF	153, 102, 255 #9966FF	153, 51, 255 #9933FF	153, 0, 255 #9900FF	153, 0, 204 #9900CC			
		102, 102, 255 #6666FF	102, 51, 255 #6633FF	102, 0, 255 #6600FF	102, 0, 204 #6600CC	102, 0, 153 #660099		
			51, 51, 255 #3333FF	51, 0, 255 #3300FF	51, 0, 204 #3300CC	51, 0, 153 #330099	51, 0, 102 #330066	
				0, 0, 255 #0000FF	0, 0, 204 #0000CC	0, 0, 153 #000099	0, 0, 102 #000066	0, 0, 51 #000033
				0, 51, 255 #0033FF	0, 51, 204 #0033CC	0, 51, 153 #003399	0, 51, 102 #003366	0, 51, 51 #003333
			51, 102, 255 #3366FF	0, 102, 255 #0066FF	0, 102, 204 #0066CC	0, 102, 153 #006699	0, 102, 102 #006666	
		102, 153, 255 #6699FF	51, 153, 255 #3399FF	0, 153, 255 #0099FF	0, 153, 204 #0099CC	0, 153, 153 #009999		
	153, 204, 255 #99CCFF	102, 204, 255 #66CCFF	51, 204, 255 #33CCFF	0, 204, 255 #00CCFF	0, 204, 204 #00CCCC			
244, 255, 255 #CCFFFF	153, 255, 255 #99FFFF	102, 255, 255 #66FFFF	51, 255, 255 #33FFFF	0, 255, 255 #00FFFF				
0, 255, 204 #CCFFCC	153, 255, 204 #99FFCC	102, 255, 204 #66FFCC	51, 255, 204 #33FFCC	0, 255, 204 #00FFCC				
	153, 255, 153 #99FF99	102, 255, 153 #66FF99	51, 255, 153 #33FF99	0, 255, 153 #00FF99	0, 204, 153 #00CC99			
		102, 255, 102 #66FF66	51, 255, 102 #33FF66	0, 255, 102 #00FF66	0, 204, 102 #00CC66	0, 153, 102 #009966		
			51, 255, 51 #33FF33	0, 255, 51 #00FF33	0, 204, 51 #00CC33	0, 153, 51 #009933	0, 102, 51 #006633	
				0, 255, 0 #00FF00	0, 204, 0 #00CC00	0, 153, 0 #009900	0, 102, 0 #006600	0, 51, 0 #003300
				51, 255, 0 #33FF00	51, 204, 0 #33CC00	51, 153, 0 #339900	51, 102, 0 #336600	51, 51, 0 #333300
			102, 255, 51 #66FF33	102, 255, 0 #66FF00	102, 204, 0 #66CC00	102, 153, 0 #669900	102, 102, 0 #666600	
		153, 255, 102 #99FF66	153, 255, 51 #99FF33	153, 255, 0 #99FF00	153, 204, 0 #99CC00	153, 153, 0 #999900		
	204, 255, 153 #CCFF99	204, 255, 102 #CCFF66	204, 255, 51 #CCFF33	204, 255, 0 #CCFF00	204, 204, 0 #CCCC00			
255, 255, 204 #FFFFCC	255, 255, 153 #FFFF99	255, 255, 102 #FFFF66	255, 255, 51 #FFFF33	255, 255, 0 #FFFF00				
255, 204, 204 #FFCCCC	255, 204, 153 #FFCC99	255, 204, 102 #FFCC66	255, 204, 51 #FFCC33	255, 204, 0 #FFCC00				
	255, 153, 153 #FF9999	255, 153, 102 #FF9966	255, 153, 51 #FF9933	255, 153, 0 #FF9900	204, 153, 0 #CC9900			
		255, 102, 102 #FF6666	255, 102, 51 #FF6633	255, 102, 0 #FF6600	204, 102, 0 #CC6600	153, 102, 0 #996600		
			255, 51, 51 #FF3333	255, 51, 0 #FF3300	204, 51, 0 #CC3300	153, 51, 0 #993300	102, 51, 0 #663300	

Key

255, 0, 0 ◄ ——— The first line shows the RGB values for each color in the chart. The format R, G, B is used.
#FF0000 ◄ ——— The second line shows the hexadecimal value for each color in the chart.

Neutral Web-safe colors

204, 153, 153 #CC9999	204, 102, 102 #CC6666	204, 51, 51 #CC3333	153, 102, 102 #996666	153, 51, 51 #993333	102, 51, 51 #663333
204, 102, 153 #CC6699	204, 51, 153 #CC3399	204, 51, 102 #CC3366		153, 51, 102 #993366	
204, 153, 204 #CC99CC	204, 102, 204 #CC66CC	204, 51, 204 #CC33CC	153, 102, 153 #996699	153, 51, 153 #993399	102, 51, 102 #663366
153, 102, 204 #9966CC	153, 51, 204 #9933CC	102, 51, 204 #6633CC		102, 51, 153 #663399	
153, 153, 204 #9999CC	102, 102, 204 #6666CC	51, 51, 204 #3333CC	102, 102, 153 #666699	51, 51, 153 #333399	51, 51, 102 #333366
102, 153, 204 #6699CC	51, 102, 204 #3366CC	51, 153, 204 #3399CC		51, 102, 153 #336699	
153, 204, 204 #99CCCC	102, 204, 204 #66CCCC	51, 204, 204 #33CCCC	102, 153, 153 #669999	51, 153, 153 #339999	51, 102, 102 #336666
102, 204, 153 #66CC99	51, 204, 153 #33CC99	51, 204, 102 #33CC66		51, 153, 102 #339966	
153, 204, 153 #99CC99	102, 204, 102 #66CC66	51, 204, 51 #33CC33	102, 153, 102 #669966	51, 153, 51 #339933	51, 102, 51 #336633
153, 204, 102 #99CC66	102, 204, 51 #66CC33	153, 204, 51 #99CC33		102, 153, 51 #669933	
204, 204, 153 #CCCC99	204, 204, 102 #CCCC66	204, 204, 51 #CCCC33	153, 153, 102 #999966	153, 153, 51 #999933	102, 102, 51 #666633
204, 153, 102 #CC9966	204, 153, 51 #CC9933	204, 102, 51 #CC6633		153, 102, 51 #996633	

Gray Web-safe colors

255, 255, 255 #FFFFFF	204, 204, 204 #CCCCCC
153, 153, 153 #999999	102, 102, 102 #666666
51, 51, 51 #333333	0, 0, 0 #000000

HTML special character codes

"	&#34;	&quot;	Quotation mark	µ	&#181;	&micro;	Micro sign	Ñ	&#209;	&Ntilde;	Capital N, tilde
&	&#38;	&amp;	Ampersand	¶	&#182;	&para;	Paragraph sign	Ò	&#210;	&Ograve;	Capital O, grave accent
<	&#60;	&lt;	Less than	·	&#183;	&middot;	Middle dot	Ó	&#211;	&Oacute;	Capital O, acute accent
>	&#62;	&gt;	Greater than	,	&#184;	&cedil;	Cedilla	Ô	&#212;	&Ocirc;	Capital O, circumflex
€	&#128;	&euro;	Euro sign	¹	&#185;	&sup1;	Superscript one	Õ	&#213;	&Otilde;	Capital O, tilde
•	&#149;	&bull;	Bullet	º	&#186;	&ordm;	Masculine ordinal	Ö	&#214;	&Ouml;	Capital O, diaeresis/umlat
–	&#150;	&ndash;	En dash	»	&#187;	&raquo;	Right angle quote, guillemot right	×	&#215;	&times;	Multiplication sign
—	&#151;	&mdash;	Em dash	¼	&#188;	&frac14;	Fraction one-fourth	Ø	&#216;	&Oslash;	Capital O, slash
			Non-breaking space	½	&#189;	&frac12;	Fraction one-half	Ù	&#217;	&Ugrave;	Capital U, grave accent
¡	&#161;	&iexcl;	Inverted exclamation	¾	&#190;	&frac34;	Fraction three-fourths	Ú	&#218;	&Uacute;	Capital U, acute accent
¢	&#162;	&cent;	Cent sign	¿	&#191;	&iquest;	Inverted question mark	Û	&#219;	&Ucirc;	Capital U, circumflex
£	&#163;	&pound;	Pound sterling	À	&#192;	&Agrave;	Capital A, grave accent	Ü	&#220;	&Uml;	Capital U, diaeresis/umlat
¤	&#164;	&curren;	General currency sign	Á	&#193;	&Aacute;	Capital A, acute accent	Ý	&#221;	&Yacute;	Capital Y, acute accent
¥	&#165;	&yen;	Yen sign	Â	&#194;	&Acirc;	Capital A, circumflex	Þ	&#222;	&THORN;	Capital Thorn, Icelandic
¦	&#166;	&brvbar;	Broken vertical bar	Ã	&#195;	&Atilde;	Capital A, tilde	ß	&#223;	&szlig;	Lowercase sharp, German sz
§	&#167;	&sect;	Section sign	Ä	&#196;	&Auml;	Capital A, diaeresis/umlat	à	&#224;	&agrave;	Lowercase a, grave accent
©	&#169;	&copy;	Copyright	Å	&#197;	&Aring;	Capital A, ring	á	&#225;	&aacute;	Lowercase a, acute accent
ª	&#170;	&ordf;	Feminine ordinal	Æ	&#198;	&AElig;	Capital AE ligature	â	&#226;	&acirc;	Lowercase a, circumflex
«	&#171;	&laquo;	Left angle quote, guillemot left	Ç	&#199;	&Ccedil;	Capital C, cedilla	ã	&#227;	&atilde;	Lowercase a, tilde
¬	&#172;	&not;	Not sign	È	&#200;	&Egrave;	Capital E, grave accent	ä	&#228;	&auml;	Lowercase a, diaeresis/umlat
	&#173;	&shy;	Soft hyphen	É	&#201;	&Eacute;	Capital E, acute accent	å	&#229;	&aring;	Lowercase a, ring
®	&#174;	&reg;	Registered trademark	Ê	&#202;	&Ecirc;	Capital E, circumflex	æ	&#230;	&aelig;	Lowercase ae ligature
¯	&#175;	&macr;	Macron accent	Ë	&#203;	&Euml;	Capital E, diaresis/umlat	ç	&#231;	&ccedil;	Lowercase c, cedilla
°	&#176;	&deg;	Degree sign	Ì	&#204;	&Igrave;	Capital I, grave accent	ð	&#240;	&eth;	Lowercase Eth, Icelandic
±	&#177;	&plusmn;	Plus or minus	Í	&#205;	&Iacute;	Capital I, acute accent	÷	&#247;	&divide;	Division sign
²	&#178;	&sup2;	Superscript two	Î	&#206;	&Icirc;	Capital I, circumflex	ø	&#248;	&oslash;	Lowercase o, slash
³	&#179;	&sup3;	Superscript three	Ï	&#207;	&Iuml;	Capital I, diaresis/umlat	þ	&#254;	&thorn;	Lowercase Thorn, Icelandic
´	&#180;	&acute;	Acute accent	Ð	&#208;	&ETH;	Capital Eth, Icelandic				

index

Note: Page numbers in italic refer to
figures or tables.

A

<A> and </A> tags, 201
"above the fold" area, 84–85, 124
active hyperlinks, 293
addresses. *See* domain names
Add Web Folder wizard, 341, *341*
Adobe GoLive, 118
Adobe Photoshop
  configuring JPEG settings, 54, *54*
  as graphics application, 119,
    120–21, *121*
  viewing color palettes, 46
advanced HTML editors, 118, *119*
advertising Web sites, 132,
  349–52, *353*
age of audience, 132
ALIGN attribute, 63, 224
alignment, text, 95
ALINK attribute, 196
Allair HomeSite, 115
ALT attribute, 95, *96,* 102, 201
Alta Vista, 350
America Online (AOL), 124, 347, 350
ampersand (&), 209
anchors, 201, 204
angle brackets (<>), 179, 196, 229
animated GIFs, 50–51, *51,* 122, 125
applications. *See* tools
archiving Web page elements,
  359–60, 364
Arizona Film Society home page, *13*
art, acquiring, 65–72. *See also*
  graphics
  custom art, 66–70, *67, 68, 69, 70*
  photographs, 70–72
  prepared art, 66
articles in title bar text, avoiding, 26
Ask Jeeves, 350
aspect ratios, 56

asterisks (*), 337
attributes, HTML
  alternative text, 95, *96,* 102
  body, 195–96
  horizontal rule, 63
  image, 224
  table, 198
  tags and, 180, 182–83, *183,* 229
attribution, 92
audience. *See also* users
  analysis of, 76–78, 102,
    130–32, 142
  writing effectively for, 34–37
audio files, 88

B

<B> and </B> tags, 181
BACKGROUND attribute, 195–96
backgrounds
  colors, 51, 89, 195–96, *196, 197*
  color selection component in
    JavaScript, 362–63, *363*
  colors in FrontPage, 292
  FrontPage, 292, *292*
  graphical patterns, 65, *65,* 191
  text and, 37
bandwidth
  audience, 77, 131
  server space and, 111
banners
  graphical text and, 64
  inserting HTML, 202–3, *203*
  programs, 122, 125
  title bar, 191, *192*
Bare Bones Software, 116
basic text and HTML editors,
  113–16, *114, 116*
BBEdit, 116

Berners-Lee, Tim, 8
BGCOLOR attribute, 170, 195
binary mode file transfer, 338
blinking text, 86
<BLOCKQUOTE> and </
  BLOCKQUOTE> tags, 219
block quotes, 219–20, *220, 221*
<BODY> and </BODY> tags, 195–96,
  196, 197
body text. *See also* content
  adding paragraph text, 217–18,
    218, 219
  creating headings, 216–17, *216,*
    217
  creating linked unnumbered lists,
    221–23, *221, 223*
  formatting block quotes and
    colored, 219–20, *220, 221*
  inserting, on home page, 216–23
  page layout and, 85, *86*
  shape of, 32–34
boldface text, 94, 181
BORDER attribute, 198, 201
borders
  hiding FrontPage table, 320–21,
    321
  HTML image, 201
  HTML table, 198
  removing HTML table, 224
brainstorming, 31–32, *32,* 38
browsers
  anomalies between, 123–25, *124*
  as FTP clients, 346–47, *347*
  Internet Explorer (*see* Microsoft
    Internet Explorer)
  plug-ins, 87
  refreshing views, 196, 202
  testing Web pages in various, 83, 123

browsers, *continued*
    viewing HTML source code in, 12,
        12, 115, 179
    visual appeal and, 88
    Web pages and, 9, 18
browser-safe colors, 51, *51,* 55, 89

 tag, 184
bulleted lists, 38, 62, *63,* 221–23,
    221, 223
BulletProof FTP, 122
bullets, 61–63, *62, 63,* 123
buttons
    adding navigation, in FrontPage,
        301–3, *302, 303*
    creating, in Word, 66–70, *67, 68,*
        69, 70
    graphics for, 190
    logos and, 60–61
    naming, 137
    as navigation tools, 90
    rollover effects, 281
    ScreenTips, 67

C

calendar pages, 151
cameras, digital, 71
case sensitivity
    of content text, 193
    of filenames and URLs, 135
    of HTML tags, 180, 193, 229
    of hyperlink filenames, 269
categories
    MSN Communities Web sites, 140
    search engines and Web site,
        350–52
CELLPADDING attribute, 198
cells, table, 197
CELLSPACING attribute, 198
character entity references, 209
chat rooms, 150–51
checklists
    home page planning, 140–41
    site planning, 136–38
    supplies, 142
    text, 33–34
classifying sites, 137
clients
    browsers as FTP, 346–47, *347*
    servers and, 15–16, *16,* 18
client/server nature of Web, 15–16,
    16, 18
    FTP and, 335
clip art
    acquiring, 66, 226

clip art, *continued*
    adding, to Word pages, 259–62,
        260, 261, 262
    copying, to Word subpages,
        262–64, *263, 264*
closing tags, 180
closing Word Web sites, 254–55
code cleanup, HTML, 114
code of conduct, MSN Communities,
    158, *158*
CoffeeCup Direct FTP, 122
COLOR attribute, 183
color look-up tables (CLUTs), 46
colors
    background, 51
    background, in FrontPage, 292
    background and link, in HTML
        documents, 195–96, *196, 197*
    background color selection
        component in JavaScript, 362–63,
        363
    colored text, 219–20, *220, 221*
    color look-up tables (CLUTs), 46
    color schemes, 88–90, 102
    editing MSN Communities Web
        page, 170
    HTML text, 183, *183,* 219–20, *220,*
        221
    hyperlink, 91, 293
    JPEG, 52
    palettes, 44–46, *44, 46*
    planning, 137
    styles and (*see* styles)
    text, 37, 94
    Web-safe, 51, *51,* 55, 89, 137, 367
    Word themes and, 249, 272
commands, HTML. *See* tags, HTML
comments, HTML, 227
community settings, 151
compressed JPEGs, 53, 54, *54*
CompuServe, 47
computers. *See* hardware; servers
computer screens, Web page
    dimensions and, 80–83, *81,* 102
conciseness, 34
connections. *See* Internet
    connections
consistency, 60, 96, 102
contact information, 92, 137. *See
    also* forms, FrontPage
content
    case of text, 193
    dynamic, 92
    HTML document, 178
    text as, 9, 22, *25, 26* (*see also* body
        text)

content, *continued*
    updating and refreshing, 87
control, HTML and, 114
copying and pasting HTML code,
    199, 204
copyright notices, 92
copyrights, 32, 66
copyright symbols, 209
CorelDraw, 121
countdown JavaScript component,
    361, *362*
counters, 282, 327–28, *327, 328*
credibility components, 91–92, 102
crop marks, *57*
cropping images, 57–58, *57,* 72
cross-platform fonts, 38, 94, 123
Ctrl+C and Ctrl+V keyboard
    shortcuts, 199
Ctrl+K keyboard shortcut, 268, 304
Ctrl+S keyboard shortcut, 187
Ctrl+X keyboard shortcut, 253, 254
custom art, 66–70, *67, 68, 69, 70*
customizing MSN Communities Web
    sites, 152, 160–62, *160, 161*
custom lists, 151
CuteFTP, 122, 335–36, *336*
CuteMAP, 122

D

dates. *See* last-modified-date
    information
dead links, 91
default.htm, 134, 255
deleting
    files and folders generated by
        templates, 241, *241*
    files uploaded with Web Publishing
        Wizard, 345, 348
    MSN Communities Web sites, 171, 173
descriptions, META tag, 351–52
design, 74–102
    audience analysis and, 76–78
    case study practice, 98, *98–101*
    color schemes, 88–90
    consistency, 96
    functional, 87
    graphics, 95, *96* (*see also* graphics)
    key points, 102
    navigation tools and hyperlinks,
        90–91
    page layout issues, 83–88, *84, 85, 86*
    planning and, 76–78, *79* (*see also*
        planning)
    standard credibility components,
        91–92

design, *continued*
    storyboarding and, 78, *79*
    text fonts, 92–95 (*see also* text)
    Web page, 80–96
    Web page dimensions, 80–83, *81*
    Web site, 96–98
    Web site structure, 97–98
design element, text as, 37–38, *39*
desktop shortcut to Web Publishing
        Wizard, 345
DHTML (Dynamic HTML), 324,
        326–27, *326*
DHTML toolbar, FrontPage, 326, *326*
dial-up Internet connections, 77, 106
digital cameras, 71
dimensions, Web page, 80–83, *81*,
        102
directories, registering with Web,
        349–50
directory structures. *See* file
        management
displays, Web page dimensions and,
        80–83, *81*, 102
dithering, 51, 52, 55, 89
documents. *See* HTML (Hypertext
        Markup Language) documents;
        text documents
DogPile, 351
domain names
    choosing, 142
    length of, 107, 109
    registering, 110–11
    uploading and, 334
    URLs and, 134
Domain Name System (DNS), 110
double-clicking HTML documents, 195
downloading
    FTP applications, 336, *336*
    graphics, 95, *96*
    image files, 148, *148*, 176, *176*,
        280, *281*
    interlaced GIFs and, 48, *49*
    JPEGs, 52
    shareware, 113
    speed, 45, 55–56, 87
    uploading vs., 335 (*see also*
        uploading)
dragging-and-dropping FrontPage
        text, 308
Drawing toolbar, Word, 67, *67*
Dreamweaver, 118
drop caps, 37
dynamic content, 92
Dynamic HTML (DHTML), 324,
        326–27, *326*

E

eBay, 109
editing
    FrontPage sites, 285
    graphics, 43, 119–21, *121*, 125
    HTML (*see* editors, text and HTML)
    MSN Communities Web site text,
        167–68, *168, 169*
    Word Web pages from Internet
        Explorer, 237
editors, text and HTML, 113–18,
        119, 125
    advanced, 118, *119*
    basic, 113–16, *114, 116*
    downloading, 113
    FrontPage as, 281–86, 329 (*see also*
        Microsoft FrontPage)
    mid-range, 116–17, *117*
    uploading with, 345–46
    Word as, 233 (*see also* Microsoft
        Word 2000)
effectiveness of text, 23–24, *23, 24*
effective writing. *See* writing, Web
e-mail
    creating Word Mail To hyperlinks,
        271–73, *272, 273*
    Hotmail, 153
    MSN Communities site, 151, 161
    Webmaster link, 92
    Web hosting providers and, 112
    Word capabilities, 233, *234*
ending tags, 180
environment, Web page creation, 118
Excite, 350
exclamation point and two dashes
        (!--), 227
expanding MSN Communities Web
        sites, 172
extensions, filename, 10, 11,
        46–47, 135
extra features, ISP, 112

F

fake names, uploading and, 358
Family site template, 152–53,
        155–57, *156*
Fetch, 123, 335
fields, FrontPage form
    configuring properties, 316–20,
        316, 317, 319
    creating, 315–16, *316*
    naming, 318–19, *318, 319*
file cabinet, 151

file management
    archiving Web page elements,
        359–60
    creating FrontPage Webs, 288–91,
        289, 290, 291
    deleting files and folders generated
        by templates, 241, *241*
    FrontPage, 329
    graphics, 66, 134, *134*, 186, *187*
    HTML documents and graphics, 186,
        187, 190–92, *190, 191, 192*, 229
    planning, 133–34, *134*
    spaces in names of folders, 249
    uploading and, 338, 353
    Web Folders (*see* Microsoft Web
        Folders)
files
    filename extensions for, 10, 11,
        46–47, 135
    graphics, 11–13, *13* (*see also*
        graphics; graphics file formats;
        graphics file sizes)
    management (*see* file
        management)
    names (*see* names)
    saving Word, as HTML documents,
        235–37, *236*
    sound, 88
    uploading (*see* uploading)
    Web pages as HTML, 8–14, *10, 11,
        13, 14* (*see also* HTML (Hypertext
        Markup Language) documents)
    zip, 176, 280
file transfer. *See* FTP (File Transfer
        Protocol) applications;
        uploading
film developers, 71
fine-tuning, HTML and, 114
Fireworks, 119
folder names, spaces in, 249
folders. *See* file management;
        Microsoft Web Folders
fonts, 92–95, 102
    browsers and, 123
    cross-platform, 38, 94, 123
    formatting, 94–95
    HTML, 183, *183*, 219–20, *220, 221*
    sizes, 93
    styles, 93–94
<FONT> tag, 183, *183*, 219
footers
    adding, in FrontPage, 303–5, *304,
        305*
    graphics in, 191
    HTML document, 207–10, *210*
    page layout and, 85, *86*

formatting
  block quotes and colored text,
    219–20, *220, 221*
  font, 94–95
  Word text documents, 244–45
forms, FrontPage, 313–21
  adding title bar and title text, 313
  configuring field properties,
    316–20, *316, 317, 319*
  creating fields, 315–16, *316*
  FrontPage Server Extensions and,
    313
  hiding borders and setting
    properties for, 320–21, *321*
  inserting form area and adding
    labels, 313–14, *314, 315*
  naming fields, 318–19, *318, 319*
forms, text in, 27
frames, 87
Frames toolbar, 251
free background patterns, 65
Freehand, 121
free online art, 66
free server space, 106–9, *108,* 125
freeware, 66, 335
FrontPage. *See* Microsoft FrontPage
FrontPage Server Extensions, 111,
    285–86, 313, 329, 346
FTP (File Transfer Protocol)
    applications, 335–39, *337*
  acquiring, 121–23, 125
  downloading, 336, *336*
  establishing connections, 336–37,
    337
  file types and, 338
  FTP client/server protocol, 335
  purchasing, 335
  risks of shareware, 336
  uploading with, 16, 338–39, 352
functional design, 87
Fusion, 118

G

GeoCities, 107
GIF Construction Set Professional,
    122
GIF (Graphics Interchange Format)
    graphics, 47–51
  animated, 50–51, *51*
  animators, 122, 125
  interlaced, 48, *49*
  key points, 72
  palettes, 44–46, *44, 46*
  saving buttons as, 69–70, *70*
  size of, 55

GIF (Graphics Interchange Format)
    graphics, *continued*
  transparent, 50, *50*
  using, 47–48, *48, 49*
GlobalSCAPE CuteMAP, 122
goals, defining, 129–30, 142
Go.com, 350
GoLive, 118
Google, 350
grammar, 36–37, 39, 92
graphical elements, 59–65, 72
  backgrounds, 65, *65*
  buttons and logos, 60–61, *61*
  creating buttons in Word, 66–70,
    67, 68, 69, 70
  graphical text, 64, *64* (*see also*
    graphical text)
  hyperlinks, 91
  icons, bullets, and horizontal rules,
    61–63, *62*
  photographs and illustrations,
    59–60, 70–72
  viewing names of, 67
graphical text
  as graphical element, 64, *64*
  as textual element, *25,* 26–27
  WordArt (*see* Microsoft WordArt)
graphic designers, 66
graphics, 40–72
  acquiring art (*see* art, acquiring)
  applications, 43, 119–21, *121,* 125
  copying, to Word subpages,
    262–64, *263, 264*
  cropping, 57–58, *57*
  design issues, 95, *96*
  downloading, 148, *148,* 176, *176,*
    280, *281*
  file formats (*see* graphics file
    formats)
  file management, 134, *134,* 186, *187*
  as files, 11–13, *13*
  file sizes (*see* graphics file sizes)
  FrontPage (*see* graphics, FrontPage)
  graphical elements (*see* graphical
    elements)
  HTML document, 190–92, *190, 191,*
    192
  hyperlinks, 91 (*see also* hyperlinks)
  inserting and linking, 223–24
  inserting banner, 202–3, *203*
  key points, 72
  mechanics of, 42–58, *59*
  MSN Communities Web sites, 153,
    173
  naming files, 66, 135
  overview of, 42

graphics, *continued*
  pixels, palettes, and colors, 42–46,
    43, 44, 46
  pop-up text (ScreenTips), 95, *96,* 102
  resizing, 56, *56,* 68
  updating, 357
  uploading, 338
  users' responses to text before, 28
  using thumbnails, 58, *59* (*see also*
    thumbnails)
  vector-based, 121
  viewing names of, 67
  Web-safe colors, 51, *51,* 55, 89
  as Word hyperlinks, 273–74, *274*
graphics, FrontPage
  adding Dynamic HTML to main
    graphic, 326–27, *326*
  adding logo and title bar graphics,
    294–96, *296*
  assembling main graphic, 324–25,
    324, 325
  background, 292, *292*
  creating links within main graphic,
    325, *326*
  keeping, together, 295, *296*
  organizing, 290
graphics file formats, 46–55
  file extensions, 46–47
  GIFs, 47–51, *47, 48, 49, 50, 51*
  JPEGs, 52–54, *52*
  key points, 72
  PNGs, 55
graphics file sizes, 55–58, *59*
  cropping graphics, 57–58, *57*
  key points, 72
  photographs, 72
  resizing graphics, 56, *56*
  using thumbnails, 58, *59*

H

<H*x*> and </H*x*> heading tags, 63,
    216
hand-coding, 114
handles, 68
hardware
  Internet as, 6–7, *6*
  scanners and digital cameras, 71
  servers (*see* servers)
  Web page dimensions and monitors,
    80–83, *81,* 102
headings
  brainstorming, 31–32, *32,* 38
  creating HTML, 216–17, *216, 217*
  graphical text for, 64
HEIGHT attribute, 201

Help, MSN Communities, 172, 173
hidaho.com, 89
hierarchical organization, 133
home pages. *See also* Web pages
  copying framework for, to
    subpages, 211–15, *211, 212, 215*
  default names for, 134, 255
  finalizing, 224–25, *225*
  FrontPage (*see* home pages,
    FrontPage)
  HTML document, 192–94, *192, 193,
    195*
  inserting banner graphic, 202–3, *203*
  inserting body text, 216–23
  as main Web page, 76
  MSN Communities, *108, 149,* 150, 153
  overloading, 88, 140
  planning, 138–41, *139, 140,* 142
  planning checklist, 140–41
  redesigned, *98, 100*
  as tables of contents, 31
home pages, FrontPage, 322–28
  adding Dynamic HTML effects to
    main graphic, 326–27, *326*
  assembling main graphic, 324–25,
    324, 325
  creating framework, 322–24, *323*
  creating links within main graphic,
    325, *326*
  inserting counter and last-modified
    date, 327–28, *327, 328*
HomeSite, 115
horizontal rules, 61–63, *62, 63,*
    259–62, *260, 261, 262*
host address, FTP, 337
hostindex.com, 111
hosting providers, 111–12. *See also*
    ISPs (Internet service
    providers); servers
HotBot, 350
HotDog Professional, 116
Hotmail, 153
HoTMetaL Pro, 118
hotspots, 312
hover buttons, 301–2, *302*
hovering, 281
HREF attribute, 205
<HR> tag, 63
HSPACE attribute, 224
HTML (Hypertext Markup Language)
  advantages of, 177
  attributes (*see* attributes, HTML)
  basics, 178–88
  bulleted lists and horizontal rules,
    62–63, *63*
  comments, 227

HTML (Hypertext Markup
    Language), *continued*
  documents (*see* HTML (Hypertext
    Markup Language) documents)
  Dynamic, 324, 326–27, *326*
  editors (*see* editors, text and HTML)
  filename extension, 135
  source code (*see* source code, HTML)
  tags (*see* tags, HTML)
<HTML> and </HTML> tags, 179–80
HTML (Hypertext Markup Language)
    documents, 174–229
  adding bulleted lists and horizontal
    rules, 62–63, *63*
  adding navigation links, 203–6,
    206, 207
  additional resources, 228–29
  advantages of knowing HTML, 177
  copying home page framework to
    subpages, 211–15, *211, 212, 215*
  creating tables, 197–99, *200*
  finalizing home pages, 224–25, *225*
  handling graphic files and, 186,
    187, 190–92, *190, 191, 192*
  HTML basics, 178–88
  inserting and linking graphics,
    223–24
  inserting and linking logos,
    200–201, *202*
  inserting footer information,
    207–10, *210*
  inserting home page banner
    graphics, 202–3, *203*
  inserting home page body text,
    216–23
  key points, 229
  main directory for, 133, *134*
  opening, 195
  planning Web sites, 188, *189*
  preparing home page, 192–94, *192,
    193, 195*
  saving, from Word, 235–37, *236*
  saving and previewing, 187–88
  specifying background and link
    colors, 195–96, *196, 197*
  standard tags, *192*
  supplies for, 176, *176*
  uploading, 338
  using tags, 178–86, *179, 181, 183,
    184–85*
  using Web sites as templates,
    226–28, *226, 227*
  Web pages as, 8–14, *10, 11, 13, 14,
    18*
HTML Editor, MSN, 170, *170*
HTTP (Hypertext Transfer Protocol), 8

hyperlinks
  active, 293
  buttons, 90 (*see also* buttons)
  dead, 91
  checking, 225, 358–59
  colors, 195–96, *196, 197,* 293, *293*
  creating, within FrontPage main
    graphic, 325, *326*
  font size and, 93
  graphical, 91
  image maps (*see* image maps)
  keywords as, 31–32, *32,* 38
  as links, 23
  logos as, 90, 200–201, *202* (*see
    also* logos)
  navigation tools as, 90–91 (*see also*
    navigation tools)
  recommended links, 357
  restricting, 34, 90
  ScreenTips, 269 (*see also* ScreenTips)
  text, 91
  as textual elements, *25, 26*
  thumbnails as, 58, *59,* 310 (*see also*
    thumbnails)
  Webmaster, 92
  Web sites and, 14, *14,* 18
  Word hyperlinks, 264–74

I
<I> and </I> tags, 181
icons
  home page, 140
  send mail, 191
  using, 61
illustration programs, 121
illustrations, 59–60
Illustrator, 121
image maps
  applications, 122, 125
  creating FrontPage, 281, 311–13,
    312
  photographs and illustrations for, 60
images. *See* graphics
images directory, 134
<IMG> tag, 200–201, *202*
index.htm, 134, 194, 255
infrared ports, 71
interface, FrontPage, 282, *283,
    284,* 329
interlaced GIFs, 48, *49*
Internet, 6–7, *6,* 18. *See also* Web
Internet connections
  audience and bandwidth
    considerations, 77, 131
  dial-up, 77, 106

Internet connections, *continued*
  FTP, 336–37, *337*
  interlacing and, 48
  ISPs and (*see* ISPs (Internet service
    providers))
  server space (*see* server space)
  T1 lines, 78
  Web Folders and, 343
Internet Explorer. *See* Microsoft
  Internet Explorer
InterNIC, 110–11
intranets, 131
inverted pyramid methodology,
  29–30, 38
Invite Someone or Recommend To A
  Friend tool, 151
ISPs (Internet service providers)
  client/server model and, 15–16, *16*
  folders, 339
  free server space, 109
  interfaces for uploading, 345–46
  servers (*see* servers)
  as Web hosting providers, 111–12
italic text, 94, 181
iwon.com, 29–30

J
jasc.com, 43
Jasc Paint Shop Pro
  configuring JPEG settings, 53–54, *54*
  cropping graphics, 57–58, *57*
  downloading, 43
  as graphics application, 119, 120,
    120
  key points, 72
  resizing graphics, 56, *56*
  saving Word buttons as GIFs,
    69–70, *70*
  viewing color palettes, 46
JavaScript components, 360–63,
  362, 363
joining online communities,
  153–55, *154,* 173
JPEG (Joint Photographic Experts
  Group) graphics, 52–54

K
keyboard shortcuts
  Ctrl+C and Ctrl+V, 199
  Ctrl+K, 268, 304
  Ctrl+S, 187
  Ctrl+X, 253, 254
keywords
  as hyperlinks, 31

keywords, *continued*
  META tag, 351–52
Kodak PhotoNet site, 71

L
<L*x*> and </L*x*> tags, 222–23
labels, FrontPage form, 313–14,
  314, 315
last-modified-date information
  adding, to FrontPage home page,
    327–28, *327, 328*
  as credibility component, 92
  on home pages, 140
  as textual element, *25,* 27–28
  updating and, 357, 358
Latin text, 95
line breaks, HTML, 184
lines. *See* horizontal rules
LINK attribute, 196
linked unnumbered lists, 221–23,
  221, 223
links. *See* hyperlinks
lists
  bulleted, 38, 62, *63*
  creating linked unnumbered,
    221–23, *221, 223*
  custom, 151
  shaping, 33
location, audience, 131
logos
  adding, in FrontPage, 294–96, *296*
  as graphical elements, 60–61, *61,*
    191
  home page, 141
  inserting and linking, with HTML,
    200–201, *202*
  as navigational tools, 90, 102
  page layout and, 85, *86*
  as textual elements, *25,* 26–27
LookSmart, 350
Lorem ipsum dolor sit amet text, 95
lossy compression, 53
lowercase. *See* case sensitivity
LView Pro, 119
Lycos, 350
Lycos Tripod online community, 107
Lynx, 125

M
Macintosh
  browser anomalies on, 124
  cross-platform fonts and, 123
  FTP client, 123, 335
  HTML editor, 116

Macintosh, *continued*
  SimpleText editor, 178, *179*
  visual appeal and, 88
  Web page dimensions and, 80–83, *81*
Magellan, 350
Mail To hyperlinks, Word, 271–73,
  272, 273
main directory, 133, *134*
maintenance, 354–64
  archiving Web page elements,
    359–60
  implementing JavaScript
    components, 360–63, *362, 363*
  key points, 364
  overview, 356
  updating Web pages, 356–59
maps, image. *See* image maps
maps, site, 97, 242, *243*
margin spacing, 123
marquee text, 282
member lists, 151
member profiles, 151
Membership Policies, 159, *159*
menu items
  as hyperlinks, 31–32, *32*
  text in, 27
message boards, 150
META tags, 351–52, 353
microsoft.com, 276, 329
Microsoft Development
  Environment, 237–38, *238*
Microsoft FrontPage
  as advanced HTML editor, 118, *119*
  advantages, 284–85
  background patterns, 65
  capabilities, 281–86
  FrontPage Server Extensions and,
    285–86
  interface, 282, *283, 284*
  Web pages (*see* Microsoft FrontPage
    Web pages)
Microsoft FrontPage Web pages,
  278–329
  adding Dynamic HTML effects,
    326–27, *326*
  adding footer information, 303–5,
    304, 305
  adding logos and title bar graphics,
    294–96, *296*
  adding navigation buttons, 301–3,
    302, 303
  adding text and thumbnail
    graphics, 307–11, *308, 309, 310*
  additional resources, 329
  assembling main graphic, 324–25,
    324, 325

Microsoft FrontPage Web pages,
    continued
  creating, using subpage layouts,
    306–21
  creating forms (*see* forms,
    FrontPage)
  creating home page framework,
    322–24, *323*
  creating home pages, 322–28
  creating image maps, 311–13, *312*
  creating links within main graphic,
    325, *326*
  creating subpage layouts, 291–305
  creating Webs, 288–91, *289, 290,*
    291
  dragging-and-dropping text, 308
  editing existing Web sites, 285
  FrontPage capabilities, 281–86
  inserting counter and last-modified
    date, 327–28, *327, 328*
  inserting tables, 297–301, *297,*
    298, 300, 301
  key points, 329
  opening subpages, 295
  organizing graphics for, 290
  planning Web sites, 286–88, *287,*
    288, 289
  publishing, 328, 346
  renaming subpages, 306–7
  saving, 294, *294*
  setting properties, 291–93, *292, 293*
  supplies for, 280, *281*
Microsoft Internet Explorer
  anomalies between other browsers
    and, 123–25, *124*
  deleting uploaded files, 345, 348
  editing FrontPage sites from, 285
  as FTP client, 346–47, *347*
  opening documents in Word from, 237
  PNG support, 55
  viewing HTML source code in, 12,
    12, 179
  visual appeal and, 88
  Web page dimensions and platforms
    for, 80–83, *81*
Microsoft Network (MSN)
  Communities (*see* MSN
    Communities Web pages)
  logo, *61*
  navigation links, *85*
  search engine, 350
Microsoft Office 2000, 116, 259, 339
Microsoft Paint, 120
Microsoft Passport, 153–55, *154,* 162
Microsoft PhotoDraw, 120

Microsoft Web Folders, 339–43, 352
  accessing and viewing, 339–40, *340*
  creating, from within Word,
    341–43, *342*
  creating, using My Computer,
    340–41, *341*
  FTP programs and, 121
  saving Word Web pages, 236
Microsoft Windows
  browser anomalies on, *124*
  cross-platform fonts and, 123
  visual appeal and, 88
  Web Folders (*see* Microsoft Web
    Folders)
  Web page dimensions and, 80–83, *81*
  Web Publishing Wizard and versions
    of, 343 (*see also* Web Publishing
    Wizard)
Microsoft Word 2000, 232–41
  creating buttons in, 66–70, *67, 68,*
    69, 70
  creating Web Folders from,
    341–42, *342*
  creating Web pages, 233–34, *234*
    (*see also* Microsoft Word 2000
    Web pages)
  creating Web pages with templates,
    238–40, *239, 240*
  creating Web pages with Web Page
    Wizard, 240–41
  as mid-range HTML editor, 116–17,
    117, 233
  saving files as HTML documents,
    235–27, *236*
  sending e-mail messages, 233
  viewing HTML source code,
    237–38, *238*
  viewing Web pages, 233, *233*
  Web capabilities, 232–41, *233, 234*
  WordArt, 25, 26–27
Microsoft Word 2000 Web pages,
    230–77
  adding clip art, 259–62, *260, 261,*
    262
  adding hyperlinks, 268–70, *269, 270*
  adding ScreenTips to hyperlinks,
    270–71
  adding text to subpages, 252–54,
    253, 254
  additional resources, 276
  copying graphics to subpages,
    262–64, *263, 264*
  creating, 233–34, *234*
  creating, with templates, 238–40,
    239, 240

Microsoft Word 2000 Web pages,
    continued
  creating, with Web Page Wizard,
    240–41, 244–51, *246, 247, 248,*
    249, 250, 251
  creating and inserting WordArt,
    255–58, *256, 257, 258, 259*
  creating Mail To hyperlinks,
    271–73, *272, 273*
  deleting files and folders generated
    by templates, 241, *241*
  editing, from Internet Explorer, 237
  formatting text documents, 244–45
  key points, 276–77
  linking graphics, 273–74, *274*
  modifying hyperlink styles, 265–68,
    266, 267, 268
  modifying navigation bars, 251–52,
    252
  planning, 241–42, *243*
  previewing, 275, *275*
  saving and closing Web sites, 254–55
  supplies for, 232, *232*
  Word Web capabilities, 232–41,
    233, 234
  working with hyperlinks, 264–74
Microsoft WordArt
  copying, to subpages, 262–64, *263,*
    264
  creating and inserting, 255–58,
    256, 257, 258, 259
  graphical elements, 64, *64*
  as text design element, 37
  textual elements, 25, 26–27
mid-range text and HTML editors,
    116–17, *117*
monitors, Web page dimensions
    and, 80–83, *81,* 102
MSN. *See* Microsoft Network (MSN)
MSN Communities Web sites, 146–73
  adding pictures to Photo Albums
    page, 165–67, *166, 167*
  additional resources for, 172
  creating, 157–60, *157, 158, 159*
  customizing, 152, 160–62, *160, 161*
  deleting, 171
  displaying HTML source code,
    169–71, *170, 171*
  editing text for, 167–68, *168, 169*
  expanding, 172
  free server space and, 107–9, *108*
  joining, 153–55, *154*
  key points, 173
  online communities and, 148–51,
    149

MSN Communities Web sites,
continued
planning, 152–53
replacing default photographs,
162–64, *162, 163, 164, 165*
returning to, 172
selecting templates, 155–57, *156*
supplies for, 148, *148*
MSN HTML Editor, 170, *170*
MSN Page Builder utility
editing text, 167–68, *168, 169,* 173
viewing HTML source code,
169–71, *170, 171*
MSN Photo Upload Control, 162–64,
162, 163, 164, 165
multifile nature of Web pages,
9–13, *10, 11, 13*
My Computer, creating Web Folders
using, 340–41, *341*
My Network Places, creating Web
Folders using, 339

N

names
default, for home pages, 134, 255
domain (*see* domain names)
for FrontPage form fields, 318–19,
318, 319
for FrontPage subpages, 306–7
FTP site, 336–37
for graphics, 67, 135, 229
for HTML files, 134–36, *136*
for online and local folders, 338
spaces in file and folder, 249
uploading files with fake, 358
URL, 134
viewing, of graphics, 67
Web Publishing Wizard and, 343–44
navigation tools, 90–91, 102
adding, with HTML, 203–6, *206, 207*
adding navigation buttons in
FrontPage, 301–3, *302, 303*
buttons, 90
graphical links, 91
logos, 90
modifying Word navigation bar
settings, 251–52, *252*
page layout and, 85, *86*
plain-text, *25,* 27
restricting, 90
safe area and, 85, *85*
text links, 91
Navigator. *See* Netscape Navigator
nested HTML tags, 181–82
Net. *See* Internet
NetFind, 350

NetObjects Fusion, 118
Netscape, 350
Netscape Navigator, 88, 123–24,
124, 125
New Frontiers for Learning in
Retirement Web pages, 98, *98,*
99, 100, 101
newspaper text methodology, 29–30
<NOBR> and </NOBR> tags, 295
nonlinear text, 28
nonstandard characters, 209
Normal template, Word, 244
NorthernLight, 350
NOSHADE attribute, 63
Notepad, 10–11, *10,* 113, *114,* 115,
178, *179*
numbered lists, 222

O

offset, 123
<OL> and </OL> tags, 222
online communities, 173
free server space on, 107–9, *108*
FTP programs and, 121
joining, 153–55, *154*
MSN Communities site and,
148–51, *149* (*see also* MSN
Communities Web sites)
online validation services, 91
opening
FrontPage subpages, 295
HTML documents, 195
opening tags, 180
Opera, 125
ordered lists, 222
organization, text, 29–34, *32*
brainstorms, headings, and
hyperlinks, 31–32, *32*
inverted pyramid methodology,
29–30
shape of body text, 32–34
organization, Web site, 132–38, *142*
file management, 133–36, *134, 136*
(*see also* file management)
models, 132–33
naming images, 135
planning checklist, 136–38
overloading of home pages, 88, 140

P

<P> and </P> tags, 181, 217
Page Builder utility. *See* MSN Page
Builder utility
page layout issues, 83–88, *84, 85, 86*
pages. *See* Web pages

Paint, 120
Paint Shop Pro. *See* Jasc Paint
Shop Pro
pairs, HTML tag, 180–81, *181*
palettes, 44–46, *44, 46. See also*
colors
paragraphs
avoiding embedded hyperlinks in, 91
shaping, 33–34
text for, 217–18, *218, 219*
Passport. *See* Microsoft Passport
passwords
FTP, 337
Passport, 154–55
Web Folders, 340
Web Publishing Wizard, 337, 344
patterns, background, 65, *65*
personal information, 92
Photo Albums pages, *108,* 150,
165–67, *166, 167,* 173
PhotoDraw, 120
photographs
acquiring, 70–72
adding, to Photo Albums page,
165–67, *166, 167,* 173
as graphical elements, 59–60
replacing default MSN
Communities, 162–64, *162, 163,
164, 165*
Photoshop. *See* Adobe Photoshop
Photo Upload Control, 162–64, *162,
163, 164, 165,* 173
PhotoWorks site, 71
picture buttons, 61
pictures. *See* graphics; photographs
pipe symbol (|), 208
pixels, 42–43, *44, 45, 45,* 72
placeholders, graphical, 95, *96,* 191
plain-text navigation elements, *25,*
27
planning, 126–42
advantages of, 128, *129*
audience analysis, 76–78, 130–32
defining goals, 129–30
design and, 76–78, *79*
file management, 133–36, *134, 136*
(*see also* file management)
FrontPage sites, 286–88, *287, 288,
289*
gathering tools and supplies, 141–42
home page checklist, 140–41
home pages, 138–41, *139, 140*
HTML document sites, 188, *189*
key points, 142
MSN Communities Web sites,
152–53, 173
naming image files, 135

planning, *continued*
    storyboarding Web sites, 78, *79,*
        136, *136*
    supplies checklist, 142
    this book and, 16–17
    Web site checklist, 136–38
    Web sites, 132–38
    Word Web sites, 241–42, *243*
plug-ins, 87
PNG (Portable Network Graphics)
    graphics, 55
pop-up text, 95, *96,* 102
posting. *See* uploading
prepared art, 66, 72
previewing
    HTML documents, 187–88, 229
    uploaded Web pages, 347–49, *348*
    using various screen settings and
        browsers, 83, 123
    Word documents as Web pages, 235
    Word Web pages, 275, *275*
printable resume versions, 242
printed graphics vs. Web graphics, 42
printed text vs. Web text, 22
Private sites, 159
programs. *See* tools
progressive JPEGs, 52, 53, *53*
pronouns, 35–36
properties
    FrontPage form, 320–21, *321*
    FrontPage form field, 316–20, *316,*
        317, 319
    FrontPage page, 291–93, *292, 293*
    FrontPage picture, 309–10
    FrontPage table cell, 299–300, *300*
    HTML (*see* attributes, HTML)
protocols, 8, 335
Public and Public Restricted sites,
    159
publicizing Web sites, 132, 349–52,
    353
publishing FrontPage Web pages,
    327, 328, 329. *See also*
    uploading
punctuation in filenames, 135
purchasing
    FTP applications, 335
    server space, 110–12, 125
purpose of Web site, 76, 141

Q

quality of Internet writing, 22
quick fixes, HTML, 114
quotation marks (""), 196, 229
quotes, block, 219–20, *220, 221*

R

readers. *See* audience; users
recommended links, 357
refreshing browser views, 196, 202
registering Web addresses, 110–11
requirements. *See* supplies
resizing graphics, 56, *56,* 68, 72
resources. *See also* supplies
    clip art, 226
    color schemes, 89
    domain registration, 110–11
    film developers, 71
    free background patterns, 65
    free online art, 66
    FrontPage, 329
    grammar, 36
    graphics applications, 43, 119–21,
        121, 125
    HTML, 228–29
    MSN Communities Help, 172
    shareware, 113
    Web hosting providers, 111
    Word, 276
reviewing. *See* previewing
rollover effects, button, 281
routers, 6
rows, table, 197
ruler, Word, 252
rules. *See* horizontal rules

S

safe area, 82–83, 85, 102
safe Web colors, 51, *51,* 89, 367
sans serif fonts, 93–94
Sausage Software, 116
saving
    archiving Web page elements,
        359–60
    buttons as GIFs, 69–70, *70*
    FrontPage Web sites, 294, *294*
    HTML documents, 187–88, 202, 229
    JPEGs, 53
    Word documents as HTML
        documents, 234, 235–37, *236,*
        276
    Word documents in Web Folders,
        341–43, *342*
    Word Web sites, 254–55
scanners, 71
scanning of text by users, 23–24,
    23, 24, 38
scheduling updates, 358
schemes, color, 88–90, 102

screens, Web page dimensions and,
    80–83, *81,* 102
ScreenTips
    adding, to Word Web site
        hyperlinks, 269–71
    buttons and, 67
    for graphics, 95, *96*
search engines
    finding free server space, 109
    finding JavaScript components, 363
    finding Web hosting services, 111
    registering with, 349–52
send mail icon, 191
serif fonts, 93
servers
    client/server nature of Web and,
        15–16, *16,* 18
    FrontPage Server Extensions and,
        285–86, 313, 329, 346
    as Internet hardware, 8
    space (*see* server space)
    Web Folders support, 339
server space, 106–12, 125. *See also*
    Internet connections
    file storage, 339
    free, 106–9, *108*
    FTP host address, 337
    purchasing, 110–12
    uploading and, 334
shareware, 113, 335, 336
shareware.com, 113
Shoebox photo album, 164, 165
SimpleText, 178, *179*
site e-mail, 151
site label, FTP, 336
site managers, 150, 157, 173
site maps, 97, 242, *243*
site planning checklist, 136–38
sites. *See* Web sites
site-specific pages, 108–9
size
    of elements, importance and, 87
    font, 93
    graphics file (*see* graphics file sizes)
SIZE attribute, 63
sketching, 78, 142
skill development, 356
software, Web as, 7–8, 18. *See also*
    tools
sound files, 88
source code, HTML. *See also* HTML
    (Hypertext Markup Language)
    viewing, in browsers, 12, *12,* 115,
        179
    viewing, in FrontPage, 282, *283*

source code, HTML, *continued*
    viewing, in MSN Page Builder,
        169–71, *170, 171*
    viewing, in Word, 237–38, *238,* 277
space, server. *See* server space
space, white, 34, 88, 90, 102
spaces in file and folder names,
    135, 249
spacing issues, HTML, 182, *183,*
    193, 208
special interests, 92
speed, download, 45, 55–56, 87
spelling, 36–37, 38, 92
spiders, 349, 350
SRC attribute, 200, 201
standard credibility components,
    91–92, 102
standard HTML tags, 192–94, *192,*
    193, 195, 229
standard JPEGs, 52, *52,* 53, *53*
stars.com, 228
starting tags, 180
storyboarding, 78, *79,* 102, 136,
    136, 289
structure, directory. *See* file
    management
structure, Web site, 97–98, 102
styles
    applying Word, 246
    font, 93–94
    modifying Word, for hyperlinks,
        265–68, *266, 267, 268*
    viewing Word, 245
    Word, 242, 244, 277
supplies, 6–14. *See also* resources;
    tools
    browsers, 9 (*see also* browsers)
    checklist, 142
    client/server model of Web and,
        15–16, *16*
    FrontPage Web sites, 280, *281*
    gathering, 141–42
    HTML documents, 176, *176*
    Internet as hardware, 6–7, *6*
    MSN Communities Web sites, 148,
        148
    uploading, 334
    viewing HTML source code in
        browsers, 12, *12,* 115
    Web as software, 7–8
    Web pages as HTML files, 8–14, *10,*
        11, 13, 14
    Word Web sites, 232, *232*
support, 112
symbols in filenames, 135

T

T1 lines, 78
<TABLE> and </TABLE> tags,
    197–99, *200*
table of contents, home pages as, 31
tables
    creating HTML, 197–99, *200*
    hiding borders of, in FrontPage,
        320–21, *321*
    inserting, in FrontPage, 297–301,
        297, 298, 300, 301
tags, HTML
    attributes for (*see* attributes, HTML)
    body, 195–96, *196, 197*
    for bullets and rules, 62–63, *63*
    META keywords and descriptions,
        351–52, 353
    standard, 192–94, *192, 193, 195,*
        229
    tables, 197–99, *200*
    using, 178–86, *179, 181, 183, 184–85*
<TD> and </TD> tags, 197
technical capabilities, audience, 77
technical features, 87
technical support, 112
templates
    default Latin text, 95
    FrontPage, 329
    HTML, 226–28, *226, 227*
    MSN Communities, 150–53,
        155–57, *156*
    page layout and, 83, *84,* 102
    using buttons as, 70
    Word, 234, 238–40, *239, 240,* 276,
        277
testing Web pages, 83, 123,
    347–49, *348*
text, 20–39
    adding, in FrontPage, 307–11, *308,*
        309
    adding, in Word, 252–54, *253, 254*
    adding title, to FrontPage form, 313
    alternative, for graphics, 95, *96*
    avoiding *thing* word variations, 36
    blinking, 86
    case of content, 193
    colors, 89
    as content, 22 (*see also* body text;
        content)
    copyrights and, 32
    default Latin, 95
    design issues, 92–95
    documents (*see* text documents)
    editing MSN Communities Web site,
        167–68, *168, 169,* 173

text, *continued*
    editors (*see* editors, text and HTML)
    font formatting, 94–95
    font sizes, 93
    font styles, 93–94
    formatting colored, 219–20, *220, 221*
    hyperlinks, 91, 141
    inserting home page body, 216–23
    key points, 38–39
    marquee, 282
    pop-up, for graphics, 95, *96,* 102
    textual elements (*see* textual
        elements)
    title (*see* title text)
    updating, 357
    users' attention to, before graphics,
        28
    users' ranking of quality of Internet
        writing, 22
    users' response and effectiveness
        of, 22–24, *23, 24*
    Web writing (*see* writing, Web)
text-based navigational elements,
    25, *27*
text documents
    formatting, 244–45
    Web pages as, 8–14, *10, 11, 13, 14,*
        18 (*see also* HTML (Hypertext
        Markup Language) documents)
textual elements, 24–28, *25,* **38**
    content, 26
    forms and menu items, 27
    graphical text, 26–27, 64, *64* (*see
        also* Microsoft WordArt)
    hyperlinks, 26, 91
    last-modified-date information,
        27–28
    logos, graphical text, and WordArt,
        26–27
    navigational options, 27
    title bars, 26
themes, Word, 249–50, *250,* **272**
thumbnails
    download speed of, 167
    FrontPage, 282, 307–11, *308, 309*
    graphics file size and, 58, *59,* 72
tiling, 65, 195
time
    gathering supplies, 141
    spent by users viewing Web pages, 23
title area, 85, *86*
title bars
    adding FrontPage, 313
    advantages of, 97
    banner graphics, 191, *192*
    FrontPage graphics, 294–96, *296*

title bars, *continued*
  as textual elements, *25,* 26
title text
  FrontPage, 291, *292*
  home page, 98
  HTML document, 237
  MSN Communities home page, 160
  Word page, 236, *236*
toolbars
  FrontPage, 282, *283,* 326, *326*
  Word, 67, 233, *233,* 251
  WordArt, 258
tools, 104–25. *See also* resources;
    supplies
  acquiring, from Web sites, 122
  browsers, 9, 123–25, *124* (*see also*
    browsers)
  categories of, 113
  FTP applications, 121–23 (*see also*
    FTP (File Transfer Protocol)
    applications)
  gathering, 141–42
  GIF animators, image map
    applications, and banner
    programs, 122
  graphics applications, 43, 119–21,
    121
  Internet connectivity and server
    space (*see* Internet connections;
    server space)
  key points, 125
  text editors and HTML editors,
    113–18, *119*
<TR> and </TR> tags, 197
transparent GIFs, 50, *50*
Tripod, 107
true color, 52
tucows.com, 113

U
<UL> and </UL> tags, 62, 222
underlined text, 94
underscore (_) in filenames, 135
Unisys, 55
unnumbered linked lists, 221–23,
    221, 223
updating, 356–59, 364. *See also*
    maintenance
  easily updated elements, 357
  reasons for, 138, 356–57
  tips and tricks, 357–59
uploading, 16, 332–53
  America Online file feature, 347
  browsers as FTP clients, 346–47, *347*

uploading, *continued*
  downloading vs., 335 (*see also*
    downloading)
  file types and, 338
  FTP applications and, 335–39, *337*
    (*see also* FTP (File Transfer
    Protocol) applications)
  FTP functions in applications and,
    343–46
  ISP folders and, 339
  ISP interfaces and HTML editor
    features and, 345–46
  key points, 352–53
  methods, 334–35
  publicizing Web sites after, 352
  publishing FrontPage Web sites,
    327, 328, 329, 346
  registering with search engines and
    directories after, 349–52
  reviewing Web sites after, 347–49,
    348
  supplies for, 334
  Web Folders and, 339–43, *340, 341,
    342*
  Web Publishing Wizard and,
    343–45, *345,* 348
uppercase. *See* case sensitivity
upper-left corners of Web pages,
    28, 84, 90, 102, 141, 200
URLs (Uniform Resource Locators),
    16, 134, 338–39
usability studies, **17, 28**
users. *See also* audience
  attention to text before graphics
    by, 28, 38
  FTP site usernames and passwords,
    337
  rankings of Internet writing quality
    by, 22
  responses to text by, 22–24, *23, 24,*
    38
  time spent viewing Web pages by, 23
  visualizing real, 76–77, 132
  Web Publishing Wizard usernames
    and passwords, 344
utilities. *See* tools

V
validation services, **91**
vector-based graphics, **121**
vendors, online art, **66**
visual appeal, **88**
visual themes, **249–50,** *250*
VLINK attribute, **196**
VSPACE attribute, **224**

W
w3.org, 229
Web. *See also* Internet
  addresses (*see* domain names)
  client/server nature of, 15–16, *16*
  dynamic nature of, 13
  hosting providers, 111–12 (*see also*
    ISPs (Internet service providers))
  online communities (*see* online
    communities)
  pages (*see* Web pages)
  servers (*see* servers)
  sites (*see* Web sites)
  as software, 7–8, 18
  writing for (*see* writing, Web)
WebCrawler, 350
Web Folders. *See* Microsoft Web
    Folders
Web hosting services, 111–12. *See
    also* ISPs (Internet service
    providers); servers
Webmaster link, 92
webmonkey.com
Web pages
  browsers and, 9 (*see also* browsers)
  client/server nature of Web and,
    15–16, *16*
  design (*see* design)
  dimensions of, 80–83, *81,* 102
  FrontPage (*see* Microsoft FrontPage
    Web pages)
  graphics for (*see* graphics)
  home pages as main, 76 (*see also*
    home pages)
  as HTML documents, 8–14, *10, 11,
    13, 14* (*see also* HTML (Hypertext
    Markup Language) documents)
  hyperlinks and, 14, *14* (*see also*
    hyperlinks)
  Internet as hardware for, 6–7, *6*
    (*see also* Internet; Internet
    connections)
  key points, 18
  maintenance of (*see* maintenance)
  MSN Communities (*see* MSN
    Communities Web sites)
  multifile nature of, 9–13, *10, 11, 13*
    (*see also* files)
  planning (*see* planning)
  resources for (*see* resources)
  skill development and, 356
  supplies for, 6–14 (*see also*
    supplies)
  templates (*see* templates)
  testing, 83, 123, 347–49, *348*

Web pages, *continued*
text for (*see* text)
this book about, 16–17
tools for (*see* tools)
uploading (*see* uploading)
users' time spent viewing, 23
viewing HTML source code (*see* source code, HTML)
Web as software for, 7–8 (*see also* Web)
Web sites as collections of, 9, 18, 76 (*see also* Web sites)
Word (*see* Microsoft Word 2000 Web pages)
Web Page Wizard
creating Web pages with, 245–51, *246, 247, 248, 249, 250, 251*
capitalization of filenames by, 269
as Word feature, 234, 240–41, 276, 277
Web Publishing Wizard
desktop shortcuts to, 345
file deletion and, 345, 348
FTP programs and, 121
passwords and, 337
uploading with, 16, 343–44, *345,* 352
Windows versions and, 343
webreview.com, 22
Webs, FrontPage, 288–91, *289, 290, 291.* See also Microsoft FrontPage Web pages
Web-safe colors, 51, *51,* **55, 89, 137**
Web sites
as collections of Web pages, 9, 18, 76 (*see also* Web pages)
design, 96–98 (*see also* design)
domain registration, 110–11
film developers, 71
free server space, 107–9, *108*
hosting providers, 111
hyperlinks and, 14, *14* (*see also* hyperlinks)

Web sites, *continued*
MSN Communities (*see* MSN Communities Web sites)
news, 29
organizing, 31–32, *32*
planning, 132–38, 142 (*see also* planning)
planning checklist, 136–38
planning HTML, 188, *189* (*see also* HTML (Hypertext Markup Language) documents)
publicizing, 352
redesign case study, 98, *98, 99, 100, 101*
registering, with search engines and directories, 349–52
saving and closing Word, 254–55
shareware, 113
site maps, 97, 242, *243*
storyboarding, 78, *79,* 102, 136, *136*
structure, 97–98
updating live, 358
using Passport technology, 154
validation services, 91
Web toolbar, Word, 233, *233*
white space, 34, 88, 90, 102
white text, 94
WIDTH attribute, 63, 198, 199, 201
windows
browser, 124
FrontPage, 282, *283, 284,* 329
Microsoft Development Environment, 237–38, *238*
Windows. See Microsoft Windows
wizards
Add Web Folder, 341, *341*
as dialog boxes, 107
Web Page (*See* Web Page Wizard)
Web publishing, 343 (*see also* Web Publishing Wizard)
Word. See Microsoft Word 2000

WordArt. See Microsoft WordArt
WordPad, 115, *116,* **178,** *179*
words, precise, 34
World Wide Web. See Web
writing, Web, 28–39. See also text
active voice, 35
avoiding *thing* word variations, 36
brainstorms, headings, and hyperlinks, 31–32, *32*
clear antecedents, 35–36
copyrights and, 32
inverted pyramid methodology, 29–30
key points, 38–39
for online audience, 32–37
organizing text, 29–34, *32*
precise words, 34
quality of, 22
shape of body text, 32–34
spelling and grammar, 36–37
strong sentences, 34–36
strong verbs, 35
resources, 36
text as design element, 37–38
user's attention to graphics vs. text, 28
Web text vs. printed text, 28
WWW. See Web
WYSIWYG editors, 113, 116, 118

Y
Yahoo!
GeoCities online community, 107
search engine, 350

Z
zip files, 176, 280
zooming of views, 45, *45,* **56**

Mary Millhollon

Mary Millhollon is the owner of Bughouse Productions and has more than enough years of publishing, design, and computer experience to count, including hands-on experience in the book, magazine, newspaper, courseware, and Web publishing industries. Mary is a freelance writer, editor, Web designer, and Internet expert, working daily (and nightly) with online technologies. Mary's educational background is a blend of art, English, journalism, and computer science, which lends itself well to today's constantly morphing computer technology. Her most recent publications include a collection of computer-related books about Internet browsers, HTML (beginning and advanced), Microsoft Office applications, online communities, Web graphics, online auctions, and other Internet, network, application, and design topics.

Jeff Castrina

Jeff Castrina is the owner of ExtraCheese (*www.extracheese.com*), a multimedia and Web design firm. Jeff has created Web sites and interactive CD-ROMs for a number of established clients. Prior to founding ExtraCheese, Jeff worked as the Multimedia Services Manager for a computer education firm in Phoenix, Arizona. Before relocating to Phoenix, Jeff held graphic design and video production positions in Rochester, New York. And before that, he jump-started his multimedia career by graduating from the Rochester Institute of Technology, where he studied film/video production and computer science.

The manuscript for this book was prepared and galleyed using Microsoft Word 2000. Pages were composed using Adobe PageMaker 6.52 for Windows, with text in Garamond Light and display type in ITC Officina Sans. Composed pages were delivered to the printer as electronic prepress files.

COVER DESIGNER
Patrick Lanfear

COVER ILLUSTRATOR
Todd Daman

INTERIOR GRAPHIC DESIGNERS
Jeff Wincapaw

for Microsoft Press
Joel Panchot, James D. Kramer

PRINCIPAL COMPOSITOR
Dan Latimer

GRAPHIC ARTISTS
Michael Kloepfer, Joel Panchot, Rob Nance

PRINCIPAL COPY EDITOR
Holly M. Viola

INDEXER
Shane-Armstrong Information Systems